BANKIMCHANDRA CHATTOPADHYAY'S
ŚRĪMADBHAGABADGĪTĀ:
Translation and Analysis

SOUTH ASIA INSTITUTE, NEW DELHI BRANCH
HEIDELBERG UNIVERSITY
SOUTH ASIAN STUDIES NO. XXXVII

Bankimchandra Chattopadhyay's *Śrīmadbhagabadgītā*:

TRANSLATION AND ANALYSIS

by

HANS HARDER

MANOHAR
2001

First published 2001

ISBN 81-7304-376-0

Published by
Ajay Kumar Jain for
Manohar Publishers & Distributors
4753/23 Ansari Road, Daryaganj
New Delhi 110002

Printed at
Rajkamal Electric Press
B 35/9 GT Karnal Road Indl Area
Delhi 110033

Contents

Preface

Baṅkim'candra Caṭṭopādhyāẏ's religious thought has attracted considerable attention among scholars from Bengal and elsewhere, and its role in the shaping of modern Hinduism has been duly recognised. Baṅkim'candra's *Śrīmadbhagabadgītā* (1886-8/1901), his fragmentary commentary on the *Bhagavadgītā*, occupies an important place among his religious writings, but has so far been neglected in the ongoing discussion. In the following thesis, my primary aim is to make the text available to interested readers and scholars without knowledge of Bengali by furnishing a critical, documented English translation of it. The introduction preceding this translation cannot claim originality: it is primarily meant to give an outline of the historical and biographical frame necessary for an evaluative and appreciative reading of the commentary. Special emphasis is placed on the mediation between Eastern and Western thought which has been so crucial in Bengali intellectual history since the beginning of the nineteenth century.

Baṅkim'candra's religious writings are closely interconnected. In my analysis following the translation, I have accordingly taken the opportunity to reconsider, in a micro-study, certain issues connected with his religious thought on the basis of the commentary while at the same time taking into account his other essays. The first chapter of the analysis contains a statement about some basic properties of the commentary, remarks on its publication history as well as a survey of prior research on the topic (so far lacking in this discussion) and notes about my procedure. In the second chapter, I have attempted to portray and critically examine a few of Baṅkim'candra's conceptions as formulated in the commentary and the surrounding writings: his view of the *Gītā* as an authoritative religious text, his use and elaboration of the terms *dharma* and *svadharma*, and his notion regarding the plurality of worship in Hinduism. The communicative set-up of the commentary is the subject of the third chapter, in which I analyse the strategies Baṅkim'candra employs in dealing with his readers, the ancient commentators, and Western Indologists. In the course of this chapter, I have tried to find some clues regarding the location of the author Baṅkim'candra in his text. The final chapter regains a broader perspective on the topic, and focuses on an explanation of the inconsistencies inherent in Baṅkim'candra's interpretation of Hinduism as worked out in the preceding analysis. I have made an attempt to demonstrate that many arguments rely on the coexistence of broad and narrow definitions of central terms, as well as normative and empirical frames of judgement, playing out against one another. This pattern is often employed by Baṅkim'candra in order to establish the superiority of Hinduism over other religions, especially Christianity. His tendency towards cultural self-assertion, I will argue, is the basic impulse of the commentary, its ultimate ratio, and an outcome of the colonial situation in which Baṅkim'candra lived. This nationalist and proto-political character of Baṅkim'candra's writings also demonstrates their relevance beyond religious studies, namely, in the study of anti-colonialism, nationalism, etc. A short examination of the appropriateness of terms such as 'neo-Hinduism' and 'modern Hinduism' concludes this chapter and the analysis.

Many of my teachers, colleagues and friends have helped me write this thesis: first of all, my teacher and examiner in Halle, Prof. Dr. Rahul Peter Das, who inspired and encouraged me to choose this particular subject. He went through all I have written more than once, and without his advice and guidance this work would have been difficult to achieve. I also wish to thank my former Bengali teacher Dr. Alokeranjan Dasgupta (Heidelberg) for his help with this thesis, as well as for the way in which he taught me — and still teaches — Bengali literature. I am also grateful to my other examiners, Prof. Dr. Walter Slaje (Halle University) and Prof. Dr. Srinivasa Ayya Srinivasan (Hamburg University), for their most valuable help and corrections. Moreover, I wish to thank the Deutsche Morgenländische Gesellschaft, who awarded me the DMG-Forschungspreis 1998 for this thesis; the editing board of South Asian Studies at the Südasieninstitut Heidelberg for accepting it for publication in this series; and the Taraknath Das Stiftung (Berlin) for generously subsidising the print of this book. Further thanks are due to the Graduiertenförderung of Hamburg University which granted me a two years' scholarship for this undertaking; Prof. Dr. Albrecht Wezler (Hamburg University) and Prof. Dr. Dietmar Rothermund (Heidelberg University) for their expertises; Dr. Melitta Waligora (Humboldt-University Berlin) for valuable comments; Raja and Sulagna Mukhopadhyay (Calcutta) for their assistance and friendship; Dr. Shivaji Bandyopadhyay (Jadavpur University), Maphidul Hak, Dr. Badruddin Umar and Prof. Anisuzzaman (Dhaka) for controversial and challenging discussions; Dr. Birgit Mayer-König, Thomas Herzog, Prof. Dr. Jürgen Paul, Prof. Dr. Walter Beltz, Dirk Moras (Halle), Christian Weiß, Jörg Watzinger, Ursula Rao (Heidelberg), Dr. Susmita Mallick (Hamburg) and many others for their assistance in various ways. A special thanks goes to Karin Harder for her support and the way in which she helped me structure my arguments and discover my thoughts.

The cover illustration of this book may need an explanatory remark. In the *Hastie Controversy* to be discussed in several instances, Baṅkim'candra, while defending idol worship, feels urged to admit that "the images we worship in Bengal are, as works of art, a disgrace to the nation. Wealthy Hindus should get their Krishnas and Radhas made in Europe." (*BR* III:216) Incidentally, thanks to Dr. Maria Schetelich from the Institut für Indologie und Zentralasienwissenschaften, University of Leipzig, I found the Art Nouveau Krishna temple "printed in Germany" around 1920 which is reproduced on the cover. The print of an anonymous painter is part of the Hertel collection which was donated to that institute by Mrs. Margarethe Hertel. I am not sure whether Baṅkim'candra would have appreciated this representation, but I could not resist the temptation to take him by his own words. I thank Dr. Schetelich and the Institut für Indologie und Zentralasienwissenschaften for allowing me to reproduce the picture.

The manuscript of this book was finished in 1997, and it must be mentioned that the delay in publication is due to several things, but not to the present publisher. I thank Mr. Ramesh Jain and the Manohar staff for their copy editing, advice and cooperation.

Halle, 10 June, 2001 Hans Harder

Abbreviations

AṣBhG	*Śrīmadbhagavadgītā aṣṭaṭīkopetā* (with the commentaries of Keśava Kaśmīribhaṭṭa, Madhusūdana Sarasvatī, Śaṅkarānanda, Śrīdhara Svāmin, Sadānanda, Dhanapati Sūrī, Daivajñapaṇḍita Sūrya and Rāghavendra), 2nd series, Part 1; ed. Lallurama, Shastri Jeevarama; Bombay, Gujarati Printing Press, 1912.
BCEIP	Chatterjee, Bhabatosh (Ed.): *Bankimchandra Chatterjee: Essays in Perspective*; New Delhi, Sahitya Akademi, 1994.
BCJ	Bhaṭṭācārya, Amitrasūdan: *Baṅkimˈcandrajībanī*; Kalˈkātā, Ānanda Publishers, 1991.
BE	Bengali era.
BhG	*Bhagavadgītā* (see *Mbh*-edition).
BhGBE	*The Bhagavadgītā in the Mahābhārata: A Bilingual Edition*; transl./ed. A.B. van Buitenen; Chicago, 1981.
BJ	Caṭṭopādhyāẏ, Śrīśˈcandra: *Baṅkim-jībanī*; Kalikātā, Pustak Bipaṇi, 1395 BE [1988] (first ed. 1318 BE [1911-2]).
BR	Caṭṭopādhyāẏ, Baṅkimˈcandra: *Baṅkim racanābalī*, 3 Vols.; ed. Bāgal, Yogeśˈcandra; Kalikātā, Sāhitya Saṃsad, Vol. I 16th ed. 1994; Vol.II 11th ed. 1397 BE (1990); Vol.III (*Bankim Rachanavali*) 2nd ed. 1990.
BSOAS	*Bulletin of the School of Oriental and African Studies.*
EPW	*Economic and Political Weekly.*
Mbh	Vishnu S. Sukthankar / S.K. Belvalkar (from 1943) (eds.): *The Mahābhārata* (critical edition), 19 Vols.; Poona, Bhandarkar Oriental Research Institute, 1927-59.
ŚaBhG	Śaṅkara: *Srīmad Bhagavad Gītā Bhāṣya of Sri Saṃkarācārya: with Text in Devanagari & English Rendering, and Index of First Lines of Verses*; transl. Warrier, A.G. Krishna; Madras, 1983.
ŚBhG	the present translation of *Śrīmadbhagabadgītā*, based on the following editions:
ŚBhG(a)	Caṭṭopādhyāẏ, Baṅkimˈcandra: *Śrīmadbhagabadgītā*; in *Baṅkim racanābalī*, Vol. II; ed. Yogeśˈcandra Bāgal; Kalikātā, Sāhitya Saṃsad, 11th ed. 1397 BE (1990): 680-775.
ŚBhG(b)	Caṭṭopādhyāẏ, Baṅkimˈcandra: *Śrīmadbhagabadgītā*; Baṅkim-śatabārṣik saṃskaraṇ; eds. Bandyopādhyāẏ, Brajendranāth and Dās, Sajanīkānta; Kalikātā, Baṅgīẏa Sāhitya Pariṣad, 2nd ed. 1357 BE (1950) [1st ed. 1347 (1941)].
ŚrBhG	Śrīdhara Śvāmin: *Srimad Bhagavad-Gita: Text, Translation of the Text and of the Gloss of Sridhara Swami*; ed./transl. Vireswarananda, Swami; Madras, 1972.
SSV	*The Sāṃkhya Sūtra Vṛtti*; ed. Garbe, Richard; Calcutta, Baptist Mission Press, 1888.
UDS	Śaṅkara's *Upadeśasahasrī*; crit. ed. with introduction and indices by Nayeda, Sengaku; Tokyo, 1973.
VP	*Śrī Viṣṇumahāpurāṇam*; ed. Rājendranātha Śarman; Delhi, Nag Publishers, 1985.
ZDMG	*Zeitschrift der Deutschen Morgenländischen Gesellschaft.*

Introduction

Historical Background and Commentator's Biography

Since Baṅkim'candra Caṭṭopādhyāẏ's[1] lifetime (1838-94), the initial part of his first name (*baṅkim*, Sanskrit *vakrima*, meaning 'bent', 'curved') has often been used for a metaphorical play with words. In an encounter with the mystic Rām'kr̥ṣṇa Param'haṃsa the following conversation is reported to have taken place:

Rām'kr̥ṣṇa (with laughter): 'Baṅkim! By whose love are you bent[2] then?'
Baṅkim'candra (laughing): 'Well, Sir, by the slaps of shoes.' (All laugh)
'I'm bent by the slaps of the *Sāhebs*' shoes.'[3]

In the Bengali literature on Baṅkim'candra,[4] this literal meaning of *baṅkim* is again and again used, alluding to his biography, literary career, social standing and the like.[5] And there are indeed several features of his life and work which justify such a designation. Baṅkim's life and development as a writer was anything but smooth; there were no clear, pre-set lines along which he could evolve, either socially, or politically, or in literature. It was rather a certain fuzziness and uncertainty, together with a multitude of possibilities, which characterised much of nineteenth century Bengal; to remove this ambiguity became one of Baṅkim'candra's aims. The heterogeneous historical setting of colonial Bengal — the cultural clash between Bengal and Britain — left little space for well-defined Bengali curricula vitae; and it is indeed largely Baṅkim's 'curvedness' that in turn provides clues for the determination of some basic characteristics of his contemporary society.

Baṅkim'candra is one of the most widely known figures in Bengali literature in Bengal and other parts of India — and recently also abroad — second only to Rabīndranāth Ṭhākur (Tagore). A huge amount of secondary literature ever since the later nineteenth century has been devoted to various aspects of his personality and work. The greatest merits with which Baṅkim is usually credited are his creation of the Bengali novel as a genre and the invention of a prose style for the Bengali language; and, despite some disputes, his importance in this area has been quite solidly established. Much attention has also been given to his role as an early nationalist, and here opinions differ considerably; the controversy over whether he is to be regarded as a 'nation-maker' or the 'father of communal thought' is still far from being settled.

[1] For the transliteration system and formal conventions used in the following, cf. the Notes on the Translation.

[2] *bā̃kā* (Beng.), the colloquial (*calit bhāṣā*) form of *baṅkim*.

[3] In Śrīma' (Gupta, Mahendranāth 1989 [1882] Part V:156). Cf. however Gopāl'candra Rāẏ (1981:38-70 in the appendix) who questions the sources and argues that Rām'kr̥ṣṇa and Baṅkim'candra never met.

[4] As is usual in publications on Baṅkim'candra Caṭṭopādhyāẏ, I will in the following text refer to him by his first name in full ('Baṅkim'candra') or abbreviated form ('Baṅkim').

[5] Thus Gopal Haldar (1994:140), for example, introduces his article by the above episode and interprets it as follows: 'The [Baṅkim's] curt reply might well imply the bashing he perforce suffered as employee of the British Raj. But it might just as well refer to the manifold layers of his personality which cannot be measured. A mind like this is naturally torn by internal conflict that manifests itself in a number of his characters. Familial, social, economic and political tensions provide the backdrop.' Cf. also the titles of two major books on Baṅkim'candra, Pramathanāth Biśī's *Baṅkim saraṇī*, meaning also 'the curved path', and Arabinda Poddār's *Baṅkim mānas*, which could be interpreted as 'the bent mind'.

Especially in Bangladesh, Baṅkim'candra has repeatedly been labeled communal and Hindu-biased; in India, on the other hand, he is quite commonly regarded as a national figure and one of the major 'nation-builders'. Superficial as such labels may tend to be, they form the bias upon — and against — which any new assessment has to be built.

Baṅkim'candra emerged from, or rather into, a very specific historical setting which is commonly called the Bengal Renaissance.[6] This epoch of Bengali history has drawn a lot of scholarly attention as an exemplary encounter between West and East characterised by cultural assimilation, modernisation and the discovery of indigenous culture in a new light. In order to be meaningful, Baṅkim'candra's biographic data and literary career, the prime object of this introduction, must be viewed in this larger perspective, and will thus in the following be embedded in a short outline of the historical situation. His *Śrīmadbhagabadgītā*,[7] being a result as well as an expression of the heterogeneity of the nineteenth century, will in this way be situated in its context.

By the beginning of the nineteenth century, the British East India Company had been present in the country for almost one and a half centuries. In the eighteenth century, trade had expanded immensely, and the former trade post Calcutta had developed into the major urban centre of Bengal. In 1757, the Battle of Plassey had marked the beginning of the gradual acquisition of political control by the British and the reduction of the Nawabs of Murshidabad to mere representatives devoid of any actual power. The demand for Indian goods in the European market had been great, and with trade flourishing, extraordinary accumulations of wealth had become possible, not only on the part of the British members of the Company, but also on that of the

[6] There is considerable dissent as to the time-span covered by this term. While its beginning is almost unanimously set at 1800 (foundation of the Fort William College), there exist many different views regarding the exact duration of the Bengal Renaissance. A narrow delimitation of the initial phase of this Renaissance has been given by David Kopf (1969:288ff.) who emphasises the role of the 'British Orientalists', i.e. the then influential faction of the East India Company favouring education in Indian languages and cultural development along classical and contemporary Indian lines, in this Renaissance. In Kopf's view, this first phase ends between 1830 and 1845, when the Orientalists had to surrender to Macaulayism and its imposition of English education on Bengal. The following phase of nascent nationalism, according to Kopf (ibid.), also marked the beginning of the mystifying historiography of that initial phase. A second demarcation has been put forth by Amiya P. Sen (1993:introduction), who considers the year 1872 to be the beginning of an era of Revivalism (but it is not clear whether, according to him, Revivalism is still incorporated in the more general term Bengal Renaissance). Similarly, Sumit Sarkar (1990-1:102) describes the sixties and seventies as a 'hiatus' between the Bengal Renaissance and the Freedom Struggle. Thirdly, the term is often used to designate the whole of the nineteenth century; the Bengal Renaissance accordingly merges into the *Svadeśī* period in 1905. Sri Aurobindo (1986 [Aug. to Nov. 1918]) has altered the term so as to apply to India in its entirety and used it in its broadest sense. According to him, this Renaissance, consisting of the synthesis between (Western) materialism and (Eastern, Indian) spiritualism, is far from being completed even in 1918 when he is writing on the topic. Gopāl Hāl'dār (1985:131), who uses the term exclusively in inverted commas, gives a still different dating: '(...) roughly from 1840 to 1890'. Further deliminations are collected in Waligora (unpublished); David M. Brookman (1990), for instance, portrays the Renaissance as a process still under way and probably lasting until the twenty-first century.

I prefer using the term in the rather limited (and fairly conventional) sense suggested by Amiya P. Sen, since in the seventies of the nineteenth century, the modes of assimilation change, and nationalism emerges as the integrative platform of identity search.

[7] This direct transliteration from Bengali (retaining the b — °*bhagabad*°) is used throughout in order to distinguish between the *Bhagavadgītā* and the name of Baṅkim's translation-cum-commentary.

Bengali intermediate traders.[8] New means of livelihood evolved and kept drawing people to Calcutta, and significantly mostly Hindus responded positively, whereas Bengali Muslims remained mostly detached from these developments; the early Muslim reform movements did their part in emphasising distancing and confrontation rather than cooperation. Calcutta had become the economic and cultural centre of the country. It became customary for rich land-owners to spend some part of the year in Calcutta residences. Economic cooperation with the British had been firmly established.

Another field of interaction before the nineteenth century had been Christian missionary work. The Company had originally made it their principle not to interfere with Indian religions and thus not to tolerate missionary activities on the territory controlled by them, but all the same, missions had been set up in the vicinity of Calcutta (e.g. the famous Danish mission at Serampur [Śrīrām'pur]), and eventually, pressure upon the Company by the British Parliament led to the abandonment of this principle in 1813. But so far, there had been little concerted, conscious response on the Bengalis' part to the changes underway. Reaction was limited, and according to Arabinda Poddar's (1970:4) opinion, consisted mostly in 'introversion and even xenophobia'. A conscious response did not evolve until the beginning of the nineteenth century, and the era of its emergence and development is what is commonly called the Bengal Renaissance.

In 1800, the Fort William College was founded by the East India Company. Its object was to teach new employees of the Company Indian languages and culture along with their duties as colonial officers. With the cooperation of Indian scholars such as Rām'rām Basu and Mṛtyuñjaẏ Bidyālaṅkār (Vidyalankar), some pioneering linguistic and educational work was achieved under the auspices of this institution. William Carey's Bengali grammar, one of the earliest of its kind, came out in 1801, and the newly established first printing press at Serampur provided for its circulation.[9] The School Book Society was founded with the aim to supply material in the Bengali language, and texts such as *Rājābalī* (1808) by Mṛtyuñjaẏ are the first samples of both Bengali prose and Bengali historiography.[10] Furthermore, the first regular newspapers and journals were started around this time in both the English and Bengali languages.

The major Indian personality of the initial phase of this Renaissance, however, was Rājā Rām'mohan Rāẏ (Rammohun Roy), who has significantly been called the first Indian intellectual.[11] Professionally a rich intermediate trader, he acquired first-hand knowledge of all major religious doctrines by extensive studies and entered into controversy with the Christian missionaries, identifying the Upaniṣads as the true basis of Hindu religion. He published English and Bengali translations of several Upaniṣads. His writings as well as his personal life reveal a new interplay and mediation between different cultures, a feature which was to become characteristic of the elite in nineteenth century Bengal.[12] Rām'mohan Rāẏ saw much of the practices of current Hinduism as

[8] By this term I denote Bengali merchants or landowners who acted as suppliers or trade assistants to the British, i.e. as go-betweens bridging the gap between producers and traders.

[9] Cf. Sisir Kumar Das (1966:21 f.).

[10] Cf. Partha Chatterjee (1995:104ff.) for a discussion of *Rājābalī*.

[11] Cf. Arabinda Poddar (1970:47) and Nirad Chaudhuri (1967:10).

[12] Wilhelm Halbfass (1990:214) stresses this point: '[...] Rammohan's translations into English and Bengali are an expression of the multilingualism that characterises his hermeneutic situation, and it corresponds to a dual motivation behind his thought and activity; the "Veds", which were thus presented

superstitions and corruptions acquired through the ages, much in accordance with the perceptions of the early British Orientalists. The notion of an ancient Golden Age of Hinduism, followed by gradual decay and resulting in present degeneration, had by all appearance initially been brought up by the first generations of European Indologists such as Wilson and Colebrooke,[13] and fit in well with indigenous notions of continuous decline in the Purāṇas. It found expression in the first comprehensive historiography of the country, James Mill's 'History of India' written in 1818,[14] and lay also at the base of the British Orientalists' perception. Rām'mohan Rāẏ was the first to react to this notion by promoting social reform, and the abolition of *satī*, the burning of widows on their husbands' pyre, was achieved largely through his initiative. His religious and social endeavours resulted in the foundation of the Brāhma Samāj in 1828, the reform movement which was one of the most important factors in Bengali society for at least the following fifty years.

The position between two cultural patterns was in fact not much of a position at all in those days, as the example of the generation of 'Young Bengal' clearly demonstrates. In 1817, the newly emerged Bengali Hindu bourgeoisie, already aware of the value of Western education, had initiated the foundation of the Hindu College in Calcutta.[15] Here the young Eurasian teacher Derozio confronted his students with English Enlightenment philosophy and thereby caused quite an upheaval. Many students denounced parts of Hindu traditional ways and took to European habits of dress and food; some converted to Christianity and got expelled from their families. The social vacuum between orthodox Hindu society and the English ruling class exposed the Derozians to great psychological strain; and it was arguably precisely this strain which forced some of them into remarkable personal achievements. A case in point is Michael Madhusūdan Datta, the first modern writer and poet of Bengal, who had used English as his medium before turning to Bengali around 1859. His aesthetics mirror his personal situation especially in his epic poetry based on Hindu epic literature; he does not continue a tradition, but approaches tradition from a distance. His shift to the Bengali language is paralleled by the increasing concern another Derozian convert, Reverend Kṛṣṇamohan Bandyopādhyāẏ, showed for Hindu religion in his later writings. Despite the creative achievements, the alienation at their root remains the most basic characteristic of this generation;[16] the Hindu community had expelled them, and the Europeans did not fully accept them but rather treated them as curiosities.[17]

---

to two different audiences, serve as vehicles of receptivity and reform as well as of self-assertion in the face of the West.'

[13] Later examples of this attitude can be found, for instance, in Wilson's *Essays and Lectures* (1861) as well as in the introduction of his translation of the *Viṣṇupurāṇa* (1864-77).

[14] Today this work is very disputed as a piece of colonial historiography. The periodisation of Indian history into Hindu India, Muslim India and British India has recently been subjected to severe criticism and is regarded as a constituent of 'divide and rule'-policy for its simplifying distinctions along the lines of dynastic religion. Cf. Romila Thapar (1977:1-23).

[15] Cf. R.C. Majumdar (1962); by contrast, David Kopf (1969:154) gives 1816 as the year of foundation.

[16] Cf. e.g. M.K. Halder (1977:71).

[17] There is much literature devoted to this time. Some Indian publications on the Derozians, and the first half of the nineteenth century in general, can be given for reference here: Svapan Basu (1985:esp.19-43); Binaẏ Ghoṣ (1984); Asit'kumār Bhaṭṭācārya (1964); K.S. Bhattacharjee (1986); Kṛṣṇakali Biśvās

In 1835, under the directives of Macaulay, the situation changed considerably. A new policy favouring exclusively English as medium of higher education was adopted, and the Orientalist faction among the British lost much of their former influence.[18] This brought to an abrupt halt the various attempts at promoting development in indigenous terms. The process once started was in this way interrupted, and when it took new shape in the late fifties, it was under different signs. The emerging *élite* was from then on officially endorsed as a class in order to mediate between the English and their uneducated Indian subjects.[19] Higher education was English, and gradually, posts for thus educated Bengalis were made available in administration, jurisdiction, etc. In this way, the social vacuum into which the Derozians had fallen was attenuated, and the interposition of Western educated Indians became instrumental to a larger civilisatory mission, namely, the dissemination of Western culture. This at least was how matters were supposed to be according to official policy; the position of the Western educated *élite*, however, grew even more complicated.

In the second phase of the Bengal Renaissance, whose beginning may be set around the middle of the nineteenth century, the main intellectual concerns remained more or less the same, religion being the prominent frame of reference. But the parameters of discussion had changed: the views expressed were no longer in conformity with the official line as in the case of the Orientalists, and the persons voicing them, increased in number, were to a considerable extent employees of the British Raj. By the time of the Mutiny (1857), after which India was put under direct control of the British Crown, the Bengali *élite* still sided entirely with the British. But soon, a growing detachment from them became perceptible. This is not to say that the influx of Western thought decreased; on the contrary, many new tendencies were taken up and became a part of common knowledge among the educated[20] and, as Nirad Chaudhuri points out, the word 'educated'[21] itself actually came exclusively to denote a person well-versed in Western culture.[22] It was rather the discrepancy between concern (revival and reform of Indian culture) and position (employees of the British Raj) which began to be perceived as a contradiction.

The development in Bengal until the sixties of the nineteenth century may thus be shortly characterised as follows. Calcutta had grown into a cosmopolitan centre and given birth to a Bengali Hindu *bourgeoisie*. New media were brought into the country and helped in elevating the Bengali language to new domains of use; modern literature began to be written in it. English higher education was made accessible to a small portion of the *bourgeoisie*, to whom their own religion and culture and its relation to

---

(1986); Sisir Kumar Das (1966 and 1974); Susobhan Sarkar (1979).

[18] Cf. David Kopf (1969), especially Part V on 'Macaulayism and the Decline and Fall of the Orientalist Movement, 1828-1835', pp. 215-72.

[19] Macaulay, in his *Minute on Education* of that year, described this class as 'Indian in blood and colour, but English in taste, in opinion, words and intellect'. This famous passage is quoted in most historiographic works on the period.

[20] The utilitarianism of Bentham and John Stuart Mill, Comte's positivism, and Darwinism were current and very influential systems of thought in Bengal in the nineteenth century.

[21] And its Bengali equivalent *śikṣita*.

[22] Cf. Nirad Chaudhuri (1967:21f.), probably with reference to Baṅkimcandra's remarks on the usage of this word.

English culture became an important preoccupation. In accepting the common notion of present India's decline, substantiated by the comparison with nineteenth century Europe and enhanced by Indological writings, this educated class reacted in several ways, from the complete abandonment of everything Hindu and Indian to religious and social reform and even retreat into orthodoxy. From the outset, the position of this *bourgeoisie* was unstable and, situated between the cultures as it was, required definition.

At this point, Baṅkim'candra enters the scene. Born in 1838 as the third of four sons of Yādab'candra Caṭṭopādhyāẏ in the village Kāṭhāl'pāṛā near Calcutta, Baṅkim'candra had spent his childhood in a fairly well-off brahmin family. His father, after studying Persian and a little English, had started his professional career in Orissa as an administrator in an English trader's salt business and been appointed Deputy Collector[23] at Medinīpur in the year of Baṅkim'candra's birth. Baṅkim'candra started primary education at home and as early as 1844 moved to Medinīpur to attend an English school. At the age of twelve, he entered Hugli College, where he showed 'Highest Proficiency' in the subjects literature, history, mathematics, natural philosophy and translation.[24] It was during this time (from 1852 onwards)[25] that he started publishing poems in the literary magazine *Saṃbād Prabhākar*, its editor Īśvar'candra Gupta being his inspiration and mentor. In 1856, Baṅkim'candra was transferred to Presidency College in Calcutta to study law, and in the following year he entered the newly founded Calcutta University. In 1858, he was one of the first two Indian students to obtain a B.A. degree.[26] After his examinations, he is reported to have taken instruction in Sanskrit *kāvya* and plays by Kālīdāsa from Śrīrām Śiromaṇi at Bhatpara (Bhāṭ'pāṛā), a centre of Sanskrit education in Bengal.[27] In the third year of his law studies, at the age of twenty, he left the college to join the Indian Civil Service in Jessore (Yaśor) as Deputy Collector and Deputy Magistrate, a position he would hold almost invariably in different parts of Eastern India throughout his life. Higher administrative positions were not available to native Indians at the time.[28]

As Śacīś'candra Caṭṭopādhyāẏ, Baṅkim'candra's nephew and first biographer, points out, there is not much material on Baṅkim's early years, except some short accounts by contemporaries[29] and a few cursory remarks by Baṅkim himself. It is known that he was married in 1849, and that his wife died when he was twenty-two, but

[23] The highest official position accessible to native Indians during the greater part of the nineteenth century.

[24] Cf. Amitrasūdan Bhaṭṭācārya's biography *Baṅkim'candrajībanī* (BCJ 1991:48f.).

[25] BCJ:50.

[26] Cf. an article in *The Hindu Patriot* in 1858 (Benoy Ghose 1978-81,V:50): 'Baboo Bunkim Chunder Chatterjea and Judoonath Bose were elected. It is the old story: — it is the Koolin Brahmin and the Koolin Kayusth who grasped the lead.'

[27] According to Haraprasād Śāstrī (1981:19).

[28] Cf. Anil Seal (1968:116ff.) for an account of the employment conditions in the Indian Civil Service in the second half of the nineteenth century. Seal — maybe not altogether seriously — makes out Baṅkim's frustation with these conditions as his prime impulse for novel-writing: 'The iron of this rung so entered his soul that he took to novel writing.' (p. 118)

[29] Collected in *Baṅkim prasaṅga* (ed. Sureś'candra Samāj'pati 1982 [1922]) and *Kācher mānuṣ baṅkim'candra* (ed. Somendranāth Basu 1989); some of these accounts have recently appeared in English translation in Chatterjee, Bhabatosh (ed.): *Bankimchandra Chatterjee: Essays in Perspective* [*BCEIP*], 1994.

his reaction is a matter of speculation. According to Śacīś'candra, he was deeply distressed and therefore strongly objected to getting married again, until his parents' order forced him to do so.[30] His relationship with his parents, again, is not very clear; for example, he is said to have held his father in great respect but, on the other hand, he supposedly once mentioned to friends that he had hardly had any relationship with his father, who had mostly been absent.[31] Anecdotes about Baṅkim's youth, classified as *janaśruti* ('rumours'; *BJ*:18), stress mainly two traits, namely, his proud and firm character[32] and his extraordinary brightness as a student.

As mentioned before, Baṅkim'candra entered the Bengali literary stage as a writer of poetry in the school of Īśvar'candra Gupta. The same is true of the famous playwright Dīnabandhu Mitra. Unlike Michael Madhusūdan Datta, Īśvar'candra's poetry was traditional in form, and it is somewhat striking that Dīnabandhu and Baṅkim, both innovators of modern genres of Bengali literature (drama and novel respectively) emerged from his group. At any rate, Bengali poetry had in the fifties already become a living mode of artistic expression, whereas the ground for literary prose and drama, according to contemporary perception, still lay fallow. Sanskrit plays and the traditional Bengali *yātrā*, besides a few adaptions of Shakespeare's plays, held the scene in drama, and it was not before 1854 that, with the appearance of Rām'nārāẏaṇ Tarkaratna's *Kulīn kul'sarbasva* ('All the Belongings of a *Kulīn* Family'), a new boom set in. The most outstanding of the dramas to appear in the following years was Dīnabandhu's *Nīl'darpaṇ* ('The Indigo Mirror', 1860).[33] It severely criticises the behaviour of contemporary English indigo planters and was even prohibited for the uproar it caused. In prose, some didactic and satirical writings had appeared, starting with Bhabānīcaraṇ Bandyopādhyāẏ's works in the 1820s, the most prominent for the time in question being Pyārīcā̃d Mitra's *Ālāler gharer dulāl* (rendered by Sukumar Sen as 'Pampered Son of a Front Rank Family', 1855-7) and Kālīprasanna Siṃha's *Hutom pyā̃cār naksā* ('Sketches by a Watching Owl', 1862). Bhūdeb Mukhopādhyāẏ's *Saphal svapna* ('The Successful Dream') and *Aṅgurīya binimaẏ* ('Exchange of Rings', both 1857) must also be mentioned.[34] However, none of these were perceived as novels in the true sense by contemporary society.[35] In fact, the impetus to write prose fiction clearly stemmed from the aquaintance with English prose. The writers apparently did not act in a void, but rather attempted to model a Bengali prose style on English examples, i.e. consciously

[30] Caṭṭopādhyāẏ, Śacīś'candra: *Baṅkim-jībanī* (*BJ*:23).

[31] Cf. Śrīś'candra Majum'dār (1964:11). Tapan Raychaudhuri even speaks of definite tensions, especially with regard to his father (1988:107).

[32] Śacīś'candra Caṭṭopādhyāẏ recounts an event during Baṅkim'candra's first school life: when the news of white men arriving at the *ghāṭ* spread in the village, everyone ran away, except he who 'stood by the side of the road close to our door, in his hand the stick given by the guru' and stayed there for half an hour until the white men left again (*BJ*:21). See Tapan Raychaudhuri (1988:113) on this pride which became vanity in the eyes of his critics, and by all appearance also included the aspect of a distinct class (and later caste) consciousness.

[33] Translated only one year after (1861) into English by Michael Madhusūdan Datta under the title *Nil Durpan or the Indigo Planting Mirror* (M.M. Datta 1990).

[34] Cf. Zbavitel (1976:238f.).

[35] Kṣetra Gupta (1991:2) gives a list of eight writers of 'novels' prior to *Durgeś'nandinī*, but points out that they had no clear conception 'what the significance of the art-form called *upanyās* [Beng. — "novel"] was'.

tried to adapt a literary genre. Accordingly, the reading public already awaited the advent of the Bengali novel. The aesthetic problem still unsolved was to conceive *sujets* and especially a suitable style of Bengali prose to fit in with the aesthetics of the new genre.

Baṅkim'candra's first attempt at the task of writing a novel was *Rajmohan's Wife*, published 1864 serially in the *Indian Field*. He had used Bengali for poetry before; his turning to English for a novel underscores the existence of conceptual difficulties involved in this choice of language. It was not this but his second novel, written in Bengali, that immediately gained him great fame. *Durgeś'nandinī* came out in 1865 and was celebrated as a major literary event.[36] It is a historical novel based on the struggle for Bengal between the Mughals and the Pathans. The language employed is different from the rather colloquial Bengali of *Ālāler gharer dulāl* as well as from the heavily Sanskritised style Bidyāsāgar (Vidyāsāgar) used in his essays. It is of course *sādhu bhāṣā*,[37] but borrowings from Sanskrit such as certain participles, long compounds, etc. are decreased. The language of *Durgeś'nandinī* and most of Baṅkim's other writings claims the status of a formal style, a certain dignity which, in Baṅkim's view, the '*ālālī*' style does not have; this status naturally corresponds with Baṅkim's notions regarding the purpose of literature.[38] On the other hand, Baṅkim'candra rejects highly Sanskritised language as the *bidyāsāgarī* style on the criteria that it lacks fluidness and intelligibility. This reasoning was not unanimously accepted at the time; but it is certainly arguable that Baṅkim'candra found the right language for novel-writing in his times, and in this way exerted a great influence on the development of modern Bengali.[39]

But *Durgeś'nandinī* is significant in several other ways, too. As a historical novel, it is indicative of the newly born sense of history in India. History was starting to be perceived as one of the most important features of modern nations, largely serving the purpose of legitimising nationhood. This process was, of course, enhanced by Western

[36] There are many testimonies to the impact *Durgeś'nandinī* had in contemporary Bengal. As an example, a passage from Ar. Cy. Dae's *The Literature of Bengal* (1877) — probably the first English monograph on Bengali literature after Rām'gati Nyāẏ'ratna's Bengali work (1872) — may be quoted: 'We all remember how, about ten or twelve years ago, the Bengali reading community was taken by surprise by the *Durgesh Nandini*, the first work of the author, and a masterwork of creative imagination. It seems as if a grand panorama had suddenly burst upon the reader's eye [...].' ibid.; 196. Also Śib'nāth Śāstrī in his *Rām'tanu lahiṛī o tat kālīn baṅgasamāj* (1967 [1903]): 'Nobody had seen before a novel [*upanyās* (Beng.)] of this kind in Bengali.' The *Brahmo Public Opinion* in 1880 (Benoy Ghose 1978-81,VII:142) stresses the merits of Baṅkim's literature (admitting however that it is not free from 'indecencies') and states: 'Babu Bankim Chunder's Durgesh Nandini was the first novel in Bengali.'

[37] I.e. the literary variety of Bengali as opposed to *calit bhāṣā*, the 'current language'. The *sādhu bhāṣā* was until about the middle of the twentieth century the most widely used medium for literary expression.

[38] In *Baṅgālā bhāṣā*, an essay published in 1878 in the *Baṅgadarśan* (*BR* II, 368-74:373), Baṅkim discusses the different styles and writes: 'Therefore it must be concluded that the height or meanness of the language should be determined according to the subject matter.' Nonetheless, he decidedly disqualifies the language of *Hutom pyā̃cār naksā* as being inadequate for literature (ibid.). Also quoted in Amitrasūdan Bhaṭṭācārya (ed.) (1986:99); the chapter *Bāṃlā gadyarīti o baṅkim'candra* (98-103) deals with the said essay. Cf. also Amiya P. Sen (1993:94).

[39] Cf. Aurobindo's statement about the results of Baṅkim's creativity: 'When a Mahratha or Gujerati has any thing important to say, he says it in English; when a Bengali, he says it in Bengali.' (Aurobindo 1954:42)

higher education, in which history was a prominent subject. Historiography was at this time given more attention, and Bengali historiography was important in framing a new, nationalist outlook.[40] As later developments show, the evaluation of historical data became very important towards the end of the century. Baṅkim'candra's historical novels and especially his essays on the topic helped in promoting this consciousness.

Furthermore, in the area of prose, *Durgeś'nandinī* was the first major writing in Bengali which turned away from satire towards a new intentional seriousness. Baṅkim's novels, however distorted some of them may seem from a modern aesthetic perspective, and despite some occasional elements of satire, are meant to be 'serious literature'; their mode of producing sense is meant to be straight, not oblique. In the case of *Durgeś'-nandinī*, of course, this mode of producing straight sense is still concerned with the past, and therefore does not, in outward appearance, directly enter the field of negotiation between the cultures. But in view of the changed consciousness regarding history, it was already assuming a political character. Enhanced by nationalist historiography,[41] history itself thus became part of the substance under negotiation. In Baṅkim's later historical novels (*Ānandamaṭh*, *Sītārām*), this character trait was to become very obvious.

The first years of Baṅkim'candra's success coincided with some new tendencies in Bengali *élite* society. Īśvar'candra Bidyāsāgar had promoted a campaign for the remarriage of widows which resulted in the Widow Marriage Act of 1856, and by his interpretations of the Śāstras, he attempted to reform the Hindus' social life from within the tradition. In 1867, the *Hindu Melā* was founded by Nabagopāl Mitra with the aim of giving due prestige to Hindu culture. Social reform, again, was one of the main concerns of the Brāhma Samāj which had since the time of Rām'mohan Rāẏ's life been a major promoter of change. But the margins between reform and revival were by no means clear-cut, and characteristically it was a Brahmo leader, Rāj'nārāẏaṇ Basu, who in 1872 first voiced Hinduism's claim for superiority among religions.[42] The dissemination of Western scientific thinking through the *Tattvabodhinī Patrikā*, and the first large-scale scholarly treatise written in the Bengali language,[43] were undertaken by Akṣaẏ'kumār Datta.

In 1872, Baṅkim first brought out his monthly journal *Baṅgadarśan*, containing his novels in instalments and essays on science, history, culture, etc., by a number of writers including himself.[44] *Baṅgadarśan* soon became one of the most influential magazines

[40] Cf. Partha Chatterjee (1995) and Sudipta Kaviraj (1993 and 1995:106ff.) for two lucid theoretical expositions of the problems of nationalist historiography.

[41] Cf. Partha Chatterjee (1995) where the beginning of nationalist historiography is traced back to *The History of India* by Tarinicharan Chattopadhyay, written as early as 1858.

[42] In a lecture entitled *Hindudharmmer śreṣṭhatā* (Rāj'nārāẏaṇ Basu: 1995:418-73); cf. also Rāj'-nārāẏaṇ's remarks in his autobiography: *Ātmacarit* (3rd edn 1952). A summary of the lecture is included in Ghatak (1991:42ff.). Baṅkim praises the lecture, which appeared as a book, in a review, but stresses that Rāj'nārāẏaṇ's *dharma* — the worship of the *brahman* — is only a fragment of Hindu *dharma*. (In his *Prāpta granther saṃkṣipta samālocan* [1872], *BR* II:873f.)

[43] *Bhārat'barṣīẏa upāsak sampradāẏ* ('The Indian Sects of Worshippers'), 2 vols.; first published in 1870 and 1883 respectively.

[44] *Baṅgadarśan* has often been highlighted as *the* literary event in the middle of the nineteenth century. Cf. Rabindranath Tagore (1961, 115): 'Then came Bankim's *Bangadarshan*, taking the Bengali heart by storm. It was bad enough to have to wait till the next number was out, but to be kept waiting further till my elders had done with it was simply intolerable!' Similarly in Śib'nāth Śāstrī (1967 [1903]:253): 'In becoming

of the time, and from the beginning the journal's educative orientation is clear. If *Baṅgadarśan* was perceived as a norm-setting medium, it was very much conceived exactly as such.

In the year 1873, an event is reported which represents quite another dimension of experience not uncommon for Bengalis of that time: Baṅkim'candra gets beaten up by an English Lieutenant Colonel for crossing a cricket ground in a palanquin.[45] Baṅkim had to suffer similar humiliations at other times of his life.[46]

Since the time of the Derozians, the educated *élite* had grown considerably in numbers, and factions had become consolidated. While one part of them took social reform as their primary concern, the other sought regeneration of the society by trying to revive ancient Hindu culture. These factions are usually called Reformers (or Progressives) and Revivalists (or Conservatives/Reactionaries), respectively.[47] Both of these groups, however, accepted very similar premises: the present inferiority of Indian culture compared to European culture, and the imperative to spread education among the 'ignorant' masses.

The *élite* were then still quite a closed circle, and the persons of repute almost all seem to have known each other personally. This is also true of Baṅkim'candra, even if he is reported to have been rather introverted and little inclined to much company. The reminiscences of some of his contemporaries give a vivid picture of many informal meetings and discussions that must have played just as important a role in the dissemination of ideas as the media of the time.[48]

Among Baṅkim's writings during the Seventies — several novels and a large number of essays on various topics — his satirical writings, compiled later under the title of *Kamalākānta*, hold a special position. Kamalākānta, a jobless opium-eater,[49] records his views about contemporary society while in a state of intoxication. This oblique or marginal mode of expression[50] permits Baṅkim to be far more outspoken about the state of things than anywhere else. Thus, *Kamalākānta* has rightly been called 'Baṅkim's mirror'[51] or his 'secret autobiography':[52] It is here that his writings escape their norm-

---

the editor of a monthly paper, he [Baṅkim] created a monthly paper which acquired a place in the homes of the Bengalis right after its publication.' On Baṅkim's role in the development of journalism and criticism, cf. (among many others) Jaẏanta Bandyopādhyāẏ (1986) and Sabitā Pāl (1994).

[45] Reported in the *Amṛtabājār Patrikā* of the 23 Oct., 1873; quoted in Arabinda Poddār (1994 [1951]:134); and in BCJ:280.

[46] Cf. Tapan Raychaudhuri (1988:114) who describes Baṅkim's experiences as 'particularly unfortunate' and gives a few examples.

[47] This terminology is, however, very problematic, especially with regard to colonised societies. What is commonly overlooked is that in a colonial situation, turning to the past assumes quite a different meaning than in independent societies. Cf. the discussions in Amiya P. Sen (1993) and Rākhāl Candra Nāth (1988).

[48] Cf. Rabindranath Tagore (1961:123) on the importance of *maj'lis* for the generations preceding his own.

[49] For this choice of narrator, *Kamalākānta* has often been compared to De Quincy's *Confessions of an Opium-Eater*, and even been claimed to be a mere Bengali version of the latter. But the similarities between these two works are rare, and the charge of plagiarism is completely unjustified.

[50] Cf. the chapter 'Humour and the Prison of Reality: Kamalakanta as the Secret Autobiography of Bankimchandra Chattopadhyay' (first 1988) of Sudipta Kaviraj (1995).

[51] In Amitrasūdan Bhaṭṭācārya (1986:77ff.).

setting function or didactic detachment and come down to plain talk. Critique of utilitarianism, of mimicry of the West, of official court language, etc., is voiced, and even a utopian vision, foreshadowing Baṅkim's later writings, comes to the opium-eater in an intoxicated dream about the goddess Durgā:

> Come, oh brothers all! Let us jump into this dark stream of time. Come, let us pick up this image[53] with 120 million arms and carry it home on 60 million heads.[54]

Durgā is addressed as *baṅgajananī* (Beng., 'mother of Bengal') or *baṅgapratimā* (Beng., 'image of Bengal'), and her return home is equated with the reawakening of the Bengalis. This is the first major instance of Baṅkim's usage of religious imagery in a proto-political context. It is still a marginal character who utters such ideas and actually regrets having taken too much opium; but soon afterwards, from the beginning of the eighties, Hindu religion comes to occupy a central place in Baṅkim'candra's various writings.

There are many indications suggesting that Baṅkim'candra's turn towards Hinduism was not an isolated phenomenon.[55] Throughout the Bengal Renaissance, religion had been a dominant concern,[56] but traditional Hinduism had been an object of polemics rather than appreciation. In the seventies of the nineteenth century, this started to change: the second great reformist movement of Hinduism, the Ārya Samāj, was founded in Bombay and soon acquired a strong footing in the north-west. In Bengal, the Brāhma Samāj split twice, in 1866 and in 1878, due to internal quarrels, and started to lose its predominant position in Bengali society.[57] Rāj'nārāẏaṇ Basu's aforementioned lecture found repercussions in progressive and conservative Hindu quarters alike,[58] and led to something Sandīp Bandyopādhyāẏ (1993) calls *śreṣṭhatvabād*, i.e. approximately 'the doctrine of superiority [of Hinduism/Indian civilisation]'. This, combined with the impact the mystic Rām'kr̥ṣṇa had on a part of educated Hindu society, was favourable to the emergence of a new attitude towards Hinduism. Many assessments of Hindu religion were published in various journals and newspapers.[59] Itinerant preachers and activists like Kr̥ṣṇaprasanna Sen and Śaśadhar Tarkacūṛāmaṇi came to Calcutta to

[52] Cf. the respective chapter in Kaviraj (1995).

[53] *pratimā* (Beng.); the image of Durgā.

[54] *Āmār durgot'sab* in *Kamalākānta* (1875); *BR* II:80.

[55] Cf. Amiya P. Sen (1993:esp. introduction) and Tapan Raychaudhuri (1988:12f.). The latter however states (p. 137) that Baṅkim's apparently rather sudden transition to a theist outlook has not been sufficiently explained yet. The answer attempted by Rabirañjan Caṭṭopādhyāẏ (1989) and Śaṅkarīprasād Basu (1990) (cf. below) does not appear to be satisfactory.

[56] Cf. e.g. Rākhāl Candra Nāth (1988:viii).

[57] To all appearance, the elitist character of the Brāhma Samāj was also partly responsible for its loss of influence. Bipin'candra Pāl attributes the increasing unpopularity of the Brāhma Samāj to Keśab'candra Sen's claim for the privileged 'authority as the ordained messengers of a New Dispensation'. Bipin Chandra Pal: *Memories of my Life and Times* (1932:237); quoted from Bhabatoṣ Datta (1961:46f.).

[58] Rāj'nārāẏaṇ Basu was not happy with some of his new supporters; e.g. he declined an offer to repeat his speech in front of a '*sākār'bādī bāṅālī sabhā*' and is amused about being addressed as *hindukul'cuṛāmaṇi* ['highest jewel of the Hindu family'] or, from another side, *kalir byās'deb* ['the R̥ṣi Vyāsa of the *kali*-age']. See Rāj'nārāẏaṇ Basu (1952:85f.).

[59] Cf. *BJ*:594.

preach the superiority of Hinduism with pseudo-scientific arguments and, apparently, a lot of success.[60] Even some of the Derozians turned back to Hinduism.[61] In the field of theatre, the earlier preponderance of a reformist critique of indigenous customs gave way to adaptions of mythical themes (e.g. the so-called *gītābhinaẏs*) with an increasingly strong nationalist touch.[62] At the same time, political participation on the part of the Indians got the first serious forum in the shape of the Indian Association, founded in 1876.[63] Like history, religion too began to assume a political aspect, and arguably this close connection has been a major factor in Indian politics ever since.

Baṅkim'candra was never active in the politics of his times and even disapproved of the Congress and the reformative zeal of the Brāhma Samāj;[64] in a discussion with Bijaẏ'lāl Datta he points out that Congress politics are confined to the *élite* and do not reach common people and pleads for a combined political, religious and social movement to ensure general uplift.[65] Baṅkim'candra's approach is rather broad: ethical renewal must precede direct political action. In his last work phase, including his last three novels, he tried to work out a model for such regeneration: philosophically based, this ethical system was largely set in Hindu religious terms.[66]

It would seem that Baṅkim'candra was drawn to his concentrated occupation with religion by a specific event.[67] In 1882, Reverend Hastie, an English missionary, published a series of letters in the *Statesman*, denouncing a huge *śrāddha* ceremony arranged by Maharaja Harendra Krishna Deb of Shobhabazar and, along with it, the whole of 'Hindu idolatry' in increasingly drastic terms. Baṅkim felt provoked and wrote a not less polemical reply under the pseudonym of Ram Chandra. Thus the so-called

[60] For a presentation and discussion of their ideas, cf. the detailed portrayal in Sunītirañjan Rāẏ'caudhurī (1981); also Amiya P. Sen (1993).

[61] Rākhāl Candra Nāth (1988:ix) mentions Dakṣiṇārañjan Mukhopādhyāẏ and Jñānendramohan Ṭhākur (the first Indian barrister) the former of whom became a *Vaiṣṇava* and the latter a 'brahmin catholic'.

[62] Cf. Zbavitel (1976:228ff.).

[63] 1875, according to Sisir Kumar Das (1984:140).

[64] Cf. Aurobindo 1954:46.

[65] Bijaẏ'lāl Datta: *Baṅkim'candra*; in Somendranāth Basu (ed.) (1989:37).

[66] The 'turn' in Baṅkim's concerns at the beginning of this last work phase was expressed by Aurobindo's famous sentence: 'The earlier Bankim was only a poet and a stylist — the later Bankim was a seer and nation-builder' (1940:9).

[67] It is true that there are many writings on religion before that date, too, e.g. in essays like *Buddhism and the Sankhya Philosophy* (1871), *Sāṃkhyadarśan* (1872) or *The Study of Hindu Philosophy* (1873). Śaṅkarīprasād Basu (1990: esp. 10-21) proves that much of the material dealt with in *Kṛṣṇacaritra* and the later writings in general can be traced to essays before the controversy, and Rabirañjan Caṭṭopādhyāẏ (1989) shows the presence of Kṛṣṇa in Baṅkim's writings starting with *Durgeś'nandinī*. But at that time Baṅkim's concern is not yet overwhelmingly religious. The discussion is far more detached than in his later writings, and neither the normative nor the didactic aspect are as important. And significantly, the claim to Hindu superiority, so common in the writings after the controversy, is still absent. Tapan Raychaudhuri (1988:146) is certainly right in stating that the Hastie controversy — the actual event under discussion — 'may have helped revive all the emotive associations which that form of worship [to Kṛṣṇa] had in the life of his family'. Cf. also Rākhāl Candra Nāth (1988:xvi) who actually sees the Hastie controversy as the starting point of what he calls *nabyahindu āndolan* ('the neo-Hindu movement', 1882-1911). Amiya P. Sen (1993:109), while clinging to the controversy as a demarcation point, remains differentiated about foreshadowings in Baṅkim's earlier life.

Hastie controversy[68] started, went on for a few polemic exchanges and then compelled Baṅkim to furnish an appreciative exposition of the Hindu religion; ultimately, Baṅkim'-candra put a halt to the controversy by claiming (with doubtful legitimation) that his opponent had sufficiently disqualified himself.

The controversy displays Baṅkim's mastery of the English language and his rhetorical skills. But besides its stylistic qualities, the controversy reveals two fundamental notions regarding the topic which may be taken as the starting point of his religious writings. First, he denies European Indologists, here F. Max Müller, the right to claim authority in matters connected with Hindu religion because, according to him, the 'inner' perspective of the believer is crucial to any right understanding (*BR* III:204). Second, he does not refer to the whole complex of Hindu culture and religion, but handles it selectively:

> Mr. Hastie may turn round upon me and say: 'You strip Hinduism of its rites, its idolatry, its caste; what do you then leave it?' — I leave *the kernel without the husk* [italics of the original]. (*BR* III:217)

These two points become almost programmatic in Baṅkim's following writings: The 'kernel' of Hinduism had to be identified, and the discussion about Hinduism had to be brought back to India.

There are also some indications that Baṅkim was more personally concerned with religion at this time than in his earlier life. His biographer Śacīś'candra Caṭṭopādhyāẏ estimates that Baṅkim's new attitude towards religion started to manifest itself at the age of forty, i.e. around 1878, and reports Baṅkim's statement in retrospect that he had been a most decided atheist (*BJ*:329). Śacīś'candra also mentions that Baṅkim for some time tried to observe rules of orthodox conduct: 'Baṅkim'candra had for some time given up fish and meat and become a *haviṣyāśin* [person eating rice and ghee]. He wore a *nāmābalī*-shawl [shawl on which names of Viṣṇu are written], remained in pure conduct, [and] always recited the *Gītā*'; Baṅkim however had to give up food restrictions for reasons of health (*BJ*:115).

By 1882, Baṅkim's most famous and controversial novel *Ānandamaṭh*[69] had come out, followed in 1884 by *Debī caudhurāṇī* and in 1887 by *Sītārām*. In all these novels, a new impact of religious imagery and ethical doctrines is evident.[70] This applies also to a certain extent to Baṅkim'candra's last work of fiction, a greatly enlarged version of his earlier novel *Rāj'siṃha* which appeared in 1893. But in contrast with former periods of his career, Baṅkim'candra became more of an essayist than

[68] Published in 1882 by Hastie in a book entitled *Hindu Idolatry and English Enlightenment*; included in *Baṅkim racanābalī* (Vol. III:186-224). Apart from Baṅkim'candra, other persons too had joined the debate (among them, at a later stage, Reverend Kṛṣṇamohan Bandyopādhyāẏ). But Hastie soon singled out 'Ram Chandra' as his main adversary. For summaries of the controversy, see Śaṅkarīprasād Basu (1990:22-8); Sisir Kumar Das (1984:158-61).

[69] This novel had been proscribed after its first edition and afterwards was brought out by Baṅkim only in attenuated versions; it was to have its full impact in militant nationalist circles only two decades later. On the history of proscriptions and confiscations of Baṅkim's later witings, cf. Chapter 5 (65-90) of Śiśir Kar (1988). — An English translation of *Ānandamaṭh* has recently been published (1992), a reprint of Basanta Koomar Roy's work of 1941; it is of hardly any use because the crucial last chapter has been left out. An English version of this chapter is included in Clark (1961).

[70] Arūp'kumār Bhaṭṭacārya (1989:117) says the last novels are decidedly influenced by *niṣkāma karman*.

novelist during the last decade of his life, and these essays were almost exclusively on religious topics. In 1884 he started a new journal called *Pracār* ('Dissemination') for the obvious purpose of spreading his ideas on culture and religion. Among these essays, the most important are *Letters on Hinduism* (in English; before 1885) and the Bengali writings *Dharmmajijñāsā* (1884); *Deb'tattva o hindudharmma* (1884-5); *Kṛṣṇacaritra* (1886/1892); *Dharmmatattva* (1888); and *Śrīmadbhagabadgītā*, his commentary on the *Bhagavadgītā*.

These latter essays are closely interconnected in their content; they were written in overlapping periods of time. Still they are quite different in character. In *Dharmmajijñāsā*, different meanings of the terms *dharma* and 'religion', and their possible equivalence, are discussed with the aim of arriving at a new definition. The essay is written as a dialogue between teacher and pupil, and thus clearly foreshadows *Dharmmatattva*; excerpts of it are included in the latter's appendices. *Deb'tattva o hindudharmma* deals with Vedic religion and its relationship to puranic Hinduism. The ideas developed in these comparatively short essays are mostly taken up again in the following voluminous writings.

Kṛṣṇacaritra ('Kṛṣṇa's Life')[71] is a study on Kṛṣṇa; its aim is to establish Kṛṣṇa as a historical figure and the ideal of mankind by extrapolation from mythology. Baṅkim'candra starts with a long argument with Western Indologists about datings and statements concerning Kṛṣṇa's historicity. Then he introduces an evaluation scale of the various textual sources regarding Kṛṣṇa. In the most 'valuable' of these, the *Mahābhārata*, he distinguishes between three layers, i.e. (a) historical content, (b) later interpolations in accordance with this content, and (c) such interpolations as could be removed without doing harm to the basic chain of events. Along these lines, he meticulously discusses the sources and dismisses everything supernatural as belonging to the third layer. The *Bhagavadgītā* is, however, not extensively discussed in *Kṛṣṇacaritra*; Baṅkim points out *Dharmmatattva* and the commentary for reference.

Dharmmatattva ('Essentials of *Dharma*'),[72] written in the form of a conversation between a teacher and a student, is the most canonical of the three texts. Here, Baṅkim systematically exposes his ideas about religion. Departing from a naturally given *dharma*, he develops an ethical system much influenced by positivist and utilitarian thought. The ultimate goal to be achieved by man through the balanced cultivation[73] of his faculties (*vṛtti*), i.e. his *dharma*, is again 'humanity' (*manuṣyatva*). This concept is adopted from Auguste Comte, the founder of positivism and the *religion de l'humanité*. On this basis, the different spheres of human activities are treated systematically and in detail, descending from *īśvarabhakti* ('devotion to God') to *deśabhakti* ('devotion to one's country').

Much less known than these latter two is the last of these essays, his *Śrīmadbhagabadgītā*. One possible reason for this is that it has remained a fragment. Out of the 18 *adhyāyas* of the *Gītā*, the commentary covers only the initial three and a part of the

[71] Bengali *caritra* as well as Sanskrit *caritram* combine the rather static meaning of 'character', '(positive) individual properties' with the more dynamic 'behaviour', '(ideal) life', the latter being more directly semantically related to √*car* ('move, walk, behave', etc.). The set-up of the book *Kṛṣṇacaritra* suggests, I think, the translation 'Kṛṣṇa's Life', though 'Kṛṣṇa's Character' would also be possible.

[72] This is the title of the English translation by Manomohan Ghosh (1977).

[73] *anuśīlan*; also the title of *Dharmmatattva* before it was published as a book.

fourth. Further, only the first and second *adhyāyas* were published during Baṅkim's lifetime (1886-8 in *Pracār*); the rest existed only in the form of manuscripts and were not published until 1902 by a relative of Baṅkim's. Besides this, the commentary's nature seems responsible for its lesser popularity. In comparison to the other religious essays, it is very heterogeneous and less organised as a text. Moreover, the coordination of the single essays published in instalments before the edition of the whole as a book is absent here; there is no final redaction as in his other writings. As a consequence, some redundancies and reiterations have remained.

Nonetheless, the commentary remains an important text for a proper understanding of Baṅkim'candra's religious ideas. For it is here that he is forced to derive his ideas directly from a textual basis, the *Bhagavadgītā*. And more than the other essays, this interpretation-in-process gives clues to the hermeneutical situation in which he found himself. It may be called a micro-study on a central text of Hinduism whose exegesis has been undertaken by many commentators, from Śaṅkarācārya to Mahātmā Gāndhī. In this way, it is apt to be made the object of another micro-study, on another level of research, about the mediation between India and Europe in religious terms. It is unlikely that the commentary itself exerted much direct influence on later interpretations of the *Gītā* or Hinduism. But there is no denying that Baṅkim's thoughts about religion had a great impact on the development of modern Hinduism; and in his commentary all of his principal concepts are present.

In short, his *Śrīmadbhagabadgītā* is revealing both as a micro-study on a central Hindu scripture and as a document of late nineteenth century thinking in Bengal. Its relevance is by no means limited to religious studies, but persists also in the greater context of intellectual history in colonised countries. Accordingly, the analysis following the translation will attempt to determine the ultimate *locus* of the commentary historically as well as conceptually; its hermeneutical interposition between two cultures, and Baṅkim'candra's ways of navigating his argumentations along such contrasted lines, will be examined in some detail.

1 Translation:

Śrīmadbhagabadgītā

First complete Bengali edition in 1902
Partly in *Pracār* from 1886 to 1888

Notes on the Translation

The translation is based on the *Sāhitya Saṃsad* edition by Yogeś candra Bāgal (*ŚBhG[a]*). In cases of doubt, the *Baṅkim-śatabārṣik* edition by Brajendranāth Bandyopādhyāẏ and Sajanīkānta Dās (*ŚBhG[b]*) has been consulted for comparison.

Priority has been given to an exact rendering of the original Bengali text. Stylistic adaptions are thus few; interpunctuation, sentence structure and paragraphs have as far as possible been kept in the translation. Where the insertion of additional conjunctions seemed necessary, these are given in square brackets. Throughout the text, including the footnotes, square brackets are reserved for the translator's comments. Passages in Latin script are marked by [Lat.]; single words in Latin script within Bengali sentences — including personal names — are given in italics and followed by [Lat.]. Sanskrit passages, including the *Bhagavadgītā* as the basis of the commentary, are given in italics, and translations of them are furnished in footnotes only when they are not translated or paraphrased in the text. In some cases, the respective portions of existing English translations have been consulted. The translations of the *Bhagavadgītā* as well as of other Sanskrit sources are direct renderings of Baṅkim's Bengali translations; only significant deviations from the original are acknowledged in footnotes. For a more accurate rendering of the *Gītā*, van Buitenen's English bilingual edition (*BhGBE*) may be consulted.

In the representation of Sanskrit passages, writing conventions due to the Bengali script and phonetics (e.g. the use of ẏ for *y*, ṙ for *ḍ*, assimilation of the *anusvāra*, etc.) have not been heeded. The reduplication of consonants after *r*, which Baṅkim uses in his Sanskrit quotations, has also been omitted. Names of Sanskrit texts (e.g. *Viṣṇupurāṇa*) and authors (e.g. Śaṅkara) as well as terms (e.g. *karman*) are given in their common Sanskrit forms. In Baṅkim candra's text of the *Bhagavadgītā*, variants deviating from the text in the critical *Mbh* edition but given in its annotations have not been notified.

In cases of problematic translations, the respective Bengali words have been given in footnotes and marked by (Beng.) in order to distinguish them from Sanskrit words, e.g. [*mahāmahopādhyāẏ* (Beng.)]. The mark is however omitted, for aesthetical reasons, with Bengali personal names (e.g. Hit lāl Miśra), titles (e.g. *Sāheb*), names of works (e.g. *Sītārām*) and names of places (e.g. Lāl dighi). In the transcription from Bengali, in contrast to Sanskrit, words are represented as spelt by Baṅkim, and thus here, the reduplications after *r* common in nineteenth century Bengali are kept (e.g. *Dharmmatattva*).

Bibliographic references of the literature Baṅkim quotes being fragmentary and sometimes erroneous in the commentary, they are given in full upon their first appearance. The quoted authors are, as far as they have been traceable, included in the bibliography.

The Sanskrit quotations have been checked; the specific editions used are given in the bibliography. Wherever Baṅkim himself gives translations of Sanskrit quotations, these have been rendered without further comments, unless the translations differ significantly in content from the respective originals.

Some terms, most prominently *dharma*, have been left without translation; this was necessary in order not to efface the inherent semantic and dialectical complexities. Where central terms are not left in the original but translated by English equivalents (e.g. 'action' which represents *karman*), my effort has been to keep one equivalent term throughout the translation, and the choices of equivalents have been documented in footnotes. In cases where this was not possible, but where it nonetheless seemed appropriate to translate a term (e.g. in the case of *karman*), other translations have been specially noted at their occurrence. In one case a term has become a loan word of the English language, and thus been represented by it: *paṇḍit* [Beng.] is translated as 'pundit' — unless *paṇḍit* [Beng.] stands for Skt. *paṇḍita*. In all such cases, however, translatory decisions have been documented. The semantic field of 'worship' is covered by the Bengali words *upāsanā*, *ārādhanā*, *pūjā* and *arcanā*. *Arcanā* has consistently been rendered by 'veneration' (or 'venerate'); in the other cases, such consistency was impossible, especially since compounds as e.g. *pratimāpūjā* and *pratimā-upāsanā* are used synonymously for Engl. 'idol-worship'.

Except in the case of proper names, capital letters in words transcribed from Indian languages are only used at the beginning of sentences.

For the rendering of Bengali words, the system of transliteration of New Indo-Aryan by Rahul Peter Das[1] is used, with a slight modification: as the latter part of conjunct consonants, Beng. *b* in *tatsama* words is rendered by *v* (e.g. *tattva*, but *bikār* instead of *vikār*).

[1] *Indo-Iranian Journal 27.1984*, p. 66, n. 2.

Preface

In the presence of the venerable Śaṅkara's and others' commentaries[1] and annotations,[2] further explanations of the *Gītā* are unnecessary. All of these commentaries and annotations, however, are written in the Sanskrit language. Nowadays there are many readers who are unable to understand Sanskrit, but are who nevertheless especially eager to read the *Gītā*. But the *Gītā* is such a difficult book that, without the aid of a commentary, it is incomprehensible to many. Therefore a Bengali commentary of the *Gītā* is required.

A Bengali commentary can be of two kinds. Firstly, a Bengali translation of the ancient commentaries and annotations by Śaṅkara and others can be provided. Secondly, a new Bengali commentary can be written. Some writers have adopted the method mentioned first. *Bābu* Hit'lāl Miśra has compiled in his translation sometimes the essential parts of Śaṅkara's commentary, sometimes those of Śrīdhara Svāmin's annotations. *Śrī Bābu* Kedār'nāth Datta, a *Vaiṣṇava* and pundit of highest order, often supplied in his translation the gist of Viśvanātha Cakravartin's commentary. For this Bengali readers are especially indebted to them. The dear *Śrīyukta Bābu* Bhūdhar'-candra Caṭṭopādhyāẏ has become engaged in another edition of the *Gītā*; I have seen in its advertisement that it will contain a translation of Śaṅkara's commentary. This is a matter of good fortune for Bengali readers.

Śrīyukta Bābu Kr̥ṣṇaprasanna adopted the second method. Along with his own translation, he published a Bengali commentary named *Gītāsandīpanī*. Fortunately, in this *Gītāsandīpanī* the inner significance of the *Gītā* has been explained the way the old pundits used to explain it; without doubt the Bengali readership should feel obliged to Śrīkr̥ṣṇaprasanna *Bābu* for this.

It may thus seem a vain effort when, despite the existence of all these translations and commentaries a person like myself sets out to publish a new translation and commentary. But if there were no genuine need I would not lay my hands on this most difficult task. I shall now explain what this need is.

Almost the majority of today's readers belong to the 'educated' class. Normally [exclusively] those are called 'educated' who are educated in Western learning; it is under the influence of current usage that I use the word 'educated' in this sense. Some may be more educated, some less; but whether it be more or less - I know that the majority of the readers in this country[3] belong to the 'educated' class. Now, the problem is that this educated class cannot understand the utterances of the ancient pundits without difficulties. Like the pundits of a *ṭol*,[4] who even in translation face difficulties understanding the utterances of Westerners, those educated in Western learning do not easily understand the sentences of their ancient Eastern pundits when confronted with a mere translation. This is not their fault, but is a natural result of their education. The Western way of thinking is so different from the ancient Indian way of thinking that the ideas[5] cannot be conveyed to them by a transformation of language. Our educated class

[1] [*bhāṣya*.]

[2] [*ṭīkā*.]

[3] [*ekhān'kār* (Beng.): literally 'from here'.]

[4] [*ṭol* (Beng.): a traditional Sanskrit school.]

[5] [*bhāb* (Beng.).]

has, from childhood on, followed the Western way of thinking, the ancient Indian way of thinking is unknown to them; the ancient ideas cannot be conveyed to them by a linguistic reversal. If they are to be taught, Western methods must be adopted, and the help of Western ideas has to be used. The aim of my commentary is thus to teach them the meaning of the *Gītā* according to Western methods and with the help of Western ideas.

Its more specific necessity lies in the fact that, in the commentaries of the ancient pundits, there is no resolution[6] of all the doubts that are likely to arise in the minds of the class [which has been] educated in Western learning. There is, indeed, no possibility of resolution, because the readers for whose benefit they had composed these commentaries could not possibly have had such doubts. All these doubts have as far as possible been resolved in this commentary.

Consequently, I do not compete with all the pundits who have circulated or circulate explanations of the *Gītā* in Bengali; my humble ambition is no more than to assist them as much as possible. I too have followed the ancient pundits as far as I could. I have written this commentary paying heed to Śaṅkara's commentary together with the annotations of Ānandagiri, Śrīdhara Svāmin's commentary, the *Rāmānuja-bhāṣya*, the commentaries of Madhusūdana Sarasvatī, Viśvanātha Cakravartin, etc. But I must also admit that there is no possibility for a person acquainted with Western literature, science and philosophy to follow the ancients at all times. I could not follow them in every case either. I have no sympathy whatsoever with those people who think that all the native ancient pundits said is true, and all what Westerners say about material principles[7] is wrong.

Commentary alone is my aim, but there can be no commentary without the original text; therefore, the original too has been provided. Many readers are not able to understand the original without a translation, for which reason this has also been supplied. There are many excellent Bengali translations of the *Gītā*; the reader may resort to whichever he considers best. My effort has usually been to translate faithfully; in a few places, however, some slight exceptions to this rule have occurred for the sake of bringing out the meaning.

Calcutta, 1293 BE [1886] Śrī Baṅkim'candra Caṭṭopādhyāẏ

[6] [*mīmāṃsā* (Beng.).]

[7] [*jāgatik tattva* (Beng.).]

First Chapter

dhṛtarāṣṭra uvāca:
dharmakṣetre kurukṣetre samavetā yuyutsavaḥ
māmakāḥ pāṇḍavāś caiva kim akurvata saṃjaya. (1)

Dhṛtarāṣṭra said:
What, O Saṃjaya, did my side and the Pāṇḍavas do, when they, desirous of fighting, gathered on the sacred land of Kurukṣetra? (1)

The *Śrīmadbhagavadgītā* is contained in the *Bhīṣmaparvan* of the *Mahābhārata*. The part from *adhyāya* 3 to *adhyāya* 43 of the *Bhīṣmaparvan* is called *Bhagavadgītāparvādhyāya*, but the *Gītā* starts in the 25th chapter.[1] Not all readers may know what happened before that, therefore I shall briefly sum it up — for if I did not do so many readers would not understand why Dhṛtarāṣṭra asked this question, and who this Saṃjaya was anyway.

Seeing the prosperity of Yudhiṣṭhira's kingdom, Dhṛtarāṣṭra's son Duryodhana invited Yudhiṣṭhira to a rigged dice-game with the intention of stealing his kingdom. Yudhiṣṭhira lost this dice-game on the stake that he and his brothers would have to live in the woods for twelve years and incognito for one year. During these thirteen years, Duryodhana would enjoy their kingdom. After this, the Pāṇḍavas would, if having been able to keep the condition, get their kingdom back. The Pāṇḍavas spent twelve years in the woods and one year incognito, but afterwards Duryodhana refused to restore their kingdom. Consequently, the Pāṇḍavas prepared to regain their kingdom by making war. Both sides collected armies, and the armies gathered on the Kurukṣetra in order to fight. The *Gītā* starts when both armies have taken their positions facing one another, the war having not yet begun.

Dhṛtarāṣṭra was not himself present at Kurukṣetra but at Hastināpura in his palace. The reason for this is that he was blind from birth, and thus also bereft of the joy of watching the war by being present at Kurukṣetra. But he was especially eager to know the course of the war. Before the war the venerable Vyāsadeva had come to greet him and had wished to bestow a favour on him by giving him the divine eye.[2] But Dhṛtarāṣṭra had refused, saying, 'I do not have the desire to watch the killing of my kinsmen, but would rather, thanks to your spiritual power,[3] hear the story of the war from beginning to end'. Then Vyāsadeva bestowed a boon upon Dhṛtarāṣṭra's minister Saṃjaya. Through this boon Saṃjaya could, while staying at Hastināpura, see all the happenings of the war at Kurukṣetra with the divine eye and started to tell Dhṛtarāṣṭra.[4] Dhṛtarāṣṭra asks questions sometimes, and Saṃjaya answers: The *Yuddhaparvans*[5] of the *Mahābhārata* are written according to this method. All of it is Saṃjaya's narration. At this point, having heard that the armies of both sides have placed themselves opposite to one another in order to fight, Dhṛtarāṣṭra asks what both sides

1 [*Adhyāya* 23, according to the critical *Mahābhārata* edition.]

2 [*divya cakṣus*: enabling one to see without regard to distance, etc.]

3 [*tejaḥprabhābe* (Beng.).]

4 [Baṅkim's summary of the antecedents ends here, as the change of tense indicates.]

5 [The books of the *Mahābhārata* narrating the course of the war.]

did. This is how the *Gītā* starts.

This matter of the divine eye is something supernatural; I do not tell the readers to believe in it. It has nothing to do with the *dharma* exposed in the *Gītā*.

In the first chapter there is nothing of that explanation of *dharma* which is the motive of the *Gītā*. In this chapter and the first eleven verses of the second, merely the circumstances in which this theory has been expounded are introduced. This part is not necessary to convey the inner significance of the *Gītā*. If they so wish, the readers may leave out this part. In accordance with my aim, I need not comment on this part; the venerable Śaṅkara too has left aside this portion. But readers of a certain class[6] might want to learn something about one or the other topic. For this reason a few lines have been written.

Kurukṣetra is a region or province. This region lies south of today's city Stāneśvar or Thāneśvar; 15 *krośas* south of Āmbālā, and 20 *krośas* north of Pānipāṭ [*sic.*][7]. Kurukṣetra and Pānipāṭ are India's battle-grounds; in these places India's fate has often been decided upon. I hope nobody will think of a *maidan*[8] when he hears the expression *kṣetra*.[9] Already in ancient times Kurukṣetra spread 5 *yojanas*[10] both in length and breadth. Therefore it used to be called Samantapañcaka.[11] Nowadays the boundary of this region has further expanded.

There was a king called Kuru from the Candra dynasty. This region was named Kurukṣetra after him. He was the ancestor of the Pāṇḍavas and Duryodhana and his brothers; that is why Duryodhana, etc., and now and then also the Pāṇḍavas, are called Kauravas. He had obtained a boon through austerities in this place, thus it was named Kurukṣetra. In the *Mahābhārata* it has been said that because of his penance, it is a sacred site. As a result, Kurukṣetra has been known as *puṇyakṣetra*[12] and *dharmakṣetra*[13] for a very long time. In the *Śatapatha-Brāhmaṇa* it says:

> *devāḥ* [*sic.*][14] *ha vai sattraṃ niṣedur agnir indraḥ somo makho viṣṇur viśvedevā anyatrevāśvibhyām. teṣāṃ kurukṣetraṃ devayajanam āsa. tasmād āhuḥ kurukṣetraṃ devayajanam.*[15] [14.1.1.1-2]

6 [*śreṇībiśeṣer pāṭhak* (Beng.).]

7 [The distances are about 45 and 60 km respectively.]

8 [Beng. *maẏ'dān*, from Ar. *maidān* ('field', 'battlefield'); the Bengali meaning, to which Baṅkim'-candra refers here, is, according to relevant lexicography, narrowed down to 'field', 'lawn' (Jñānendramohan Dās 1994,II: 1726), or 'extended lawn' (Haricaraṇ Bandyopādhyāẏ 1988(1966),II:1734).]

9 [Literally 'field'.]

10 [Equivalent to about 30 km.]

11 [Literally: 'entirely consisting of five'. Baṅkim refers in this etymology to its extention over 5×5 *yojanas*. Another, arguably more convincing, etymology derives from the existence of five lakes in this region. See *Paurāṇik abhidhān* (Sudhīr'candra Sar'kār 1981-2:538).]

12 [Literally approximately 'place of ethical merit'.]

13 ['Place of *dharma*', i.e. 'righteousness', etc. See Chapter 2.2 of the analysis on the difficulties of translating this term.]

14 [This quotation is not according to the sandhi rules since the *visarga* should be eliminated here: *devā ha*, etc.]

15 ['The gods Agni, Indra, Soma, Makha, Viṣṇu and the Viśvedevas, except the *Āśvins*, sat for a *satra*-sacrifice. Their place of sacrifice to/of the gods was Kurukṣetra. Therefore, they call Kurukṣetra the place of sacrifice to/of the gods.']

That is: The Gods used to perform sacrifices here, therefore it is called 'Place of the Sacrifices of the Gods'. In the chapter *Tīrthayātrā* of the *Vanaparvan* of the *Mahābhārata* it is said that Kurukṣetra is the principal sacred site in the Three Worlds. In the *Vanaparvan*, the boundaries of Kurukṣetra are described thus: 'There is the Sarasvatī to the north, the Dṛṣadvatī to the south; between these two rivers lies Kurukṣetra.' (Chapter 83). In the *Manusaṃhitā* this very boundary has been set forth for the famous Brahmāvarta:

sarasvatīdṛṣadvatyor devanadyor yad antaraṃ
taṃ devanirmitaṃ deśaṃ brahmāvartaṃ pracakṣate.[16] (2.17)

Consequently Kurukṣetra and Brahmāvarta are one and the same. This can also be understood from the following poem by Kālidāsa:

brahmāvartaṃ janapadam atha cchāyayā gāhamānaḥ
kṣetraṃ kṣatrapraghanapiśunaṃ kauravaṃ tad bhajethāḥ
rājanyānāṃ śitaśaraśatair yatra gāṇḍīvadhanvā
dhārāpātais tvam iva kamalāny abhyavarṣan mukhāni.[17]
(*Meghadūta* 49)[18]

But in the *Manusmṛti* it says differently as follows:

kurukṣetraṃ ca matsyāś ca pañcālāḥ śūrasenakāḥ
eṣa brahmarṣideśo vai brahmāvartād anantaraḥ.[19] [2.19]

In relatively recent times[20] the Chinese traveller Hsüan-Tsang also called it *dharmakṣetra* in his book.[21]

Even today, Kurukṣetra is known as a *puṇyatīrtha* in India; many *yogins* and *saṃnyāsins* wander about there. There are many different sacred sites at Kurukṣetra, and among these quite a few are memorials of the war of the *Mahābhārata*. The place where *Abhimanyu* was killed through unfair battle by the *saptarathī*[22] is now called Abhimanyukṣetra or Amin. Still today, women longing for children offer worship to *Āditi* there in the *Āditi*-temple. The part of the *kṣetra* where the funeral rites of the warriors killed in the war of Kurukṣetra were performed [and] which was scattered with bones, is still called Asthipur.[23] The spot where the fierce battle between *Sātyaki* and *Bhūriśravas* took place and where Arjuna unjustly severed *Bhūriśravas*'s arm in order to save *Sātyaki*, is called Bhor today. A popular saying has it that birds took with them *Bhūriśravas*'s cut off arm. Among the ornaments of this hand was a very precious jewel;

16 ['The country prepared for/by the gods which lies between the divine rivers, Sarasvatī and Dṛṣadvatī, is called Brahmāvarta.']

17 ['Now, intruding with your shadow upon the region Brahmāvarta, resort to that *kauravic* field betraying the unfolding of the warriors, where the one whose bow is the *Gāṇḍīva* berained with hundreds of sharp arrows the faces of the nobles, as you (do) the lotuses with torrential showers.']

18 [The serial number varies according to the respective recensions of the *Meghadūta*.]

19 ['Kurukṣetra and (the region of) the Matsyas, the Pañcālas and the Śūrasenakas: this indeed is the country of the *brahmarṣis*, immediately adjoining Brahmāvarta.']

20 [In the seventh century A.D.]

21 M. Stanislaus [*sic.*] Julien [Lat.] [1853] wrote in his translation: '*Le champ du bonheur*' [Lat.], i.e. *dharmakṣetra.*

22 [*saptarathī*: the seven warriors of the Kaurava army who, after luring Arjuna's son *Abhimanyu* into a special battle-formation called *cakravyūha*, killed him mercilessly.]

23 [*asthipur* (Beng.): 'city of bones'.]

this was the *Kohinūr* which today adorns the body of the Queen of India.[24] It is needless to say that there is no proof of this saying's truth.

The name of Kurukṣetra is on the tongue of each and every Bengali; when seeing any tumult Bengali females say: 'It's a Kurukṣetra.' But then nobody knows anything more specific about Kurukṣetra. Especially English authors such as Thomson, Wheeler and others, lacking exact knowledge, have created a good deal of confusion; this is why Kurukṣetra has been treated here in such detail.[25]

saṃjaya uvāca:
dṛṣṭvā tu pāṇḍavānīkaṃ vyūḍhaṃ duryodhanas tadā
ācāryam upasaṃgamya rājā vacanam abravīt. (2)

Saṃjaya said:
After seeing the arrayed army of the Pāṇḍavas, King Duryodhana approached the master and spoke thus. (2)

Droṇa, son of Bharadvāja, was the teacher[26] of the art of using weapons to Duryodhana and his brothers. He was the guru of the Pāṇḍavas as well. He was a brahmin, and yet he was incomparable in military science. It is not correct that the art of using weapons belonged only to the kṣatriyas. Droṇācārya, Paraśurāma, Kṛpācārya, Aśvatthāman — all these were brahmins, and all the same they have usually been described as outshining the kṣatriyas in battle. This will have to be remembered when, later, the topic of fulfilling one's *svadharma* comes up.

The arraying of an army for a battle is called *vyūha*:
samagrasya tu sainyasya vinyāsaḥ sthānabhedataḥ
sa vyūha iti vikhyāto yuddheṣu pṛthivībhūjām.[27]

In modern European war, the construction of the battle- formation [*vyūha*] is the main task of the commander-in-chief.

paśyaitāṃ pāṇḍuputrāṇām ācārya mahatīṃ camūm
vyūḍhāṃ drupadaputreṇa tava śiṣyeṇa dhīmatā. (3)

O *Ācārya*, behold this huge army of the Pāṇḍavas, arrayed by your disciple, the talented son of Drupada. (3)

[24] [The *Kohinūr* is a huge diamond very much desired throughout the history of Mughal India. In 1849, with the surrender of the Pañjāb, it became the possession of Queen Victoria of England.]

[25] In order to give an example of the mistakes of the *Sāhebs*, I shall quote two lines from the commentary of Thomson [1855], translator of the *Gītā*. About Kurukṣetra he writes: 'A part of Dharmmakshetra, the flat plain around Delhi, which city is often identified with Hastinapur, the Capital of Kurukshetra.' [Lat.]

In this small text there are five mistakes: (1) There is no independent *kṣetra* called *Dharmakṣetra*. (2) Kurukṣetra is not just a part of *Dharmakṣetra*. (3) '*The flat plain around Delhi*' [Engl.] is not Kurukṣetra. (4) Delhi is not Hastināpur. (5) Hastināpur is not the capital of Kurukṣetra. We did not know that it was possible to unite so many mistakes in such a tiny space.

[26] [*ācārya*.]

[27] ['The arrangement, however, of the whole army according to the difference of the site is well-known, with reference to wars, as a *vyūha* among kings.' (Source not identified.)]

Drupada's son was Dhṛṣṭadyumna, one of the commanders of the Pāṇḍavas. It was he who had arranged the battle-formation. It is said that his birth took place as the consequence of a sacrifice his father performed out of desire for the murder of Droṇa. He is described as Droṇa's disciple. This will have to be remembered when talking about the fulfilment of one's *svadharma*. Droṇa gave education to an enemy produced for his own murder; the *dharma* of a master is to hand over knowledge.

atra śūrā maheṣvāsā bhīmārjunasamā yudhi
yuyudhāno virāṭaś ca drupadaś ca mahārathaḥ. (4)

dhṛṣṭaketuś cekitānaḥ kāśīrājaś ca vīryavān
purujit kuntibhojaś ca śaibyaś ca narapuṃgavaḥ. (5)

yudhāmanyuś ca vikrānta uttamaujāś ca vīryavān
saubhadro draupadeyāś ca sarva eva mahārathāḥ. (6)

In it[28] there are the heroes great in archery and in battle comparable to Bhīma and Arjuna, [namely,] Yuyudhāna (i); Virāṭa (ii); Drupada, the great warrior; Dhṛṣṭaketu (iii); Cekitāna, the mighty king of Kāśī; Purujit· Kuntibhoja (iv); Śaibya, the best of men; the valiant Yudhāmanyu; the mighty Uttamaujas; the son of Subhadrā (v); and the sons of Draupadī, all of whom are great warriors. (4) (5) (6)

(i) Yuyudhāna: the great hero Sātyaki from the lineage of Yadu.
(ii) Drupada, Virāṭa, Sātyaki, Dhṛṣṭaketu, etc., were all commanders of an *akṣauhiṇī*.[29]
(iii) Dhṛṣṭaketu has been described in the *Mahābhārata* as the emperor of the country Cedi. There is another description as well (*Mbh*, *Udyogaparvan*, Chapter 171 [?]).
(iv) Kuntibhoja is the name of a lineage. The old Kuntibhoja was the son of the maternal aunt of Śūra, father of Vasudeva.[30] Kuntī, the mother of the Pāṇḍavas, had been brought up in his house. Through this relation, Purujit· is the maternal uncle of the Pāṇḍavas.
(v) The famous Abhimanyu.

asmākaṃ tu viśiṣṭā ye tān nibodha dvijottama
nāyakā mama sainyasya saṃjñārthaṃ tān bravīmi te. (7)

O Best of the twice-born, know those who are best among us and who are the leaders of my army. To make you conscient of them I shall tell you their names. (7)

bhavān bhīṣmaś ca karṇaś ca kṛpaś ca samitiṃjayaḥ
aśvatthāmā vikarṇaś ca saumadattir jayadrathaḥ. (8)[31]

28 [I.e. in the army of the Pāṇḍavas.]

29 [According to the *Bāṅgālā bhāṣār abhidhān*, an *akṣauhiṇī* is 'a division of an army consisting of 109 350 foot-soldiers, 65 610 horses, 21 870 chariots and 21 870 elephants.' (Jñānendramohan Dās 1994:13)]

30 [Vasudeva is the father of Kṛṣṇa.]

31 There is another variant that reads *saumadattis tathaiva ca* ['and also Saumadatti indeed'].

You, Bhīṣma, Karṇa, Kṛpa, the winner of wars (vi), Aśvatthāman (vii), Vikarṇa, Saumadattaputra (viii) and Jayadratha (ix). (8)

(vi) He too was a brahmin and the Kauravas' teacher in the art of using weapons.
(vii) Son of Droṇa.
(viii) He is the famous Bhūriśravas.
(ix) The husband of Duryodhana's sister.

anye ca bahavaḥ śūrā madarthe tyaktajīvitāḥ
nānāśastrapraharaṇāḥ sarve yuddhaviśāradāḥ. (9)

Also many other heroes have given their lives (that is, are ready to give their lives) for my sake; they all are equipped with various weapons and well-versed in warfare. (9)

In the first chapter of the *Gītā*, there are no principles[32] of *dharma*; but the first chapter is excellent in its *kāvya*-part. It is a device of the poet that here the names of the many talented commanders of both sides have been brought to the memory of the readers. From now on, preparations are being made to convey to the readership the compassionate and beautiful devotion of Arjuna written down later on.

aparyāptaṃ tad asmākaṃ balaṃ bhīṣmābhirakṣitam
paryāptaṃ tv idam eteṣāṃ balaṃ bhīmābhirakṣitam. (10)

This army of ours guarded by Bhīṣma is insufficient,[33] and their army guarded by Bhīma is sufficient.[34] (10)

The words *paryāpta* and *aparyāpta* have been interpreted in accordance with Śrīdhara Svāmin's commentary. Others have interpreted them as 'limited'[35] and 'unlimited'.[36]

ayaneṣu ca sarveṣu yathābhāgam avasthitāḥ
bhīṣmam evābhirakṣantu bhavantaḥ sarva eva hi. (11)

All of you position yourselves according to your respective divisions at the entrances to the formation, and safeguard Bhīṣma from all sides. (11)

Bhīṣma was Duryodhana's commander-in-chief.

tasya saṃjanayan harṣaṃ kuruvṛddhaḥ pitāmahaḥ
siṃhanādaṃ vinadyoccaiḥ śaṅkhaṃ dadhmau pratāpavān. (12)

32 [*tattva*.]

33 [*asamartha* (Beng.).]

34 [*samartha* (Beng.).]

35 [*parimita* (Beng.).]

36 [*aparimita* (Beng.).]

Gladdening Duryodhana's heart, the eldest of the Kurus and grandfather (Bhīṣma) roared like a lion and blew his conch. (12)

In former times the warriors used to blow conches before battle. Bhīṣma was the brother of Duryodhana's grandfather.

tataḥ śaṅkhāś ca bheryaś ca paṇavānakagomukhāḥ
sahasaivābhyahanyanta sa śabdas tumulo 'bhavat. (13)

Then all of a sudden conches, kettle-drums, trumpets, drums and horns — all instruments blared, and the sound became tremendous. (13)

tataḥ śvetair hayair yukte mahati syandane sthitau
mādhavaḥ pāṇḍavaś caiva divyau śaṅkhau pradadhmatuḥ. (14)

Then, situated on a great chariot with two white horses, Kṛṣṇa and Arjuna[37] blew their heavenly conches. (14)

pāñcajanyaṃ hṛṣīkeśo devadattaṃ dhanaṃjayaḥ
pauṇḍraṃ dadhmau mahāśaṅkhaṃ bhīmakarmā vṛkodaraḥ. (15)

anantavijayaṃ rājā kuntīputro yudhiṣṭhiraḥ
nakulaḥ sahadevaś ca sughoṣamaṇipuṣpakau. (16)

Kṛṣṇa blew the conch called *Pāñcajanya*, Arjuna *Devadatta*, and Bhīma, known for his terrible deeds, the great conch called *Pauṇḍra*. (15)

King Yudhiṣṭhira, son of Kuntī, blew the conch *Anantavijaya*, Nakula that called *Sughoṣa* and Sahadeva that called *Maṇipuṣpaka*. (16)

kāśyaś ca parameṣvāsaḥ śikhaṇḍī ca mahārathaḥ
dhṛṣṭadyumno virāṭaś ca sātyakiś cāparājitaḥ. (17)

drupado draupadeyāś ca sarvaśaḥ pṛthivīpate
saubhadraś ca mahābāhuḥ śaṅkhān dadhmuḥ pṛthak pṛthak. (18)

The King of Kāśī, the great archer, the great warrior Śikhaṇḍin, Dhṛṣṭadyumna, Virāṭa, the unconquered Sātyaki, Drupada, the sons of Draupadī and the mighty-armed son of Subhadrā — all these, O Lord of the earth, blew each his respective conch. (17) (18)

sa ghoṣo dhārtarāṣṭrāṇāṃ hṛdayāni vyadārayat
nabhaś ca pṛthivīṃ caiva tumulo 'bhyanunādayan. (19)[38]

This sound pierced the hearts of the sons of Dhṛtarāṣṭra, and made heaven and earth

[37] [Mādhava and Pāṇḍava respectively in the Sanskrit original.]

[38] A different variant reads *tumulo vyanunādayan* [identical translation].

resound. (19)

atha vyavasthitān dṛṣṭvā dhārtarāṣṭrān kapidhvajaḥ
pravṛtte śastrasaṃpāte dhanur udyamya pāṇḍavaḥ
hṛṣīkeśaṃ tadā vākyam idam āha mahīpate. (20)[39]

Then, oh Lord of the earth,[40] the monkey-bannered Arjuna saw the sons of Dhṛtarāṣṭra prepared, took up his bow, and, ready to loose weapons, said these words to Hṛṣīkeśa.[41] (20)

Śrīdhara Svāmin has written as explanation of the word *vyavasthita*[42] 'established in preparation for battle.'

arjuna uvāca:
senayor ubhayor madhye rathaṃ sthāpaya me 'cyuta. (21)

yāvad etān nirīkṣe 'haṃ yoddhukāmān avasthitān
kair mayā saha yoddhavyam asmin raṇasamudyame. (22)

yotsyamānān avekṣe 'ham ya ete 'tra samāgatāḥ
dhārtarāṣṭrasya durbuddher yuddhe priyacikīrṣavaḥ. (23)

Arjuna said:
Place my chariot so far between the two armies that I can examine those who are present in order to fight, (that I can see) those with whom I shall have to combat, and that I can see all those who have come to the war in favour of the son of Dhṛtarāṣṭra.[43] (21) (22) (23)

saṃjaya uvāca:
evam ukto hṛṣīkeśo guḍākeśena bhārata
senayor ubhayor madhye sthāpayitvā rathottamam. (24)

bhīṣmadroṇapramukhataḥ sarveṣāṃ ca mahīkṣitām
uvāca pārtha paśyaitān samavetān kurūn iti. (25)

Saṃjaya said:
O Bhārata,[44] having thus been told by Guḍokeśa,[45] Hṛṣīkeśa placed the excellent

[39] [Baṅkim's way of counting in this instance is unusual; normally the third line figures as the first *pada* of *śloka* 21.]

[40] I presume the reader remembers that Saṃjaya is speaking. He is telling Dhṛtarāṣṭra the story of the war of Kurukṣetra.

[41] [Kṛṣṇa.]

[42] ['prepared', according to Baṅkim.]

[43] [That is, Duryodhana.]

[44] In this book both Dhṛtarāṣṭra and Arjuna are addressed as 'Bhārata' since they are from the lineage of Bharata, the son of Duṣmanta.

chariot between the two armies in front of Bhīṣma, Droṇa and all the rulers and said: 'O Pārtha,[46] look at these assembled Kurus.' (24) (25)

tatrāpaśyat sthitān pārthaḥ pitṝn atha pitāmahān
ācāryān mātulān bhrātṝn putrān pautrān sakhīṃs tathā
śvaśurān suhṛdaś caiva senayor ubhayor api. (26)

Then Arjuna saw fathers, grandfathers, masters, maternal uncles, brothers, sons, grandchildren, fathers-in-law, associates[47] and well-wishers standing there in the two armies. (26)

tān samīkṣya sa kaunteyaḥ sarvān bandhūn avasthitān
kṛpayā parayāviṣṭo viṣīdann idam abravīt. (27)

Seeing all these friends present, this son of Kunti became overwhelmed with pity and said this out of sorrow. (27)

arjuna uvāca:
dṛṣṭvemān svajanān kṛṣṇa yuyutsūn samavasthitān[48]
sīdanti mama gātrāṇi mukhaṃ ca pariśuṣyati. (28)

Arjuna said:
O Kṛṣṇa, seeing these kinsmen assembled and desirous to fight, my limbs are exhausted and my mouth gets dry. (28)

vepathuś ca śarīre me romaharṣaś ca jāyate
gāṇḍīvaṃ sraṃsate hastāt tvak caiva paridahyate. (29)

My body is trembling, my hair is standing up, *Gāṇḍīva*[49] is falling from my hands, and my skin is burning. (29)

na ca śaknomy avasthātuṃ bhramatīva ca me manaḥ
nimittāni ca paśyāmi viparītāni keśava. (30)

O Keśava,[50] I am unable to contain myself, my mind seems to be deluded, and I see all kinds of adverse omens. (30)

[45] [Arjuna.]

[46] [Literally: Descendant of *Pṛthu*; Arjuna.]

[47] There is of course a distinction between associates [*sakhā*] and well-wishers [*suhṛd*]. Associates are such persons one has obtained help from.

[48] There is a variant *dṛṣṭvemaṃ svajanaṃ kṛṣṇa yuyutsuṃ samupasthitam* ['seeing this kinsman come up desirous to fight'].

[49] [Name of Arjuna's bow.]

[50] [Kṛṣṇa.]

na ca śreyo 'nupaśyāmi hatvā svajanam āhave
na kāṅkṣe vijayaṃ kṛṣṇa na ca rājyaṃ sukhāni ca. (31)

I do not see any good in killing relatives in war; O Kṛṣṇa, I do not desire victory, nor the joy of sovereignty.[51] (31)

kiṃ no rājyena govinda kiṃ bhogair jīvitena vā
yeṣām arthe kāṅkṣitaṃ no rājyaṃ bhogāḥ sukhāni ca. (32)

ta ime 'vasthitā yuddhe prāṇāṃs tyaktvā dhanāni ca
ācāryāḥ pitaraḥ putrās tathaiva ca pitāmahāḥ. (33)

mātulāḥ śvaśurāḥ pautrāḥ śyālāḥ sambandhinas tathā
etān na hantum icchāmi ghnato 'pi madhusūdana. (34)

When the teachers, fathers, sons, grandfathers, maternal uncles, fathers-in-law, grandsons, brothers-in-law and other relatives, for whom sovereignty, enjoyment and happiness can be desired, have sacrificed their wealth and life to be present in this war, then, O Govinda,[52] what need have we of sovereignty, enjoyment or life? O Madhusūdana,[53] if I die, let it be so; still I do not wish to kill them. (32) (33) (34)

The significance of the phrase 'If I die, let it be so (*ghnato 'pi*)' is this: 'If I do not kill them they might indeed kill me. If this happens, it is all right; still I shall not kill them.' This is in fact how Arjuna fought with Bhīṣma and Droṇa. We often hear of Arjuna's 'soft war'.

api trailokyarājyasya hetoḥ kin nu mahīkṛte
nihatya dhārtarāṣṭrān naḥ kā prītiḥ syāj janārdana. (35)

Not to speak of this earth, even for sovereignty of the three worlds, O Janārdana,[54] what joy would it bring to kill the sons of Dhṛtarāṣṭra? (35)

pāpam evāśrayed asmān[55] *hatvaitān ātatāyinaḥ*
tasmān nārhā vayaṃ hantuṃ dhārtarāṣṭrān sabāndhavān[56]
svajanaṃ hi kathaṃ hatvā sukhinaḥ syāma mādhava. (36)

If we destroy these aggressors, sin shall come upon us; thus, we cannot kill the sons of

[51] [The Sanskrit enumerates *rājya* and *sukhāni* as separate items; there is further 'highest good ... after having killed' instead of 'any good'.]

[52] [Kṛṣṇa.]

[53] [Kṛṣṇa.]

[54] [Kṛṣṇa.]

[55] [Misprinted as *admān* in the original.]

[56] There is a variant *svabāndhavān* ['my friends'].

Dhṛtarāṣṭra and their friends. O Mādhava,[57] how, having killed our our own ones, could we be happy? (36)

Six persons are called agressors [*ātatāyin*]:

agnido garadaś caiva śastrapāṇir dhanāpahaḥ
kṣetradārāpahārī ca ṣaḍ ete ātatāyinaḥ.

'The incendiary, the poisoner, the one with weapon in hand, the thief of wealth, the thief of land and the abductor of women, these six are aggressors.'[58] According to the *Arthaśāstra*, the aggressor is punishable with death. The commentators explain Arjuna's utterance as meaning that even if an aggressor is to be killed according to the *Arthaśāstra*, still the guru and others are not to be killed according to the *Dharmaśāstra*. The *Arthaśāstra* is subordinate to the *Dharmaśāstra*; consequently even if Bhīṣma, Droṇa, etc., are aggressors sin would be embodied [in us][59] through their killing. Today we distinguish between '*Law*' and '*Morality*' [Lat.]; this consideration is exactly the same. '*Morals*' are above '*Law*' [Lat.]. In the English Penal Code too it is written that under certain circumstances, there is no punishment for killing an aggressor. However, the killing of the aggressor in such a case is not always compatible with today's moral code.[60] Ānandagiri has given another explanation of this *śloka* . He says that it might also means that when killing the guru, etc.,[61] we become aggressors; therefore we accumulate sin: *gurubhrātṛsuhṛtprabhṛtīn etān hatvā vayam ātatāyinaḥ syāma.*

yady apy ete na paśyanti lobhopahatacetasaḥ
kulakṣayakṛtaṃ doṣaṃ mitradrohe ca pātakam. (37)

kathaṃ na jñeyam asmābhiḥ pāpād asmān nivartitum
kulakṣayakṛtaṃ doṣaṃ prapaśyadbhir janārdana. (38)

Even if they, bewildered by greed, do not see the harm in the destruction of the family and the crime that lies in hostility to friends; we however, O Janārdana, see the evil that lies in the destruction of the family, so why should we not be endowed with the comprehension of refraining from this sin? (37) (38)

kulakṣaye praṇaśyanti kuladharmāḥ sanātanāḥ
dharme naṣṭe kulaṃ kṛtsnam adharmo 'bhibhavaty uta. (39)

By the destruction of the family, the eternal *dharma* of the family[62] is destroyed. When *dharma* is destroyed, the remaining family falls prey to *adharma*.[63] (39)

[57] [Kṛṣṇa.]

[58] [Source not identified.]

[59] [*pāpāśraẏ haïbe* (Beng.).]

[60] [*nītiśāstra* (Beng.).]

[61] [Ānandagiri's original has: '(...) guru, brothers, friends, etc.']

[62] [*kuladharma*, *kula* also meaning 'clan'.]

[63] [The opposite of *dharma*, i.e. vice, disorder, etc.]

The eternal *dharma* of the family — i.e. the *dharma* of the family received through ancestral tradition.

adharmābhibhavāt kr̥ṣṇa praduṣyanti kulastriyaḥ
strīṣu duṣṭāsu vārṣṇeya jāyate varṇasaṃkaraḥ. (40)

O Kr̥ṣṇa, by being overcome by *adharma*, the women of the family become corrupt; and once the women have been spoiled, O Vārṣṇeya,[64] the mixture of *varṇas* arises. (40)

saṃkaro narakāyaiva kulaghnānāṃ kulasya ca
patanti pitaro hy eṣāṃ luptapiṇḍodakakriyāḥ. (41)

The mixture of *varṇas* leads the destroyers of the family and the family itself to hell. Because of the vanishing of the ancestral rites, their forefathers [too] fall into hell. (41)

doṣair etaiḥ kulaghnānāṃ varṇasaṃkarakārakaiḥ
utsādyante jātidharmāḥ kuladharmāś ca śāśvatāḥ. (42)

Through this fault of the destroyers of the family, leading to the mixture of *varṇas*, the generic *dharma* and the eternal *dharma* of the family decays. (42)

utsannakuladharmāṇāṃ manuṣyāṇām janārdana
narake niyataṃ vāso bhavatīty anuśuśruma. (43)

O Janārdana, we have heard that the men whose *kuladharma* decays are forever made to live in hell. (43)

The five *ślokas* (39), (40), (41), (42) and (43) will not sound good to today's cultured readers. This may seem, to them, to be full of ancient superstitions against the mixture of *varṇas*, moreover containing such embellishments as the phrase *luptapiṇḍodakakriyāḥ*.[65] A particular hate of the creator of the *Gītā* against the mixture of *varṇas* is apparent; he has placed the censure of *varṇa*-mixing even in the mouth of the Lord Himself. We shall try to understand the significance of this statement when we engage ourselves in the discussion of the Lord's statement on this topic. For the present, it is sufficient to grasp the rough meaning of Arjuna's utterance. It can often be seen that once the men of a clan [*kula*] have died the women of that clan become adulterous. When the women of a clan of descent become adulterous, offspring produced from the semen of mean people continue to issue from their wombs. The lineage gets filled with mean offspring, consequently the *dharma* of the clan disappears. Even those who do not see any harm in the mixture of castes; who do not believe that the ancestral rites bring one into heaven;[66] and even those who do not believe in heaven, hell and the like

[64] Kr̥ṣṇa is born from the lineage of Vr̥ṣṇi, therefore he is called Vārṣṇeya.

[65] ['whose ancestral rites have vanished'.]

[66] [The phrase is: *piṇḍādir svargakārakatāẏ yāhārā biśvās'bān nahen* (Beng.).]

either, should, I presume, accept as much as this.[67] The rest is the language of the epoch and embellishments.[68] The whole is very coarse indeed. There is something of a reason to place this in Arjuna's mouth: the Lord, in answer to Arjuna's boasting of *kuladharma*, will take up the subject of *svadharma*;[69] this is the author's device. However, after the ambrosia-like sentence *na kāṅkṣe vijayaṃ kṛṣṇa na ca rājyaṃ sukhāni ca*[70] this is not worthy to be said.

aho bata mahat pāpaṃ kartuṃ vyavasitā vayaṃ
yad rājyasukhalobhena hantuṃ svajanam udyatāḥ. (44)

Alas! Out of greed for the happiness of sovereignty, we are preparing to kill our own; we have resolved to commit a great crime. (44)

yadi mām apratīkāram aśastraṃ śastrapāṇayaḥ
dhārtarāṣṭrā raṇe hanyus tan me kṣemataraṃ bhavet. (45)

It would be relatively more beneficial for me even if the armed sons of Dhṛtarāṣṭra were to kill me in battle while I was unwilling to offer resistance and unarmed.[71] (45)

saṃjaya uvāca:
evam uktvārjunaḥ saṃkhye rathopastha upāviṣat
visṛjya saśaraṃ cāpaṃ śokasaṃvignamānasaḥ. (46)

Saṃjaya said:
Having spoken thus, Arjuna, thoroughly grief-stricken, laid down his bow and arrows and sat down on the chariot situated on the battle-field. (46)

67 'The women, for instance, whose husbands, friends and relations have been all slain in battle, no longer restrained by law, seek husbands among other and lower castes, or tribes, causing a mixture of blood, which many nations at all ages have regarded as a most serious evil; but particularly those who — like the Aryans, the Jews and the Scotch — were at first surrounded by foreigners very different to themselves, and thus preserved the distinction and genealogies of their races more effectively than any other.' (Thomson's *Translation of the Bhagavadgita* [1855], p. 7) [Lat.].

'By the destruction of the males the rites of both tribe and family would cease, because women were not allowed to perform them; and confusion of castes would arise, for the women would marry men of another caste. Such marriages were considered impure (Manu, x. 1-40). Such marriages produced elsewhere a confusion of classes. Livy tells us that the Roman patricians at the instance of Canuleius complained of the intermarriages of the plebeian class with their own, affirming that "*omnia divina humanaque turbari, ut qui natus sit, ignoret, cujus sanguinis, quorum sacrorum sit.*"'
(Davies' *Translation of the Bhagavadgita* [1882], p. 26.) [Lat.]

68 'In bringing forward these and other melancholy superstitions of Brahmanism in the mouth of Arjuna, we are not to suppose that our poet — though as much Brahman as philosopher in many unimportant points of belief — himself received and approved of them.' (Thomson [1855], p. 7.) [Lat.].

69 [One's own *dharma*; see below.]

70 [*Gītā* 1.31.]

71 [The *Gītā* has literally: 'It would be better for me if', etc.]

iti śrīmadbhagavadgītāsu upaniṣatsu brahmavidyāyāṃ yogaśāstre śrīkṛṣṇārjunasamvāde arjunaviṣādo[72] *nāma prathamo 'dhyāyaḥ.*[73]

I have said that there are no principles of *dharma*[74] in this first chapter; but this chapter is an excellent piece of *kāvya*. All the ingredients of a *kāvya* have been very beautifully arranged here. Both fully equipped armies have confronted[75] each other on the Kurukṣetra. Duryodhana, seeing that the huge Pāṇḍava army has been arrayed, shows his teacher the excelling best of warfare. Somewhat worried, he says to the teacher:[76] 'See to it that my commander-in-chief Bhīṣma is safeguarded.' But the old Bhīṣma is even more enthusiastic than the youngsters — at this moment, he roars like a lion and blows his conch (conches were the *bugles* [Lat.] of those days). Hearing this all the warriors of both armies, either encouraged or reacting, blow their conches. Various instruments of battle burst forth on both sides; the heavens are split by the tumult of conches, drums and other instruments; heaven and earth reverberate. At this moment of great enthusiasm, equanimous Arjuna, carrying on his back the burden of the victory over the Kauravas, says to Kṛṣṇa, his charioteer: 'Place the chariot between both armies; let me see with whom I shall have to fight.' Kṛṣṇa places the great chariot pulled by white horses between both armies, and he, the omniscient doer of all deeds[77] says: 'Look here.' Arjuna sees his near and dear on both sides, all the paternal uncles, grandfathers, sons, grandsons, maternal uncles, fathers-in-law, brothers-in-law, friends and comrades, and his body starts to tremble, his hair stands on end, his mouth becomes dry, he feels benumbed and dizzy, and the huge bow *Gāṇḍīva* slips out of his hand. He says: 'Kṛṣṇa, what is the use of sovereignty through killing those for whom sovereignty is wanted? I will not make war!' This battlefield, two huge armies on two sides, this tumultuous noise, war-cries and extreme enthusiasm, and at this point first the calmness of this great hero, then this compassionate and great, peaceful feeling in this heart — a scene of this impact is indeed rare in the world of literature. Who else[78] has anywhere heard an ambrosia-filled voice compared to this one: *na kāṅkṣe vijayaṃ kṛṣṇa na ca rājyaṃ sukhāni ca.*[79]

[72] There is a version *sainyadarśanaṃ* ['inspection of the army'] in some books.

[73] 'This is the first chapter called *Arjuna's grief* in the *Yogaśāstra* [taught as] a dialogue between Kṛṣṇa and Arjuna with regard to the knowledge of the *brahman*, in the secret teachings sung by the Lord.'

[74] [*dharmmatattva* (Beng.).]

[75] [The synoptic present tense is used in the translation here contrary to Baṅkimcandra, who uses the narrative imperfect.]

[76] [Duryodhana's teacher (*ācārya*) is Droṇa.]

[77] [*sarbbakartā* (Beng.).]

[78] ['Who else *than we Indians*' is probably the implication intended here; the word order makes the interpretation 'Where else has anybody' (*ke kothāẏ ār*) appear unlikely.]

[79] [*Gītā* 1.31.]

Second Chapter

saṃjaya uvāca:
taṃ tathā kṛpayāviṣṭaṃ aśrupūrṇakulekṣaṇam
viṣīdantam idaṃ vākyam uvāca madhusūdanaḥ. (1)

Saṃjaya said:
Then Madhusūdana spoke to him (Arjuna) who was overwhelmed with pity, whose eyes were full of tears and who was sad, as follows. (1)

śrībhagavān uvāca:
kutas tvā kaśmalam idaṃ viṣame samupasthitam
anāryaṃ juṣṭam asvargyam akīrtikaram arjuna. (2)

The Lord said:
O Arjuna, where has this illusion[1] of yours, which is not suitable for *āryas*, obstructs the way to heaven and causes ill fame, come from in this predicament? (2)

mā klaibyaṃ gaccha kaunteya[2] *naitat tvayy upapadyate*
kṣudraṃ hṛdayadaurbalyaṃ tyaktvottiṣṭha paraṃtapa. (3)

O Kaunteya,[3] do not yield to unmanliness,[4] this does not befit you. O Paraṃtapa,[5] shake off this mean weakness of the heart and get up! (3)

arjuna uvāca:
kathaṃ bhīṣmam ahaṃ saṃkhye droṇaṃ ca madhusūdana
iṣubhiḥ pratiyotsyāmi pūjārhāv arisūdana. (4)

Arjuna said:
O Madhusūdana, killer of your enemies, how shall I fight back in battle with arrows against Bhīṣma and Droṇa, who are worthy of reveration? (4)

gurūn ahatvā hi mahānubhāvāñ
śreyo bhoktuṃ bhaikṣyam apīha loke
hatvārthakāmāṃs tu gurūn ihaiva
bhuñjīya bhogān rudhirapradigdhān. (5)

It would be better even to depend on alms in this world while not killing these high-minded gurus, and the enjoyment of wealth and fulfilment of desires which may be obtained by killing gurus are smeared with blood. (5)

[1] [Baṅkim translates the Sanskrit *kaśmala* ('sorrow, dejection of mind') as *moha*, which basically means 'illusion' and seems somewhat inaccurate here.]

[2] The version taken up by Ānandagiri runs *klaibyaṃ mā sma gamaḥ pārtha.*

[3] ['Son of Kunti'; epithet of Arjuna.]

[4] [*klībatā* (Beng.).]

[5] [Another common epithet of Arjuna meaning 'Scorcher of the others', i.e. of the enemies.]

na caitad vidmaḥ kataran no garīyo
yad vā jayema yadi vā no jayeyuḥ
yān eva hatvā na jijīviṣāmas
te 'vasthitāḥ pramukhe dhārtarāṣṭrāḥ. (6)

We cannot understand which of the following is better — whether we should win or they should defeat us; the sons of Dhṛtarāṣṭra, killing whom we would not want to live afterwards, are assembled in front of us. (6)

kārpaṇyadoṣopahatasvabhāvaḥ
pṛcchāmi tvāṃ dharmasaṃmūḍhacetāḥ
yac chreyaḥ syān niścitaṃ brūhi tan me
śiṣyas te 'haṃ śādhi māṃ tvāṃ prapannam. (7)

I have been overcome by the fault of misery,[6] and my consciousness of *dharma* has become confounded. Tell me definitely what is good. I am your disciple, I have taken refuge in you — instruct me. (7)

Kārpaṇya means misery.[7] In the *Vācaspatyam*,[8] Tārānātha, when indicating this meaning, has quoted as an example the present words of the *Gītā*. I hope none of my readers shall take 'misery' for [economic] poverty here. 'Miserable' means 'in great misfortune'. Take for example another sentence Tārānātha has quoted from the *Rāmāyaṇa*: *mahad vā vyasanaṃ prāpto dīnaḥ kṛpaṇa ucyate.*[9] Ānandagiri says: *yo 'lpaṃ svalpam api svakṣatiṃ na kṣamate sa kṛpaṇa* — someone who cannot accept an insignificant loss is called *kṛpaṇa.*[10] Śrīdhara Svāmin has explained in this way: '*Kārpaṇya* is Arjuna's thought: "Should I keep my life after killing my friends and relatives?"' He has interpreted the compositum *kārpaṇyadoṣa* as a *dvandva* — *kārpaṇya* and *doṣa*. The word *doṣa* should be understood as the sin of destroying one's clan mentioned above. The other commentators have not interpreted it in this way.

na hi prapaśyāmi mamāpanudyād
yac chokam ucchoṣaṇam indriyāṇām
avāpya bhūmāv asapatnam ṛddhaṃ
rājyaṃ surāṇām api cādhipatyam. (8)

I cannot see by what means the sorrow that would dry up my senses, even when attaining a prosperous kingdom without rivals in this world and even lordship of the lords, should disappear. (8)

6 [The term is *kārpaṇya*, literally 'poverty, wretchedness'.]

7 [*dīnatā*.]

8 [Name of a well-known Sanskrit dictionary (1962 [1873-84]).]

9 ['Or a miserable (person) fallen into great misfortune is called *kṛpaṇa*', *kṛpaṇa* being the respective adjective to the abstractum *kārpaṇya* (*Vācaspatyam* 1962 [1873-84]).]

10 Kashinath Trimbak Telang [1990 (1882)] has 'helplessness' [Engl. in the original] as the equivalent of *kārpaṇya*.

saṃjaya uvāca:
evam uktvā hṛṣīkeśaṃ guḍākeśa paraṃtapaḥ
na yotsya iti govindam uktvā tūṣṇīṃ babhūva ha. (9)

Saṃjaya said:
Arjuna,[11] the conqueror of his enemies, having thus spoken to Hṛṣīkeśa, said to Govinda: 'I shall not fight' and then became silent. (9)

tam uvāca hṛṣīkeśaḥ prahasann iva bhārata
senayor ubhayor madhye viṣīdantam idaṃ vacaḥ. (10)

O Bhārata,[12] Hṛṣīkeśa smilingly said these words to the sorrowstricken Arjuna between the two armies. (10)

śrībhagavān uvāca:
aśocyān anvaśocas tvaṃ prajñāvādāṃś ca bhāṣase
gatāsūn agatāsūṃś ca nānuśocanti paṇḍitāḥ. (11)

The Lord said:
You speak like a wise man; but you sorrow for those whom it is not just to sorrow for. The wise do not sorrow for anybody whether living or dead. (11)

This is the real beginning of the *Gītā*. Let us examine which topic appears now.

Duryodhana and his brothers have unjustly robbed the kingdom of the Pāṇḍavas. There is no possibility of its recovery except war. Is, then, war a duty[13] here?

This issue has been thoroughly considered in the *Udyogaparvan* of the *Mahābhārata*; war has been judged to be a duty. Thus these two armies have been assembled and are facing one another.

We would accept the accuracy of the Pāṇḍavas' resolution also when having to judge by modern moral standards whether, in this case, war is a duty or not. Of all the various kinds of actions that exist in this world, war is usually the most inferior. But then, there is such a thing as *dharmayuddha*.[14] The war Washington fought in America, William the Silent in Europe, and Pratāp Siṃh in India, were *dharma* of the highest order, better even than charity, etc. The Pāṇḍavas' inclination to fight also belongs to this class of *dharma*. I have discussed this in detail in *Kṛṣṇacaritra* — it is unnecessary to repeat it here.[15] My argument there was roughly that it is one's *dharma* to protect to the best of one's abilities one's right sanctioned by *dharma*. Protection means that nobody can rob or obstruct it unjustly; if anybody does so, its recovery and his punishment stand as a duty. If people, self-interestedly depriving others of their rights, are allowed to freely rob and thereafter enjoy others' property, then society cannot last

[11] In the original it says *Guḍākeśa*. *Guḍākeśa* is a name of Arjuna. The commentators interpret it as 'the conqueror of sleep', but also other meanings have been attributed to this.

[12] [I.e. Dhṛtarāṣṭra.]

[13] [*karttabya* (Beng.).]

[14] ['righteous war'.]

[15] See also *Nabajīban*, Vol. I. [where *Kṛṣṇacaritra* was serially published.]

for even one day. In such a case all humans would suffer infinitely. Consequently, it is a duty to recover one's property. If there exists any means superior to war [to achieve this], it must be resorted to with priority; but if such means does not exist, force must be used. In this case, force is *dharma*.

In the *Mahābhārata* we can see that up to this point, Arjuna has always been in favour of war. It is a natural misconception for an honest person that on the sight of the faces of his relatives, when the time of their killing in the war has arrived, he would feel afflicted and turn his back on strategic considerations.

We can also see in the *Mahābhārata* that Kr̥ṣṇa made special efforts in order to prevent the war. Later on when the war became inevitable he refused to take a vow for any particular side in the war and accepted only to drive Arjuna's chariot. But even if he was disinclined to make war, he was an excellent knower of *dharma*; consequently he was bound to tell Arjuna in this instance which was the path of *dharma*. Thus he is telling Arjuna that in this case, to make war is *dharma*, whereas not to fight is *adharma*.

It is hard to believe that this discussion between Kr̥ṣṇa and Arjuna really did take place at the beginning of the war on the battlefield. But it seems acceptable that the creator of the *Gītā*, using his imagination in this way, inserted the compiled essentials of the *dharma* proclaimed by Kr̥ṣṇa into the *Mahābhārata*.

All of Kr̥ṣṇa's instructions to Arjuna indicating the intention to make war are contained in this second chapter. It is true that also in the other chapters the Lord sometimes concludes his sentences with the instruction to make war, but those sentences do not have any special relationship with the obligation to fight. Rather it seems that the reader is occasionally reminded of the war in order to conceal his feeling the artificiality of the device by which the author has connected this explanation of *dharma* with the *Mahābhārata*. It is not the genuine intention of this book to support the cause of war, but, under the pretext of supporting war, to proclaim the true knowledge of the entire *dharma* of mankind.

It seems that if this is examined separately the reader shall understand implicitly that there is great doubt whether there has really been any discussion of this kind between Kr̥ṣṇa and Arjuna in the chariot placed between the two armies on the battlefield. It also does not seem very likely that, at the time when two opposite armies in battle-formation are ready to attack each other, a commander of one side should place his chariot between both armies and listen to eighteen chapters on *yoga* and *dharma*. But whether the coherence of this be accepted or not accepted, it is my duty to remind the readers of some other points.

(1) There is no doubt that the *dharma* proclaimed by the Lord has been compiled in the *Gītā*; the book called *Gītā*, however, was not written by the Lord but by some other person.

(2) It is not very trustworthy either that the author of this book should have been present at the time of Kr̥ṣṇa's and Arjuna's discussion and heard all of it with his own ears, and should then have written it down right there, or learnt it by heart like a *smr̥tidhar*.[16] Thus it cannot be believed that all the words the author has manifested through the mouth of the Lord were in their entirety ever uttered by the Lord. It is possible that in many parts the author expressed his own opinion through the mouth of the Lord.

[16] ['container of memories'.]

With those who say that this book, belonging to the *Mahābhārata*, was written by the Maharṣi Vyāsa, who through the force of *yoga* was omniscient and infallible, and that for this reason such doubt is out of place here, we cannot enter into discussion. I can only remark that this commentary has not been written for readers of this category.

(3) In all Sanskrit books one can find instances of interpolated *ślokas*. No *śloka* can have been interpolated from the time of Śaṅkarācārya's commentary, for the current original is identical with his. But the *Gītā* already existed one thousand or even more years before the time of Śaṅkarācārya; so how can we say that no *śloka* was interpolated during that time? Sometimes we shall find *ślokas* that seem interpolated.

If we do not keep these things in mind we will not be able to understand the true significance of the *Gītā*. I have therefore said these things beforehand. Let us now see what the essence of Kr̥ṣṇa's explanation to Arjuna concerning the righteousness[17] of war is.

It is needless to say that the method we, influenced as we are by the moral code of the nineteenth century, used above to explain briefly the righteousness of this war, is not the one followed by Kr̥ṣṇa. The rough meaning of his words are that everyone's duty is to fulfil his *svadharma*. But first we must understand what kind of thing this *svadharma* is.[18]

For Śaṅkara and the other old pundits it had been very easy to explain this theory. Arjuna is a kṣatriya, consequently his *svadharma* is the *dharma* of the kṣatriyas, i.e. war. His saying that rather than making war he would depend on alms shows his desire for others' *dharma*; for begging is the *dharma* of the brahmins.[19] But what has this explanation actually taught us? We seem to have understood that the *svadharma* of the Hindu *dharma*, which depends upon the *varṇa*-system, can be determined according to the divisions of the *varṇas*. But what is *svadharma* for non-Hindus? The sum of all brahmins, kṣatriyas, vaiśyas and śūdras is still a very minor part of the world population. Most people on earth are outside the four *varṇas*; do they not have any *svadharma*? Has God not prescribed any *dharma* for them? Has He created millions and millions of people to provide only Indians with *dharma* and leave everybody else deprived of it? Is the *dharma* proclaimed by the Lord only for Hindus? Are the *mlecchas*[20] not His children? The divine *dharma* is not as narrow-minded as this.

Whoever believes in this sort of fall from *dharma* by the Lord of the world is comparable to the Christians.[21] And whoever does not believe it will undoubtedly look out for another meaning of *svadharma*.

The *dharma* one has is one's *svadharma*. Now what is man's *dharma*? Whatever

[17] [*dhammyatā* (Beng.).]

[18] [*svadharmma sāmagrīṭā ki?* (Beng.)]

[19] *śokamohābhyāṃ hy abhibhūtavivekavijñānaḥ svata eva kṣatradharme yuddhe pravr̥tto 'pi tasmād śuddhād upararāma paradharmaṃ ca bhikṣājīvanādikaṃ kartuṃ pravavr̥te.* — Śaṅkarabhāṣya. ['It was because his discrimination and practical knowledge were undermined by grief and delusion that Arjuna refrained from fighting, though he had voluntarily undertaken to fight his opponents as the duty of the Kṣatriyas, and instead got ready to live conforming to an alien law of life (*paradharma*).' (*ŚaBhG*:19)]

[20] ['foreigner, barbarian, non-Aryan, man of an outcast race, any person who does not speak Sanskr̥it and does not conform to the usual Hindū institutions' (Monier-Williams 1899).]

[21] The Christians believe that the Lord of the world throws him who does not honour Jesus Christ into hell for eternity.

has to do with humanity.[22] What has to do with humanity? Man has body and mind.[23] What is body, and what is mind? The body is a conglomerate of a number of substances and has a number of powers. When these powers disappear from the body, humanity does not remain; for one can hardly say that there is humanity in a man's corpse. Therefore one has to leave out the substances — those physical powers alone are the true constituents of the human body. Elsewhere[24] I have called them 'physical faculties'. The human mind too is such an aggregate of powers or faculties. Let these be called 'mental faculties'. Now it can be seen that man, or the humanity of man, consists in these physical and mental faculties.

If that be so, then the prescribed cultivation of all these faculties is man's *dharma*.

What do we do through the use[25] of these faculties? Either we act, or we acquire knowledge. There are no fruits of human life except action[26] and knowledge[27] [28]

Therefore, knowledge and action are man's *svadharma*. If all were to make use of all their faculties in a prescribed fashion, both knowledge and action would be the *svadharma* of all men. But usually this does not happen during the undeveloped state of a society.[29] Someone gives knowledge the main status of his *svadharma*, another likewise mainly adopts action as his *svadharma*.

The highest goal of knowledge is the *brahman*. The whole world lies in the *brahman*. This is why those whose *svadharma* is the acquisition of knowledge can be called brahmins. The word *brāhmaṇa* has been formed from *brahman*.

Action can be divided into three categories. But in order to understand this, action must be clearly conceived. In the world, there are inner and outer objects.[30] The inner objects cannot be submitted to action, only the outer ones are objects of action. Whether it be a number or all: these outer objects are consumable[31] by man. Human action resorts[32] to consumable objects. This resorting is of three kinds: (1) production, (2) connection or collection, and (3) protection. (1) Those who produce are those having agriculture as their *dharma*; (2) those who conneet or collect are those having

[22] [*yāhā laïyā manuṣyatva* (Beng.).]

[23] The word *'man'* [Beng., Skt. *manas*] is quite current, therefore I have used it here. This current word is only the translation of the English 'mind'. If the language of the Indian philosophical systems were to be used here, the three words *buddhi*, *manas* and *ahaṅkāra* would have to be given in its place. It is better instead to follow the distinction between 'matter and mind' [Lat.].

[24] [In *Dharmmatattva*, *BR* II:591, etc.]

[25] [*sañcālan* (Beng.): lit. 'motion' or 'setting in motion'.]

[26] [*karman*.]

[27] [*jñāna*.]

[28] Comte and other Western philosophers have made a threefold distinction of the development of mind into 'Thought, Feeling, Action' [Lat.]; this is reasonable. But 'Feeling' gets finally transformed into 'Thought' or 'Action'; consequently it is also justified to speak of the twofold result, that is knowledge and action.

[29] I apply this term 'undeveloped state of a society' also for nineteenth century Europe.

[30] [*antarbbiṣaẏ* and *bahirbbiṣaẏ* (Beng.) respectively.]

[31] [*bhogya*.]

[32] [*āśraẏ kare* (Beng.).]

war as their *dharma*. Can the readers accept that their other names are vice versa kṣatriyas, vaiśyas, and śūdras?

There is one objection against such an acceptance. According to the Dharmaśāstras of the Hindus and also to the situation in this *Gītā*, agriculture is not the *dharma* of the śūdra, but both commerce and agriculture are the *dharma* of the vaiśyas; the *dharma* of the śūdras is serving the other three *varṇas*. Nowadays we can see that agriculture is mainly the *dharma* of the śūdras; but also serving the other three *varṇas* is the śūdras' *dharma*. When the actions[33] of those whose *dharma* is knowledge, war, commerce or agriculture are so abundant as to disable the respective agents to discharge all of their daily and other[34] necessary actions, then a number of people get employed in their service. Consequently, action is of five kinds, namely, (1) acquisition of knowledge and education, (2) war or the protection of society, (3) industry or commerce, (4) production or agriculture, and (5) service.

In every society there are accordingly, in some transformation, five classes [*jāti*]. But, Hindu society differs from other societies in that in it *dharma* is passed on patrilinearly. But it is not true that only Hindu society is like that, for also among the Muslims in contact with Hindu society this has happened. The *dar'jis*[35] sew, the *jolās*[36] weave, and the *kalus*[37] sell oil in patrilinear succession respectively. When affairs are in this way bound to patrilinear tradition, the following defect occurs: once the population of a certain class increases, the determined occupations are no longer sufficient, and unless the field of action is changed, the means of living are no longer provided for. In comparison to ancient times, the population of the śūdra-class has especially increased, which can be proved historically.[38] The śūdras have thus become farmers by leaving service. On the other hand, in former times the majority of the Aryan people were craftsmen, merchants or farmers for similar social reasons; and it is they who are called vaiśyas.

However this may be, people are, according to knowledge or action, divided into brahmins, kṣatriyas, merchants, craftsmen, farmers and servants. If looking at the social circumstances you say that men are either brahmins, kṣatriyas, vaiśyas or śūdras, nothing can be objected too. Substantially, man pursues no other than this six-, five- or four-fold action. If there is anything else, it is evil action.[39] Whichever one of this six-fold action someone adopts, be it as a means of livelihood or for whatever other reason, and whichever one's[40] burden one choses to carry, that is one's action to be executed,[41] one's

[33] [*karman*.]

[34] [*dainikādi* (Beng.).]

[35] [Muslim tailors.]

[36] [Muslim weavers.]

[37] [Muslim oil-men.]

[38] I am not only speaking of the growth of population in the course of time. In some articles on the subject of *bāṅālir utpatti* [Beng., 'The origin of the Bengalis' (*BR* II:344-63)] I published in the *Baṅgadarśan* I tried to prove that all non-Aryan races [*jāti*], when converting to the Hindu *dharma*, were transformed into śūdras. The ancient non-Aryan race named *puṇḍra*, for example, has become *puṛā* (Beng.) in some places and *pode* (Beng.) in others. This is how the number of śūdras gradually increased. A totally different reason for this increase is the mixture of *varṇas*.

[39] As stealing, etc.

[40] [This refers to the various actions.]

whichever one's[40] burden one choses to carry, that is one's action to be executed,[41] one's '*Duty*' [Lat.]; that is one's *svadharma*. This is to my understanding the liberal interpretation of *svadharma* exposed in the *Gītā*. Those who limit themselves to point out only its significance for ancient Hindu society consider the words of the Lord to be extremely narrow. The Lord is never narrow-minded.

When the words of the Lord — be it the *Gītā* or the *Bible* [Lat.], be they uttered by the incarnate Lord Himself or by the person[s] favoured by him — are proclaimed, they become manifest in the language of those days, and the meaning sanctioned by the condition of public education and customs of contemporary society is accepted then. But the condition of a society, public education and the whole set of customs change in the course of time. Then the interpretation of the Lord's words has to be extended. For, *dharma* is eternal, and so is its connection with society. It can never be the intention of God that the *dharma* proclaimed by Him is *dharma* only for some specific society or condition of society, that it does not function in other conditions, and that, therefore, society has to be kept in its original condition. In the process of time, according to social change, an interpretation of the words of the Lord is required which suits the knowledge of [that] society and is helpful for knowledge. The meaning of *svadharma* exposed by Kṛṣṇa encompasses *varṇāśramadharma*[42] as well as [the aspects] I have mentioned, since these are merely an extension of *varṇāśramadharma*. But a modern interpretation of the words of the Lord must be based on an understanding of *varṇāśrama* in ancient times; a modern interpretation is possible only by comprehending exactly in the way I have explained above.

If we have understood at least in some way what *svadharma* is, then we shall now have to understand why we should observe *svadharma*.

Kṛṣṇa resorts to two different kinds of considerations when explaining this concept to Arjuna. One is *jñānamārga*, the other *karmamārga*.[43] The *ślokas* 12 to 38 are dedicated to the praise[44] of *jñānamārga*, thereafter it is the turn of *karmamārga*. The rough essence of *jñānamārga* is the indestructibility of the *ātman*; this topic appears in the following *śloka*.

na tv evāhaṃ jātu nāsaṃ na tvaṃ neme janādhipāḥ
na caiva na bhaviṣyāmaḥ sarve vayam ataḥ param. (12)

It is not true that I have never been; neither is it true that you and these kings have never been; nor also is it true that all of us shall not be after this. (12)

Arjuna was grieved on seeing the possibility of killing his relatives in the war. Thereupon, Kṛṣṇa told him in the preceding *śloka*: 'You sorrow for those who are not to be sorrowed for.' The present *śloka* explains why it is not right to sorrow for someone who shall die. Its gist is this: 'Look, nobody dies. I, you, and these kings, i.e. everybody

[40] [This refers to the various actions.]

[41] [*anuṣṭheya karma* (Beng.).]

[42] [The *dharma* of the different *varṇas* and stages of life (*āśrama*).]

[43] ['way of knowledge' and 'way of action' respectively.]

[44] [*kīrtan* (Beng.).]

is everlasting; all of us existed before and shall exist after the destruction of this life. If they shall not die but continue to exist, why should you sorrow for them?'

This is the substantial thing about Hindu *dharma*, its inherent main essence. It is the essence not only of Hindu *dharma* but of Christianity, Buddhism, Islam and all other *dharmas*. This essence is that there is an *ātman* apart from the body, etc., and that this *ātman* is indestructible. Also if the body decays, the *ātman* stays alive after death. There are, and may be, controversies concerning the condition of the *ātman* after death, but Hindus, Christians, Buddhists, Brāhmas, Muslims and all others agree that the *ātman* is apart from, but still present in the body, that it is infallible to destruction and eternal. This is the basic foundation of all these *dharmas*.

The main opposers of this theory are the scientists. They say that there is nothing except the body; there is no proof of there being an *ātman* apart from the body. Today, it is the scientists who are powerful. All *dharmas*[45] of the earth stand on one side, and they stand on the other; through their tremendous influence all *dharmas* on earth are about to disappear. Still, *dharma* is greater than science.[46] On the other hand, we cannot abandon science by calling *dharma* greater. Both *dharma* and science are true. Consequently we shall have to consider in this instance how much truth there is on each side. Especially the educated Bengalis, whether they know about science or not, are stricken with unshakeable devotion towards it. Through science, railways and telegraphs are constructed, ships move, machines run, cloth is produced, and money comes in in different ways; thus, science (*bijñān* [Beng.]) is higher to them than knowledge (*jñān* [Beng.]). Since this commentary is being written for educated Bengalis, it is fair to consider the counter-arguments of science against the theory of *ātman*.

In the course of this consideration, it is our duty to understand first what it is exactly that is called *ātman*, and how the Hindus conceive it.

The Hindu philosophers say about the *ātman*: *ahampratyayaviṣayāspadapratyaya-lakṣitārthaḥ*[47] — i.e. what we mean when we say 'I', that is the *ātman*. I am quoting what I have written earlier concerning this topic. This is merely a paraphrase of this sentence.

> I am suffering - but who am I? Nothing is perceptible to your senses except the outer world. You say, 'I am suffering badly', or 'I am very happy'. But I cannot see any substance to address as 'you' apart from a human body. Only your body and the processes of your body are accessible to my knowledge. Shall I then attribute this feeling of happiness and pain to your body only?
>
> If you die this body of yours shall lie there, but at that time no symptoms of its feeling happiness or pain shall be visible. Imagine furthermore, someone has insulted you; your body is not affected in any way, still you are unhappy. So it is not your body that suffers pain. That which suffers pain is independent. That is you. Your body is not you.
>
> It is likewise with anything animate.[48] Consequently it can be seen

[45] [Obviously used in the sense of 'religion' here.]

[46] It is suitable here to remind the readers that, according to common usage, I am using and shall use *bijñān* (Beng.) as the equivalent of *Science* [Lat.].

[47] [Cf. Śaṅkara: *UDS* II.2.52.]

[48] [*sakal jīber* (Beng.).]

> that a certain part of the world is perceptible through the senses, whereas another part is not, but only inferable; this latter enjoys happiness and suffers pain. That which feels happiness, pain, etc., is the *ātman.*[49]

This fundamental conception concerning the theory of *ātman* is contained in Christianity as well as in any other *dharma*. But another conception, very subtle and astonishing, is found only in the Hindu *dharma*. This theory is extremely elaborate, liberal and pure; man fulfils the purpose of his birth just by believing it. No other nation [*jāti*] except the Hindus managed to realise this most important essential. This is one among the very important factors which make Hindu *dharma* superior to all other *dharmas*. I shall now explain this theory.

Everyone has an *ātman*. Since I am different from you, then your *ātman* is inevitably different from mine. But while different they are again not truly different. Imagine a great number of empty vessels. There is space[50] in each one of them. The space in one vessel is different from that in another. But although being different, all the spaces enclosed in vessels are a part of universal space. Once the vessels are broken, all difference vanishes; all enclosed spaces merge in universal space. Likewise, all the different *ātmans* enclosed in animate beings, while being separated still belong to the universal ātman; when someone frees himself from bondage, he merges in the universal *ātman*. The Hindu philosophers call this universal *ātman* '*paramātman*'. As long as the *ātman* in the body of anything animate does not merge in the *paramātman*, it is called *jīvātman*.

Now, is this *jīvātman* perishable? Is it destroyed with the destruction of the body? The simple reply to this is that whatever is a part of the imperishable can never be perishable. If cosmic space is imperishable, then so is the space in an earthen pot. If the *paramātman* is imperishable, then so is its part, the *jīvātman*.

So far for *hindudharma*; no other *dharma* has been able to come even near to this most elaborate theory. We shall demonstrate later that it is in no way inadequate to say that, among the theories known to mankind, there is no concept more elaborate than this. The ancient *ṛṣis* could say: 'If we had not done anything, if we had only departed [from this world] after propagating this theory, even then we would have been worthy of residing above all men.'[51] Actually, when one is discussing this theory one cannot count them among humans, but feels inclined to call them gods.

Let us see now what the scientists say about this. In the first place, they say, there is no proof of the existence of *ātman*. In the absence of proof, nothing has to be accepted. If the existence of the *ātman* cannot be accepted,[52] then its indestructibility, the *jīvātman*, the *paramātman* - all this would definitely have to be counted as fancy. A world-famous writer of this class explains in detail objections against accepting the existence of *ātman*:

> Thought and consciousness, though mentally distinguishable from the body, may not be a substance separable from it, but a result of it, standing in relation of it, like that of a tune to the musical instrument on which it

[49] *Prabandha pustak*. [*Sāṃkhyadarśan*, *BR* II, 221-34:225.]

[50] [*ākāśa*.]

[51] It is, I assume, not necessary to say that the theory I have expounded is not the foreign *pantheism* [Lat.].

[52] [According to *ŚBhG(b)*:31; *nā* is erroneously omitted in *ŚBhG(a)*:697.]

> is played; and that the arguments used to prove that the soul does not die with the body, would equally prove that the tune does not die with the instrument but survives its destruction and continues to exist apart. In fact, those moderns who dispute the evidence of the immortality of the soul, do not in general believe the soul to be a substance per se, but regard it as a bundle of attributes, the attributes of feeling, thinking, reasoning, believing, willing and these attributes they regard as a consequence of the bodily organization which therefore, they urge, it is as unreasonable to suppose surviving when that organization is dispersed, as to suppose the colour or odour of a rose surviving when the rose has perished. Those, therefore, who would deduce the immortality of the soul from its own nature have first to prove that the attributes in question are not attributes of the body, but of a separate substance. [Lat.][53]

The reader should try to understand somewhat subtly here. The meaning of this consideration is that proof of the *ātman*'s existence is lacking, and that therefore its existence is unverified. Apart from this, the non-existence of the *ātman* is in no way proved by this. Neither Mill nor anybody can say that the *ātman* does not exist. Mill himself observes that, by the consideration quoted above, the non-existence of the *ātman* is not proved:

> In the first place, it does not prove, experimentally, that any mode of organization has the power of producing feeling or thought. To make that proof good, it would be necessary, that we should be able to produce an organism, and try whether it would feel, which we cannot do. [Lat.][54]

And again:

> There are thinkers who regard it as a truth of reason that miracles are impossible; and in like manner there are others who, because the phenomena of life and consciousness are associated in their minds by undeviating experience with the action of material organs, thinking it an absurdity per se to imagine it possible those phenomena can exist under any other conditions. But they should remember that the uniform co-existence of one fact with another does not make the one fact a part of the other or the same with it. The relation of thought to a material brain is no metaphysical necessity; but simply a constant co-existence within the limits of observation. And when analysed to the bottom on the principles of the associative Psychology, just as much as the mental functions, is, like matter itself, merely a set of human sensations either actual or inferrible as possible... Experience furnishes us with no examples of any series of states of consciousness without this group of contingent sensations attached to it; but it is as easy to imagine such a series of states without, as with, this accompaniment, and we know of no reason in the nature of things against the possibility of its being thus disjoined. We may suppose that the same thoughts, emotions, volition and even sensations which we have here, may persist or recommence somewhere else under other

[53] *Three Essays on Religion*, p. 197 [Lat. (John Stuart Mill 1969:460)]. Since this commentary is written for the educated class, no translation from the English shall be given here.

[54] [Mill 1969:460f.]

> conditions, just as we may suppose that other thoughts and sensations may exist under other conditions in other parts of the universe. And in entertaining this supposition we need not be embarrassed by any metaphysical difficulty about a thinking substance. Substance is but a general name for the perdurability of attributes; wherever there is a series of thoughts connected together by memories, that constitutes a thinking substance. [Lat.][55]

The objection of the materialists has been swept away by this consideration; not even a trace of it has been left. And yet, just by this the supporters of the theory of *ātman* win. It has been proved by this that nobody has a right to deny the existence of a separate *ātman* or to call it destructible. Still, is has not been proved that the *ātman* is an independent substance, and that it is imperishable. When you speak of an independent and indestructible *ātman*, then how can this be proved?

This proof has been collected for many thousands of years among all the civilised races of the world. The scientists dismiss it as insufficient. The scientists are followers of truth, and they are good judges in matters of proof. Consequently we have to understand once and for all why they say this.

In order to understand them we shall first have to make clear what a proof is. A proof is that by which the knowledge of any object is produced. I am able to know that this flower exists, because I can see it. Direct sight is the proof of the flower's existence in this case. While lying inside the house I heard thunder, from this I knew that there are clouds in the sky.[56] Here, not the cloud is the object of my direct perception [*pratyakṣa*],[57] but the sound of the cloud. While in this latter case direct perception is lacking, the reason for the knowledge about the cloud is inference from former direct perception. Whenever, on hearing the sound of thunder, I have looked at the sky, I have always seen a cloud there.

Thus we get to see proof of two kinds: (1) direct perception, and (2) inference. Indians accept also another kind of proof, which I shall discuss later. Scientists or materialists, however, do not accept any other sort of proof. Concerning inference they add that any inference which is not based on direct perception is invalid, or cannot be made at all. The Europeans have, for the handling[58] of this doctrine,[59] established a most curious and fascinating philosophy, which cannot be dealt with in detail here for lack of space.

Now it shall of course have to be admitted that the *ātman* has never been anybody's object of direct perception. The body is perceptible, but the *ātman* inside this body is devoid of perceptibility. Likewise, nobody has ever perceived an *ātman* freed from the body. No inference based on perception can be made regarding a thing which is no object of perception. And not only this: men do not possess any kind of knowledge produced from any sort of direct perception about any object other than the *ātman* that would enable them to infer the existence of the *ātman* from it. So all the proofs that

[55] [Mill 1969:461f.]

[56] [The tense structure has been left as in the original.]

[57] That which is perceptible to the senses is an object of direct perception. The flower was perceived optically, the sound of the cloud acoustically.

[58] [*mīmāṃsā* (Beng.).]

[59] [*tattva* (Beng.).]

have been applied here and in Europe do not stand the test. As a result, there is no proof of the existence of the *ātman*.[60]

So science does not find the *ātman*. Science follows truth. Science searched as far as was possible for it, but while being genuinely in search of truth and trying as hard as it could, it missed the *ātman* all the same. It did not find it because science lacks the power to go that far. No one can move further than [the extent of] his reach. The diver enters the ocean by tying a cord to his waist; he can go as far as the cord reaches, not further; he does not have the capacity of picking up all the jewels in the ocean. Now the cord of proof is tied to the waist of science; where should science find the *ātman* that is inaccessible to proof? Science has no right in an area where it does not reach; it is an illusion to search for any scientific proof at all at that lowest step where science sits and makes its life meaningful, while behind it there is a huge building.

> Our victorious Science fails to sound one fathom's depth on any side, since it does not explain the parentage of *mind*.[61] For mind was in truth before all science, and remains forever the seer, judge, interpreter, even father of all its systems, facts, and laws. Our faculties are none the less truly above our heads because we no longer wonder like children about processes we do not understand. Spite of category and formula of Kant and Hegel, we are abashed before our own untraceable thought. The star of heaven, the grass of the field, the very dust that shall be man, foils our curiosity as much as ever, and none the less for yielding to the lens, the prism and the polariscope of science ever now triumphs for our pride and delight. [Lat.][62]

When science fails to prove the existence of a particle of dust,[63] then how should it prove the existence of the *ātman*? He who does not find God in his heart will not find him through[64] science. And he who has found God in his heart does not feel any necessity of a scientific proof regarding the theory of *ātman*.

Now the scientists will reply that this judgement is very unjust. When you say that proof is the only means of knowledge, you will certainly agree that there is nothing knowable without proof. When the theory of *ātman* is beyond proof, and when no proof can be furnished for the existence of the *ātman*, then men have no knowledge of it and

[60] But in all countries, common people believe that the *ātman* freed from the body of a dead person is sometimes perceptible to the human senses. When an *ātman* freed from the body thus is perceived by men, it is in certain conditions called a ghost or spirit. The scientists say that all this is an error of the mind, mistaken knowledge like taking a cord for a snake, and that such illusion is the reason for belief in the independence of the *ātman*. But at present [we testify to] the appearance of the discipline of *Spiritualism* [Lat.] in Europe and America, and the theory of ghosts has become a branch of science; famous scientists like Crookes and Wallace have examined and categorised all proofs regarding this so marvellously that they have left their contrahents somewhat perplexed. Much discussion of this is going on. But it may be stated that scientists still usually do not accept the authenticity of direct perception of ghosts; therefore I could not resort to it for proving the existence of the *ātman*. But then, I do not consider it desirable to build the foundation of a *dharma* upon such proofs, for *dharma* is not science; its foundation is even firmer.

[61] *ātman*.

[62] *Oriental Religions, India*, p. 447. [Lat. (S. Johnson 1885)]

[63] In the opinion of a number of European philosophers, there is no proof for the existence of the outer world.

[64] [*bijñāne* (Beng.): locative or instrumental case; the alternative reading is thus 'in science'.]

cannot possibly have it. Consequently, we have no other means of saying than that we do not know whether the *ātman* exists or not.

Two answers can be given to this. One is that of the ancient Indian philosophers, the other that of the contemporary Germans. In philosophy, these two are the best races of the world. Both races have realised that direct perception and inference based on perception have a very limited capacity and can in no way delimit human knowledge. Therefore, the Hindu philosophers also accept other kinds of proof. The *Naiyāyikas*[65] say that there are two other kinds of proof, namely, *upamāna*[66] and *śābda*.[67] The *Sāṃkhyas*[68] do not accept *upamāna*, but have *śābda* as their third kind of proof. I cannot tell my readers to believe that *upamāna* (*Analogy*) [Lat.] is a separate kind of proof. In many cases, instead of verified knowledge, erroneous knowledge is produced by it. Wherever *upamāna* functions as a proof, it is no separate proof in itself, but only a special kind of inference.[69] As for *śābda*, I shall now explain what it is.

Authoritative teaching is *śābda*; i.e. an utterance devoid of illusion, error, etc., is a proof of the third kind. If we can accept the Vedas, etc., as devoid of illusion and error, then the existence and indestructibility of the *ātman* can easily be taken for granted, for they have been proclaimed in the Vedas. If, on the other hand, the Vedas, etc., are utterances of humans they cannot be accepted as devoid of illusion and error, because then they are subjected to human illusions, errors, etc. Basically, only God alone is *puruṣa* devoid of illusion, error, etc. If we can acknowledge an utterance as divine, then that is a genuine *śābda* proof. The Christians too accept this as an excellent proof; its English term is *Revelation* [Lat.]. In fact, when an utterance can be acknowledged as divine, it is, as a proof, superior even to direct perception and inference. Because direct perception and inference can be deluding, which God can never be. If then someone deems this *Gītā* a divine utterance, he shall not have to search for any other proof regarding the existence and indestructibility of the *ātman*; this *Gītā* will be an irrefutable proof. But an atheist scientist would not accept the divinity of the *Gītā* or any other texts. Is he therefore not obliged to believe in the existence of the *ātman*?

For this [category of persons], there is an answer by the German philosophers. There is no place here to expose Kant's variegated philosophy to the readers. But Kant and a couple of successive well-established philosophers are of the opinion that there are other means of knowledge than direct perception and inference based on perception. They say that a number of principles[70] are *per se* proved[71] in the human mind. And they do not only claim this; the proof Kant has given of this theory provides us with a marvellous exposition of the human mind. Kant also says that, apart from that which we call the intellect[72] or the power through which we consider our perceptions, etc., with the help of obtained knowledge, we possess another power superior to it. That which is

[65] [The philosophers of the *Nyāya* school.]

[66] ['analogy'.]

[67] [Literally 'oral', 'verbal'. Bankim candra's explanation follows below.]

[68] [The philosophers of the *Saṃkhyā* school.]

[69] [*anumāna*.]

[70] [*tattva*.]

[71] [*svataḥsiddha*.]

[72] [*buddhi*.]

unattainable through consideration we can get to know through this power. It provides us with knowledge concerning the unity of God, the *ātman* and the world. This '*Transcendental Philosophy*' [Lat.] is not undisputed among the various schools. Consequently, there are many persons who cannot easily acquire belief in the existence and indestructibility of the *ātman*. But I feel obliged here to say what according to my knowledge and belief is true: I believe that **when all the faculties of the mind are adequately purified, this knowledge regarding the *ātman* is proved *per se*** [bold type of the original].[73]

A devotee has no need of all these quarrels. A devotee of God does not depend on miserable philosophy to accept the independence and indestructibility of the *ātman*. For the devotee it is sufficient that God exists and that He has proclaimed Himself to be the *paramātman* and to have descended among all living beings. However, my reason for engaging in this long argument is that many take the shelter of imperfect science to ridicule the theory of the *ātman*. They should know that the theory of *ātman*, though it may be beyond it, is not contrary to science.

dehino 'smin yathā dehe kaumāraṃ yauvanaṃ jarā
tathā dehāntaraprāptir dhīras tatra na muhyati. (13)

Just as the possessor of a body [attains] childhood, youth and old age in this body, so does he attain another body. The wise one is not deluded[74] by this. (13)

The first main theory proclaimed in the *Gītā* is the indestructibility of the *ātman*. In this *śloka*, the second great theory has been said: the doctrine of reincarnation. Just as we are bound to gradually attain stages such as childhood, youth and old age, in the same way is the attainment of a different body after death merely the attainment of a different condition. In other words, death is only a different condition; just as youth follows childhood, and old age follows youth, the present body decays, and another body comes [instead]. And, when nobody sorrows for the arrival of youth after childhood, or the arrival of old age after youth, why then should we sorrow at the time when, after this present body's decay, a new body is attained?

Through these words it has been acknowledged that, despite dying, there is rebirth. Just as the indestructibility of the *ātman* is the first essence of Hindu *dharma*, the doctrine of reincarnation is its second. But unlike the indestructibility of the *ātman* which is accepted in Christianity and all other main *dharmas*, the doctrine of reincarnation is not undisputed. On the other hand it is also not true that the doctrine of reincarnation belongs exclusively to Hindu *dharma*. It represents a main essence of Buddhism and existed or exists in other *dharmas* too. But in Europe this concept is unacceptable, and there is no scientific proof of it. This is why the educated Bengalis do not approve of this concept.

Just as there is in fact no scientific proof of the existence of the *ātman*, neither is there any such proof regarding reincarnation. On the other hand, like the existence of

[73] Many will ask now whether all the mental faculties of persons like Huxley, Tyndall [Lat.], etc., have not been adequately purified. Answer: No, not all have.

[74] [*mugdha*: the Sanskrit meaning 'deluded' is probably more dominant in this instance than the Bengali meaning 'astonished'.]

the *ātman*, reincarnation also cannot be disproved. But be that as it may, something that lacks proof is not bound to be believed by anyone. Neither can I hold that belief in this theory is proved *per se* through the adequate cultivation of all the mental faculties. But a believer in heaven and hell is in no way more powerful than a supporter of reincarnation. Like the doctrine of reincarnation, heaven, hell, etc., also admit of no other proof than authoritative teaching. It is a matter of astonishment that in this country, many educated persons, emulating the Europeans, believe in heaven and hell despite the absence of proof — that is, in a specific otherworldly condition characterised by pleasure or suffering respectively — but rigourously refuse to believe in reincarnation.

We need to discuss this topic somewhat in detail. We are not arguing with those who do not believe in the existence of the *ātman*, for those, consequently, cannot accept reincarnation. But in front of those who believe in the existence and indestructibility of the *ātman*, a very important question imposes itself automatically:

If the *jīvātman* is indestructible, then what is the course it takes after death?

Concerning this, there are many opinions current in the world:

1. Birth as a ghost is attained. This is usually the belief of uncivilised races.
2. Other worlds such as heaven and hell are attained. This is the opinion of the Christians and Muslims.
3. Reincarnation is attained. This is the opinion of the Buddhists.
4. [The *ātman*] gets dissolved in the *parabrahman* or attains *nirvāṇa*.

In the Hindu *dharma*, the three last-mentioned conceptions are current. Let me explain the way these three conceptions are coordinated. The Hindus say that the *jīvātman* is not freed after death, but obtains another body according to its done actions,[75] and attains reincarnation. Now, when the *jīvātman* has acquired a state worthy of merging in God, then it is no longer reborn but attains God or *nirvāṇa*. This is usually called *mukti* or *mokṣa*.[76] And the means by which these can be attained form the major issue of the philosophies like the *Sāṃkhya*. The Hindus also say that when the *jīvātman* has not yet reached the condition of liberation, or when it has done some good deed so as to make it worthy to enjoy heaven, then it stays in heaven for a time according to the amount of good done by it, and thereafter is reincarnated.

At present, all these things may seem implausible to many of those who have received a Western education. But it will seem different after some more consideration.

The doctrine of reincarnation is extremely strong in Hindu *dharma*. All kinds of Hindu *dharma*, whether that proclaimed in the Upaniṣads or the *Gītā*, whether the Hindu *dharma* of the Purāṇas or philosophical[77] Hindu *dharma*, are based on it. Just like pearls are lined up on a cord, all the principles[78] of Hindu *dharma* are lined up on this cord. Consequently, we shall have to understand it with care; it is of major importance, and extremely difficult. We have heard it continually from our childhood; it

[75] [*karman*; the theory of *karman* is being introduced here. All the same, the translation 'action' is retained, for this is obviously the meaning implied here, especially since the adjective *kṛta* ('done') is attributed to it.]

[76] ['liberation'.]

[77] [*dārśanik* (Beng.).]

[78] [*tattva*.]

belonged to our socialisation,[79] therefore we do not usually sense its importance. But pensive pundits from other countries and following other *dharmas* have, by freeing themselves from prejudices, been overcome by astonishment when discussing it. Thomson *Sāheb* [1855], translator of the *Gītā*, remarked in this context: 'Undoubtedly it is the most novel and starting [*sic.*] idea ever started [*sic.*] in any age or country.' [Lat.] Tylor *Sāheb* praises it by calling it 'One of the most remarkable developments of ethical speculation'. [Lat.][80]

If the topic is as important as this, then let us make an attempt at understanding it a little better.

It has been mentioned that, according to the Hindu Śāstras, the *jīvātman* is a part of the *paramātman*. How has this part of the *paramātman* or *parabrahman* been separated from it? And why is it bound to the body? I am explaining the answer to this [as] contained in the Śāstras. God has infinite powers. One of these powers is *māyā*. I shall explain elsewhere what this *māyā* is. Through this *māyā*, He has converted His identity[81] into the world. He is full of consciousness, and there is no consciousness apart from Him; consequently, the consciousness we perceive in the world is a part of Him. This part has through His desire to create become subordinate to *māyā*, separated and bound to the body. Now if this separated consciousness or *jīvātman* in any way manages to come free from the fetters of *māyā*, why should its separation persist? The separation disappears, and the *jīvātman* merges again in the *paramātman*.

Now it may be asked how the *jīvātman* is to transcend *māyā*. If it is captured by God's will or initiative, is it then within its possibilities to liberate itself again? The answer to this is that it is not God's intention to keep the *jīvātman* forever captured by *māyā*. Among all the laws He enacted, He provided also for the means to overcome *māyā*. There is disagreement regarding what this means consists of. Some say *māyā* can be overcome only through knowledge, others say through action, and again others say through devotion. We shall decide later which among these opinions is true and which is false. Let us at present suppose that all of them are true. If then these are the means to merge in God, a person who does not adequately pay heed to knowledge, action and devotion in this life shall not dissolve in God or attain liberation. So where should such a person's *ātman* go after death? The *ātman* is imperishable, therefore an *ātman* cut off from the body will have to go somewhere.

One possible answer to this is that the *ātman* cut off from the body goes to heaven or to hell according to its *karman*. Other worlds like heaven or hell lack proof. But let us leave aside proof for a while. Let us accept that the *ātman* goes to heaven or to hell according to its actions. Then it must be enquired whether the *jīvātman* goes to heaven or hell for a limited time or for eternity.

If you say that it goes there for a limited time, then where should it return to? You cannot answer this question without accepting reincarnation. You cannot say anything except that the *jīvātman* either spends a time suitable for the fruit of its actions in heaven or hell and then is born again, or that it shall stay in heaven or hell eternally.

The Christians say so; they claim that God by His judgement sends the sinners to eternal hell and the virtuous to eternal heaven.

[79] [*bālya-saṃskār* (Beng.).]

[80] Primitive Culture, Vol. I, p. 12. [Tylor 1871 (1913), *Vol. II* (probably Baṅkim's quoting mistake)]

[81] [*sattā* (Beng.).]

This leads to great confusion. There is no one among humanity who never did any good deed or any bad deed. Everybody commits some sin and does some virtuous deeds. Now it must be asked whether someone who has done some bad and some good should be sent to eternal heaven or to eternal hell. If he goes to eternal heaven, I shall ask why his sins have not been punished; if, on the other hand, you say that he goes to eternal hell, then I have to inquire why his virtuous deeds have not been rewarded.

And if you say that he whose sin is greater goes to hell and he whose virtue is greater to eternal heaven, you accuse God of misjudgement. For in such a case, on the one hand virtue has not been rewarded, and on the other hand sin has not been punished.

And it is not so that God is accused only of misjudgement; He is also accused of enormous cruelty. Can there be any graver misjudgement and cruelty than His — Whom we call merciful — decreeing eternal punishment for sins committed in a human life limited to a short time? Such cruelty cannot be found even among the most debased of this life.

If you say that he whose sin exceeds the virtue should stay in heaven for a time according to his good and then move to hell for eternity, and respectively in the opposite case, you have still not managed to erase all those objections. For limited time, and if it be millions and millions of ages,[82] is nothing in comparison to eternity. Maybe the misjudgement and cruelty have been somewhat mitigated, but they have not been done away with. So if you accept heaven and hell you have all the same to admit that an eternal stay in either one of them cannot be just. The utmost you can say is that a being stays in heaven or hell for a limited time according to the amount of its sin and virtue, or that it stays in both heaven and hell in regular succession. But then the answer to the old question remains outstanding: Where does the *jīvātman* go after the termination of this limited period? It cannot merge in the *parabrahman*; for if knowledge, action, etc., are the means of liberation, then in heaven and hell it is unattainable because of the impossibility of achieving anything there through these means.[83] The reason for this is that heaven and hell are only enjoyment or suffering;[84] they are no field of action, and the *ātman* which is devoid of the body lacks the senses of knowledge and action[85] and therefore lacks knowledge and action in heaven and hell. Thus, the question remains as to where the *jīvātman* goes after the termination of this limited time.

The Hindu Śāstras say in answer to this question: The *jīvātman* returns to the world of beings and acquires a new body. The intention of Hindu *dharma* and especially of the *dharma* proclaimed by the *Gītā* is that the *jīvātman*, after the usual decay of the body, is born again in a new body. In the course of this acquisition of a new body, good or bad birth is undergone depending on the fruits of former actions[86] and on the proportion of sin and virtuous deeds. Usually, the fruits of actions extend their effects on future births, but there are a number of actions that can result in securing one a place in heaven, and also a number of such actions as result in suffering hell. One has

82 [*koṭi koṭi yug* (Beng.): lit. 'ten millions and ten millions of ages'.]

83 [*se upāẏer sādhanābhābe* (Beng.).]

84 [*bhog* (Beng.) has been translated by two English terms.]

85 [*jñānendriya* and *karmendriya* respectively.]

86 [*karmmaphalānusāre* (Beng.).]

to go to heaven and hell according to the action one has done. One stays in heaven or hell only for a time according in amount to the fruits of actions and then returns to the world of beings and takes birth.

But still not all the objections of a person who does not believe in reincarnation have been removed. He will say: 'What you have told me is merely speculation. I accept that an eternal stay in heaven or hell is inconsistent; I did not believe in heaven and hell in the beginning, for they lack proof. But why should I believe in reincarnation just because I do not believe in heaven or hell? I admit that the *ātman* is imperishable. You ask where the imperishable *ātman* should go unless it is reincarnated. And I shall answer you that I do not know where it goes. I do not know anything about the time after death. And that which I do not know, which is without proof, I do not believe. Give me a proof of reincarnation, then I shall believe in it. The absence of proof of an alternative is no proof of reincarnation. That you are not Rām and Śyām does not prove that you are Yādab or Mādhab. What proof is there that reincarnation exists?'

This is very difficult. All the proofs that supporters of reincarnation state or might state in this context I have as far as possible collected below.

(1) In this country, this opinion is usually supported by pointing out how destiny discriminates between people. Someone is sad without any sin, another is happy despite a thousand sins; the natives of this country cannot see any other reason for such inequality than the good and bad deeds in another birth. The destined inequality in this world cannot be entirely explained by saying that in the other worlds, i.e. heaven and hell, good deeds are rewarded and bad deeds are punished. Someone is miserable for his whole life, he has been born in the house of a foodless [family]; another is fortunate, being the only son of a king; why is this inequality already present at birth? If it is a fruit of a being's actions, then these are not actions of this present life, for in the case of a new-born baby, there are no actions of this life.[87] As a result, they consider here the fruits of actions committed in a former life.

The objector will not be satisfied by this decision. Imagine that he would say: 'Is everything the fruit of actions? If that be so, then also death must be deemed the fruit of actions. But then, no being has ever been spared by death. Consequently it is proved that there is no such action or non-action by which death can be escaped. Therefore death can be no fruit of actions. And if death is no fruit of actions, why should I then call birth a fruit of actions? That which is a fruit of actions and that which is not — all happens according to God's laws. This does also. A child is born due to conjugal cohabitation in a certain set of circumstances, in a king's house just as in a carrier's house. This too has happened for that reason. Why should I in such a case look for the fruits of actions of persons born?'

The discussion does not end here. The supporter of former births could reply: 'I agree that everything happens according to God's laws. But I say that in this matter, God's law is precisely that all these inequalities occur as the fruit of the actions committed in former lives. But I do not accept the law you mentioned. A birth takes place as soon as the reason for it appears, whether this be in a queen's or a poor woman's womb. But can you explain the entire essence of birth by this law? One is born with beauty, splendour, intellect and good qualities; another ugly, ignorant and bereft of [good] qualities. If you say that this kind of difference is often the result of education

87 [*ihajanmakṛta karmma* (Beng.).]

subsequent to birth, then my answer is that some disparities do indeed come into being through this difference of education, but education cannot account for all of them. For it can be observed in many instances that one kind of education, bestowed on different characters, leads to very different results. More than that, even before the beginning of education, physical and intellectual differences can be noticed. This difference can be perceived already among six-month-old children. I know you will say that this disparity which cannot be explained as a result of education is genetic,[88] i.e. a result of the natural qualities of the father, the mother or the ancestors. I also admit that we are bound to receive the natural qualities of our parents or the ancestors preceding them, and even their socialisation,[89] and that Western scientists have proved this. But the disparity between men I am speaking of is not completely intellegible through your genetic theory. See: many brothers are born from one mother's womb and one father's semen. There is no difference whatsoever among them regarding their parents or ancestors, and nevertheless, considerable disparity can be observed among them. In answer to this you can say of course that the physical condition of the parents at the time of conception and the mother's physical and mental condition during pregnancy as well as all the events during this time cause this disparity. I might accept even this; but can you give any reasons for the disparity of this same kind which can be noticed also among twins?'

The scientist has an answer to this, too. He can remark that when these disparities have as far as this been comprehensible as subjected to natural laws known to men, then it is just to consider also the rest as subjected to natural laws knowable by men; it is unnecessary to imagine former births. Up to now science has not advanced so far as to be able to explain the reasons of this disparity in every instance, but it can be trusted that someday it will.

Here the supporter of reincarnation can object: 'This is mere speculation on your part. It is mere speculation that science is generally able to explain, or shall be able to explain in the future, respectively, what it cannot explain at present. I do not believe this.'

This sort of discussion is interminable and cannot be won by either side. The scientist cannot defeat the supporter of reincarnation here, and vice versa; the situation of both becomes comparable. Both must resort to that which is unknown, but especially that which the supporter of reincarnation must resort to is unknown and unprovable to a high degree. We cannot admit that reincarnation is proved by this argument.

(2) Many say that the belief of the common people is to be judged as the truth. People of other *dharmas* usually believe in rebirth, let the Christians and Muslims say what they may. When looking for it on the earth it can be seen that various races in various countries believe in reincarnation.[90]

[88] [*baijik* (Beng.): literally 'seminal'.]

[89] [*saṃskār* (Beng.).]

[90] 'It has been accepted, in some form, by disciples of every religion in the world. It is common to Greek philosophers, Egyptian priests, Jewish Rabbins and several early Christian sects. It appears in the speculations of the Neo-Platonists, of later European mystics, even of socialists like Fourier, who elaborated a fanciful system of successive lines mutually related by numerical relation. It reaches from the Eleusinian mysteries down to the religions of many rude tribes of North America and the Pacific isles. Not a few dreams of the cultivated imagination are subtly associated with it, as in Plato, Giordano Bruno, Herder, Sir Thomas Browne, and specially notable is Lessing's conception of gradual improvement of the human type

It is superfluous to remark that this proof too will not seem reliable to many people. A public belief is not always true, as is widely known. Take for example [the belief that] the earth is the centre of rotation of the sun, etc.

(3) As long as the *ātman* has not shaken off sin by action, knowledge, etc. acquired in many lives, it is not worthy to attain the *brahman*. Not all obtain in one life the mental purity required for this. This is our indigenous concept, but the Greek philosophers too have tried to demonstrate the truth of the doctrine of reincarnation by this argument. Those who would like to read about this in detail should study Socrates' words in the famous book *Phædon* [Lat.]. The scientists however will once again state a lack of proof.

(4) Many believe that men who are *siddhas*[91] through *yoga* can recall the stories of their former lives. But there is no trustworthy proof that any *siddha* person has had any such recollections. It goes without saying that all the narrations of the Purāṇas are not authoritative.[92] And if any *siddha* person really says that he has recollections from former lives, even then our proof is not complete. For two doubts remain: (a) whether he speaks the truth or not, and (b) even if he does not lie deliberately, is this recollection of his merely an aberration of the brain caused by affliction?

(5) Even if one does not believe in the recollections from former births of *yogins*, there is, however, another manifestation of such recollections. It happens to many that when arriving at some new place it seems to them that they have been to this place before, or, when something new happens, it seems that this event has taken place before. However, they remember with certainty that in their present birth they have never come to this place, or that such an event has not taken place. In such an instance, many judge that they have come to this place or that this event has happened in a former life, for otherwise where should such a recollection come from?

It is true that such memories occur; I can say this after having enquired. Many of my present readers also should be able to say that such recollections have every now and then arisen in their minds. Western science too accepts its truth. The scientists say that all these are '*Fallacies of Memory*' [Lat.] or *Double actions* [Lat.] of the brain. I shall explain the way in which such recollections come into being by quoting two examples from Carpenter *Sāheb*'s book *Mental Physiology* [Lat., 1869].

> Several years ago the Rev. S. Hansard, now Rector of Bethnal Green, was doing clerical duty for a time at Hurstmonceaux in Sussex and while there,

---

through metamorphosis in a series of future lives.' Oriental Religions: India, p. 517. [Lat. (Johnson, 1885)]

Anyone who wishes to see the first detailed collection of all these topics should study the twelfth chapter of the book *Primitive Culture* [Lat.] by Tylor [1913 (1871), Vol. II, 1-43: *Animism*]

[91] [*siddha* refers to a person who has attained the highest degree of accomplishment.]

[92] But I must admit that also authors of various countries talk of such recollections from former lives. 'Pythagoras is made to illustrate in his own person his doctrine of metempsychosis, by recognising where it hung in Here's temple the shield he had carried in a former birth, when he was that Euphorbos whom Menelaus slew at the siege of Troy. Afterwards he was Hermotimos, the Klazomenian prophet, whose funeral rites were so prematurely celebrated while his soul was out, and after that, as Lucian tells the story, his prophetic soul passed into a cock. Mikyllos asks this cock to tell him about Troy — were things there really as Homer said? But the cock replies: "How should Homer have known, O Mikyllos? When the Trojan war was going on, he was a camel in Baktria."' Tylor's *Primitive culture*, Vol. II, p. 13 [Lat.; 1913 (1871)].

We need not point out that these are just pleasant tales.

> he one day went over with a party of friends of Pevensey Castle, which he did not remember to have previously visited. As he approached the gateway he became conscious of a very vivid impression of having seen it before and he 'seemed to himself to see' not only the gateway itself but donkeys beneath the arch and people on top of it. His conviction that he must have visited the castle on some former occasion - although he had neither the slightest remembrance of such a visit, nor any knowledge of ever having been in the neighbourhood previously at his residence at Hurstmonceaux - made him inquire from his mother if she could throw any light on the matter. She at once informed him that being in that part of the country when he was about *eighteen months* old, she has [*sic.*] gone over with a large party and had taken him in the pannier of a donkey, that the elders of the party having brought lunch with them, had eaten it on the roof of the gateway, where they would have been seen from below, whilst he had been left with the attendants and the donkeys. - This case is remarkable for the vividness of the sensorial impression (it may be worth mentioning that Mr. Hansard has a decidedly artistic temperament) and for the reproduction of details which were not likely to have been brought up in conversation, even if he had happened to hear the visit itself mentioned as an event of his childhood, and of such mention he has no remembrance whatsoever. [Lat.]

If this person's mother had not been alive, it would not have been possible to furnish any certainty as to where this recollection had come from. No doubt, supporters of reincarnation would take this for a recollection from a former birth. There are many such recollections we do not see any reason for, but whose reason we can find in this life after some enquiry. I am quoting another example of such a successful enquiry from this book by Carpenter *Sāheb* [1869].

> In a Roman Catholic town in Germany a young woman who could neither read nor write, was seized by a fever and was said by the priests to be possessed of the devil, because she was heard talking Latin, Greek and Hebrew. Whole sheets of her ravings were written out and found to consist of sentences intelligible in themselves, but having slight connection with each other. Of her Hebrew sayings only a few could be traced to the Bible and most seemed to be in Rabbinical dialect. All trick was out of the question; the woman was a simple creature; there was no doubt as to the fever. It was long before any explanation, save that of demonical possession, could be obtained. At last the mystery was unveiled by a physician who determined to trace back the girl's history and who after much trouble discovered that at the age of nine she had been charitably taken by an old Protestant pastor, a great Hebrew scholar, in whose house she lived till his death. On further inquiry it appeared to have been the old man's custom for years to walk up and down a passage in his house into which the kitchen opened, and to read to himself with a loud voice out of his books. The books were ransacked and among them were found several of the Greek and Latin Fathers together with a collection of Rabbinical writings. In these books so many of the passages taken down at the young woman's beside were identified that there could be no reasonable doubt as to their source. [Lat.]

Had it been in this country, there would have been no enquiry; the Latin, Greek and Hebrew would have been deemed to be a part of the 'learning of the woman's former life', and would have been established as such. On the other hand it cannot be said either that all similar recollections can on investigation be put down to this present life; we are not able to say anything definite here until more research has been done. Not much research has been done so far. As long as it is not done we cannot be certain about how far this proof is acceptable.

Whatever the results of such research, there is another debate that might open up. Is memory a function of the brain or of the *ātman*? If you say it is a function of the *ātman*, then why does not a detailed recollection of our former lives arise in our minds? Why should one have to speak of some slight, unclear recollection arising sporadically in our minds? The *ātman* is the same, so where can its recollections have gone? And if you say memory is a function of the brain, then how can even this slight and unclear recollection possibly come up? For the brain which contained the former life's recollections decayed with the body and does not exist anymore.

This objection can be resolved well. But there is no need, since it is not even proved that all these recollections are from former lives.

The conclusion is that those who accept the eternity of the *ātman* have no alternative other than to accept reincarnation. [For] if the *ātman* is eternal, then it definitely existed before. Where? It cannot be sustained that it was merged in the *paramātman*, for whatever is merged in the *paramātman* is not a *jīvātman* and has no separate existence. And if you say that it was in another world then you must call its birth in this world reincarnation; if you do not hold it to have been in another world then of course you have to maintain that it was in this very world in another body.

There might be someone who, while accepting the indestructibility of the *ātman*, does not accept its eternity. That is to say, such a person would argue that the *ātman* is born with the body and persists once it is born, but that it might not be true that the *ātman* existed also before birth. Those who think like this imagine a new creation in every birth of a being. Such imagination is contradicted by science, for the basic principle of science is that every universal law is eternal, and no disorder ever happens here. Now one of the laws which is especially proved is that, in the world, nothing is created anew. Things are not created anew, but merely transformed through the effects of eternal laws.[93] We cannot maintain that this living body, by being born or being conceived in the female womb, constitutes a new creation; it is no more than a new combination of the respective inanimate substances that also existed before. Other things have only been transformed. One cannot call the *ātman* which has been born with the body to be the transformation of anything. For the *ātman* is no inanimate substance, and consequently no transformation[94] of the inanimate. All the *ātmans* born before are indestructible too, so it is no transformation of them, either. Thus it would have to be called a new creation, but a new creation goes against natural laws. Therefore, if one considers the *ātman* to be indestructible, one has, as a consequence, to accept its eternity and beginninglessness. By calling it eternal and beginningless one has consequently

[93] *nāvastuno vastusiddhiḥ* ['(There is) no accomplishment of a thing out of nothing.' Origin unidentified.]. And: *Ex nihilo nihil fit* [Lat.; a slightly altered version of the (especially Epicurean) materialist position in classical antiquity, as formulated in Lucretius' *De Rerum natura* (1.150).].

[94] [*bikār* (Beng.) instead of the previously used *rūpāntar* (Beng.).]

to accept reincarnation.

And those who do not believe in the independence and indestructibility of the *ātman* shall certainly also reject reincarnation. I have to tell them that the doctrine of reincarnation, even if unprovable, cannot be contemptible to them. Let us hear what the European pundits who actually belong to their community say about it.[95] The Buddhologist *Rhys Davids* [Lat., 1877] writes:

> The doctrine of Transmigration in either the Brahmanical or the Buddhist form, is not capable of disproof; while it affords an explanation, quite complete to those who can believe in it, of the apparent anomalities and wrong in the distribution of happiness or woe.[96] The explanation can always be exact, for it is scarcely more than a repetition of the facts to be explained; it may always fit the facts, for it is derived from them; and it cannot be disproved,[97] for it lies within a sphere beyond the reach of human enquiry. [Lat.]

Tylor *Sāheb* [1913 (1871)] writes:

> The Buddhist Theory of 'Karma', or 'Action', which controls the destiny of all sentient beings, not by judicial rewards and punishment, but by the inexhorable result of cause into effect, where the present is ever determined by the past in an unbroken line of causation is indeed one of the world's most remarkable developments of ethical speculation. *Primitive Culture*, Vol. II, p. 12. [Lat.].

There is a deeper meaning in this quotation. The Christians do not believe in reincarnation; they say that God, while sitting in heaven, judges sin and virtuous deeds and determines the punishment of the guilty and the reward of the righteous. The significance of Tylor *Sāheb*'s text is that compared to a God who sits like a judge on the bench and issues decrees, this destiny of beings bound to cause and effect is indeed the more scientific theory. This should be well understood. The universe's procedure of ruling consists in there being a number of universal laws. They are eternal, are never disordered. By their effects all natural processes are maintained; God never needs to intervene in order to accomplish any action Himself. It is also true that every action is performed by Him, but hidden behind these laws. If I say that He, engaged in the work of judgement, issues decrees concerning the destiny of beings after their death, sending some to heaven, some to hell, then a thing has been imagined which contradicts the universe. Here, nothing is accomplished by any law; God Himself has to act. The prescriptions of punishment or reward for every single being are each actions of God unregulated[98] by laws, i.e. *miracles* [Lat.]. But in the doctrine of reincarnation, this objection does not occur. God's law is that such and such a sinner earns such and such

[95] Many modern European writers have supported the doctrine of rebirth. The most prominent among them are *Herder* [Lat.] and *Lessing* [Lat.]. Apart from them, the names of many other writers can be mentioned, like *Fourier, Soame, Jenyns, Figuier, Dupont de Nemours, Pezzani* [Lat.], etc.

[96] *Buddhism*, p. 100 [Lat.].

[97] If you say the parapsychologist [*pret'tattvabid* (Beng.)] pundits prove that a human *ātman* devoid of its body sometimes appears [in a form] perceptible to the senses of men, even then the doctrine of reincarnation is not refuted. The supporters of reincarnation do not claim that the *ātman* enters a new body always immediately after death. If it is so that every now and then there is some delay regarding the acquisition of a new body, then reincarnation is not disproved by this.

[98] [*aniẏam'siddha* (Beng.).]

a birth. Action is the cause, and the specific birth is the effect.[99] Reincarnation is established by the results of actions bound to the relation of cause and effect; *'miracle'* [Lat.] is unnecessary.

Schlegel is a very orthodox Christian, but one of Europe's greatest writers and scholars. I am quoting the English translation of his statement on this topic.

> In this doctrine, there was a noble element of truth — the feeling that man, since he had gone astray, and wandered so far from his God, must needs excert [*sic.*] many efforts, and undergo a long and painful pilgrimage before he can regain the source of all perfection; — the firm conviction and positive certainty that nothing defective, impure, or defiled with earthly stains can enter the pure region of perfect spirits, or be eternally united to God; and that thus before it can attain to the blissful end, the immortal soul must pass through long trials and many purifications. It may now well be conceived, (and indeed the experience of this life would prove it) that suffering, which deeply pierces the soul, anguish that convulses all the members of existence, may contribute, or may even be necessary, to the deliverance of the soul from all alloy, and pollution, or to borrow a comparison from natural objects, the generous metal is melted down in fire and purged from its dross. It is certainly true that the greater the degeneracy and the degradation of man, the nearer is his approximation to the brute; and when the transmigration of the immortal soul through the bodies of various animals is merely considered as the punishment of its former transgressions, we can very well understand the opinion that man who by his crimes and the abuse of his reason, had descended to the level of the brute should at last be transformed into the brute itself. [Lat.][100]

Finally I quote the statement of Samuel Johnson *Sāheb* who lives in America. Writers of his erudition are rare.

> The Transmigration faith was so widely spread in the elder world, because it had its roots in natural and profound aspirations. It combined the two-fold intuition of immortality and moral sequence with that mystic sense of the unity of being which is a germ of the highest religious truth. [Lat.][101]

I shall now summarise the gist[102] of what has been said.

1. The doctrine of reincarnation cannot be disproved.
2. In a certain way, there are also some proofs in its favour.
3. Its authoritativeness is irrefutable to those who accept the indestructibility of the *ātman*.
4. This theory cannot be comtemptible even to those who do not believe in the indestructibility of the *ātman*, for there is no other current theory concerning the life after death coherently connected with the universal, eternal laws.

[99] [*karmma kāraṇ, yonibiśeṣ, tāhār kāryya* (Beng.).]

[100] *Philosophy of History* — translated by Robertson — Bohn's Edition, pp. 157-8 [Lat., 1846].

[101] *Oriental Religions: India*, p. 539. [Lat., 1885]

[102] [*sthūl marmma* (Beng.).]

All these discussions are unnecessary for a devotee; when this *śloka* represents the sense of divine speech, then that is sufficient reason for his belief. He would have to consider whether the doctrine of reincarnation as it is proclaimed in the *Gītā* is really divine speech or just the author's belief, i.e. whether he has inserted his personal belief in God's words.

If someone has doubts as to whether these are God's words or not, and if he does not believe in reincarnation despite the discussion of all the proofs above, then he should ask himself whether the *dharma* of the *Gītā* can be accepted even without believing in reincarnation.

The answer to this is very easy. This *dharma* proclaimed by the *Gītā* is for all men. It is the best *dharma* for him who believes in reincarnation just as well as for him who does not. It is the best *dharma* for him who is devoted to Kṛṣṇa as well as for him who is not. It is the best *dharma* for him who believes in God, and also for him who does not; for purification of the mind and constraint of the senses is the best *dharma* for atheists too, and this purification of the mind is the *Gītā*'s goal. Such a universal[103] and all-embracing *dharma* has never again been proclaimed on earth. Everybody should take from it according to his right. And where a person does not believe, there his right expires. Everybody shall receive from that to which he has a right.

mātrāsparśās tu kaunteya śītoṣṇasukhaduḥkhadāh
āgamāpāyino 'nityās tāṃs titikṣasva bhārata. (14)

O Kaunteya, the senses and their contact with the sense-objects:[104] this is what creates the pleasure and pain of cold and hot. All this has birth and destruction and is thus not eternal; so bear it all, O Bhārata. (14)

In the eleventh *śloka* it was said: 'You are sorrowing for that which one should not sorrow for.' In the twelfth, the reason for making such an admonition has been indicated. This reason is that nobody dies, for the *ātman* is indestructible. Even if you are hewn down, he [i.e. the individual] will remain, for his *ātman* will remain. The eleventh *śloka* shows us that reincarnation was accepted in society at the time the *Gītā* was written. Here the Lord fears Arjuna's objection and destroys it. Arjuna could say: 'So maybe the *ātman* remains; but when the body dies, where then does my relative for whom I sorrow remain? When reborn he will have become a different person.' Fearing this objection the Lord says in the thirteenth *śloka* that it is not right to imagine such a division, for just like childhood, youth and old age are but different conditions of a person, likewise also the acquisition of a new body is merely another condition. Arjuna can object to this, too: 'Alright, I accept that the embodied being[105] also keeps its unity in a future body — but there is such a thing as a pain and suffering of death. Should I not sorrow when remembering that these relatives have to undergo this pain? Should I not feel sad in their absence?'

In reply to this, the Lord says in this fourteenth *śloka*: 'All you call sorrow is born

103 [*biśvalaukik* (Beng.).]

104 *mātrāś ca sparśāś ca iti — Śaṅkaraḥ* ['The senses and their objects [...]' (*ŚaBhG*:30f.) — Śaṅkara('s explanation)].

105 [*dehin*.]

from the link of the senses with sense-objects. As long as there is this link this sorrow persists; when the link is lacking, the sorrow disappears; just as when the skin is in contact with the heat of the sun, etc., or the cold of snow we feel pain in the form of heat or cold, but when the sun, etc., disappear, this pain does not remain. And that which does not persist, which is perishable, should be endured. Why should we be troubled because of the pain which just by enduring comes to an end?'

Life becomes pleasant as soon as this quality of tolerance or patience is there. If one trains then no pain is considered a pain anymore. Then human life is overflowing with unlimited joy through the blissful devotion proclaimed in the *Gītā*. No trace of pain is left. This tolerance towards pain is the foundation of making one's life pleasant — without it, nothing can be attained. The joy derived from the contact of the senses with outer sense-objects, like pleasure, enjoyment, luxury, etc., must be considered pain too, for when passion for them is produced, their absence too is felt as pain. This is why 'cold and heat, [and] pleasure and pain', have been enumerated together here.[106]

yaṃ hi na vyathayanty ete puruṣaṃ puruṣarṣabha
samaduḥkhasukhaṃ dhīraṃ so 'mṛtatvāya kalpate. (15)

O best[107] of men, that wise man alone who maintains equanimity in pleasure as well as in pain and is not afflicted by all these is capable of attaining liberation.[108]

Why is one fit for liberation when being able to endure pleasure and pain? It is freedom from pain which is freedom or liberation. The *saṃsāra*[109] is full of pain. Even those who say that, in *saṃsāra*, pleasure exceeds pain will have to admit that pain exists in *saṃsāra*. For this reason reincarnation too means pain, because when returning to the *saṃsāra* one has to suffer pain. Therefore, freedom from rebirth too is freedom or liberation. Roughly, the attainment of freedom from suffering pain is liberation. This is why the author of the *Sāṃkhyakārikāḥ* has said in the very first *sūtra*: *trividhaduḥkha-*

106 Here, the word *mātrā*, and the sentence-element [*pad* (Beng.)] *mātrāsparśa* of the original can be interpreted in two different ways. By it, the senses as well as the sense-objects can be designated. Śaṅkarācārya says: *mātrā* [']*ābhir mīyante śabdādaya*['] *iti śrotādinīndriyāṇi, mātrāṇāṃ sparśāḥ śabdādibhiḥ saṃyogāḥ*. ['*Mātras* are the sense-organs like the ears, etc., by which objects like sounds are measured. Touches (*sparśāḥ*) of these *mātrās* (means) their contacts with objects like sounds.' (Cf. *ŚaBhG*:31)] Śrīdhara Svāmin likewise says: *mīyante jñāyante viṣayā ābhir iti mātrā indriyavṛttayas tāsāṃ sparśā viṣayaiḥ saha sambandhāḥ (mātrāsparśāḥ)*. ['Those by which the objects of the senses are perceived are called *mātrā*, i.e. the functions of the senses; 'their contact' (means) connection with the objects.' (Cf. *ŚrBhG*:36)] Also Madhusūdana Sarasvatī says exactly this. On the other hand, Viśvanātha Cakravartin says: *mātrā indriyagrāhyaviṣayāḥ*. ['The *mātrās* are the objects perceivable through the senses.'] This would not matter much, had not an English translator called Davies [1882] reminded us that the word *mātrā* is *Materia* [Lat.] in Latin and *matter* [Lat.] in English, and consequently written '*Matter-contacts*' as a translation of *mātrāsparśāḥ*. Doubtlessly, sense-objects are necessary for quantitative knowledge [*parimāṇ-jñān* (Beng.)]. The significance of the word *tanmātra* of *Sāṃkhya* philosophy must be considered here. It is needless to say that I follow Śaṅkarācārya and Śrīdhara Svāmin here while rejecting Viśvanātha Cakravartin and Davies *Sāheb*.

107 [literally: 'steer'.]

108 ['Liberation' is a rendering of Baṅkim's translation *mokṣalābh*; the *Gītā* however has *amṛtatva* here, which means 'immortality'.]

109 [i.e. the transmigratory world.]

syātyantanivṛttir atyantapuruṣārthaḥ.[110] Now, when one learns to endure pain he attains freedom from pain, for he no longer considers that thing a pain which he has learnt to endure. He has attained liberation because he no longer has any pain. Consequently one does not have to die in order to attain liberation; once one can endure pain, or, in other words, is not pained by pain,[111] one attains liberation already in this life.

nāsato vidyate bhāvo nābhāvo vidyate sataḥ
ubhayor api dṛṣṭo 'ntas tv anayos tattvadarśibhiḥ. (16)

Unreal things do not exist;[112] there is no non-being[113] of real things.[114] Those who know the essence have in this manner seen the end[115] of both. (16)

The word *sat*[116] stems from the root *as*. Whatever will be is *sat*; and whatever is not or will not be, *asat*. The *ātman* is *sat*, whereas pleasure and pain, etc., such as cold and hot, etc., are *asat*. In the eternal *ātman* the perishable heat, cold, pleasure and pain cannot persist, for the *asat* cold and hot, etc., are contradictory to the *dharma*[117] of the *ātman*. Śrīdhara Svāmin has explained thus: *asato 'nātmadharmatvāt avidyamānasya śītoṣṇāder ātmani na bhāvaḥ.*[118] We have followed him.

It is a duty of the readership, too, to discuss with profound attention the way in which Śaṅkarācārya has explained *sat* and *asat* intellect with regard to this *śloka*. From this you[119] shall be able to understand the difference between the point of view our ancestors had of all these topics and the one we have now. Śaṅkara's commentary on this *śloka* is extremely difficult. A translation of it is given below.

> Since they come into being from causes and are thus of an *asat* nature, such effects[120] as cold, hot, etc., have no existence. It is ascertained by proof that cold and hot are produced by a cause, therefore they cannot be *sat* substances. The reason for this is that they are merely transformations,[121] and transformations can always be seen to allow of transgressions (i.e. sometimes the transformation exists and sometimes it does

110 ['The final release from threefold pain is the final goal of man.' (*SSV* 1.1)]

111 [*duḥkhe duḥkhita* (Beng.).]

112 [*astitva nāi* (Beng.).]

113 [*abhāva*; the word *abhāb* (Beng.) employed here denotes *abhāva* 'non-being' rather then merely 'lack' in which sense it is usually used in Bengali.]

114 [The *Gītā* has: 'There is no becoming of what does not already exist, there is no unbecoming of what does exist' (*BhGBE*:75).]

115 [i.e. boundary.]

116 [Present participle meaning 'being'.]

117 [*dharma* is used here in the sense of 'property'.]

118 ['Since non-existing is no quality (*dharma*) of the *ātman*, non-existing (qualities) such as heat and cold have no existence in the *ātman*.' (Cf. *ŚrBhG*:38)]

119 [*āp'nārā* (Beng.).]

120 [*kāryya* (Beng.).]

121 [*bikār* (Beng.).]

not). Just as as soon as one sees them through the eyes, substances like vessels are not realised as anything but clay,[122] in the same manner transformations of all kinds are *asat* for their not being realised as anything except their cause. Before their production and after their destruction, effects like vessels that are produced from causes like clay are not realised. Now again all these causes for their not being realised as anything separate from their causes are also *asat*. It could be objected here that when the causes are *asat* in this manner, all substances become *asat* (nothing at all remains *sat*). The refutation of such an objection is that two kinds of knowledge [*jñān* (Beng.)][123] are produced in every case, the knowledge of [something] as *sat* and the knowledge of [something] as *asat*. The entity[124] whose cognition is not transgressed, i.e. the entity of which it seems that, once it 'exists', it does not again 'not exist', is called *sat*. And the entity of which it seems that, once it exists, it again does not exist, is called *asat*. In this manner the mental apparatus[125] is divided into the two parts of *sat* and *asat*, and everybody everywhere realises this because he acquires knowledge of these two kinds. When a qualifier and a qualified[126] are present in the same case they become without differentiation, as e.g. the meaning of *nīlaṃ utpalaṃ* ['blue lotus'] is not different from 'the lotus is blue', i.e. once the knowledge of this lotus is acquired, simultaneously, without differentiation, the knowledge of its blueness too comes into being. When in this way the knowledge of 'being a vessel', 'being a cloth', 'being an elephant'[127] is produced, then the knowledge of 'being'[128] arises inseparably with that of the vessel. Consequently the imagination of *buddhi* divided into *sat* and *asat*, that was being considered, is senseless.[129] But people do not realise inseparably in this way. It has been shown that among the two *buddhis*, the *buddhi* of the vessel, etc., is transgressed;[130] the *buddhi* of *sat* is not transgressed. Therefore, the substances which like vessels are objects of *buddhi*, are *asat* because of their being transgressed, and since they are not untransgressable they cannot be objects of *buddhi*.

[122] That is, when the knowledge of the vessel is on the point of arising, the knowledge of clay arises simultaneously. Without the knowledge of clay arising, the knowledge of the vessel does not arise; thus, the vessel is *asat*, [and] its cause, clay, is *sat*.

[123] [As the Bengali translation of Sanskrit *buddhi* (throughout the quotation, unless where *buddhi* is left in the Bengali text) (Cf. *ŚaBhG*:32).]

[124] [*bastu* (Beng.); not present in *ŚaBhG*.]

[125] [*buddhitantra* (*ŚaBhG*:32 and translation).]

[126] [*biśeṣaṇ* and *biśeṣya* (Beng.); 'adjective' and 'noun' in modern Bengali grammar.]

[127] ['*ghaṭaḥ san*', '*paṭaḥ san*', '*hastī san*'. — Śaṅkarācārya has the reverse order, i.e. *san ghaṭaḥ*, etc. (*ŚaBhG*:32ff.)]

[128] [Here, *sat* clearly means 'being'.]

[129] [The Bengali translation Baṅkim quotes is not very accurate here; it is more an interpretation than a direct rendering. Śaṅkara's point is the following: Contrary to the case *nīlam utpalam*, where the relation is that of a qualifier and a qualified, *san ghaṭaḥ*, etc., merges both cognitions.]

[130] [*byabhicār haẏ* (Beng.).]

If you say that, with the transgression of the *buddhi* of the vessel at the time of its destruction, the *buddhi* of *sat* is also transgressed (that is, in the opinion of the objector the *buddhi* of the vessel and that of *sat* are not different, therefore the *buddhi* of *sat* should be transgressed with the *buddhi* of the vessel), then this objection cannot apply; for at this time, the *buddhi* of *sat* is present in the vessel, etc. (and consequently it is not transgressed). That *buddhi* of *sat* is present in the form of a qualifier, therefore it is not destroyed (with the destruction of the qualified).

If you say that, as regards the *buddhi* of *sat*, there is also, rationally, the *buddhi* of vessels in other vessels after one vessel has been destroyed, and, therefore, 'the *buddhi* of the vessel is *sat*', then this objection cannot apply here, because this *buddhi* of the vessel, etc., is not in cloth, etc.

If you say that, after the destruction of a vessel, the *buddhi* of *sat* too is not visible, then this is no strong objection. The *buddhi* of *sat* is present in the form of a qualifier; a qualifier cannot be where there is no qualified. If it is, what happens to its object? If the object is wanting, the *buddhi* of *sat* cannot be. If you say that, even in the absence of a qualified, the vessel is *sat* because the qualifier can be mentioned as the qualified in the same case, then the answer is that in the case of mirages, etc., too, *sat idaṃ udakaṃ* [*sic.*]; 'this water is existent [*sat*]' can be used in the same case even when both the *buddhi* of *sat* and water are absent (by this the mention in the same case is proof for neither *sat* nor *asat*).

Consequently, combinations[131] like the body are produced from causes and therefore *asat*; they do not exist. And the *ātman* which is *sat* is lacking in no part, for it is not transgressed anywhere. This is the determination in the form of *sat* and *asat*, and of the *ātman* and the *anātman*. Whatever is *sat*, is *sat*; whatever is *asat*, is *asat*.[132]

As world-conquering a pundit as Śaṅkarācārya was, this philosophical argument is indeed suitable for him. But it is not very compatible with Western education of the nineteenth century. Pleasure and pain, whether you call them *sat* or *asat*, do exist. It is true that they do not persist; but their inexistence is out of the question. Still it is the main thing[133] that they do not last. But they are only destroyed if one can endure them.

'— The darkest day,
Wait till to-morrow,
Will have passed away.' [Lat.][134]

Some objections can now be raised if one does not understand well what has been said in the *ślokas* 14, 15 and 16. The first objection is that, if pain must be endured, should it not be prevented? Arjuna's pain is the killing of relatives and friends; this pain is warded off by simply not fighting, which is an easy means for the prevention of pain. What kind of instruction is it when in this situation the Lord does not instruct him to

131 [*dvandva* (Beng.).]

132 We have been presented this translation from Śaṅkarācārya's commentary by a certain friend. [For the Sanskrit text and an English translation, cf. *ŚaBhG*:32ff.]

133 [*baṛa kājer kathā* (Beng.).]

134 [origin?]

sickness?

No, this is not the case. It is not forbidden to prevent pain; but where one by preventing pain causes *adharma*, there one must not prevent pain but endure it. The war Arjuna is engaged in is a *dharmayuddha*.[135] A kṣatriya has no higher *dharma* than *dharmayuddha*. Through the abandonment of *dharma* there is *adharma*. Consequently, in this case, preventing pain instead of enduring it leads to *adharma*. This is why pain must here be endured and not prevented.

The second objection is that one may endure pain, but how is it that one endures pleasure? Should we regard pleasure and pain as the same? Is then the Lord's instruction that in this world, no pleasure leads to [true] pleasure? What is *asceticism* [Lat.] then? What is gained by a *dharma* devoid of pleasure?

I have already written the reply to this above. The pleasure that depends on the sense-organs is the cause of pain and is therefore to be regarded as such. The pleasure independent of the senses, the joys derived from knowledge, devotion, friendship, mercy, etc., is, according to the *dharma* proclaimed in the *Gītā*, not to be abandoned but is instead its goal. And even the pleasures derived from the senses actually are not to be abandoned according to this *dharma*; this abandonment is also not the goal of the *dharma* of the *Gītā*. The non-attachment to them is the goal of the *dharma* proclaimed in the *Gītā*, not their abandonment.

rāgadveṣavimuktais tu viṣayān indriyaiś caran
ātmavaśyair vidheyātmā prasādam adhigacchati. 2.64 [*Gītā*][136]

We shall say some more about this topic when discussing this 64th *śloka*.

We see that in the twelfth *śloka* the first principle[137] of Hindu *dharma* has been indicated: the indestructibility of the *ātman*. In the thirteenth *śloka*, [we have] the second principle, the doctrine of reincarnation. In the *ślokas* 14, 15 and 16 the third principle is indicated: the 'non-*ātman*-ness' [*anātmadharmitā*] and transitoriness of pleasure and pain. I shall explain the relation of pleasure and pain with the *ātman* in the way I have done before on the occasion of an explanation of the *Sāṃkhyadarśana*.

> The *puruṣa* is apart from the body, etc. But pain is related to the body, etc.; there is no pain whose reasons are not in the body, etc. Outer substances are the root of what we call mental pain. If you have been insulted by my words, [then because] my words are a natural substance you received through your organs of hearing; your pain is through this. So there is no pain except in the *prakṛti*; but why is the pain produced through the *prakṛti* in the *puruṣa*? *aṅgo*[138] *'yam puruṣaḥ*. The *puruṣa* is alone, he is not connected with anything (first chapter, fifteenth *sūtra*.). All conditions are of the body, not of the *ātman* (ibid., fourteenth *sūtra*.). *na bāhyāntarayor uparajyoparañjakabhāvo 'pi deśavyavadhānātsrughnastha-pāṭaliputrasthayor iva* [*SSV* 1.28]. [That is,] between the inside and the outside there is no relation as between a colourant and that which is to be

[135] [A war in accordance with *dharma*.]

[136] ['When he experiences the objects with senses that neither love nor hate and are under his control, he [i.e. the *vidheyātman*] attains serenity.' (*BhGBE*:81)]

[137] [*tattva*.]

[138] [Probably misprint for *asaṅgo*; cf. *SSV* 1.15.]

pāṭaliputrasthayor iva [*SSV* 1.28]. [That is,] between the inside and the outside there is no relation as between a colourant and that which is to be painted; for they are not in touch with each other, they are spatially divided. Their distance is like that between one person who lives in the town of Pāṭaliputra and another who lives in the town of Srughna. So why does the *puruṣa* suffer pain? His contact with the *prakṛti* is the cause of pain. There is indeed a spatial distance between the inside and the outside, but it is not true that there is no contact. It is the same kind of contact as the contact between flower and vessel one can speak of when one places a china-rose near a crystalline vessel and the vessel takes on the colour of the flower. Even when they are spatially divided, the colour of the vessel can be altered; this is similar. Obviously this contact is not eternal; so it can be broken. Once it is broken, pain is eliminated. Thus the destruction of this contact is the means of removing pain and, consequently, it is the ultimate goal.[139] *yad vā tad vā taducchittiḥ puruṣārthas taducchittiḥ puruṣārthaḥ*[140] (6.7 [*SSV* 6.70]).[141]

avināśi tu tad viddhi yena sarvam idaṃ tatam
vināśam avyayasyāsya na kaścit kartum arhati. (17)

Know as imperishable that by which all this is pervaded. No-one can bring about the destruction of this immutable [principle]. (17)

'That by which' i.e. through the *paramātman*. 'All this', i.e. the world. This whole world is pervaded by the *paramātman*, in the same way, according to Śaṅkara, as vessels, etc., are pervaded by ether.[142]

That which is all-pervading cannot be destroyed, for as long as anything exists, this all-pervading existence[143] also will persist. This all-pervading existence will be all-pervading as long as anything exists. Thus it is immutable. Space is all-pervading; we cannot even imagine its destruction or perishing in our minds. Space is indestructible and immutable. He who is all-pervading and by whom, therefore, space too is pervaded, is also indestructible and immutable. Nobody can bring about his destruction.

Now, this topic leads to a couple of other topics. All these are substantial topics of Hindu *dharma*, for which reason they should be taken up here.

Firstly, it is proved through this *śloka* that God is formless, that He cannot have a shape. That which has a shape cannot be all-pervading. The shaped is perceptible to the sense-organs. We know that there is no shaped all-pervading substance perceptible to the senses. Thus, if God is all-pervading, He is not in possession of any shape.

It is the *Gītā*'s opinion that God is shapeless. And it is not only the *Gītā*'s common conception, but that of the Hindu Śāstras and of Hindu *dharma* [as a whole].

139 [*puruṣārtha*.]

140 ['It is the ultimate goal of man to eliminate whatever there might be.']

141 Quoted from the *Prabandha-pustak*. [The quoted passage is from Baṅkim's essay *Sāṃkhyadarśan*, *BR* II:225.]

142 [*ākāśa*.]

143 [*sattā* (Beng.); translated as 'identity' above (*ŚBhG*:51).]

The Upaniṣads and the philosophical systems are of this opinion. In all these, God has been indicated as all-pervading consciousness.[144] It is true, of course, that in the Purāṇas and Itihāsas, Brahmā, Viṣṇu and Śiva have been imagined as consciousness having a form and in many cases worshipped as God.[145] It is not necessary here to investigate for which reasons the need for or origin of imagining such images of God had come about. It must only be said that the authors of the Purāṇas and Itihāsas do not want to establish the formedness of God, even when Śiva, etc., have been described as having shape; they never forget that God is formless. He is formless also in the Purāṇas and Itihāsas.

The significance of my words can be understood as soon as I give an example. Let us thus take the character of Prahlāda of the *Viṣṇupurāṇa* for this purpose. There, Viṣṇu is God. Prahlāda praises him by saying *namas te puṇḍarīkākṣa*.[146] In another place he clearly accepts the formedness of God, namely:

brahmatve sṛjate viśvaṃ sthitau pālayate punaḥ
rudrarūpāya kalpānte namas tubhyaṃ trimūrtaye. [*VP* 1.19.66][147]

And finally Viṣṇu clad in yellow cloth shows himself in his corporeal form to Prahlāda. But still Viṣṇu is shapeless in this biography of Prahlāda; his name is *Ananta*,[148] he is 'all-pervading'. He who is endless and all-pervading can only be shapeless, and not corporeal; and it has been repeated again and again that He is devoid of qualities and shape, as for example:

namas tasmai namas tasmai namas tasmai parātmane
nāmarūpaṃ na yasyaiko yo 'stitvenopalabhyate. Etc. ([*VP*] 1.19.79)[149]

And again, Viṣṇu is *anādimadhyāntaḥ*,[150] therefore, shapeless.

It is like this in all the Purāṇas. Thus it is more or less certain that it is the gist of Hindu *dharma* that God is formless.

But is there no adoration[151] of corporeal [gods] in Hindu *dharma*? We do find idol worship daily in every village; India is full of the veneration of idols. How can we then say that there is no doctrine of corporeality[152] in Hindu *dharma*?

The answer to this is that, whatever be the situation in other countries, the Hindu veneration of idols is not worship of the shaped, and the Hindu who venerates an idol will, unless he is utterly ignorant or uneducated, never imagine the idol to be God, or that God is shaped like this and that this is God's genuine image. If a person who

[144] [*sarbbabyāpī caitanya* (Beng.).]

[145] [*īśvara*.]

[146] ['Homage to you, O lotus-eyed (epithet of Viṣṇu)'.]

[147] [Wilson (1865, Vol. II:57) translates: 'To him who, as Brahmā, creates the universe; who, in its existence, is its preserver; be praise! To thee, who, at the end of the Kalpa, takest the form of Rudra; to thee, who art triform; be adoration!']

[148] ['Endless.']

[149] [Wilson (1865, Vol. II) translates: 'Glory be to the great spirit, again and again; to him who is without name or shape; who sole, is to be known by adoration.']

[150] ['Without beginning, middle and end.' Cf. e.g. *VP* 1.17.151.]

[151] [*upāsanā* (Beng.). In the present passage, *pūjā* (Beng.) has been rendered by 'worship' and *arcanā* (Beng.) by 'veneration'.]

[152] [*sākāravāda*.]

adores a *Kālī* made of a lump of clay has only the slightest idea about the adoration offered by himself, then he knows that this painted lump of clay is not God and not His image, and he knows that it cannot possibly be the portrait of God.

So why does he worship a lump of clay? He does not find the One he wants to worship; He is invisible, unthinkable, not attainable by meditation and thus beyond adoration. So he calls Him and says: 'O world-pervading, omnipresent primordial energy! You are everywhere, but I cannot see you; you can manifest[153] yourself everywhere, so manifest yourself in something I can see. Manifest yourself in this form which I made when imagining you; let me worship you. Otherwise I cannot make up my mind where to put the sandal paste.'

For this idol-worship the English, our teachers, are very angry with us, and their pupils, the new Indians, as well. The reason for the anger of the English is that the Bible forbids it. The educated Indians are angry because the English are angry. What the English blame must of course be blamed by 'us'. The English blame idol-worship, thus it must be blamed by 'us'; there is no need of [independent] investigation. The English say that India has been ruined because of this idol-worship, and shall be utterly ruined if it is not abolished;[154] thus we, too, are bound to believe this; there is no need of further [independent] investigation. It is true that ancient states like Rome, Greece, etc., had developed despite their worshipping of idols; but the English maintain that India will be ruined through idol-worship, so India will definitely be ruined by idol-worship; considerations on this topic are unnecessary. Many members of the educated class think like this. Judging differently is, to them, the result of wrong education, perverted intelligence and depravedness.

We cannot approve of such utterances. God is omniscient and inside of all.[155] He can enter into everyone and accept all kinds of adoration; no-one, whether he be an adorer of the shaped or the shapeless, can know His true nature. He is unthinkable. Therefore in His eyes, the adoration of an adorer of the shaped or the shapeless is comparable; none knows Him. If this be true, if devotion is the essence of adoration and if devotionless adoration is quite unacceptable to Him, then the devoted adoration of an adorer of the corporeal is acceptable for Him; whereas the devotionless adoration of an adorer of the formless will not reach Him. So it is our belief that if an Indian is devoted to God, then none will be ruined, even if enmeshed in the state of adoration of the corporeal; and there is no doubt that he is ruined by devotionless adoration of the formless. In our opinion, neither adoration of the unmanifest nor that of the manifest is fruitless, and there is no superiority or inferiority among the two. Consequently it is needless to consider the question of superiority or inferiority.

The adorers of the manifest keep saying that there is no such thing as adoration of the unmanifest. We cannot grasp the infinite with our minds, therefore to meditate or think of Him is not possible for us. This, too, does not seem to require much consideration, for if there is anybody who is capable of meditation upon or thought of the Infinite through his limited power of thought, and who also manages to be devoted to Him, then let that person adore the unmanifest. Whoever cannot do this will consequently have to turn to the adoration of the manifest. Hence there is no reason for

153 [*ābhirbhūta*.]

154 [*dhvaṃsa nā haïle* (Beng.).]

155 [*sakaler antaryyāmī* (Beng.).]

discussions, controversies and mutual hatred between the two kinds of adorers, [those] of the corporeal and the formless.

The readers should remember that I do not use 'doctrine of the corporeal' and 'supporter of the corporeal' but only 'adoration of the corporeal' and 'adorer of the corporeal' respectively, because the 'doctrine of the corporeal' is of course to be abandoned. It has been said before that God is not corporeal.

The question might come up that if God is not corporeal, what happens to the doctrine of avatāras in Hindu *dharma*? Let us take Kṛṣṇa, the speaker of this *Gītā*, as an example. God is formless, but Kṛṣṇa is corporeal; how can he then be called an avatāra of God? I have answered this question as far as possible in my book *Kṛṣṇa-caritra*, therefore there is no need to repeat all that here. God is almighty, and thus to maintain that He cannot adopt forms according to His will means to limit His powers.

Through sentences like *yena sarvam idaṃ tatam*, etc., many might be deluded to think that *European Pantheism* [Lat.] and the theism of Hindu *dharma* are perhaps the same. This delusion shall be removed elsewhere.

antavanta ime dehā nityasyoktāḥ śarīriṇaḥ
anāśino 'prameyasya tasmād yuddhasva bhārata. (18)

These bodies of the eternal, indestructible and immeasurable *ātman* are said to be perishable. Therefore, O Bhārata, fight! (18)

Eternal, i.e. always constant in this form (Śrīdhara).

Immeasurable means undivided: not to be divided by direct perception or other proofs; beyond direct perception, etc.

Śrīdhara explains the *śloka* like this:

> The body of this *ātman* which is eternal, i.e. always in one form and therefore indestructible, and immeasurable, i.e. undivided, is subject to pleasure, pain, etc.; this has been said by the philosophers;[156] since the *ātman* cannot be destroyed and stands in no relation with pleasure and pain, let go of the sorrow produced from illusion and fight, i.e. do not abandon your *svadharma*.

Special attention is due to Śaṅkara's words subsequent to the commentary on this *śloka*. He says:

> The obligation to fight is not prescribed by this. Although about to fight, he is restrained by the illusion of sorrow[157] and is silent; the Lord is merely removing the obstacles to [his exercise of] duty.[158] Thus 'Fight!' is not a rule but just an illustration [of that rule].[159]

Many hold that the basic goal of this work [called] the *Gītā* is to stimulate men for cruel affairs like war. It goes without saying that they have not tried to understand the *Gītā*.

[156] [*tattvadarśin*.]

[157] [*śokamohapratibaddha*: the translation of this compound as a *tatpuruṣa* seems preferable to a *dvandva*.]

[158] [*karttabyapratibandha* (Beng.).]

[159] [Cf. *ŚaBhG*:39.]

The *Gītā* is not a cheap[160] novel whose entire significance one can grasp in a single reading. It cannot be understood without specially discussing it. The purpose of this part of the *Gītā* is to establish the indispensability of the exercise of *svadharma*. The educated class might have difficulty in understanding when I use the word *svadharma*; I suppose that by hearing its equivalent *Duty* [Lat.] this difficulty should be done away with. The purpose of this part of the *Gītā* then is to establish the necessity to exercise that *Duty* [Lat.] — *dharma*. The *svadharma* is not the same for all men; some have punishment as their *svadharma*, others forgiveness. The soldier's *svadharma* is to wound the enemy; the doctor's is to treat such wounds. There are as many kinds of *svadharma* as there are actions[161] of men. But it is war which is the cruelest matter among all these different *svadharmas*. War is nobody's duty[162] when it can be avoided. But there occur situations when such a cruel undertaking becomes unavoidable and indispensable. When for example Taimurlang or Nādir comes to burn down and rob the country, then for whoever knows how to fight, war is his unavoidable and indispensable *svadharma*. Therefore the author of the *Gītā*, taking resort in what English philosophy calls *Crucial instance* [Lat.] with regard to upholding *svadharma*, explains the indispensability of *svadharma* and, in this connection, also the most hidden secret of the whole *dharma*. As an example the most cruel and terrifying *svadharma* of all, to which every virtuous person feels *per se* uninclined, has been taken. And not only this — he has taken as an example the most cruel and terrifying war among wars, which not even a person of a cruel nature would easily undertake. A *Crucial instance* [Lat.] indeed. The *Gītā* wants to demonstrate that *svadharma* is definitely to be observed even when as cruel, terrifying and apparently contradictory to the disposition of virtuous persons as this.

But I suppose the intention of the *śloka* has still not been made clear. What do the words 'The *ātman* is indestructible, nobody can destroy it; therefore, fight', mean? Is it not a sin to kill a person because the *ātman* is indestructible? This is not the intention of the Lord's words. Its intention is that which has been said in Śaṅkara's commentary quoted above. Arjuna is ready for war but, overcome by illusion, is being dissuaded from it by the pain of having to kill men. The Lord is explaining that there is no reason for pain whatsoever, for no-one will die. True, the body will be destroyed, but the body is perishable anyway; even if Arjuna does not fight it will perish some day. But a man does not die when his body dies; that which possesses the body is eternal, nobody can kill it. Consequently, the objection to the war which Arjuna presents is produced only by an illusion. Therefore, he can fight.

ya enaṃ vetti hantāraṃ yaś cạinaṃ manyate hatam
ubhau tau na vijānīto nāyaṃ hanti na hanyate. (19)

He who knows Him as a slayer and he who knows Him as slain are both ignorant. He does not slay and is not slain. (19)

The ancient commentators explain this *śloka* as follows: Arjuna's sorrow due to the death of Bhīṣma, etc., is by this sentence removed. In response to the pain from [the

160 [*bājārer* (Beng.): lit. 'of the market', i.e. to be purchased on the market.]

161 [*karman*: i.e. 'occupations'.]

162 [*karttabya* (Beng.).]

assertion that] 'I am the agent of their killing', which has been proclaimed by Arjuna in the *ślokas* 34, 35, etc., of the first chapter, the Lord now explains that, just like the *ātman* is not killed by anyone, so it does not kill anyone either, for it is unalterable.[163]

I am following here the interpretations of Śaṅkarācārya, Śrīdhara and other great luminaries. I shall interpret the following *śloka* accordingly, too. It will also be discussed whether other interpretations are possible. The commentators say that the proof of the *ātman* being unalterable is given in the subsequent *śloka*.

na jāyate mriyate vā kadācin nāyaṃ bhūtvā bhavitā vā na bhūyaḥ
ajo nityaḥ śāśvato 'yaṃ purāṇo na hanyate hanyamāne śarīre. (20)

It is not born and does not die, has never come into existence, has no present and will not be in future. It is unborn, eternal, constant and ancient; it is not killed when the body is killed. (20)

The commentators say that the unalterability of the *ātman* is being underscored through its devoidness of the alterations of the six *bhāvas* [modes of being]. It is birthless — herewith birth has been disproved. It does not die — its destruction has been disproved. It has never come into existence, therefore it has no present. Whatever is born can be said to be present; but it [the *ātman*] exists from before by itself in its own true form, which is why it does not have the presence that comes from being produced. And therefore it will not be born again. This is why it is unborn, i.e. birthless, is constant, i.e. always in one form, eternal, i.e. free from decay, ancient, i.e. free from deliminators.

If now the readers turn their minds to these two *ślokas*, they can observe that in the original there is no clear statement about the doctrine of the *ātman*'s unalterability. There is an unclear *nāyaṃ hanti*, but it is not the case that this is unambiguous. If no-one dies, then of course the *ātman* does not kill anyone either.

It is an opinion of ancient philosophy that the *ātman* is unalterable. The theory could be explained to the readers, but it does not seem necessary to take up that context here. The reason that it does not seem necessary is that we are engaged in the interpretation of the *Gītā*, but these two *ślokas* are not from the *Gītā*; they are from the *Kaṭha-Upaniṣad*. The 19th *śloka* of the *Gītā*'s second chapter is the 19th *śloka* of the second *vallī* of the *Kaṭha-Upaniṣad*; and the 20th *śloka* of that chapter of the *Gītā* is the 18th *śloka* of that *vallī* of the *Kaṭha-Upaniṣad*. The *ślokas* of the *Gītā* and those of the *Kaṭha-Upaniṣad* can be written side by side:

Gītā:

ya enaṃ vetti hantāraṃ yaś cainaṃ manyate hatam
ubhau tau na vijānīto nāyaṃ hanti na hanyate. (2.19)

na jāyate mriyate vā kadācin nāyaṃ bhūtvā bhavitā vā na bhūyaḥ
ajo nityaḥ śāśvato 'yaṃ purāṇo na hanyate hanyamāne śarīre. (2.20)

[163] [*abikriẏa* (Beng.).]

Kaṭha-Upaniṣad:

hantā cen manyate hantuṃ hataś cen manyate hatam
ubhau tau na vijānīto nāyaṃ hanti na hanyate. (2.19)

na jāyate mriyate vā vipaścin na ayaṃ kutaścin na babhūva kaścit
ajo nityaḥ śāśvato 'yaṃ purāṇo na hanyate hanyamāne śarīre. (2.18)

These two *ślokas* have been taken from the *Kaṭha-Upaniṣad* [and put] into the *Gītā*, not vice versa. This does not need further consideration, I suppose. We shall see that many *ślokas* from the Upaniṣads have been put into the *Gītā*. This is at least the opinion of the ancient commentators. Śaṅkarācārya has written *śokamohādisaṃsārakāraṇanivṛtty-arthaṃ gītāśāstraṃ na pravartakaṃ ity etat pārthasya sākṣībhūte ṛcāv ānināya,*[164] and Ānandagiri wrote *hantā cen manyate hantuṃ ity ādyām ṛcam arthato darśayitvā vyācaṣṭe ya enam iti.*[165]

Now I am bound to remark upon two things about these *ślokas*.

Firstly, [the concept of] *karmayoga* must be cast away if the *ātman* is not the agent. It is needless to say that this is Śaṅkarācārya's purpose. The readers can consider this when reading about *karmayoga*.

Secondly, the unalterability of the *ātman* is a philosophical [*dārśanik* (Beng.)] notion. In antiquity, *darśana*[166] used to claim the position of *dharma*[167] in all countries, and *dharma* used to follow *darśana*. This was harmful to both. *Darśana* and *dharma* both develop only when they are independent from one another, otherwise they do not. Comte and his pupils helped both *darśana* and *dharma* by proving this theory. We as well should follow this path.

Whatever may be the philosophical [*dārśanik* (Beng.)] concept, the common Hindu concept is that the *ātman* is the agent. In order to prove this, statements could be quoted for a hundred pages. We shall mention only two statements, one from the Upaniṣads and one from the Purāṇas.

ātmā vā idam eka evāgra āsīt
nānyat kiñcana miṣat
sa īkṣata lokān nu sṛjā iti. (1) [1.1]
sa imāṃl lokān asṛjata ambho marīcīr maram [1.2] *ityādi.*[168]

Ṛgvedīya Aitareya-Upaniṣad

[164] ['In the presence of Arjuna, the Lord has cited these two *mantras* that testify to the fact that the science of the *Gītā* purports to remove the cause of transmigratory life consisting of grief, delusion, etc., and not to compell (anyone to undertake any action).' (Cf. *ŚaBhG*:39)]

[165] ['(Śaṅkara,) after having shown the first *ṛic* "*hantā cen manyate hantuṃ*", etc., according to its meaning, explains "*ya enam*".']

[166] [Obviously used in the sense of 'philosophy'.]

[167] ['religion' here.]

[168] ['This indeed is the *ātman*, he was all alone before; nothing else was winking; he looked (*īkṣata*), thinking (*iti*): let me create the worlds. (1) He created these worlds: water, light rays, death, etc.' (*īkṣata* is an injunctive in seemingly imperfective function: cf. Hofmann 1967:108.)]

The *ātman* has created everything, therefore it is the agent.

I am taking the second example from the Purāṇas. Comparing it with the *śloka* of the *Kaṭha-Upaniṣad*, the readers shall see what a painful experience it is to look for unity in the Hindu scriptures:

kaḥ kena hanyate jantur jantuḥ kaḥ kena rakṣyate
hanti rakṣati caivātmā hy asat sādhu samācaran.

Viṣṇupurāṇa (1.18.29)[169]

vedāvināśinaṃ nityaṃ ya enam ajam avyayam
kathaṃ sa puruṣaḥ pārtha kaṃ ghātayati hanti kam. (21)

Whom can a man who knows that the *ātman* is indestructible, eternal, unborn and immutable, slay or cause to be slain? (21)

Significance: He who knows that the embodied [self] is not destroyed simply because the body is destroyed, should not grieve by thinking 'I have become the reason for his destruction' if he becomes the reason for the destruction of someone's body. For, the *ātman* is indestructible. It has not been destroyed through the destruction of the body.

However, if you say: 'It is fair enough if the *ātman* is not destroyed, but still the body does undergo destruction. Why should I become the reason even of bodily destruction?', then the answer to this is given in the following *śloka*.

vāsāṃsi jīrṇāni yathā vihāya navāni gṛhnāti naro 'parāṇi
tathā śarīrāṇi vihāya jīrṇāny anyāni saṃyāti navāni dehī. (22)

Just like a man discards a worn-out piece of clothing and gets another new dress,[170] so does also the *ātman* leave the old body and get united with a new body. (22)

This means that, whether someone tears up your worn-out dress or not, you will in any case have to discard the worn-out dress and get a new one; likewise, whether you fight or not, the warriors will definitely give up their bodies; the destruction of their bodies will not be avoided by your non-engagement in the war. So why should you not fight?

It is our duty to remember that all these sentences are to be applied in the case of a person who is overcome with the illusion of pain because he shall have to kill, and

169 [Wilson (1865, Vol. II:48) points out the parallel to the *Gītā* and translates: 'What living creature slays, or is slain? What living creature preserves, or is preserved? Each is his own destroyer, or preserver, as he follows evil, or good.']

170 'It was [as] if my soul were thinking separately from the body; she looked upon the *body as a foreign substance, as we look upon a garment.*' [Lat.] Wilhelm Meister [Goethe], Carlyle's Translation [1842], Book VI. [Lat.] The readers should reflect on the words I have written in italics; the words of the *Gītā* will be understood well.

therefore turns away from [participating in] a *dharmayuddha*.[171] Otherwise, by saying that the *ātman* is imperishable and only the body perishable, it is not implied that there is no sin in someone murdering another. The decision of whether murdering constitutes a sin or not stands in no relation whatsoever to this argument, and cannot possibly stand in relation. That which is to be considered here is whether there is reason for the illusion of pain or not in a *dharmayuddha*. The answer is that there is not, since the *ātman* is imperishable and the body perishable. The embodied self shall merely receive a new dress, so what is there to cry about?

nainaṃ chindanti śastrāṇi nainaṃ dahati pāvakaḥ
na cainaṃ kledayanty āpo na śoṣayati mārutaḥ. (23)

This (*ātman*) is not cut by weapons, burned by fire, wetted by water nor dried by the wind. (23)

The *ātman* is bodiless and therefore beyond [the reach] of weapons, etc.

acchedyo 'yam adāhyo 'yam akledyo 'śoṣya eva ca
nityaḥ sarvagataḥ sthāṇur acalo 'yam sanātanaḥ
avyakto 'yam acintyo 'yam avikāryo 'yam ucyate. (24)

It is not cutable, burnable, wetable or dryable; (it is) said to be eternal, all-pervading, stable, immovable, constant, unmanifest, unthinkable and unchangeable. (24)

Stable, i.e. of a fixed nature. Immovable: not leaving its previous form. Constant: never-ending, beginningless. Unmanifest: not an object of the five perceptive senses like the eye, etc. Unthinkable: not an object of the mind.[172] Unchangeable [and] immovable: not an object of the organs of action.

Śaṅkara explains this *śloka* like this: The *ātman* cannot be cut, etc., therefore the *ātman* is eternal; eternal, therefore all-pervading; all-pervading, therefore of a fixed nature; of a fixed nature, therefore immovable; immovable, therefore constant, etc.

tasmād evaṃ viditvainaṃ nānuśocitum arhasi. (25)

Therefore, knowing it to be such, do not grieve. (25)

atha cainaṃ[173] *nityajātaṃ nityaṃ vā manyase mṛtam*
tathāpi tvaṃ mahābāho nainaṃ[174] *śocitum arhasi*. (26)

And when you think that the *ātman* is born and dies constantly, even then, O Mighty-Armed, do not grieve for it. (26)

171 ['righteous war'.]

172 [*man* (Beng.).]

173 [Misprinted as *caina* in *ŚBhG(a)*:720.]

174 There is a variant *naivaṃ*.

Why should he not sorrow even then? Because death is certain, Śaṅkara says. This is also what the subsequent *śloka* has. But there, the indestructibility of the *ātman* is also indicated by the sentence *dhruvaṃ janma mṛtasya ca.*[175] Where then has the destruction of the *ātman* been accepted? And what on earth is new in this? Therefore, Śrīdhara has interpreted in a different manner by saying that, if the *ātman* too died, you would no longer have to bear the fruits of your bad and virtuous actions; so what is there to be sad about?

The next *śloka* explains why he should nevertheless turn away from grieving.

jātasya hi dhruvo mṛtyur dhruvaṃ janma mṛtasya ca
tasmād aparihārye 'rthe na tvaṃ śocitum arhasi. (27)

Whoever is born dies for sure, and whoever dies is born for sure; so do not grieve for what is unavoidable. (27)

The indestructibility of the *ātman* has penetrated the author of the *Gītā* to the bones. Even while accepting the statement *nityaṃ vā manyase mṛtam,*[176] he again answers *dhruvaṃ janma mṛtasya ca.* If after dying one will definitely be born again, then the *ātman* is indestructible; it no longer works to say *nityaṃ vā manyase mṛtam.* However, if we accept Śrīdhara's explanation this objection does not arise.

avyaktādīni bhūtāni vyaktamadhyāni bhārata
avyaktanidhanāny eva tatra kā parivedanā. (28)

All beings are unmanifest in the beginning, manifest (only) in between, and (again) unmanifest through their annihilation; what do sorrow and lamentation[177] [have to seek] there? (28)

The meaning of the word 'unmanifest' has been explained before. Śaṅkara interprets: *avyaktam adarśanam anupalabdhir yeṣāṃ bhūtānām,* i.e. (the condition in which) the beings cannot be seen or perceived. Śrīdhara interprets: *avyaktaṃ pradhānaṃ tad evādy-utpatteḥ pūrvarūpaṃ,* i.e. all beings are unmanifest before their coming into being in the form of causes. All the others have followed either Śrīdhara or Śaṅkara. As soon as we accept Śaṅkara's interpretation, the meaning can easily be understood.

The *śloka* means that, when all beings were beyond the senses such as the eyes, etc., in the beginning — that is before birth —, became manifest in between only for a few days by attaining birth, and will in the end, after death, again be beyond the senses such as the eyes, etc., why should we grieve about that any longer? *pratibuddhasya svapnadṛṣṭavastuṣv iva śoko na yujyate* (Śrīdhara Svāmin): Grievance for a being is as inappropriate as grievance for an object seen in a dream after awaking.

Here too, the doctrine of the indestructibility of the *ātman* shines brightly.

āścaryavat paśyati kaścid enam āścaryavad vadati tathaiva cānyaḥ

175 [See following *śloka.*]

176 [See preceding *śloka.*]

177 [*śok-bilāp* (Beng.) — Baṅkimcandra's translation of *parivedanā.*]

āścaryavac cainam anyaḥ śṛṇoti śrutvāpy enaṃ veda na caiva kaścit. (29)

One sees this (*ātman*) as a wonder, another speaks of it as a wonder, still another hears of it as a wonder. Another again has not been able to know it even after having heard. (29)

The significance of this *śloka* is this: despite the indestructibility of the *ātman* the wise, too, grieve for the dead. But the reason for this is that even they do not know the true doctrine[178] of the *ātman*. The *ātman* is merely an object of curiosity to them; they consider it as a wonder. This is an illusion all have as a consequence of the *ātman* being extremely difficult to understand.

This could provoke the objection that in utterances like 'the *ātman* is indestructible' and 'it is no sense-object', there is nothing to render them unintelligible even to pundits. But the purpose of the Lord's words is not to accomplish mere abstruseness. Even when we are able to understand the indestructibility of the *ātman*, this does not readily enter our hearts. The belief concerning it does not govern our whole life. We do not develop this belief into anything ever-shining, living and thoroughly blossoming in the heart. *This* is the purpose of the Lord's words.

dehī nityam avadhyo 'yaṃ dehe sarvasya bhārata
tasmāt sarvāṇi bhūtāni na tvaṃ śocitum arhasi. (30)

O Bhārata! The *ātman* in everyone's body is eternal and indestructible. Therefore, your sorrow for all beings is inappropriate. (30)

This *śloka* is the conclusion of what has been said about the indestructibility of the *ātman*.

svadharmam api cāvekṣya na vikampitum arhasi
dharmād dhi yuddhāc chreyo 'nyat kṣatriyasya na vidyate. (31)

Keep your eyes fixed on your *svadharma* and do not be afraid; there is nothing better for a kṣatriya than a righteous war. (31)

Now we shall have to remember what has been said in the commentaries to the *ślokas* 11 and 22 [of this chapter]. I have explained before what *svadharma* is. The *svadharma* of a kṣatriya, i.e. of a professional warrior, is war. But it is not the case that, because of his *svadharma* being war, the warrior has to engage in it whenever a war takes place. Many kings fight in order to rob others' property. To engage in such a war is not sanctioned by *dharma*; but because of the defects of human society, a professional warrior has to engage in it too. The warriors are subject to the king's or general's orders; each subordinate warrior is bound to make war according to their orders. But even when fighting in such conditions, they share in the sin of robbing others' property or the like. Most wars are such unrighteous wars.[179] The warrior can in no way obtain

[178] [*tattva*.]
[179] [*adharmayuddha*.]

release from this. In this *Mahābhārata*, there is the narration of a highly righteous person such as Bhīṣma becoming engaged in an unrighteous war on the side of the Kauravas because he had relied on them for his livelihood.[180] If one were to search in European armies, thousands and thousands of warriors entangled in conditions comparable to Bhīṣma's can be found. Thus it is the warrior's great misfortune that he often has to get entangled in *adharma* when trying to obey his *svadharma*. A righteous warrior considers this a tragedy. But there is also such a thing as a *dharmayuddha*. Wars arise for the protection of oneself, one's relatives, society, the country, all the subjects, or *dharma*. In such wars, the warrior gains not *adharma*, but highest *dharma*. This is not solely a matter of observing one's *svadharma*, but infinite merit is acquired along with it. The warrior whose fate furnishes him a *dharmayuddha* is extremely fortunate. Such a time has come for Arjuna; a non-engagement in this war would be severe *adharma*, a senseless desertion of *svadharma*. Arjuna is prepared for major *adharma* in the form of senseless desertion of his *svadharma*. The reason for this is nothing but the fear of his relatives' death. The Lord has explained that there is no reason to be afraid, sad or overcome with illusion on account of this fear; He has made clear that no-one will die, for the embodied self is immortal. Only the empty body will perish, but this is no more than a mere worn-out dress. Thus it is not proper for him to disregard his *svadharma* by fearing the killing of his relatives. There is no other affair as auspicious for a kṣatriya as this *dharmayuddha*. This is the meaning of the *śloka*.

yadr̥cchayā copapannaṃ svargadvāram apāvr̥tam
sukhinaḥ kṣatriyāḥ pārtha labhante yuddham īdr̥śam. (32)

Only fortunate kṣatriyas, O Bhārata, obtain a war like this which is an open door to heaven and has come about all by itself. (32)

atha cet tvam imaṃ dharmaṃ saṃgrāmaṃ na kariṣyasi
tataḥ svadharmaṃ kīrtiṃ ca hitvā pāpam avāpsyasi. (33)

And if you do not fight in this righteous war, then you will acquire sin by betraying your *svadharma* and your reputation. (33)

These two *ślokas* can be clearly understood by what has been written in the commentary of *śloka* 31.

akīrtiṃ cāpi bhūtāni kathayiṣyanti te 'vyayām
sambhāvitasya cākīrtir maraṇād atiricyate. (34)

People[181] will proclaim your eternal ill-fame. Death is better than the ill-fame of a capable person. (34)

bhayād raṇād uparataṃ maṃsyante tvāṃ mahārathāḥ
yeṣāṃ ca tvaṃ bahumato bhūtvā yāsyasi lāghavam. (35)

180 [*annadāsatvavaśataḥ*.]

181 [*bhūtāni*: 'beings'; Baṅkim translates as *loke* (Beng.).]

The great warriors will think you fled the battle out of fear. You shall be disgraced in the eyes of those who honour you greatly. (35)

avācyavādāṃś ca bahūn vadiṣyanti tavāhitāḥ
nindantas tava sāmarthyaṃ tato duḥkhataraṃ nu kim. (36)

Your enemies will malign your capacity and say many unsayable thing; what is more painful than that? (36)

hato vā prāpsyasi svargaṃ jitvā vā bhokṣyase mahīm
tasmād uttiṣṭha kaunteya yuddhāya kṛtaniścayaḥ. (37)

If you are killed you will attain heaven; if you win you will govern the earth. So, O Kaunteya, arise with the determination to fight. (37)

It is incomprehensible how the *ślokas* 34, 35, 36 and 37 have appeared here. These four *ślokas* are unworthy of the *Gītā*. In the *Gītā*, there is the theme of *dharma* and also philosophical theory; the topic of these four *ślokas* is neither *dharma* nor philosophical theory![182] There is nothing else in this except the shallow, despicable words that wealthy persons often use as their instruction. It is full of severe egotism; it is nothing else except that.

Up to *śloka* 33, the Lord has given Arjuna the most holy instruction concerning the doctrine[183] of the *ātman*. And from *śloka* 38 again most holy instructions regarding knowledge and action will be expounded. Neither of these two has any connection whatsoever with these four *ślokas*. The fear of public censure is demonstrated instead. It goes without saying that the fear of public censure is not any kind of *dharma*. It is indeed true that, in all modern societies, *dharma* has become so weak that the fear of public censure often appropriates the position of *dharma*. Many thieves, while desiring to steal, ultimately do not steal only for fear of public censure; and many adulterous persons remain controlled only for fear of public censure. But even so, it has not become *dharma*; when brass is gilded, it can be circulated as gold for a few days, but brass does not become gold for that reason. And on the other hand, public censure is the cause of a lot of sins. Nowadays abortion and the killing of women are to a large extent produced from this fear of public censure. At one time in France it was the lack of adultery which used to be a reason for public censure among the upper class. Among the *siẏāpoṣ*[184] Kafirs, whoever has not cut off the head of at least one Muslim, i.e. is not homicidal, is censured in society and cannot be married. Thousands and thousands of sins in all societies are produced from the fear of public censure, because the

[182] [*dārśanik tattva* (Beng.).]

[183] [*tattva*.]

[184] [Beng. rendering of Pers. *siyāpuš*, 'black-clad': reference to the Abbasids of the Khalifat at Bagdad (A.D. 750-1258)? In that case, the background of Baṅkim's remark is probably the Abbasid revolution against the Umayyads, and possibly the formers' suppression of the Shiism of Southern Iran. But the denomination of the Abbasids as Kafirs ('infidels') is striking, and Baṅkim's statement concerning homicide as a *rite de passage* seems out of place. — Another possible point of reference might be sought among the tribal populations of the Hindukush.]

common people are ignorant and censure even that which is good. Precisely because men now search for that which people call good, they have not the time or concentration necessary for righteous conduct.[185] It can continually be noticed that many cannot do righteous conduct because of the fear of public censure, and that shallow people threaten those prepared for righteous conduct with public censure. He who engages in a war out of fear of public censure is an incarnate human devil. It is impossible that the Lord Himself should instruct Arjuna to commit this great sin. No knowledgeable person at all will accept this as the Lord's words. It cannot be accepted as the personal statement of the author of the *Gītā* either, for, whoever the author may be, he is most knowledgeable and initiated in the *dharma* of the Lord; such a sinful utterance can in no way be from him. If anyone calls these four *ślokas* interpolated, then he shall have to admit that they must have been interpolated before[186] Śaṅkara. Abhinavaguptācārya has called these few *ślokas* the 'worldly law'.[187] If even *Śrīkṛṣṇa* Himself does not abandon the 'worldly law', then on which ground are we supposed to stand? At any rate, words like *eṣā te 'bhihitā sāṃkhye buddhir yoge*, etc., seem very unconnected indeed after this talk of public censure and governing the earth. Consequently, we are not willing to quarrel with those who would like to call these four *ślokas* interpolated.

It only remains to be said: even if in the 37th *śloka* the fear of public censure is not shown, it is nevertheless full of egotism. Inciting someone to *dharma* by enticing him with heaven or a kingdom is quite comparable to inciting a boy to good deeds by promising him sweets; both are merely the excitement of base egotism.

sukhaduḥkhe same kṛtvā lābhālābhau jayājayau
tato yuddhāya yujasva naivaṃ pāpam avāpsyasi. (38)

Therefore you should know pleasure and pain, gain and loss, and victory and defeat as alike and prepare to fight. Otherwise you will be touched by sin. (38)

If war is *svadharma* and therefore unavoidable, then it must be executed by regarding pleasure and pain, gain and loss, and victory and defeat as alike; for that which is to be executed,[188] whatever its fruit may be, is certainly a duty. It is not one's duty to consider whether pleasure or pain, or gain or loss, results from it. This is proclaimed as *karmayoga* below, as for example:

siddhyasiddhyoḥ samo bhūtvā samatvaṃ yoga ucyate. ([2.] 48)[189]

The readers shall see that after the 37th *śloka*, [we] are in tune again. Now we find the glorious sound in the true *Bhagavadgītā*. This is the real sound of Kṛṣṇa's flute. What a difference between the 34th-37th *ślokas* and the 38th!

[185] [*dharmmācaraṇ* (Beng.).]

[186] [Both editions (*ŚBhG[a]* and *[b]*) have *par* (Beng., 'after': '*...śaṅkarer par prakṣipta haiẏāche*'), which is definitely erroneous since the *ślokas* are there in Śaṅkara's commentary. Since this contradicts Baṅkim's related statements, this mistake must be due to inattention and has thus been corrected.]

[187] [*laukik nyāẏ* (Beng.).]

[188] [*anuṣṭheẏa* (Beng.).]

[189] [Baṅkim's translation below (*BhG* 2.48): '[Act] while considering success and failure as equal. Such equanimity is called *yoga*.']

eṣā te 'bhihitā sāṃkhye buddhir yoge tv imāṃ śṛṇu
buddhyā yukto yayā pārtha karmabandhaṃ prahāsyasi. (39)

This knowledge has been given to you in the *sāṃkhya*; hear this (what I will tell you) in[190] (*karma-*) *yoga*. When you become associated with it, O Pārtha, you shall be freed from the bondage of actions.[191] (39)

Firstly: what is *sāṃkhya*? *'samyak khyāyate prakāśyate vastutattvam anayeti saṃkhyā. samyag jñānaṃ tasyāṃ prakāśamānam ātmatattvaṃ sāṃkhyam'* (Śrīdhara). That by which the essentials of matter[192] are fully revealed is *saṃkhyā*. The essentials of the *ātman*[193] which fully reveal its knowledge are *sāṃkhya*.[194] Nowadays the name '*Sāṃkhya*' is usually only used in connection with a particular philosophical system; because of this, English scholars fall prey to great confusion. In the *Gītā*, the word *sāṃkhya* is basically used in the sense of 'knowledge of the essentials',[195] and this seems to be its original meaning.

Secondly, what is *yoga*? Like *sāṃkhya* is nowadays the name of Kapila's philosophical system, *yoga* also is the name of Patañjali's philosophy. Today, when we conduct *yoga* we usually understand the word *yoga* in the sense Patañjali has used it.[196] But the word is not used in that sense in the *Gītā*. If it were so, words like *karmayoga*, *bhaktiyoga*, etc., would have no meaning at all. In fact, it cannot be said either that the word *yoga* is used in only one sense throughout the *Gītā*. According to the meaning in which it is normally employed in the *Gītā*, it can be understood that *yoga* is either worship of God, or the various means for liberation, or a particular kind of striving. Knowledge is such a means or striving, action is another similar means, and devotion is the third, etc. — therefore, words like *jñānayoga*, *karmayoga*, and *bhaktiyoga* are used. Usually this is the meaning, but in this *śloka* it is not employed in this sense. Here, '*yoga*' means *karmayoga*. In the *Gītā*, we shall see words like *yoga*, *yogin* and *yukta* used in this sense. In other instances, it will be observed that the word '*yoga*' also means *jñānayoga*, etc.

So we have understood the two [central] words of this *śloka*: *sāṃkhya* is knowledge, and *yoga*, action. Now some discussion on the nature of man is necessary.

Western pundits have divided all there is in human life into three classes: *Thought, Action and Feeling* [Lat.]. Maybe we are not supporters of the opinion of

[190] [The Sanskrit locative (*sāṃkhye, yoge*) can assume the meaning of 'with regard to'. This aspect seems to be intended in the present *śloka*. However, the Bengali locative does not cover this meaning, and Baṅkim appears to have used the case in its locative (as opposed to the instrumental) aspect. This makes his translation inadequate in this instance. Cf. *BhGBE*:77 where the locative is rendered as 'according to', and *sāṃkhya* as 'theory', *yoga* as 'practice'.]

[191] [*karmabandhan* (Beng.): this could in fact also be rendered as 'bondage of *karman*' in the conceptualised sense *karman* or rather *karma* has as a loan word.]

[192] [*bastutattva* (Beng.).]

[193] [*ātmatattva* (Beng.).]

[194] [Possible translations: 'calculation', 'reason'. Cf. the translation in *ŚrBhG*:53.]

[195] [*tattvajñān* (Beng.).]

[196] *yogaś cittavṛttinirodhaḥ*. ['*Yoga* is the restraint of the dispositions of the mind.' *Pātañjalayogadarśanam* (1.1.2.)]

Western pundits, but when discussing human life for ourselves we shall see that there is nothing else in it. These three can be fixed on God; all three, if God wishes,[197] can lead to God. *Jñānayoga* is when *Thought* [Lat.] is fixed on God, *karmayoga* when *Action* [Lat.] is, and *bhaktiyoga* when *Feeling* [Lat.] is, respectively. Let us leave aside *bhaktiyoga* for the moment. Up to *śloka* 34, the Lord explained knowledge to Arjuna; in fact, this second chapter is called '*Sāṃkhyayoga*'.[198] After this teaching on knowledge, the Lord now, from the 39th *śloka*,[199] instructs Arjuna regarding action. Now listen to what He says.

The commentators say that this action is the attainment of knowledge (Śrīdhara) or a means of its attainment (Śaṅkara). That is, the Lord first tells Arjuna what the knowledge of the essentials[200] is, and then says that 'if the knowledge of the essentials is not unconcealed to Arjuna, then this *karmayoga* is the means for it to arise through the purification of the mind' (Hit'lāl Miśra). It is needless to say that there is no such utterance here in the original. But in other places there is indeed, such as:

āruruksor muner yogaṃ karma kāraṇam ucyate. ([*BhG*] 6.3)[201]

But again, in other places different statements can also be found, such as:

yat sāṃkhyaiḥ prāpyate sthānaṃ tad yogair api gamyate. ([*BhG*] 5.5)[202]

The significance of all these words shall soon be understood.

The fruit of *karmayoga* too has been proclaimed in this *śloka*. This fruit is the liberation from the 'bondage of action'.[203] What is the bondage of action? Whenever one acts one has to bear the fruits of this action. Supporters of reincarnation say that the fruits of that which is done in the present life have to be borne in another life. The fruits of actions need not be borne only when one is not reincarnated. Only then is liberation from the bondage of action reached. Therefore, only he who has attained liberation is free from the bondage of action.

But even a person who does not believe in reincarnation can accept the liberation from the bondage of action as the highest goal of this life. We do not know what happens after death or in a reincarnation, but all of us know that we bear the consequences of all actions in this present life. All of us know that the contact [of the body] with cold produces a cold in this life, [and] we all know that a disease is cured by treating it. We all know, too, that when we behave as someone's enemy, then that person will be our enemy as well in this life; and if we help somebody, then that person is likely to help us in exchange in this life. Everybody knows that the collection of wealth allows one to 'lord it' in this life, and that by studying assiduously one can acquire learning in this life. The fruits of all kinds of actions can thus be acquired in this present life.

But there are a number of actions from which we have been educated to especially expect fruits; these actions one usually calls sin and merit. Indeed, all the

[197] [*tinii īśvarārpita haïle* (Beng.; *ŚBhG[a]*:724) is a misprint for *tin'i* ... (*ŚBhG[b]*:72), which underlies my translation.]

[198] The fourth chapter is called '*Jñānayoga*'. We shall see later what the difference is.

[199] Indeed, do not the four *ślokas* in between appear interpolated?

[200] [*tattvajñān* (Beng.).]

[201] ['When a sage wishes to rise to this discipline, action is called his means' (*BhGBE*:93).]

[202] ['The place which is attained by the *sāṃkhyas* is also reached by the *yogas*.']

[203] [*karmabandha*.]

fruits we have learnt to expect from them are indeed not acquired in this life. We have learnt that through charity, heaven is attained; but no-one ever attains heaven in this life. Some suppose that one can receive ten times that which one has given, but in this life one does not even get half of what one gives. It has been heard that through stealing a great sin is committed. But not all who have stolen are officially punished in this life, and not all are able to see some sort of punishment for this sin. But it is not so that, since not everybody is able to see it, there is no punishment whatsoever for theft in this life, no fruit of action; and it is also not so that there is no reward at all for charity. There is mental benefit:[204] by repeated charity, the mind develops and magnanimity increases. I have explained the way in which one gets the appropriate respective fruits for one's sins and merits in this life in another book,[205] so I need not repeat that. Whoever wishes may look in that book.

I have also shown, in that book, that one can already attain liberation in this life by a perfectly righteous conduct. I have also explained in that book how and in which form this liberation is attained. I shall not repeat all that here. As a consequence of it the doctrine[206] of liberation in the midst of life[207] is nothing outside the Hindu *dharma*. The *Gītā* itself has it that liberation in the midst of life is attainable. We shall understand that step by step. The procedure[208] by which it can be attained is *karmayoga*. This too we shall see. Therefore, even those who do not believe in rebirth can, through *karmayoga*, attain liberation. It has been mentioned before that the *dharma* proclaimed by the *Gītā* is universal.

In conclusion it must be said that another kind of fruit of action is mentioned. Hindus keep performing sacrifices and observances in order to obtain the fruits of actions. We do not say that in this world no fruit at all is attained by all this. When observing the *ekādaśīvrata*, bodily health can be obtained, and [likewise] some kind of bodily or mental fruit may be obtained from various sacrifices and observances. But the fruits Hindus usually aspire to when performing such rituals can, of course, not be obtained in this life. I hope that no reader of this commentary will appear who expects an answer to this question.

nehābhikramanāśo 'sti pratyavāyo na vidyate
svalpam apy asya dharmasya trāyate mahato bhayāt. (40)

In this (*karmayoga*) there is no destruction of undertaking and no sin; even a little bit of this *dharma* saves from great fear. (40)

Such a thing cannot be said about knowledge, because little knowledge does not bear any fruits, but there is sin.[209] When one of mediocre knowledge searches for God, for example, atheism occurs; this has often been seen.

204 [*cittaprasād* (Beng.).]

205 *Dharmmatattva*.

206 [*tattva*.]

207 [*jīvanmukti*.]

208 [*anuṣṭhān* (Beng.).]

209 [*pratyabāẏ* (Beng.).]

vyavasāyātmikā buddhir ekeha kurunandana
bahuśākhā hy anantāś ca buddhayo 'vyavasāyinām. (41)

O descendant of Kuru! In this (*karmayoga*) the determined (positive)[210] *buddhi* is one, whereas the *buddhi* of the undetermined is divided into many branches and infinite. (41)

Śrīdhara says that the positive *buddhi* [as in a sentence like] 'I shall definitely obtain succour by devotion to God' is determined *buddhi*. It is one, that is, single-minded; it does not run towards many themes. But the wishes of those who are undetermined, i.e. who do not have this determined *buddhi*, i.e. who are averse to the worship of God and full of wishes, are all infinite; and the fruits of actions and characteristics are of different kinds. Therefore, their *buddhi* too becomes divided into many branches and infinite, that is, there is no end of the directions in which it goes. Those who are subject to wishes, and being thus subjected to wishes keep performing actions for fulfilling their wishes,[211] such persons' *buddhi* of worshipping God is not single-minded but flows towards various themes.

The basic meaning of this is the following: The Lord is revealing *karmayoga*, but Arjuna might think that the performance of actions for fulfilling wishes is *karmayoga*, for in that time, only the Vedic actions for fulfilling wishes were known as *karman*. *Karman* denotes all these actions [*karman*]. Thus right at the outset, the Lord makes clear that *karmayoga* is not those actions for fulfilling wishes but their contrary. He shall explain later what *karman* is; but beforehand, in the following,[212] He removes the common misconception concerning this topic.

yām imāṃ puṣpitāṃ vācaṃ pravadanty avipaścitaḥ
vedavādaratāḥ pārtha nānyad astīti vādinaḥ. (42)

kāmātmānaḥ svargaparā janmakarmaphalapradām
kriyāviśeṣabahulāṃ bhogaiśvaryagatiṃ prati. (43)

bhogaiśvaryaprasaktānāṃ tayāpahṛtacetasām
vyavasāyātmikā buddhiḥ samādhau na vidhīyate. (44)

O Pārtha! The inconsiderate persons [who] pronounce these pleasant-to-hear sentences full of specific actions which are the means of realising enjoyment and wealth, and are 'birth-action-fruit-giving',[213] [and] who are supporters of the Veda, [and] who say that 'there is nothing (except it)', are full of desires, eager for heaven, addicted to enjoyment and wealth; and those whose mind is carried away by this cannot remain without doubt in their concentration. (42) (43) (44)

These three *ślokas*, the two *ślokas* subsequent to them as well as *śloka* 53 are of special

[210] [*niścayātmikā.*]

[211] [*kāmya karman*, i.e. 'ritualistic action', 'rites'.]

[212] [*pare* (Beng., literally 'afterwards'.]

[213] [*janmakarmaphalapradā*; this compound is explained below by Baṅkim candra.]

importance, for in these six *ślokas*, a specific historical truth[214] is concealed. And this is especially necessary in order to understand the greatness of the *Gītā* and of Kṛṣṇa. Consequently I solicit the readers' special attention towards them.[215]

First let us understand the words employed in these three *ślokas*.

We were discussing ritualistic action [*kāmya karman*]. This is still going on. Words about *kāmya karman* are said to be momentaneously pleasant to hear, for it is generally said that by doing this, heaven is attained, and by doing that sovereignty, etc.

All these words are 'birth-action-fruit-giving'. Śaṅkara interprets this thus: *janmaiva karmaṇaḥ phalaṃ janmakarmaphalaṃ, tat pradadātīti janmakarmaphalapradā*. Birth is the fruit of action; that which gives it is 'birth-action-fruit-giving'. Śrīdhara interprets differently: *janma ca tatra karmāṇi ca tatphalāni ca pradadātīti*. That which gives birth, action and its fruit. Some translators followed Śaṅkara, others Śrīdhara; both interpretations can be accepted.

Thereafter, those words about ritualistic action have been called 'abounding in special rites[216] leading to the attainment of enjoyment and wealth'. It is not hard to understand this. Its meaning is merely that there is an abundance of special rites for the attainment of enjoyment and wealth in all those rules.

These words are like this: those who utter the words are 'entangled in the Vedist doctrine'.[217] All the words about ritualistic action are in the Vedas themselves, or at least were there at that time; and even now, all those rites are famous and authoritative as based on the Vedas. Those who are attracted by ritualistic action invoke the Vedas alone and say that 'there is nothing else except the Vedas'. In other words, their opinion is that there is no other *dharma* except the *dharma* of ritualistic action which is proclaimed in the Vedas. They are 'full of desires' or subject to desire, and 'wish for heaven', i.e. their highest goal is heaven; they have no inclination towards God, and no aspirations concerning liberation. They are attached to enjoyment and wealth; therefore they desire heaven, because they believe heaven to be a place of enjoyment and wealth. The flowery words about ritualistic action cast a spell over their minds. Persons of this kind are inconsiderate or stupid. Such an intellect [as theirs] does not become firm in *samādhi*, the facing of God, or concentration on Him, in one's mind.

Now we can understand the significance of the three *ślokas*. There are various rules regarding ritualistic action in the Vedas; the Vedas have it that, as a fruit of this manifold ritualistic action, various kinds of enjoyment and wealth such as heaven, etc., are obtained, which makes these words very attractive at first glance. The minds of those

214 [*tattva*.]

215 Since these three *ślokas* are of special importance it is better to give another translation beside mine in order to remove suspicions of the readers. Therefore, this part of Kālīprasanna Siṃha's [1882-3] translation of the *Mahābhārata* has also been given here. One cannot say it is without defects, but it is an expert [work] indeed.

'The *buddhi* of these inconsiderate and stupid persons who are attracted to apparently pleasing and pleasant-to-hear words, to whom only those sentences of the Vedas which show manifold fruits are dear, who do not accept anything but action [*karman*] bringing forth fruits like heaven, etc., who are addicted to desire, whose highest human goal is heaven, whose mind is carried away by words describing birth, action, and various deeds for the accomplishment of enjoyment and wealth, and who are solely attached to enjoyment and wealth, cannot be free of doubt regarding concentration.'

216 [*kriyā*.]

217 [*vedavādarata*.]

who are subject to desire, look for their own enjoyment and wealth, and consequently wish for heaven, become enthralled by such words. They spend time invoking nothing but the Vedas, claiming that there is no *dharma* except this. They are stupid. Their intellect can never fix itself upon God, for, as has been said in the preceding *śloka*, their intellect is 'divided into many branches' and 'infinite'.

This is most awful and curious. India is ruled by the Vedas even in this nineteenth century. Even now, the might of the British Government is not even one thousandth of that of the Vedas. In that ancient time, the might of the Vedas was even a thousand times greater than now. The author of the *Sāṃkhya* does not believe in God and has unhesitatingly dared to proclaim that God does not exist; [but] even he does not have the courage to negate the [authority of] the Vedas and has been obliged to invoke the Vedas repeatedly. [And now] Śrī Kr̥ṣṇa unhesitatingly says that these supporters of the Vedas are stupid and given to luxury, that they are not worthy to worship God!

There is a [piece of] historical truth[218] hidden in this. Before explaining it, it is necessary to say two other things. Firstly such an utterance by Kr̥ṣṇa is no criticism of the Vedas, but criticism of the supporters of the Vedic ritualistic doctrine.[219] It is criticism of those who maintain that only that kind of action which is named in the Vedas is *dharma* (as for example, the horse sacrifice, etc.), that only that is to be performed. But it is not true that there is nothing in the Vedas except rules for sacrifices such as the horse sacrifice. The *Gītā* entirely follows the highly developed doctrine of the *brahman* in the Upaniṣads; their doctrine of knowledge[220] has often been quoted, compiled, extended[221] and brought into agreement with the doctrines of *niṣkāma karman* and devotion in the *Gītā*. Thus it is inappropriate to interpret Kr̥ṣṇa's criticism as applying to the whole Vedas. But secondly it must be stated that Kr̥ṣṇa is not among those who say that all there is in the Vedas is *dharma*, and that nothing else is *dharma*, respectively. He says: (1) I admit that there is *dharma* in the Vedas, but (2) there are many things in the Vedas that are not genuine *dharma*, as for instance the flowery description replete with different special 'birth-action-fruit-giving' rites.[222] Furthermore, He says that (3) while, on the one hand, there are many things in the Vedas that are not *dharma*, there are, on the other hand, many principles[223] which are true principles of *dharma*, but are not contained in the Vedas. We shall have examples of this in the *Gītā* itself. But [they] can also be found in other parts of the *Mahābhārata*; I quote two *ślokas* from the *Karṇaparvan* as an example:

> *śrutir dharma iti hy eke vadanti bahavo janāḥ*
> *tat te na pratyasūyāmi na ca sarvaṃ vidhīyate.* (56) [8.49.48]

218 [*aitihāsik tattva* (Beng.).]

219 [*baidik karmmabādī* (Beng.).]

220 [*jñānabād* (Beng.).]

221 [*samprasārita* (Beng.).]

222 [*kriyā* (Beng.).]

223 [*tattva*.]

prabhavārthāya bhūtānāṃ dharmapravacanaṃ kr̥tam. (57) [8.49.49][224]

If anyone wants to label this criticism of the Vedas, then Kr̥ṣṇa is a criticiser of the Vedas, and there is [indeed] criticism of the Vedas in the *Gītā* and in other parts of the *Mahābhārata*. As a matter of fact, it is criticism of the Vedas insofar as, through it, the incompleteness of the Vedas is indicated.

So we may to this extent just as well call it criticism of the Vedas. I already mentioned that there is a [piece of] historical truth hidden in it which I have explained in my book *Dharmmatattva*. But since this book has only recently been published and thus might not be easily available to the readers, I am quoting the relevant passage below:

> The relation which is usually observed between the worshipper[225] and the worshipped god[226] exists between worshipped and worshipper in the Vedic *dharma*, too. 'O Lord! Drink this *Soma* juice offered by me! Eat *havis*,[227] and give me wealth, give me property, give me a son, give me a cow, give me grain, and destroy my enemy." The utmost they said was 'Destroy my sins'. The Vedic people used to perform sacrifices, etc., to please the gods with such intentions. Performing sacrifices for the sake of desired objects in this way is called ritualistic action.[228] The worship[229] involving actions for desired objects is usually called ritualistic action.
>
> [']This particular action has this fruit, thus the action has to be done[']: this sort of procedure of acquiring *dharma* is called *karman*. Towards the end of the Vedic period, this *karman*-oriented[230] *dharma* had become very prevalent. Through the tyranny of sacrifices, the true sense of *dharma* had disappeared. In that situation, talented high-class persons realised that this *karman*-oriented *dharma* was vain. Many among them had understood that the imagination of the Vedic gods and goddesses does not help in comprehending the existence of the world, and that there is an eternal and inscrutable reason behind [it]. They engaged in finding that reason.
>
> For all those reasons, many lost faith in *karman*. They produced a three-fold revolution. Even today Asia is governed by the results of that revolution. One group was that of the Cārvākas. They said: 'All this ritualistic part of the Vedas [*karmakāṇḍa*] is in vain; eat and drink, and wander about dancing'. The founder and leader of the second group[231]

224 'Many point out the *śruti* as a proof of *dharma*. I do not fault this, but the *śruti* is not prescribed as the whole principle [*tattva*] of *dharma*. Therefore *dharma* has to be determined in many places by inference.' — Kālīprasanna Siṃha's translation [1882-3]; *Karṇaparvan*, Chapter 70. According to the edition *Mahodaẏ* Siṃha consulted while translating, these two *ślokas* belong to the seventieth chapter; elsewhere, however, they are found in Chapter 71 [*Mbh* 8.49 in the critical edition].

225 [*upāsak* (Beng.).]

226 [*upāsya deb* (Beng.).]

227 [an oblation offered into the fire.]

228 [*kāmya karman*.]

229 [*upāsanā* (Beng.).]

230 [i.e. ritualistic.]

231 [*sampradāẏ* (Beng.).]

> was Śākyasiṃha;[232] he said: 'I do believe in the fruit of action, but pain comes from action; rebirth comes from action. Therefore destroy action, resist thirst,[233] and attain *nirvāṇa* by following the eightfold path and controlling your mind'.[234] The third revolution was brought up[235] by the philosophers. They were mostly supporters of the doctrine of the *brahman*. They realised that the consciousness which is the eternal cause of the world, in whose pursuit they were engaged, was extremely difficult to know. If one could know that *brahman* — if one could know what our relationship with that *antarātman* or *paramātman* of the world is, and what the world's relationship with it or with us is, then it may be understood what is to be done with this life. That is difficult — to know it is *dharma* — therefore, knowledge is *dharma* — knowledge is the highest. The part of the Vedas which can be called the Upaniṣads is the achievement of these first supporters of the doctrine of knowledge. The determination of the *brahman* and the knowledge of the *ātman* is the goal of all the Upaniṣads. Afterwards this doctrine of knowledge was further developed and circulated by the six philosophical systems. Even if in Kapila's *Sāṃkhya* the *brahman* has been rejected, this philosophical system is based on the doctrine of knowledge.[236]

Kṛṣṇa is amongst these supporters of the doctrine of knowledge. But He, the knower of the infinite, realised what other gnostics are unable to see: He realised that knowledge is not within the scope for all, that it is at any rate extremely hard to acquire for many. And furthermore He realised that there are also other paths of *dharma*; depending on qualification, they are even more difficult than knowledge. Finally He also realised, or demonstrated, that the path of knowledge and the other paths are in the end all the same. These are the few things the *Gītā* is about.

traiguṇyaviṣayā vedā nistraiguṇyo bhavārjuna
nirdvaṃdvo nityasattvastho niryogakṣema ātmavān. (45)

O Arjuna, all the Vedas have the *traiguṇya* as their object;[237] be without the *traiguṇya*. Be free from opposites,[238] be always fixed in *sattva*, be indifferent towards acquisition and preservation and be self-possessed. (45)

Since it is necessary to explain in detail the words used in this *śloka*, they could not be made clear at all in the translation. Firstly, what is *traiguṇyaviṣaya*? The three *guṇas* are *sattva*, *rajas* and *tamas*; their aggregate is *traiguṇya*. Where do we observe the aggregate

232 [i.e. the Buddha.]

233 [i.e. longing.]

234 [*citta*.]

235 [*upasthit haïyāchila* (Beng.).]

236 [*jñānabādātmak* (Beng.). The passage is from *Dharmmatattva*, *BR* II:623 (Chapter 11).]

237 [*traiguṇyaviṣaya*.]

238 [*nirdvandva* (Beng.).]

of these three *guṇas*? In the world.[239] That whose object, i.e. that which is to be expressed (Subject [Lat.]), is the world, is *traiguṇyaviṣaya*.

This is how Śaṅkara has explained [this *śloka*]. He says: *traiguṇyaviṣayāḥ traiguṇyaṃ saṃsāro viṣayaḥ prakāśayitavyo yeṣāṃ te vedās traiguṇyaviṣayāḥ*.[240] This too sounds a little like blame of the Vedas. So Śaṅkara's commentator Ānandagiri, considering this a calamity, wrote the following in order to keep all sides unimpaired: *vedaśabdenātra karmakāṇḍam eva gṛhyate. tadabhyāsavatāṃ tadanuṣṭhānadvārā saṃsāradhrauvyān na vivekāvasaro 'stīty arthaḥ*, that is, 'Here the meaning of the word Veda must be understood as its part dealing with sacrifices.[241] Those who practise it have no chance [to attain] consciousness through that practice of theirs because of the constancy of the world.' We do not have any objections concerning these words of Ānandagiri, provided that no confusion occurs as to how much of the Vedas is the part on sacrifices, and how much that on knowledge.

Śrīdhara Svāmin says: *triguṇātmakāḥ sakāmā ye adhikāriṇas tadviṣayāḥ karmaphalasambandhapratipādakā vedāḥ*.[242] Following this explanation, the ancient Bengali translator Hit'lāl Miśra has explained that 'because of (!) the *adhikārins* [who were] dominated by the three *guṇas* and thus with desire, all the Vedas are confirmative regarding the fruits of actions'.[243] And in pursuance of Śrīdhara Svāmin's words, Kālīprasanna Siṃha's *Mahābhārata* translation [1882-3] has this half *śloka* like this: 'The Vedas are the confirmation of the fruits of actions for desirous persons.' Others too have followed this path.

Both interpretations are essentially the same. Let us then accept this interpretation and try to understand the first half of this *śloka*. In this case, its meaning stands as: 'O Arjuna, all the Vedas are confirmative of the world or of the fruits of actions. Transcend the Vedas and become desireless regarding the world and the fruits of actions.' Let us remember what was being discussed. Having firstly explained *sāṃkhyayoga* to Arjuna, the Lord thereafter expressed the intention of explaining *karmayoga*. But He has not yet said what *karmayoga* is, because it is [his] duty to remove first one important common misconception concerning action[244] that used to prevail (and still does). Otherwise Arjuna will not understand what genuine action is. This common misconception has it that the ceremonial rites of all the sacrifices, etc., that have been proclaimed and prescribed in the Vedas are action. The Lord wants to explain that this is not genuine action. Rather, those who give their mind to this fail to achieve concentration in worshipping the Lord. Therefore this is no action for a genuine *karmayogin*. The same point is being repeated in this 45th *śloka*. The Lord is saying that 'all the Vedas are to be followed by those who are worldly, that is who search for the pleasure of the world. Do not look for such wordly pleasures. Transcend the *traiguṇya*.'

The way in which one can transcend the *traiguṇya* is proclaimed in the second

[239] [*saṃsāre* (Beng.).]

[240] ['The scope of the *guṇas* covers all transmigratory life. It is what the Vedas set forth.' (*ŚaBhG*:67)]

[241] [*karmakāṇḍa*.]

[242] ['The aspirants characterised by the three *guṇas* and with desire — those are the objeccts to whom the Vedas explain the connection between action and fruit.' (Cf. the translation in *ŚrBhG*:59.)]

[243] [*karmaphala*.]

[244] [*karman*.]

half of the *śloka*. The Lord says: 'Be free from opposites, be always fixed in *sattva*, be indifferent towards acquisition and preservation, and be self-possessed.' Now if just these few words are comprehended, the *śloka* is understood.

(1) *nirdvaṃdva* - cold and heat, pleasure and pain, etc., are called opposites, as has been said before. He who regards all of these as equal is free from opposites.

(2) *nityasattvastha* - always resting in the *sattvaguṇa*.

(3) *yogakṣemarahita* - the gaining of that which is not [yet] obtained is called acquisition [*yoga*], and the safeguarding of that which is obtained is called preservation [*kṣema*]. That is, be without the worry connected with gaining and safeguarding.

(4) *ātmavān* - or sober.[245]

yāvān artha udapāne sarvataḥ saṃplutodake
tāvān sarveṣu vedeṣu brāhmaṇasya vijānataḥ. (46)

I have not given any translation of this *śloka* here. The translation can be found in the commentary. The reason is that a few objections arise concerning the conventional meaning for this *śloka*; it would not be rational to give a translation without resolving these.

I shall explain three different interpretations of this *śloka*.

First: I shall first explain the interpretation which has been conventional from the beginning, and which is sanctioned by Śaṅkara and Śrīdhara Svāmin.

Second: I shall put another, new interpretation in front of the reader for his judgement. If it does not seem appropriate, the reader may abandon it.

Third: I shall also explain the way modern English translators have interpreted [it].

Briefly, these three interpretations are the following:

1. *sarvataḥ saṃplutodake udapāne yāvān arthaḥ*[,] *vijānato brāhmaṇasya sarveṣu vedeṣu tāvān arthaḥ*. This is the the English translators' translation. It does not make any sense.

[245] I have explained this the way it seemed to be in accordance with the original to my humble intellect. But in order to demonstrate how persons who want to interpret this *śloka* while keeping intact the glory of the Vedas understand this, I am quoting below the interpretation by *Bābu* Kedārnāth Datta as an example. The reader may accept the meaning that seems more appropriate to him.

'The Śāstras have two kinds of subjects; namely, aimed-at [*uddiṣṭa* (Beng.)] subjects and indicated [*nirdiṣṭa* (Beng.)] subjects. Whatever subject is the highest aim of a Śāstra, is its aimed-at subject. The subject that is indicated so as to point to the aimed-at subject is called indicated subject. In the place where *Arundhatī* is the aimed-at subject, the dense stars that are first noticed in her vicinity are the indicated subject. All the Vedas point to the quality-less principle as the aimed-at subject, but as the quality-less principle is not perceived easily, they usually first indicate some principle with quality. This is why, at first sight, the *māyā* consisting in the three *guṇas sattva*, *rajas* and *tamas* seems to be the subject of all the Vedas. O Arjuna, do not be enmeshed in this indicated subject, but obtain the aimed-at subject in the form of the quality-less principle [*tattva* (Beng.)] by accepting the *nistraiguṇya*. In the Veda śāstras [or Vedas and śāstras: '*bed śāstre*' (*ŚBhG[a]*:730)], in some places action characterised by the guṇas *rajas* and *tamas*, in others knowledge characterised by the *guṇa sattva*, and in some special places devotion to the quality-less has been prescribed. Free yourself from the feelings of opposites such as honour, dishonour, etc., which are pervaded by the *guṇas*, and obtain eternal *sattva*, i.e. *nistraiguṇya*, with the help of *buddhiyoga* by joining my devotees and giving up the search for acquisition and preservation as to be searched according to the *karma*- and *jñānamārgas*.'

2. *sarvataḥ saṃplutodake sati udapāne yāvān artha*, etc., as above. This interpretation is new.
3. *udapāne yāvān arthaḥ sarvataḥ saṃplutodake tāvān arthaḥ. evaṃ sarveṣu vedeṣu yāvān arthaḥ*[,] *vijānato brāhmaṇasya tāvān arthaḥ*. This interpretation[246] is ancient and conventional.

First I shall explain the conventional interpretation. But a Bengali translation could not be furnished; since its lack might cause problems for those who do not know Sanskrit, I shall at first quote below the translation by the ancient translator Hit'lāl Miśra as an example of the conventional interpretation:

> That from which water can be drunk is to be denoted by the word *udapāna*, i.e. ponds and wells, etc. In the way in which the needs for bathing, drinking, etc., are met separately by moving about between all those wells, etc., for the reason that it is impossible to fulfil all [those] needs together by the little water contained in these, and in which way all these needs can be met together by a big lake which is to be denoted by the word *saṃplutodaka*, likewise the goal[247] in the form of the fruits of actions contained[248] in all the Vedas can be achieved together through a person with devotion to the Lord and steadfast in the *brahman*.

Both Śaṅkara and Śrīdhara have interpreted in this way, thus all the others have wandered on this path. We are quoting the interpretation by Śrīdhara:

> *udakaṃ pīyate yasmiṃs tad udapānaṃ vāpīkūpataḍāgādi. tasmin svalpodake ekatra kṛtsnārthasyāsambhavāt tatra tatra paribhramaṇena vibhāgaśo* ***yāvān*** *snānapānādir arthaḥ prayojanaṃ bhavati* ***tāvān*** *sarvo 'py arthaḥ sarvataḥ saṃplutodake mahāhrade ekatraiva yathā bhavati evaṃ* ***yāvān*** *sarveṣu vedeṣu tattatkarmaphalarūpo 'rthas* ***tāvān*** *sarvo 'pi vijānato vyavasāyātmikābuddhiyuktasya brāhmaṇasya brahmaniṣṭhasya bhavaty eva.*

The rough significance of this is that **as many** limited needs can be fulfilled by moving about from one small body of water to another, **so many** are also fulfilled by just one big lake. Accordingly, **as many** needs are fulfilled by all the Vedas, **so many** are fulfilled by being steadfast in the *brahman* with a determined[249] mind.[250]

We are of humble intellect, and so I am setting forth the confusion we had to undergo when trying to understand this interpretation, paying reverence to the lotus-

[246] [*artha* (Beng.) instead of the usual *byākhyā* (Beng.).]

[247] [*artha* (Beng.).]

[248] [*kathita* (Beng.): lit. 'spoken about'.]

[249] [*vyavasāyātmikā*.]

[250] The language employed by Śaṅkarācārya is somewhat different. Explaining the second half of the *śloka*, he says:

> '*sarveṣu vedeṣu vedokteṣu karmasu yo 'rtho yat karmaphalaṃ so 'rtho brāhmaṇasya sannyāsinaḥ paramārthatattvaṃ vijānato yo 'rthaḥ yat vijñānaphalaṃ sarvataḥ saṃplutodakasthānīyaṃ tasmiṃs tāvān eva saṃpadyate ityādi*.'

Later on I will explain the other tricks and devices [hidden] in this. At present I beg the readers to pay attention to the way Lord Śaṅkara has explained '*sarveṣu vedeṣu*'. '*Sarveṣu vedeṣu*' [in all the Vedas] means '*vedokteṣu karmasu*' [in all the rites said in the Vedas]. The reason for Ānandagiri's saying '*vedaśabdenātra karmakāṇḍam eva gṛhyate*' [see above] made him say too that '*sarveṣu vedeṣu*' means '*vedokteṣu karmasu*'.

feet of the ancient masters.[251] He who does not dare express his doubts cannot acquire any knowledge; neither is there any possibility of such an acquisition.

The words *yāvat* and *tāvat* are indicators of quantity. But no quantity can be understood when there is only *yāvat*. Whenever there is a *yāvat* there must be a *tāvat*. Whenever there is a *tāvat* there must be a *yāvat*. It often happens that only *yāvat* is explicit, and *tāvat* must be implied, as for example in 'You stay here as long as I do not come [back]'. The actual meaning of this is 'You stay here (so long) as long I do not come [back]'. Thus, be it explicitly or implicitly, whenever there is an 'as long' [*yāvat*] there must be a 'so long' [*tāvat*]. In the same way, whenever there is a *tāvat*, there must be a *yāvat*.

The interrelation of the words *yāvat* and *tāvat* is such that the quantity of both things, that accompanied by *yāvat* and that accompanied by *tāvat*, is described as the same or identical. So whenever there are *yāvat* and *tāvat* it must be understood that there are two things comparable or to be compared. The sentence 'You stay here (so long) as long I do not come [back]' really means 'The time until my return and the time of your staying here, both shall be identical'. Here, these two periods of time are comparable or to be compared.

Accordingly, where there is a *yāvān* and a *tāvān*,[252] we are to understand that two things are being compared to one another. If we see *yāvān* and *tāvān* again after this, then we definitely have to understand that again two other things are being compared to each other. This can never be otherwise.

Now, in the original of this *śloka* there is one *yāvān* and one *tāvān*; thus we are to understand that only two things are being compared to one another, namely, (1) as much as, in a certain situation, the quantified need of a pond or a small body of water is felt, (2) so much is the need of all the Vedas in a certain situation. But in the interpretations written by the ancient commentators, of which examples have been quoted above, we notice two *yāvān* and two *tāvān*.[253] So we have to understand that, after two things have first been compared, two things have again been compared. Firstly, all the Vedas are not compared to small bodies of water, but to a large lake. Then again all the Vedas, giving up their relationship with small bodies of water, are compared to the steadfastness in the *brahman*. Is any confusion of meanings occurring here or not?

Usually, the answer to this question is that no confusion of meanings is occurring. For even where *yāvān* and *tāvān* are absent, the commentator has to place them according to the needs of the interpretation; an example of this has been given before. Two objections to this statement are coming up here.

The first objection is this. I accept that the commentator can place *yāvān* and *tāvān* according to the needs of the interpretation. But can he substitute *tāvān* for *yāvān* or *yāvān* for *tāvān*? If I say 'As long [*yāvat*] as I do not come back, you stay here', then the commentator may insert the word *tāvat* and say 'so long [*tāvat*] you stay here'. But if he substitutes *tāvat* for *yāvat* and *yāvat* for *tāvat*, if he says that this sentence means 'I will not come back so long as long you stay here', then his interpretation must be labelled unacceptable and contrary to the original.

Let us clarify the matter even further through another example.

251 [*mahāmahopādhyāy* (Beng.).]

252 [Nominative masculine of *yāvat* and *tāvat* respectively.]

253 I have printed these four words in bold letters; the reader may verify.

'As long as your life is, so long is my pleasure.' (a)

Take this sentence as an example and mark it by (a). Then substitute *tāvat* for its *yāvat* and *yāvat* for its *tāvat*. In that case the sentence becomes the following:

'Your life is so long, as long is my pleasure.' (b)

Now look how much confusion has occured to the meaning of the sentence. The real meaning of the sentence marked (a) is 'As long as you live, so long will I be happy, thereafter I will not be happy anymore.' The sentence marked (b) really means 'As long as I will be happy, so long will you live, afterwards you will not live anymore.' A complete confusion of the meaning has occured.

Thus the commentator is never allowed to ever substitute *tāvān* for *yāvān* or vice versa. But here the commentator has done exactly this. In order to understand this, let us mark the *caraṇas* of the *śloka* in serial order by (a), (b), (c) and (d). Then the *yāvān* in the *śloka* falls under (a), and the *tāvān* under (c).

(a) *yāvān artha udapāne*
(b) *sarvataḥ saṃplutodake*
(c) *tāvān sarveṣu vedeṣu*
(d) *brāhmaṇasya vijānataḥ*

In explaining this the commentator has produced

(a) *yāvān artha udapāne*
(b) *tāvān sarvataḥ saṃplutodake*
(c) *yāvān sarveṣu vedeṣu*
(d) *tāvān brāhmaṇasya vijānataḥ*

Now the reader may compare the (c) portions to see for himself whether *yāvān* has been substituted for *tāvān* or not.[254]

The second objection is this: When required for the interpretation, the commentator may explain by inserting *yāvān* and *tāvān*. But may he insert them needlessly? Where a simple explanation without inserting new *yāvān* and *tāvān* makes sense, must one insert *yāvān* and *tāvān* there too? Does [this *śloka*] not make sense without inserting *yāvān* and *tāvān*? Of course it does. There is a very simple meaning.

yāvān artha udapāne sarvataḥ saṃplutodake
tāvān sarveṣu vedeṣu brāhmaṇasya vijānataḥ.

I understand its simple meaning as this:

sarvataḥ saṃplutodake sati udapāne yāvān arthaḥ
vijānato brāhmaṇasya sarveṣu vedeṣu tāvān arthaḥ.

That is, as much as there is need of a pond, i.e. a small body of water, when all places are flooded by water, so much are the Vedas needed by the one knowing the *brahman* and steadfast in the *brahman*.

[254] It is true that Śaṅkara was careful to avoid employing the word *yāvān* instead of *tāvān*, but he used the word *yad* in its place. So the result is the same.

It seems unlikely to me that the great masters, the ancient ṛṣi-like commentators and annotators did not take into consideration this simple meaning. To me it seems that they thoroughly considered this meaning and, being extremely far-sighted pundits knowing place, time and people, rejected this simple meaning. The reader can see that as soon as he carefully examines the genuine meaning of the two interpretations. What is the significance of the latter simple interpretation? When all places are flooded by water, what need do people have for a small body of water? There is no need at all. For all places are flooded, water is available anywhere. When one can get water sitting in one's home, no-one must any longer go out to tanks, wells, etc. Likewise, he who has realised the Lord has no need whatsoever for all the Vedas. Now we, disciples of the English in the nineteenth century, may daringly utter that there is no need for the Vedas; but could Śaṅkarācārya or Śrīdhara Svāmin have said such words? The Vedas are self-originated, superhuman, eternal and bearing every fruit. The ancient Indians erected the Vedas themselves as the real form of God.[255] Kapila was able to reject God, but he could not reject the Vedas. Bṛhaspati or Śākyasiṃha, etc., who rejected the Vedas, were cast out of Hindu society. Therefore there was never any possibility on either Śaṅkarācārya's or Śrīdhara Śvāmin's part of an utterance proclaiming that the Vedas are needless for anyone, be he a knower of the *brahman* or whatever else. Consequently, they had to interpret in such a way as to show that what is [acquired] through the knowledge of the *brahman* is also [acquired] through the Vedas, and that the results are identical. By this the status of the Vedas was kept intact. The interpretation given last means that in comparison to the knowledge of the *brahman*, the knowledge of the Vedas is quite irrelevant. In this instance the reader may recall the sentences *vedokteṣu karmasu*, *vedaśabdenatra karmakāṇḍam eva gṛhyate*,[256] etc., as interpretations of *sarveṣu vedeṣu*. He will [then] understand the motives of the ancient commentators.

Now the reader has to decide: There are two interpretations; for one the original does not have to be altered in any way, its meaning can be brought out by interpreting it just as it is. But there is no supporter of this interpretation at all. For the other interpretation, some new things have to be inserted and some curtailing is required. But all commentators, annotators and translators and the whole scholarly group of great masters are in favour of that interpretation. Which interpretation should be accepted? I am not recommending [the reader] to take any particular side. I have explained the way my humble intellect has understood. I have explained both sides; the reader may choose whichever interpretation seems plausible to him. Some more things could be said in support of the new interpretation, but there appears to be nothing necessitating this much effort. It is enough if the reader understands the relation between the *dharma* stated in the *Gītā* and the Vedic *dharma*. I have said before what this relation is.

Thirdly, the English translators have explained this *śloka* in still another way. Instead of the reading *sarvataḥ saṃplutodake sati udapāne yāvān arthaḥ*, they understand *sarvataḥ saṃplutodake udapāne yāvān arthaḥ*, etc. That is, the inflected compound *saṃplutodake* is only an attribute of *udapāna*. Whether the readers have respect for the other English translators or not, Kashinath Trimbak Telang [1990 (1882)] may be respected. He has translated this *śloka* as follows:

[255] [*īśvar'svarūp* (Beng.).]

[256] [Cf. above 2.45 and in the present commentary.]

> To the instructed Brahmana there is in all the Vedas as much utility as in a reservoir of water into which waters flow from all sides.

It is only unfortunate that this makes no sense. There is no significance. The translator, too, feels compelled to admit this. He has written a commentary to this *śloka* in which he says:

> The meaning here is not easily apprehended. I suggest the following explanation: — Having said that the Vedas are not concerned with actions for special benefits, Krishna compares them to a reservoir which provides water for various special purposes — drinking, bathing &c. The Vedas similarly prescribe particular rites and ceremonies for going to heaven, or destroying an enemy &c. But, say[s] Krishna, man's duty is merely to perform the actions prescribed for him among these, and not entertain desires for the special benefits named.

It is not necessary to quote yet another translation from any English translator after that of Telang. It is enough to say that the other *Sāhebs* like Davies and Thomson have translated like Telang. But there is even more flavour in the small glosses they have attached to those translations. It will suffice to present the little gloss written by Thomson [1855] to the readers. I am quoting it:

> As a tank full of fresh water may be used for drinking, bathing, washing one's clothes and numerous other purposes, so the text of the Vedas may be turned to any object of self-interest by a Brahman who is well acquainted with them and knows how to wield them. We may exemplify this general fact by the uses made of texts from our scriptures in the mouths of the Puritans on the one hand, and of the Cavaliers on the other. Our author must not, however, be understood to reject the use of the Vedas by what he here says. He merely advises a careful use of them. Kapila himself admits them as a last source of proof of the truth when others fail.

I openly admit that a humble person like myself is unable to understand or explain the inner significance[257] of the *Gītā*. Nevertheless, remembering the sentence *svalpam apy asya dharmasya*,[258] etc. I have set out on my undertaking. But whether I am able to explain [it] or not, I hope that at least from all the great utterances of the ancient commentators I quote, the reader will understand its inner significance. Whether he thereby understands or not, I entreat the reader with folded hands not to go to the English to understand the meaning of the *Gītā*. I say this only because I have seen well-educated Bengalis reading translations of the *Gītā* by Englishmen; and it is merely for the destruction of that inclination that I have quoted so much English in this place.

There is a saying that after the proclamation of the Purāṇas, etc., the venerable Vyāsa was sitting by the seashore one day and pondering over something. Like the succession of huge waves in the sea, deep worries came up in his mental sea, too, and put his mind to unrest. At that time, the celestial saint Nārada appeared before him. Vyāsa described his state of mind to Nārada, saying: 'Lord, for the welfare of the world I have made easy and circulated the *dharma* of the Vedas which is unintelligible for the common people, and by the device of stories I have taken the teachings of the Vedas and composed the Purāṇas [thereof]; the greater part of my lifetime has been spent on

[257] [*marmmārtha* (Beng.).]

[258] [*BhG* 2.40.]

this. Nonetheless I now feel that maybe my duty has not in the least been fulfilled, but I cannot determine what I should do. Therefore my mind is extremely anxious; I have come to the seashore with a restless mind. Lord, give peace to my restless mind by advising me as to where I have failed in my duty and what other duty remains to be done by me.' 'Preach devotion, the main pillar of *dharma*, in the world', advised the celestial saint and disappeared. It is said that Vyāsa then composed the *Bhāgavata*[-*purāṇa*] and the *Bhagavadgītā* and depicted the ideal for the devotee in a few other Purāṇas. This is why some infer that the *Mahābhārata* has been composed earlier than the *Gītā*.

The *Gītā* and the *Bhāgavata*[-*purāṇa*] are works dominated by devotion. Vyāsa realised that devotion is the highest goal of life and the only means of salvation.

Now we have to recall once what was being talked about. The Lord, after explaining *jñānayoga* to Arjuna, said in the sentence *eṣā te 'bhihitā sāṃkhye* [2.39], etc., Now I shall tell you about *karmayoga*'. Praising *karmayoga* slightly, he firstly became engaged in wiping out a common and conventional error. The error is that people are mentally absorbed in all the ritualistic actions said in the Vedas; such people cannot concentrate their minds on God. So the Lord said to Arjuna: 'All the Vedas have the *traiguṇya* as their object. Be without the *traiguṇya* and transcend the objects of the Vedas. For, just as no-one needs tanks, wells and ponds when all places are flooded, likewise he who is steadfast in the *brahman* does not need the Vedas any longer.' Thus demonstrating the lack of relation between *karmayoga* and Vedic *karman*, the Lord now speaks on *karmayoga*; —

karmaṇy evādhikāras te mā phaleṣu kadācana
mā karmaphalahetur bhūr mā te saṅgo 'stv akarmaṇi. (47)

You are entitled to *karman*,[259] but may you never be (entitled) to the fruits. Do not be *karmaphalahetu*; may you not become attached to *akarman*. (47)

In order to understand this *śloka* we have to understand what *karman*, *karmaphalahetu* and *akarman* mean.

Once *karman* is understood, the other two are understood as well. He whose inclination or motivation is the fruits of *karman* is *karmaphalahetu*. The absence of *karman* is *akarman*. I shall explain afterwards what *karman* means.

So the meaning of the *śloka* is [']Do *karman*, but do not desire the fruits of *karman*. May the acquisition of the fruits of *karman* not be the reason for your engaging in *karman*[']. But since there is no probability of anyone engaging in *karman* without expectations of the fruits of *karman*, this too has been forbidden at the end of the *śloka*. Here it is said that 'You should not abstain from *karman* by saying that you do not want the fruits of *karman*'. That is, 'You must of course indulge in *karman*, but you must not indulge in *karman* desiring the fruits of *karman*.'

I assume the *śloka* has been understood by now. This is the famous theory of *niṣkāma karman* [desireless action]. Such an elevated, holy utterance of *dharma*, bene-

[259] [In the present commentary to *BhG* 2.47, *karman* is not, as elsewhere, translated as 'action' but left in transcription (together with the compounds containing it), because its main object is precisely the specification of this term. In 2.48 and 49, too, *karman* had to be given in transcription in some instances.]

ficial for man and of great dignity, has never again been proclaimed on earth. It is only through the grace of the Lord[260] that the Hindus have obtained such a holy doctrine of *dharma*.[261]

But although the Hindus have obtained it, it has not been particularly fruitful for them. This is because even in such cases, much confusion has occurred due to our errancy of intellect. Even today we have not yet been able to understand it well.

I am not saying that I have understood it completely or that I can explain it completely to the reader. Only he can understand it on whom the Lord bestows such favour. But there is apparently no harm in attempting an explanation as far as I can.

The first confusion in this case is about the meaning of the word *karman*. The conventional meaning of the word *karman* is, 'that which can or must be done is *karman*.' But several Hindu writers of Śāstras or commentators on Śāstras have created confusion. Thanks to them, we are to understand in all these instances that *karman* means sacrifices, etc., prescribed in the Vedas. 'Actions' [*karman*] alone are not *karman*; only the sacrifices, etc., prescribed in the Vedas and Śāstras are *karman*.

If this be so, then one has to understand the meaning of this *śloka* as: 'Perform the sacrifices prescribed in the Vedas and so on, but do not desire heaven, etc., which are the fruits of all those sacrifices.' This meaning having been long current, well-educated Anglophiles have also understood such a meaning. The very erudite pundit Kashinath Trimbak Telang [1990 (1882)] has written in the commentary to the preceding *śloka*:

> The Vedas ... prescribe particular rites and ceremonies for going to heaven and destroying an enemy &c. But, says Krishna, man's duty is merely to perform the actions prescribed for him among these, and not entertain desires for the special benefits named.

If this is the meaning of *karman*, then the reader must be somewhat confused. The reader will ask:[262] 'If I do not desire that fruit of *karman* whose fruit is heaven, etc., and which has no other purpose, then why should I perform that *karman* at all? What is *niṣkāma kāmya karman* ['desireless desirous[263] action']? Why should I perform desirous *karman* desirelessly?'

Thus it becomes obvious that when taking the ritualistic *karman* said in the Vedas as the meaning of *karman*, we can not arrive at any comprehensible theory.[264] And in the discussion of the third chapter of the *Gītā* it is very evident that the ritualistic *karman* mentioned in the Vedas is not meant by the *niṣkāma karman* of the *Gītā*. The title of this third chapter is '*karmayoga*'. In it, it has been said about *karman*:

> *na hi kaścit kṣaṇam api jātu tiṣṭhaty akarmakṛt*
> *kāryate hy avaśaḥ karma sarvaḥ prakṛtijair guṇaiḥ*. (5)

'No-one can ever even for a moment be without performing any action; for the properties originating in nature or inherent compel all to act.'

260 [*bhagavatprasādāt*.]

261 [*dharmmatattva* (Beng.).]

262 [*balilen* (Beng.; *ŚBhG[a]*:736 and *ŚBhG[b]*:89): misprint for *baliben*.]

263 [In this instance, *kāmya* obviously means 'desirous' rather than 'ritualistic'.]

264 [*tattva*.]

Now it can be seen that this can never be said about the sacrifices, etc., mentioned in the Vedas. This can only be said about what we usually call *karman* — that which is called *kāj* [Beng.][265] in the [spoken] language[266] and *action* [Lat.] in English. No-one can ever be without doing an action; even if he refrains from all other action, still, subject to inherent nature [*svabhāva*] or *prakṛti* (*nature* [Lat.]), he definitely has to perform some actions, such as eating, sitting, lying, respiration, inhalation, etc., Consequently, the word *karman* clearly denotes that which is usually called *karman* [i.e. 'action'], and not sacrifices, etc.

Again it has been said in the eighth *śloka* of that chapter:

niyataṃ kuru karma tvaṃ karma jyāyo hy akarmaṇaḥ
śarīrayātrāpi ca te na prasidhyed akarmaṇaḥ. (8)

'Act as a rule; action is superior to non-action [*akarman*]; by non-action even your body cannot be maintained.'

Here, too, action is definitely action of all kinds or *kāj*, not sacrifices, etc. The body can be — and is — maintained by everyone without sacrifices, etc., but it cannot be maintained without that *kāj* or *action* [Lat.] which one may usually denote as *karman*.

There is more proof of this kind that can be quoted from the *Gītā*.[267] If the proof is faultless, one proof is sufficient; so more is unnecessary.

Thus it is proved that in his explanation of *karmayoga*, the Lord intends as the meaning of *karman* that which is usually called *karman*, i.e. *kāj* [Beng.] or *action* [Lat.], and not Vedic sacrifices.

If this be so, then the meaning of *śloka* 47 is that all necessary[268] actions have to be performed. But one[269] must not desire their fruits; one must act desirelessly. Let us now try to understand the real significance of this great sentence.[270]

There are two commands in it: Firstly, actions must be performed; secondly, all actions must be performed desirelessly. Let us understand them one after the other. Firstly, actions must be performed.

Why must actions be performed? This has been explained by the two *ślokas* of the third chapter I have quoted above. Action is our rule of life — *Law of Life* [Lat.]; nobody can exist for one moment without performing actions. All are bound to act by

[265] ['work', 'action'.]

[266] [*bhāṣā*, Beng. 'language'; Baṅkim uses it here in the Sanskrit sense, i.e. 'spoken language', which later meant 'language other than Sanskrit', 'vernacular'.]

[267] On the other hand, in the eighth chapter we have also the sentence *bhūtabhāvodbhavakaro visargaḥ karmasaṃjñitaḥ* [*BhG* 8.3]. The conventional meaning of this is indeed in favour of sacrifices, but I think the reader will understand hereafter that this conventional meaning is erroneous too. I am not talking of explaining it; the reader will understand easily. Furthermore I am also bound to admit that sometimes the word *karman* denotes the Vedic ritualistic action in the *Gītā*, too, as in *dūreṇa hy avaraṃ karma* in *śloka* 49 in the present chapter. But here too it can be understood most clearly that this *karman* and *karmayoga* stand contrasted. I have already said that in the *Gītā*, many words have been used with various meanings in different places.

[268] [*karttabya* (Beng.).]

[269] [The grammatical construction of this sentence leaves open ambiguities and allows of two other coherent interpretations regarding the (unmentioned) subject: (a) Arjuna; and (b), taking the inflected verb as 2nd pers. singular, 'you'.]

[270] [*mahākābya* (Beng.; *ŚBhG[a]*:737) is a misprint for *mahābākya* 'great sentence' (cf. *ŚBhG[b]*:91).]

natural properties.[271] Without action, the body is not maintained. Thus all must act.

But must all actions be performed? A number of actions we call good deeds, others we call bad deeds. Must bad deeds also be performed?

Bad deeds do not belong to the rule of maintaining our life, they are not our *Law of Life* [Lat.]. It is untrue that one cannot exist for a moment without doing bad deeds, and no-one's maintenance of his body is endangered if he abstains from bad deeds. It is untrue that one cannot live without theft or adultery. Thus, bad deeds do not have to be performed. [This] can be understood from those two *ślokas* of the third chapter quoted above; more will be understood later.

On the other hand, it can also be questioned whether that which we call good deeds is actually our rule of living.[272] Some [deeds] we call good, as benevolence, etc.; and some we call bad, as adultery, etc.; and some we call neither good nor bad, as sleeping, eating, etc. It has been well understood that there is no need of performing actions of the second group, and that the actions of the third group are necessary and thus have to be performed. But why should we perform the actions of the first group? What makes the good deeds a rule of human life?

I have answered this question in detail in my book called *Dharmmatattva*, so there is no need of repetition. I have explained in that book that what we call good deeds is the main component of humanity. Therefore they are a rule for the maintenance of human life.

In fact, *karman* cannot be divided into these three categories. Only two are necessary for humanity, namely, the [actions] we call good, and those we call neither good nor bad, but which we are bound to perform. Therefore in *Dharmmatattva*, I called these two 'actions to be performed'.[273] I shall continue to do so in this commentary.

Now the question may come up who is to decide which action is to be performed and which is not. The approximate law for such decision-making is laid down in the *Gītā* as we will see later on; and in the said book *Dharmmatattva* I relied on that law for resolving this problem to some extent.

This, at present, is enough for the first rule said in this *śloka*, 'actions must be performed'; I shall now explain the second rule in general. The second rule is: 'The actions you perform must be performed desirelessly.' Let us give an example.

Benevolence is an action to be performed. Many practise benevolence with the following intention: 'He whom I have helped will help me in return.' This is an action with desire. It is contrary to this rule.

Many practice benevolence through donations, etc. with the motive of collecting merit and, as a result of that, attaining heaven, etc. This too is action with desire and contrary to this rule.

Many [again] practice benevolence with the motive of making God pleased with them and, being pleased, do good to them. That is possible; God will no doubt be pleased and may also do good to the benevolent. But this is no desireless action. It is with desire and contrary to this rule.

The *niṣkāmakarmin* does not want even this, he does not want anything at all except to perform his own action to be performed. 'Benevolence is my action to be

271 [*prakṛtija guṇe* (Beng.).]

272 [*jīban/yātrār niẏam* (Beng.), not *jībaner niẏam* (Beng.; 'rule of life').]

273 [*anuṣṭheẏa karmma* (Beng.).]

performed, and therefore I will practise it; I do not want any fruit whatsoever.' This is the desireless attitude.[274]

In *Dharmmatattva* I have explained through other examples that all kinds of actions to be performed can be desireless. So a repetition is superfluous.

This is a first glance at desireless action. This theory[275] will gradually become more transparent and will be elaborated upon.

yogasthaḥ kuru karmāṇi saṅgaṃ tyaktvā dhanaṃjaya
siddhyasiddhyoḥ samo bhūtvā samatvaṃ yoga ucyate. (48)

O Dhanaṃjaya, be firm in *yoga*, give up attachment and then act. (Act) while considering success and failure as equal. (Such) equanimity is called *yoga*. (48)

In the preceding *śloka*, action devoid of aspirations for its fruits has been prescribed. Now three rules concerning doing such action are pointed out:

Firstly, you shall act while being firm in *yoga*.
Secondly, you shall act after giving up attachment.
Thirdly, you shall consider success and failure as equal.

Let us try to understand these three rules successively.

First: 'You shall act while being firm in *yoga*'. What is *yoga*? I have already said that the word *yoga* has been used with various meanings in different places of the *Gītā*. I need not explain to the reader that that which the venerable Patañjali called 'the restraint of the dispositions of the mind'[276] is not mentioned here.

In Śrīdhara Svāmin's opinion, the word *yoga* here means 'immersion in the highest God alone.'[277] Śaṅkarācārya, too, has explained thus. He says: *yogastha san kuru karmāṇi kevalam īśvarārtham.*[278] But when interpreting the latter part of the *śloka* he has *ko 'sau yogo yantrasthaḥ kurv ity uktam idam eva tat siddhyasiddhyoḥ samatvaṃ yoga ucyate.*[279]

In fact, what is the use of searching for other different meanings when the Lord has in this *śloka* itself explained the meaning of *yoga*? Equanimity towards success and failure is *yoga*. We will understand this as soon as we understand the third rule. The third rule is only an extension[280] of the first rule. An extension cannot, [however], be called a repetition.

Let us understand the second rule before the third. 'You shall act after giving up

274 [*cittabhāb* (Beng.).]

275 [*tattva*.]

276 [Cf. the commentary to 2.39: *cittavṛttinirodha*.]

277 [*parameśvaraikaparatā*.]

278 ['Established in Yoga, do works, O Arjuna! just for the sake of God.' (*ŚaBhG*:70)]

279 ['What is this *yoga* (about which is) said "*yantrasthaḥ kuru*"? It is that one. Equanimity in success and failure is called *yoga*.' (Cf. the translation in *ŚaBhG*:70.)]

280 [*samprasāraṇ* (Beng.).]

saṅga.' What is *saṅga*? Śrīdhara says *kartṛtvābhiniveśaḥ*.[281] I shall act after giving up the absorption [in the concept that] I am an agent, and by taking the shelter of God, i.e. by knowing that He alone is the agent.

Śaṅkara says '*yogasthaḥ san kuru karmāṇi, kevalam īśvarārthaṃ tatrāpīśvaro me tuṣyatv iti saṅgaṃ tyaktvā*'; act only for God, but act while giving up the desire that God should therefore do good to you. Therefore, the abandonment of the desire for fruits is the abandonment of *saṅga* [attachment]; it can be seen that the word '*saṅga*' is repeatedly used in this sense in the *Gītā*.

Let us now understand the third rule. The equanimity consisting in considering the success and failure of action [to be] alike is *yoga*. There is no special profit for ignorant people such as ourselves in understanding the way Śaṅkara, who preaches the doctrine of knowledge,[282] has explained this. His opinion is that the acquisition of knowledge is the success of action. So he says that *sattvaśuddhijā jñānaprāptilakṣaṇā siddhiḥ*, and *tadviparyayajā asiddhiḥ*.[283] Śrīdhara too is following Śaṅkara in this instance. He says *karmaphalasya jñānasya siddhyasiddhyoḥ*, etc.[284]

At present there is no need to decide whether or not knowledge is the fruit of action. We shall have to reach this decision at another place. For the moment, we will gain most if we are able to understand the straightforward meaning of the words under discussion. The commentator Madhusūdana Sarasvatī has explained that simple meaning. He says: *siddhyasiddhyoḥ samo bhūtveti phalasiddhau harṣaṃ phalāsiddhau ca viṣādaṃ tyaktvā*, etc. [I.e.:] The abandonment of elation in success and the abandonment of sorrow in failure, this is equanimity towards success and failure. This will seem to be the coherent meaning to the common reader. He who is desireless, who does not desire the fruits, cannot be overcome by elation in the case of success and sorrow in the case of failure. As long as he feels joy at the attainment of fruits, it be understood that he desires the fruits of actions; for why should he be elated about the successful attainment of fruits if he did not desire them? When a doer of actions is desireless, he feels no elation in case of successful attainment of fruits and no pain in case of failure. Success and failure are alike to him. This equanimity is *yoga*. Thus being firm in *yoga*, perform actions — this is the first rule.

dūreṇa hy avaraṃ karma buddhiyogād dhanaṃjaya
buddhau śaraṇam anviccha kṛpaṇāḥ phalahetavaḥ. (49)

O Dhanaṃjaya, action is by far inferior to *buddhiyoga*. Pray for a refuge in *buddhi*. Those who are with desire are inferior.[285] (49)

It has not yet been said what is meant by *buddhiyoga*. Śrīdhara says that *buddhiyoga* is

[281] ['mental absorption in one's agency'.]

[282] [*jñān/bādī* (Beng.).]

[283] ['Success (is) characterised by attainment of knowledge, born of purity consisting in *sattva*', (...) 'failure (is) born from its opposite.' (*ŚaBhG*:70)]

[284] ['(...) of the knowledge of the fruits of action in success and failure (...)' (Cf. *ŚrBhG*:62)]

[285] [misprint *ŚBhG(a)*:739 — *tāhā* should read *tāhārā*.]

karmayoga with a determined intellect. Śaṅkara says, *samatvabuddhi.*[286] *samatvaṃ yoga ucyate.*[287] When action has been said to be much more inferior to this, we are to understand that the word *karman* here denotes ritualistic action.[288] The commentators say so. Thus the meaning of the first half of the *śloka* is that ritualistic action is much more inferior to the *karmayoga* I have talked about.

In the second half of the *śloka* it is said that one should take refuge in the intellect or use the intellect. By the word *buddhi*, *buddhiyoga* must be understood here. The commentators say the intellect of reasoning [*saṃkhyābuddhi*] or knowledge. If that is true, then it is also fair to understand the word *buddhi* as 'knowledge' in the first part. Then there will not be any confusion in the sentence *jyāyasī cet karmaṇas te matā buddhir janārdana*, etc. in the beginning of chapter three either. There will be some confusion, however, in the subsequent *śloka* 50.

buddhiyukto jahātīha ubhe sukṛtaduṣkṛte
tasmād yogāya yujyasva yogaḥ karmasu kauśalam. (50)

He who is *buddhiyukta* abandons both deeds done well and done badly in this birth. Therefore, apply *yoga*. *Yoga* is skill in action.

buddhiyukta — i.e. applying oneself to *buddhiyoga*. All the actions having heaven, etc., as their fruits are deeds done well, and all the actions having hell, etc., as their fruits are deeds done badly. He who applies himself to *buddhi* abandons both kinds of actions, those which lead to heaven and to hell. This does not signify that he does not do any good deeds or that he does not do any deeds at all, whether good or bad. It means that he does not perform any action out of the desire for heaven, etc., or out of the fear of hell, etc. Whatever he does, he does because it is to be performed.

'Therefore, apply *yoga*. *Yoga* is skill in action.' The ancient commentators have given this the meaning that action leads to bondage, for whenever one acts, the fruits of actions must be endured by being born again. But if even such bondage can be transformed, with the help of worship to God, into a means of salvation, then that indeed can be called skill or cleverness in action.

In the nineteenth century, we are not ready to interpret like this. We understand that he is a *yogin* who is skilful in action, that is, who exercises all his actions to be performed as prescribed. *yogaḥ karmasu kauśalam* — it is this meaning of this phrase which seems simple and coherent. Wherever there is a simple meaning, we shall bow from afar to the commentators, the great masters, and follow that simple meaning.

karmajaṃ buddhiyuktā hi phalam tyaktvā manīṣiṇaḥ
janmabandhavinirmuktāḥ padaṃ gacchanty anāmayam. (51)

The knowers who are *buddhiyukta* abandon the fruits born from action, become free from the bondage of birth and attain the *anāmaya pada*. (51)

[286] ['the attitude of equanimity'.]

[287] ['Equanimity is called *yoga*' — cf. *ŚaBhG*:70 (2.48)]

[288] [*kāmya karman*.]

buddhiyukta — following *buddhiyoga*.
anāmaya pada — the state of Viṣṇu free from all disturbance. (Śrīdhara)

yadā te mohakalilaṃ buddhir vyatitariṣyati
tadā gantāsi nirvedaṃ śrotavyasya śrutasya ca. (52)

When your intellect [*buddhi*] transcends the garden of illusion, then you shall attain indifference towards that which is to be heard and that which is heard. (52)

How can this state free from all affliction be attained by the abandonment of the desire for the fruits? When illusion and the false conception of the manifest[289] are left behind, indifference or desirelessness towards all things heard and to be heard is produced. One does not have to be spell-bound when hearing about any object, be it the joy of heaven, etc., or the wealth of a kingdom, etc.

śrutivipratipannā te yadā sthāsyati niścalā
samādhāv acalā buddhis tadā yogam avāpsyasi. (53)

When your '*śrutivipratipannā*' intellect is immobile in *samādhi* and (therefore) motionless, you will attain *yoga*. (53)

'*śrutivipratipannā*'. The meaning of *vipratipannā* is *bikṣipta* [Beng.].[290] But what is *śruti*? *Śruti* is that which has been heard, and *śruti* is what the Vedas are called. The ancient commentators cannot accept that the Vedas should be a reason for distraction of the intellect; consequently, they explain the word *śruti* as 'that which has been heard'. Rāmānuja's opinion is straightforward: [']*śruti* just means hearing.['] Madhusūdana says a little more, namely, that *śruti* is 'the hearing of various fruits [of action]'. Śaṅkarācārya says the same, the greater part, however, consisting in the brilliance of the words of his polished pen. He says, '*śrutivipratipannā anekasādhyasādhanasambandhaprakāśanaśrutibhiḥ śravaṇair vipratipannā*'.[291] Śrīdhara, somewhat more daring than all the others, says '*nānālaukikavaidikārthaśravaṇair vipratipannā*'.[292]

The English do not understand anything of the *Gītā*, and there is no possibility for such an understanding. But often, the pundit does not see any harm in listening to the words of the ignorant. I am quoting what Davies[293] [Lat.] *Sāheb* has said in this matter.

The *Sāheb* first boasts a little:

> I, too, have consulted Hindu Commentators largely (*at times*)[294] and have found them deficient in critical insight and more intent on finding or

[289] [*dehābhimān* (Beng.).]

[290] *Anglice* — distracted [Lat.].

[291] ['*śrutivipratipannā*: perplexed by the *śruti*, (i.e.) by the hearing, which discloses the relationship between various means and goals.' (Cf. *ŚaBhG*:74)]

[292] ['perplexed by the hearing of various worldly and *Vedic* objects'.]

[293] [Misprinted as 'Davis' (*ŚBhG[a]*:740 and *ŚBhG[b]*:96).]

[294] [Baṅkim's inserted Bengali comments are given in italics.]

> forming Vedantist doctrines in every part than in giving the true sense of the author. (*Many native people, too, say this about Śaṅkara's commentary.*) I have examined their explanations with the freedom of inquiry that is common to western habits of thought, and thus while I have sometimes followed their guidance, I have been obliged to reject their comments as misrepresenting the doctrine of the author. I append some instances of this kind, that my readers may be able to form their own judgement.

After this anouncement, the *Sāheb* quoted this very *śloka* as an example in the second chapter. He explained *śruti* as meaning Veda. And in support of the statement written above he says:

> Here the reference is to *Sruti* which means (1) hearing, (2) revelation. Hindu commentators say that the meaning is, what you have heard, about the means of obtaining desirable things; assuming as a certain proposition that the Vedas could not be attacked. The doctrine of the Bhagavadgita is, however, that the devotee (*yogin*), when fixed in meditation lays aside the Vedas and Vedic ritual.

Davies is an insignificant creature — there was no need to waste paper by quoting his statement. But this opinion is that of one of the best scholars of Europe — of Lassen himself. He too translated the verse *śrutivipratipannā* in this way. The other insignificant translators have followed his path. Apart from this, there is one invaluable expression in Davies' self-praise; that priceless theory which has not yet existed in India and still does not. 'FREEDOM OF ENQUIRY' [Lat. (*sic.*)] — for the sake of this invaluable expression we do not abstain from quoting the self-praise of an author of his kind.

The foreign opinion matches more coherently than the native Kṛṣṇa's opinion concerning the Vedas as we have understood or explained it. But if he wishes, the reader may place Śrīdhara in the foreign group here.

Apart from *śrutivipratipannā*, only one more term in this *śloka* requires explanation. *Samādhi* is that in which the mind [*citta*] is completely absorbed. When reading the translation now, the reader will presumably be able to understand the meaning of the *śloka*.

arjuna uvāca:
sthitaprajñasya kā bhāṣā samādhisthasya keśava
sthitadhīḥ kiṃ prabhāṣeta kim āsīta vrajeta kim. (54)

Arjuna said:
O Keśava, what are the characteristics of someone who, immersed in *samādhi*, has become steady-minded?[295] How does a person firm in wisdom[296] speak, how does he take his place, how does he walk? (54)

Having spoken on *sāṃkhyayoga* beforehand, the Lord has now explained *karmayoga* to Arjuna. His final statement concerning *karmayoga* has been: 'Your mind has become distracted by all you have heard about *karmayoga* (be it in the Vedas or elsewhere). As long as you stay like this you will not attain *karmayoga*. But when your mind becomes

[295] [*sthitaprajña*.]
[296] [*sthitadhī*.]

steady in *samādhi*[297] (in the Lord) you shall attain *yoga*. He whose *buddhi*[298] has thus become steady may be called a steady-minded person or a person firm in wisdom.' Arjuna is now inquiring about the characteristics of such a person who is immersed in deep meditation and steady-minded.

śrībhagavān uvāca:
prajahāti yadā kāmān sarvān pārtha manogatān
ātmany evātmanā tuṣṭaḥ sthitaprajñas tadocyate. (55)

[The Lord said:
O Pārtha,][299] when all kinds of mental desires are given up and a person is satisfied by himself or (his *ātman*), then one may call him a steady-minded person. (55)

We can see that the pleasure of man consists in the fulfilment of desires. What pleasure remains for him who has abandoned desire? Śaṅkarācārya says that, having attained the sight of the *paramārtha*, all other joy is needless. In the Vedas such a person has been called *ātmārāma*.

We are satisfied with another simple answer. We admit that the *parameśvara* is joy. He is bliss. But the outer world is also not separated from God. Why should it not be possible to feel joy about outer objects when one is desireless? Does not he who is devoid of desire become enchanted at the sight of the world's beauty? Or, does he not feel joy at the acquisition of knowledge? Or is he not delighted about the accomplishment of a good deed? The mere performance of action is joyful; and when in addition to this there is the knowledge of the similarity of success and failure, this joy never again decreases. And such joy is in the *ātman*, it does not depend on anyone.

Whoever does not thoroughly understand this will deem all these utterances of the *Gītā*, the present *śloka* and the few succeeding ones to be *Ascetic Philosophy* [Lat.]. In fact, this is no *Asceticism* [Lat.]. This theory is helpful in the unhindered enjoyment of what pleasure there is in the world. The obstacle in the enjoyment of what enjoyable pleasure[300] there is in the world is the intensity of desire and of the senses, etc. When this is controlled, no more hindrance in the enjoyment of all the wordly pleasures persists; the world is transformed into a holy and pleasant field of action.[301] I have made a special effort to elaborate this theory in my *Anuśīlan'tattva* (first part of *Dharmmatattva*), so there is no need of repetition. In the succeeding *ślokas* this will be made especially clear.

duḥkheṣv anudvignamanāḥ sukheṣu vigataspṛhaḥ
vītarāgabhayakrodhaḥ sthitadhīr munir ucyate. (56)

He who is unperturbed in pain, who is devoid of wishes in pleasure, who has no more

[297] ['deep meditation'.]

[298] ['intellect'.]

[299] [Left out of Baṅkim's translation.]

[300] [*upabhogya ye kichu sukh* (Beng.).]

[301] [*karmakṣetra*.]

passion, fear and anger, may be called a *muni* of firm wisdom. (56)

None of this is *Asceticism* [Lat.]; this doctrine is pain-destroying and (thus) a means of increasing pleasure. Only he who is afflicted by pain is pained. He whose mind is unperturbed by pain has conquered pain, he does not have pain anymore. He who wishes pleasure is very pained, for the wish for pleasure often yields no fruits, and even if it does, the fruits are not those hoped for. In both of these cases that wish for pleasure is transmuted into pain. Therefore, the wish for pleasure is merely a cause for the increase of pain. It goes without saying that fear and anger are causes of pain. 'Passion' [*anurāga*] should not be understood here in the sense of all kinds of passion. That which is passion for God can never be forbidden. By 'passion', only passion for 'desirable' [*kāmya*] objects, i.e. objects to be enjoyed by the senses, etc., is to be understood here. It is superfluous to say again that passion for all such objects is a cause of pain.

It remains only to be said that, if the wish for pleasure is given up, pleasure itself is not yet abandoned. And other than the abandonment of the wish for pleasure, the abandonment of the enjoyment of pleasure is not being ordained here. He who is devoid of wishes for pleasure can enjoy every sort of pleasure, and indeed does so. The Lord of the world Himself is devoid of all kinds of wishes, but enjoys infinite pleasure. But regarding man, the objection may come up that if man becomes devoid of wishes for pleasure, he will not attempt the attainment of pleasure; and if he does not attempt it, he will not attain pleasure. Someone who has understood *karmayoga* will never raise this objection. The central meaning of *karmayoga* is that one should perform actions desirelessly. The fruit of action is pleasure; he who accomplishes an action to be executed also attains the pleasure born from it. [On the other hand,] he who is dominated by desires or wishes when acting, attains no pleasure; desires and wishes are causes of action not to be executed and thus of sin and pain. Therefore, act desirelessly and devoid of wishes for pleasure — pleasure will come by itself. The Lord Himself has said this in *śloka* 70, as we shall see later.

yaḥ sarvatrānabhisnehas tat tat prāpya śubhāśubham
nābhinandati na dveṣṭi tasya prajñā pratiṣṭhitā. (57)

He who is free from affection everywhere, who is not joyous at the attainment of good or filled with hate at the attainment of the bad, is a steady-minded person. (57)

'Free from affection everywhere': Śrīdhara says that 'everywhere' means 'even with regard to sons, friends, etc.'.[302] Śaṅkara says, 'even with regard to the body, life, etc.'.[303] Śaṅkara's interpretation seems to be the genuine one. It does not have to be explained that the mind of that person who feels no joy or hate in good and evil of the body, life, etc., is likely to become fixed on God.

yadā saṃharate cāyaṃ kūrmo 'ṅgānīva sarvaśaḥ
indriyāṇīndriyārthebhyas tasya prajñā pratiṣṭhitā. (58)

302 [*putramitrādiṣv api* (*putrādiṣu*, acc. to *AṣBhG*:193)].

303 [*dehajīvitādiṣv api*.]

He who, like the tortoise withdrawing all its limbs from all objects, withdraws all the senses from all objects of senses, has a steady mind. (58)

We need no commentary on this statement. There is no righteous conduct[304] without the subdual of the senses, this is the first page of all books of scripture and the first step of all the temples of *dharma*.[305] In all Śāstras the matter of the subdual of the senses comes first. Only slight attention must be paid to this simile of the tortoise. The tortoise keeps its hands, feet, etc. withdrawn; it does not destroy them, and it maintains its vital functions through them as required. The same is true for the senses, etc. Their subdual is *dharma*, not their destruction. I have explained this in *Dharmmatattva*.

viṣayā vinivartante nirāhārasya dehinaḥ
rasavarjaṃ raso 'py asya paraṃ dr̥ṣṭvā nivartate. (59)

The objects (of the senses, etc.) are turned away from the person[306] without food, but the passion towards them does not perish. It (only) disappears through the encounter with the *brahman*. (59)

'Without food' — he who abstains from enjoyment of the objects of the senses, etc.

There exists a very dreadful state of mind, which, unfortunately, can continually be seen in the world. The enjoyment[307] disappears, but not the longing.[308] The ancient commentators have given the example of the sick, etc. He who is blind[309] or sick is unable to enjoy, and thus has no enjoyment. But there is no lack of the longing for enjoyment. Unfortunately, we can daily see examples more regrettable than this. Many give up enjoyment for fear of public censure, or pretend to a holy character, or accept the *dharma* of *saṃnyāsa*, etc., but cannot abandon their longings. Then, one day, the dam of sand breaks, and all dissolves in a flood of sin. The difference between such a person and a person engaged in enjoyment is very small. Such a state of mind is quite difficult to overcome. But it is removed when passion for God comes into being. The statement *paraṃ dr̥ṣṭvā* does not signify that God is to be perceived visually.

This obstacle of *dharma* is so serious that, in the subsequent *ślokas*, the Lord makes it even clearer.

yatato hy api kaunteya puruṣasya vipaścitaḥ
indriyāṇi pramāthīni haranti prasabhaṃ manaḥ. (60)

[304] [*dharmmācaraṇ* (Beng.).]

[305] 'All ethical gymnastic consists therefore singly in subjugating the instincts and appetites of our physical system in order that we remain their masters in any and all circumstances hazardous to morality; a gymnastic exercise rendering the will hardy and robust and which by the consciousness of regained freedom makes the heart glad.' Kant: *Metaphysics of Ethics* [1836] — translated by Semple [Kant 1991:§35 of the *Ethische Elementarlehre*].

[306] [*dehin*: lit. 'the one possessing a body'.]

[307] [*upabhog* (Beng.).]

[308] [*bāsanā* (Beng.).]

[309] [*jaṙa* (Beng.), also 'mute', 'unconscious', 'ignorant', etc.]

tāni sarvāṇi saṃyamya yukta āsīta matparaḥ
vaśe hi yasyendriyāṇi tasya prajñā pratiṣṭhitā. (61)

O Kaunteya, even if a discerning man takes care himself, the agitating senses carry his mind away by force. (60)

He who has controlled all those senses, is freed by *yoga*,[310] sits meditating upon me, and whose senses are all subordinated, is indeed a steady-minded person. (61)

So much for the inborn powers of the senses. Even he who is discerning cannot, even by taking care, easily bring them under control; they carry the mind away by force. And those who do not take care, who outwardly do not enjoy, but inwardly meditate only on those objects of the senses all the time, fall prey to complete destruction. This is said in the succeeding two *ślokas*.

dhyāyato viṣayān puṃsaḥ saṅgas teṣūpajāyate
saṅgāt saṃjāyate kāmaḥ kāmāt krodho 'bhijāyate. (62)

krodhād bhavati saṃmohaḥ saṃmohāt smṛtivibhramaḥ
smṛtibhraṃśād buddhināśo buddhināśāt praṇaśyati. (63)

When thinking of the objects (of the senses), attachment to them is produced. From attachment, desire is born; from desire, anger is born. (62)

From anger arises delusion, from delusion confusion of memory, from confusion of memory destruction of the intellect, and from destruction of the intellect, destruction [of the person concerned] happens. (63)

Attachment[311] will arise towards that to which one again and again gives room in one's mind. When attachment has arisen, one wishes to obtain it, i.e. desire is produced. If one does not obtain it, anger regarding the obstructive objects is produced. Through anger, ignorance or stupidity concerning what is to be done or not to be done is produced. Through such delusion, one must forget the mutual relationship of cause and effect. If one has forgotten the relationship of cause and effect, the destruction of the intellect takes place. Through the destruction of the intellect, destruction [of the person concerned] comes about.[312]

The senses must be restrained, and no room must be given to the objects of the senses, etc., even in one's mind. Is, then, the enjoyment of the senses, etc., absolutely forbidden? If so, then what is this *dharma* proclaimed in the *Gītā* but *asceticism*[313] [Lat.]? In that case, human society must be transformed into a monastery for *saṃnyāsins*.

310 [*yogamukta* (Beng.).]

311 [*āsakti* (Beng.).]

312 The present writer has tried to illustrate these words by the example of the character of *Sītārām*. [Protagonist of Baṅkim's last novel.]

313 *Asceticism* is somewhat different from what we call *vairāgya* or *sannyāsa*. Therefore, I have used the English term above.

It is not so, the enjoyment[314] of the senses is not forbidden; a special rule for this is given in the next *śloka*.

rāgadveṣavimuktais tu viṣayān indriyaiś caran
ātmavaśyair vidheyātmā prasādam adhigacchati. (64)

He who is *vidheyātman* is free from passion and hate and attains serenity by enjoying objects through his controlled senses. (64)

vidheyātman — whose *ātman* or innermost heart[315] is subdued.

The senses of such a person are subject to his orders; they cannot forcibly take away his mind. All his senses are free from passion and hate towards the objects to be enjoyed — all the senses are under his control, he is not under theirs. Such a person attains serenity or peace[316] by enjoying the objects of the senses, etc. In other words, the enjoyment he has is no cause of pain, but of pleasure. Therefore I was saying that this *dharma* proclaimed in the *Gītā* is no *Ascetic Philosophy* [Lat.]; it is a genuinely meritorious[317] and delightful *dharma*. The enjoying of the objects is not forbidden in it, but its measure and suitable rules are mentioned.

One thing remains to be explained. All the senses of a man who is *vidheyātman* have been called *rāgadveṣavimukta* — devoid of passion and hate. It is unnecessary to explain why a man who is *vidheyātman* must be devoid of passion in the object to be enjoyed. But what is the reason for saying 'devoid of hate'? Passion for enjoyable objects is the natural *dharma* ['property'] of the senses, hate is unnatural; it can never be shown. Why should the unlikely be forbidden? And if hate for the objects to be enjoyed does occur in the senses, then that is only good, because in that case, no inclination towards sensual pleasures can persist. So why this prohibition?

It is not true that hate of the thing to be enjoyed does not occur. The sick person's distaste for food and the lazy person's distaste for the pleasure of exercise can be given as examples. These are characteristics neither of physical health, nor of mental health. We can see many who will not at any price wear a bordered *dhoti*, and who do not put anything on their feet except sandals. Their mind has not, even today, become devoid of aberrations, just like the minds of those abnormal persons who will not wear anything but a very fine *dhoti* with a black border. When all is known as alike, then they will no longer have such objections.

In fact, the matter is not as unimportant and insignificant as it seems from all these trifling examples. I will now demonstrate its importance by a greater example. The teachers of Roman Catholic *dharma* despise the satisfaction of certain senses[318] — if not in deed, then certainly in rules. Therefore, celibacy was ordained for them. The disorder which resulted from this is known to every reader of history. But the Aryan *ṛṣis* were really steady-minded men; neither did they have passion towards any sense,

314 [*upabhog* (Beng.).]

315 [*antaḥkaraṇ* (Beng.).]

316 'Makes the heart glad,' vide Kant's utterance quoted above.

317 [*pūṇyamaẏ* (Beng.).]

318 [*indriẏabiśeṣ* (Beng.).]

nor hatred. Thus, in due course, after completing *brahmacarya*, they used to take wives. But they were just as devoid of passion towards the senses as hateless, and therefore only married in accordance with *dharma* for the mere sake of giving birth to offspring; and except [in the case of] the temporal law prescribed by nature for this purpose, they never satisfied the senses.

Besides *Asceticism* [Lat.], the *dharma* proclaimed in the *Gītā* is also adverse to *Puritanism* [Lat.]. For *Puritanism* originates from the idea[319] of hatred. In the *dharma* of the *Gītā*, there is no way for any kind of hypocrisy to run its course.

prasāde sarvaduḥkhānāṃ hānir asyopajāyate
prasannacetaso hy āśu buddhiḥ paryavatiṣṭhate. (65)

In serenity, all his pain comes to be destroyed. The intellect of him who has a serene mind quickly becomes firm. (65)

It has been said in the preceding *śloka* that serenity is attained through the enjoyment of objects by senses under control of the self and devoid of passion and hatred. Serenity denotes a happy mind, or peace. Now it is being said that all pain is destroyed by that serenity, [and] that a steady-minded state comes into being in such a serene person.

nāsti buddhir ayuktasya na cāyuktasya bhāvanā
na cābhāvayataḥ śāntir aśāntasya kutaḥ sukham. (66)

The uncontrolled person[320] has no knowledge [*buddhi*]. The uncontrolled person has no reflection [*bhāvanā*]. He who has no reflection is without peace. He who has no peace has no pleasure. (66)

Uncontrolled means having a heart not wholly immersed in meditation (devoid of *yoga*). *Bhāvanā* [reflection] is contemplation,[321] thought.[322] He whose innermost heart is not immersed in meditation, and whose senses have not been subdued, does not acquire knowledge [*buddhi*] in the discussion of the Śāstras, either. A person without knowledge cannot think (the commentators say: has no assiduity towards knowledge of the self). He who has no power of thinking has no peace; if there is no peace, there is no pleasure.

It contradicts the common meaning of the word *buddhi* [intellect, knowledge] that a person devoted to the senses should have no *buddhi*. Many persons devoted to the senses have become known in the world as being *buddhimān* [intelligent (Beng.)]. But such a *buddhi* never makes them happy. The *buddhi* which does not make happy is no *buddhi* at all.

indriyāṇāṃ hi caratāṃ yan mano 'nuvidhīyate
tad asya harati prajñāṃ vāyur nāvam ivāmbhasi. (67)

[319] [*buddhi*.]

[320] [*ayuktir* (Beng., *ŚBhG[a]*:745): printing error for *ayukter* (Beng.) (cf. *ŚBhG[b]*:103).]

[321] [*dhyāna*.]

[322] [*cintā*.]

He whose mind follows the senses[323] wandering towards the objects — as the wind immerses a boat in water, so do (the senses) rob his insight.[324] (67)

Comments are not necessary.

tasmād yasya mahābāho nigṛhītāni sarvaśaḥ
indriyāṇīndriyārthebhyas tasya prajñā pratiṣṭhitā. (68)

Therefore, O Mighty-Armed, he is a steady-minded person whose senses are in every way detached from the sense-objects. (68)

Comments are not necessary.

yā niśā sarvabhūtānāṃ tasyāṃ jāgarti saṃyamī
yasyāṃ jāgrati bhūtāni sā niśā paśyato muneḥ.[325] (69)

The man of self-control is awake in what is night for all beings. And when all beings are awake, it is night for the *muni* endowed with sight. (69)

The translation of the creator of the [Bengali] *Mahābhārata*[326] is an abundant commentary of this *śloka*. 'The *yogins* who have conquered their senses remain awake in the state of the *brahman* appearing as night to persons whose intellect is enveloped by the darkness of ignorance. And the day, appearing as the state of being given to sense-objects,[327] in which the beings are awake, is night to the *yogins* seeing the essence of the self.'

āpūryamāṇam acalapratiṣṭhaṃ samudram āpaḥ praviśanti yadvat
tadvat kāmā yaṃ praviśanti sarve sa śāntim āpnoti na kāmakāmī. (70)

Only he obtains peace into whom all enjoyments enter, just as all the rivers enter into the eternally stable ocean being filled [with water]; he who desires enjoyments does not obtain [peace]. (70)

The ocean does not go out in search of water; the rivers by themselves enter into the ocean with their water and keep it filled. Likewise the enjoyments by themselves take refuge in him who has controlled his senses; for this reason, only he attains peace. He who is driven by the senses and thus subject to desire can never attain this peace. Now remember what I have said in the commentary to *śloka* 56. The abandonment of desire is the reason for the attainment of pleasure born from the fruits of action. The pleasure born from the fruits of action by itself takes recourse to him. Only such pleasure gives

323 [Literally: 'He whose mind is followed by the wandering senses', etc.]

324 ['Immerses' is not in the original, and the subject of 'rob' is clearly *manas* ('mind').]

325 [Misprinted as *munoḥ* in *ŚBhG(a)*:745.]

326 [Kālīprasanna Siṃha 1882-3.]

327 [*biṣaẏ/niṣṭhāsvarūp* (Beng.).]

peace. In the pleasure born from desire, there is no peace; therefore that pleasure is no pleasure at all.

vihāya kāmān yaḥ sarvān pumāṃś carati niḥspṛhaḥ
nirmamo nirahaṃkāraḥ sa śāntim adhigacchati. (71)

Only he who dwells wishless by abandoning all desires, is free of self-ness and egotism, obtains peace. (71)

Free of self-ness — free of pride.[328]

eṣā brāhmī sthitiḥ pārtha naināṃ prāpya vimuhyati
sthitvāsyām antakāle 'pi brahmanirvāṇam ṛcchati. (72)

O Pārtha, this is the state of being given to the *brahman*. Having obtained it, one need no longer be deluded. Just through becoming firm in it, even in one's ultimate moment, one can attain extinction in the *brahman*. (72)

So the state of being given to the *brahman* has come in just a few words. Control of the senses and abandonment of desire: that is the state of being given to the *brahman*. It must be remembered that this is only a characteristic of the mind absorbed in God - the abandonment of desire does not happen without worship of the Lord. Thus, the genuine state of being given to the *brahman* is the placing of the mind on God, with controlled senses, and desireless. The execution of desireless action, together with control of the senses and bestowal of the mind to God, is the actual[329] state of being given to the *brahman*.

If this is so, *dharma* becomes complete. This indeed is the essence of Hindu *dharma*. Whatever else is in the *Gītā* is merely an extension of this, merely the choice of method according to different qualifications. Whatever else there is in the Hindu *dharma* or in any other *dharma* is no necessary part of *dharma*. It is either fiction,[330] or superstition, or social custom, or nonsense — it is better to abandon it. It is manageable by everyone; no study of the Vedas, no twilight-*gāyatrīs* are required for it. It is accessible to women or the fallen, śūdras or unbelievers, Muslims or Christians — to all. It is the only *dharma* in the world; it alone is the only *Catholic religion* [Lat.].

iti śrīmahābhārate śatasāhasryāṃ saṃhitāyāṃ vaiyāsikyāṃ bhīṣmaparvaṇi śrīmadbhagavadgītāsūpaniṣatsu brahmavidyāyāṃ yogaśāstre śrīkṛṣṇārjunasaṃvāde sāṃkhyayogo nāma dvitīyo 'dhyāyaḥ.[331]

328 [*abhimān* (Beng.).]

329 [*yatheṣṭa* (Beng.): usually 'enough'; lit. 'as is wished'.]

330 [*upanyās* (Beng.).]

331 ['This is the second chapter called *Sāṃkhyayoga* in the *Yogaśāstra*, taught as a dialogue between Kṛṣṇa and Arjuna, with regard to the knowledge of *brahman*, in the secret teachings sung by the Lord in the *Bhīṣmaparvan* of Vyāsa's *Saṃhitā* (consisting of) 100 000 (*ślokas*), in the *Mahābhārata*.']

Third Chapter

arjuna uvāca:
jyāyasī cet karmaṇas te matā buddhir janārdana
tat kiṃ karmaṇi ghore māṃ niyojayasi keśava. (1)

Arjuna said:
O Janārdana, if in your opinion *buddhi* is superior to action, then why, O Keśava, do you engage me in this violent action? (1)

Buddhi must again be understood as knowledge here. The Lord has told Arjuna to make war, but in the last few *ślokas* of the second chapter, i.e. with regard to the characteristics of a steady-minded person, Arjuna has understood that knowledge is better than action. So he asks: 'If knowledge is indeed superior to action, then why do you engage me in action, especially in such mean action as a war?'

How such a doubt has arisen in Arjuna has been explained by Śrīdhara in the following way: After the topic of *dehātmavivekabuddhi* for the attainment of liberation has first been taken up through the sentences *'aśocyān anvaśocas tvam'* (see *śloka* 11 of the second chapter), etc., action too has been treated in the sentences *'eṣā te 'bhihitā sāṃkhye buddhiḥ'* (see *śloka* 39 of the second chapter), etc. But it has not been clearly shown which of these is the condition with superior qualities. Thus, having interpreted the Lord's intention to be [an assertion regarding] the superiority of knowledge among knowledge and action, [namely,] through the praise of the characteristics of the steady-minded person endowed with knowledge, such as inactivity, sense-control and non-egotism, etc., [as well as] the eulogising conclusion *'eṣā brāhmī sthitiḥ pārtha'* (see *śloka* 72 of the preceding chapter), Arjuna enquires in this way.

In fact, nowhere in the second chapter has [Kṛṣṇa] said explicitly that knowledge is better than action. But some confusion is indeed created by *śloka* 49,

'dūreṇa hy avaraṃ karma buddhiyogād dhanaṃjaya.'

I have also explained, at the time of interpretation of the said *śloka*, that the commentators have taken *buddhi* here in the sense of resolute *karmayoga*. If this meaning is given up there and if *buddhi* is understood as knowledge, no confusion remains. Otherwise, as I mentioned before, confusion is created here. Ānandagiri too has especially pointed out the *śloka 'dūreṇa hy avaraṃ karma'*, etc., in his annotation to the commentary on this first *śloka* of the third [chapter].

In any case, the utterances of the Lord in the second chapter concerning the superiority of knowledge or action are indeed somewhat *'vyāmiśra'* (*anglice ambiguous* [Lat.]). It seems that the Lord has intentionally not clarified this topic at first, but waited for the answer to this question. Because the resolution regarding the differences and the mutual relationship between knowledge and action, given at the occasion of the answer to this question in the next few chapters, is infinitely beneficial for man and must be accepted as stemming from a superhuman mind. Never has such a generally beneficial[1] *dharma* been proclaimed anywhere in the world.

Arjuna expressly refers to that *vyāmiśra* utterance:

[1] [*sarbbamaṅgal'maẏ* (Beng.).]

vyāmiśreṇeva vākyena buddhiṃ mohayasīva me
tad ekam vada niścitya yena śreyo 'ham āpnuyām. (2)

You are confusing my intellect by ambiguous (dubious) statements. Therefore, definitely tell me the one (one kind of position)[2] by which I can obtain salvation.[3] (2)

śrībhagavān uvāca:
loke 'smin dvividhā niṣṭhā purā proktā mayānagha
jñānayogena sāṃkhyānāṃ karmayogena yoginām. (3)

[The Lord said:][4]
O sinless one, I have said before that there are two kinds of positions[5] in this world; i.e. I mentioned *jñānayoga* for the *sāṃkhyas* and *karmayoga* for the (*karma-*) *yogins.* (3)

All this has been explained once [before]. A repetition is not necessary.

na karmaṇām anārambhān naiṣkarmyaṃ puruṣo 'śnute
na ca saṃnyāsanād eva siddhiṃ samadhigacchati. (4)

One does not attain freedom from action by abstaining from doing this,[6] and perfection is not attained by the mere abandonment of action. (4)

Arjuna's question was: 'If knowledge is better than action, then why do you engage me in action?' The Lord's answer: 'If knowledge is indeed superior, then must I therefore tell you to give up action? Having given yourself to knowledge, will you be able to give up action? Will you obtain freedom from action by merely not performing actions? Or will you attain perfection by the mere acquisition of non-action?'

The Lord continues by speaking on why non-action is not obtained by performing action.

na hi kaścit kṣanam api jātu tiṣṭhaty akarmakṛt
kāryate hy avaśaḥ karma sarvaḥ prakṛtijair guṇaiḥ. (5)

No-one can exist even for a moment without performing an action. All are bound to act by the properties originated in *prakṛti.* (5)

'O Arjuna, you say that I am telling you to act despite the superiority of knowledge; but can you be without acting? Does nature let you? Exhalation, inhalation, eating, sleeping, bathing, drinking — what are all these but actions? Can all these be given up by becoming a follower of the path of knowledge?'

[2] [*niṣṭhā.*]

[3] [*śreẏa* (Beng.).]

[4] [Left out by Baṅkim (*ŚBhG[a]*:747 and *ŚBhG[b]*:107).]

[5] [*niṣṭhā.*]

[6] [*anuṣṭhānī* (Beng., *ŚBhG[a]*:747) is a misprint for *ananuṣṭhānei* (Beng.) (cf. *ŚBhG[b]*:107).]

The inquisitive might say here that, although the actions one has to perform due to nature cannot certainly be abandoned, cannot the knower or *saṃnyāsin* give up those actions[7] which are subordinate to his will?

The simple answer to this is that nobody can give up an action to be executed. The meditation on God depends on one's own will; can it be given up by the follower of the path of knowledge? What then is the purpose of knowledge?

Many will say that that which is usually called *karman* is not intended here. In the Hindu-Śāstras, *karman* is *śrauta karman* and *smārta karman*.[8] But it is not true [that] one cannot exist for even a moment without performing *śrauta karman* or *smārta karman*; none of this is natural[9] [in the sense] that one would be obliged to do it by a drive of nature. Therefore, that which is usually called *karman*, namely, anything that can be done, is indeed the object of discussion here. I have said this before and repeat it here. Whenever one says *karman* in an interpretation of the *Gītā*, only *karman* ['action'] must be understood; it can be seen in this very *śloka* that it is not only *śrauta* and *smārta karman* which are intended by the Lord.

karmendriyāṇi saṃyamya ya āste manasā smaran
indriyārthān vimūḍhātmā mithyācāraḥ sa ucyate. (6)

He whose *ātman* is deluded, who maintains control only over his organs of action while remembering the sense-objects in his mind,[10] is a practiser of falsehood. (6)

The Lord has said that non-action[11] is not attained by merely refraining from action, and that perfection is not attained by mere abandonment of action. The Lord gives this proof that non-action is not achieved by refraining from action: Even if you do not perform actions, you are bound to perform actions by [your] nature. And he gives this proof that perfection is not attained by the mere abandonment of action: Even if one controls all the organs of action and remains idle, saying 'I will not act', all the objects enjoyable by the senses can arise in one's mind. In such a case, this is only the practice of falsehood. Through it, no perfection is possible.

If neither action can be abandoned nor, even through the abandonment of action, perfection be attained, then what is to be done? Indeed, this is what is said now:

yas tv indriyāṇi manasā niyamyārabhate 'rjuna
karmendriyaiḥ karmayogam asaktaḥ sa viśiṣyate. (7)

O Arjuna, he who has controlled all senses through his mind, is unattached and performs *karmayoga* through his organs of action, is the best. (7)

[7] [*kārya* (Beng.).]

[8] [i.e. sacrifices according to *śruti* and *smṛti* respectively.]

[9] [*svābhābik* (Beng.).]

[10] [*man* (Beng.).]

[11] [*naiṣkarman*; also 'state of freedom from *karman*'.]

niyataṃ kuru karma tvaṃ karma jyāyo hy akarmaṇaḥ
śarīrayātrāpi ca te na prasidhyed akarmaṇaḥ. (8)

Perform action as a rule. Action is superior to devoidness of action. By devoidness of action, even your vital functions cannot be kept up. (8)

'tat kiṃ karmaṇi ghore māṃ niyojayasi keśava!'[12] To Arjuna's question, the Lord has given this answer. The answer is that no-one can abandon action, and that only by abandoning it, perfection is not attained. If you do not act, it is not possible to keep up your vital functions. Therefore, perform actions. But since you have to act, act in such a way that your actions are beneficial. Two rules have been proclaimed as to what makes actions bring about the best: Act — firstly — having controlled all the senses[13] by the mind, and — secondly — being unattached. Apart from that, there is another rule; it is the most excellent, the best of all and the focal point of *karmayoga*. It is said in the succeeding *śloka*.

yajñārthāt karmaṇo 'nyatra loko 'yaṃ karmabandhanaḥ
tadarthaṃ karma kaunteya muktasaṅgaḥ samācara. (9)

All action except that directed towards *yajña* is a cause of bondage in this world. Therefore (for the purpose of *yajña*), O Kaunteya, perform actions being unattached. (9)

The interpretation of this *śloka* depends on the meaning of the word *yajña*. Formerly, the rituals mentioned in the Vedas were usually called *yajña*, as the *aśvamedhayajña*, etc. Nowadays, the rituals mentioned in all kinds of Śāstras are called *yajñas*.

The ancient commentators Śaṅkara and Śrīdhara do not accept this meaning. Śaṅkara says: *'yajño vai viṣṇur iti śruter yajña īśvaraḥ'*.[14] Śrīdhara accepts that meaning. Madhusūdana Sarasvatī too explains likewise. Rāmānuja does not say so; he calls an action for the gain of anything material, etc., a *yajña*.

If one accepts the meaning of the word *yajña* stated by Śaṅkara and others, this *śloka* means that all actions, except those directed towards God, are only bondage for the enjoyment of the fruits of action. Therefore you should be unattached and only perform actions directed towards God.

In that case, the *śloka* under consideration means that any action, except that directed to the worship of God, is just bondage to the enjoyment of the fruits of action. Therefore act only for the worship[15] of God.

In this instance, it may be enquired: 'Is that possible? The Lord Himself says that we must also act as driven perforce by nature, and for the maintenance of our vital functions. Can the worship of God be the object of all such actions? What relation can bathing, drinking, eating, physical exercise, etc., through which I maintain my vital

[12] [*BhG* 3.1.]

[13] Only the organs of knowledge [*jñānendriya*], say the commentators.

[14] ['"The sacrifice is indeed Viṣṇu" — from (this sentence of) the *śruti* [*Taittirīya Saṃhitā* 1.7.44] (it is understood that) the sacrifice is God.' (Cf. *ŚaBhG*:108)]

[15] [In this passage, 'worship' renders the Bengali *ārādhanā*, not *pūjā* which is elsewhere translated as 'worship'.]

functions, have with the worship of God?'

Before understanding this we have to determine what worship of God means. When worshipping a human, we engage in praise and eulogy of the person to be worshipped. But we cannot imagine God to be similarly low-minded and fond of flattery. If by praising and eulogising him we acquire happiness or the elevation of our minds, then there is no objection at all against engaging in such praise and eulogy, and it is definitely a duty in this kind of case. But it cannot therefore be called genuine worship of God. In the same way, what we usually call offerings and sacrifices[16] — flowers and sandal, food-offerings, the sacred fire, sacrificial animals, festivals — is no worship of God.

Worship of God is, of course, His satisfaction, but His satisfaction cannot be achieved through flattering. The execution of the action intended by Him and the observance of His rules are His satisfaction; these are the genuine worship of God. What do we call the execution of the action intended by Him and the observance of His rules? In the *Viṣṇupurāṇa*, Prahlāda has in one word given a very beautiful answer to this question:

'sarvatra daityāḥ samatām upeta
samatvam ārādhanam acyutasya.'[17]

Impartiality concerning all beings is genuine worship of God; we shall gradually see again and again that this is also the worship of God related in the *Gītā*: impartiality regarding all beings, knowledge that all beings are similar to oneself, and beneficence towards all beings.

Thus the only purpose of the action of a *karmayogin* is beneficence towards all beings.

The agent is himself also included in all beings. Therefore self-protection is also intended by God. The Lord of the world has loaded the burden of self-protection on each and every one. I have explained all this in detail in *Dharmmatattva*, so there is no need of repetition.

It is being said in this ninth *śloka* that all actions except *'yajña'* (in whatever sense) are only bondage. It remains to be explained what 'bondage'[18] is. It is not being said that action of other kinds is fruitless or sinful; it is being said that it is equal to bondage. In order to understand this bondage, we have to remember the doctrine of reincarnation. As soon as one acts, one has to partake of the fruits thereof in another life. For partaking of the fruits of action — no matter whether these be good or bad — the being must participate in reincarnation. As long as birth follows birth, there is no salvation for the being. Because it is a hinderance of salvation, action is only bondage.

Now it might be enquired: What if there is no reincarnation? Is the *niṣkāma karman* of the *Gītā* even then sanctioned by *dharma*? Or are desireless action[19] and action with desire[20] just the same?

I have answered this in *Dharmmatattva*. There is no humanity without desireless action. And without humanity, there is no steady pleasure in this birth or world.

16 [*yāg*/*yajña* (Beng.): *yāg* is the modern Indo-Aryan form of *yajña* (sacrifice).]

17 ['Always, O *Daityas*, devote yourselves to *samatā*. *Samatā* is the worship of *Acyuta* [Viṣṇu].']

18 [*bandhan* (Beng.).]

19 [*niṣkāma karman*.]

20 [*sakāma karman*.]

Consequently, this *dharma* proclaimed in the *Gītā* is universal.

sahayajñāḥ prajāḥ sṛṣṭvā purovāca prajāpatiḥ
anena prasaviṣyadhvam eṣa vo 'stv iṣṭakāmadhuk. (10)

In former times, Prajāpati created the creatures along with the *yajña* and said: 'You will grow by this, it will fulfil your desires.' (10)

Here the word *yajña* no longer means 'God' or 'worship of God'. Only sacrifices, that is *śrauta*[21] and *smārta*[22] performances, are *yajña*; and in the following *ślokas* 12, 13, 14 and 15, *yajna* means only those sacrifices. After using a word in one meaning [*sic.*][23] in one *śloka*, no-one takes it in a different meaning in the subsequent line. Therefore, many modern scholars take 'sacrifice' as the meaning of *yajña* in the ninth *śloka*. Kashinath Trimbak Telang [1990 (1882)], in his translation, has written *sacrifice* [Lat.] for *yajña*. Thereafter, in the commentary on the tenth *śloka*, he has written: 'Probably the sacrifices spoken of in this passage (the ninth *śloka* [Beng.]) must be taken to be the same as those referred to in this passage.' [Lat.] Davies *Sāheb* [1882] also follows this path. He has revealed to us in his notes that although having consulted Śaṅkara's commentary, he has not heeded it. On the other hand, he has written *kamduk* [Lat.] in the place of *kāmadhuk*! Not once, but again and again!!!

So far, the Lord has been engaged in censure of action with desire and praise of desireless action. But sacrifices are with desire. Therefore, if 'God' is not understood to be the meaning of *yajña*, we are to understand that the Lord gives an instruction to perform action with desire. Thus the venerable Śaṅkara took it from the Vedas that in the ninth [*śloka*], *yajña* means 'God'. He knew the four Vedas by heart.

Now, one thing concerning this *śloka* needs to be explained. It has been said that Prajāpati created together with the *yajña*. Nobody should understand that the *yajña* is a being or thing; when Prajāpati created man, he created it, too. The meaning of this is that there are sacrificial rules in the Vedas, and when Prajāpati created the creatures, these Vedas were also there. Orthodox Hindus will be satisfied with just this, but the majority of my readers are not of this category. My readers will say: 'First of all, I do not believe in the creation of the creatures at all; after all, man has evolved from the monkey. Second, I do not believe either that the Vedas are eternal, or superhuman, or contemporary to the creation of creatures. And, finally, I do not accept that *Prajāpati*, after creating the creatures, held a speech on *yajña*.'

There is no necessity of believing this. I do not believe it either. Neither does Kṛṣṇa tell us to believe it. It will gradually become clear. I shall discuss all this and the true significance of the succeding *ślokas* after *śloka* 16.

He says, again relying on customary belief:[24]

21 [Vedic, according to the *śruti*.]

22 [According to the *smṛti*.]

23 [*ekārthe* (Beng., 'in one meaning') and *arthabiśeṣe* (Beng., 'in a particular meaning') are both used in the sentence, which is untranslatable.]

24 [*laukik biśvās* (Beng.).]

devān bhāvayatānena te devā bhāvayantu vaḥ
parasparaṃ bhāvayantaḥ śreyaḥ param avāpsyatha. (11)

Enrich the gods by *yajñas*; may the gods enrich you. By thus enriching each other, you shall attain utmost good. (11)

Śrīdhara Svāmin says in his commentary: 'You shall enrich the gods by portions of clarified butter, and the gods shall also enrich you by producing food through rain, etc.' It is known, after all, that we do not survive without food. The gods, too, allegedly drink the sacrificial clarified butter and thereby nourish themselves. This is said in the Vedas. Be it so.[25]

iṣṭān bhogān hi vo devā dāsyante yajñabhāvitāḥ
tair dattān apradāyaibhyo yo bhuṅkte stena eva saḥ. (12)

He who enjoys the desired enjoyment which the gods, enriched through sacrifices, will give to you, without giving them that (the nourishment) given by them, is a thief. (12)

Śaṅkara and Śrīdhara Svāmin say (there appears to be no particular need to do so) *pañcayajñādibhir adattvā*: '[He who] enjoys without giving through the five sacrifices, etc. is a thief.'[26] The five sacrifices, namely:

adhyāpanaṃ brahmayajñaḥ pitṛyajñas tu tarpaṇam
homo daivo balir bhauto nṛyajño 'tithibhojanam.[27]

That is, *brahmayajña* or teaching, *pitṛyajña* or oblation of water, *daiva yajña* or oblation into fire, *bhūtayajña* or animal sacrifice, and *nṛyajña* or feeding of guests. It must be kept in mind that Śrīdhara does not say *pañcayajñair adattvā* but *pañcayajñādibhir adattvā*.[28]

yajñaśiṣṭāśinaḥ santo mucyante sarvakilbiṣaiḥ
bhuñjate te tv aghaṃ pāpā ye pacanty ātmakāraṇāt. (13)

Those good people who eat the residues of the sacrifice are freed from all sin; those sinners who cook only for themselves eat sin. (13)

annād bhavanti bhūtāni parjanyād annasaṃbhavaḥ
yajñād bhavati parjanyo yajñaḥ karmasamudbhavaḥ. (14)

From food, all living beings[29] are created. Food is born from Parjanya, Parjanya from

25 [*thākuk* (Beng.): also 'Let's leave it at that'.]

26 [Contrary to Baṅkim's indication, the five sacrifices are not mentioned in Śaṅkara's commentary but only in Śrīdhara's. (*AṣBhG*:242)]

27 [Origin not identified.]

28 [Cf. above: 'without giving through the five sacrifices, etc.'.]

29 [*bhūta*.]

the sacrifice. The sacrifice is produced by action.[30] (14)

Parjanya is a Vedic divinity. He makes rain. Here, it suffices if Parjanya is understood as rain.

The beings[31] are produced from food. This statement may not be quite scientific, but it is not untrue, and it is indeed[32] comprehensible. The commentators say that food is transformed into semen and blood,[33] and that through these a being is born. That is sufficient.

Then, food comes from rain. This too may be accepted, for without rain, there are no crops. But the coming forth of the rain from the sacrifice is a statement that a scientist will not accept. The commentators say that clouds are produced from the smoke of the sacrifice. Clouds can [however] also be produced from other smoke, and most clouds form without any smoke. Even in countries where no sacrifices are performed, there are clouds and rain. But be that as it may, the scientific doctrine is not being discussed in this place. Are, consequently, the words of the Lord untrue and unscientific? I shall explain exactly this in due course.

karma brahmodbhavaṃ viddhi brahmākṣarasamudbhavam
tasmāt sarvagataṃ brahma nityaṃ yajñe pratiṣṭhitam. (15)

Know action to have originated from the *brahman*; the *brahman* has arisen from the imperishable. Thus the all-pervading *brahman* eternally rests in the sacrifice. (15)

The commentators say that the word *brahman* means the Vedas here, and *akṣara* ['imperishable'] the *paramātman*. But some create confusion by understanding *brahman* to denote the Vedas in the first line, and the *parabrahman* in the second. Otherwise it makes no sense. The creator of the [Bengali] *Mahābhārata*, Kālīprasanna Siṃha [1882-3], and other translators have followed this opinion. But Śaṅkarācārya himself has clung to the *brahman* meaning the Vedas in the second line also; therefore this *śloka* can be interpreted in two ways.

Firstly, in the opinion of Śrīdhara and others, 'Action has come from the Vedas, and the Vedas from the *parabrahman*; therefore, the all-pervading *brahman* always rests in the sacrifice.'

Secondly, in the opinion of Śaṅkara, etc., 'Action has come from the Vedas, and the Vedas from the *parabrahman*; therefore the Vedas, because they bring out all meanings, always rest in the sacrifice.'

The reader may adopt whichever interpretation he likes; no harm is done by either of them to the basic significance of the [*śloka*].

evaṃ pravartitaṃ cakraṃ nānuvartayatīha yaḥ
aghāyur indriyārāmo moghaṃ pārtha sa jīvati. (16)

30 [*karman*.]

31 [*jīb* (Beng.).]

32 [*bale* (Beng.): *ŚBhG[a]* — misprint for *baṭe* (Beng.) (cf. *ŚBhG[b]*:113).]

33 [Obviously the 'blood' (i.e. the menstrual fluid) which unites with semen to create a child.]

He who does not follow this cycle once started, O Pārtha, leads a sinful life and is an *indriyārāma*, [and] lives in vain. (16)

(He is an *indriyārāma*, whose delight consists in the pleasure of the senses.)

The Vedas come from the *brahman*, action from the Vedas, sacrifice from action, clouds from sacrifices, nourishment from clouds, and beings from nourishment. The commentators have called this *jagaccakra*.[34] This universal cycle is followed by doing action; because sacrifice will come from action, clouds from sacrifice, and nourishment from clouds. Through nourishment, the vital functions will be maintained. This is one part of the cycle. This part is not true, for we know that by [just] doing an action, no sacrifice[35] is produced, that by merely performing a sacrifice, no clouds are produced, and that by the mere presence of clouds, no grain is produced (not in all clouds is there rain, and there is also excessive rain), etc. On the other hand, there is action apart from sacrifice, clouds are also produced without sacrifices, grain also grows without clouds (as the winter crops), the vital functions can also be maintained without grain (for example, all uncivilised and half-civilised races live by hunting or rearing livestock) and so on.

The second part of the cycle is that the Vedas arise from the *brahman*, and action from the Vedas. This, too, is an issue of contention. Many, instead of saying that the Vedas have come from the *brahman*, call the Vedas superhuman. Many may say that the Vedas are neither superhuman nor originated in the *brahman*, but merely formulated by the ṛṣis, the proof of which is in the Vedas themselves. Further, the statement regarding the origin of action from the Vedas does not apply for any kind of action except *śrauta karman*.[36] The reader will notice that from the tenth to this sixteenth *śloka* we are caught in a severe whirlpool of supernatural statements. It is all *abaijñānik* (*unscientific* [Lat.]). Here none of the ancient, maharṣi-like commentators comes to our aid; they have set the sails of belief and passed over easily. We are pupils of the *mlecchas*; we do not have this means of succour. But we will easily be able to understand that the *Gītā* is not a book on science. It has not been written by Huxley or Tyndale [both Engl. in the original] for the circulation of a pure scientific doctrine. In a book which has been written three thousand years ago, science of the nineteenth century cannot be expected to be found.

Nevertheless the reader may say: 'All you call utterances of the Lord should be devoid of errors and untruths. Unscientific means untrue. How is it possible that God's words should be untrue?'

But I cannot say that these seven *ślokas* are utterances of the Lord. I have said before that it is misleading to believe that all there is in the *Gītā* are words of the Lord. I have said that the *dharma* proclaimed by Kṛṣṇa has been compiled by someone else. He who made this compilation, of course, had his own opinions. It is impossible that, in a book compiled by him, he nowhere circulated his own opinion. Regarding the compilor, even a commentator like Śrīdhara Svāmin said that *'prāyaśaḥ śrīkṛṣṇamukhād*

[34] ['universal cycle'.]

[35] If you say that only *śrauta* and *smārta karman* is *karman* [action] and that, therefore, there is no action apart from sacrifice, then sentences like *'na hi kaścit kṣanam api jātu tiṣṭhaty akarmakṛt'* (*śloka* 5) and *'śarīrayātrāpi ca te na prasidhyed akarmaṇaḥ'* (*śloka* 8), etc., make no sense.

[36] [That is Vedic sacrifice, ritualistic action.]

viniḥsr̥tān eva ślokān alikhat', and thereby accepted that '*kāṃscit tatsaṅgataye svayaṃ ca vyaracayat*'.[37] Here we can see that these seven *ślokas* are particularly contradictory to the *niṣkāma dharma* proclaimed by Kr̥ṣṇa. Therefore I believe that these are not utterances of the Lord but the opinion of the compilor.

But I must also say that if these are really Kr̥ṣṇa's words, then I do not believe that they should be in harmony with nineteenth century science. I have shown in *Kr̥ṣṇacaritra* that Kr̥ṣṇa carries out his earthly actions through human power, not through divine power. God's assuming a human body cannot be understood except in the context of the development of the ideal of humanity. If Kr̥ṣṇa is God in a human body, then it is impossible for him to act through his divine power instead of his human power; because no human has divine power, and this cannot be a part of the ideal of humans. In a doctrine of *dharma* which is the fruit of only human powers, the scientific truths current three thousand years later cannot be expected. This is not intended by God.

And there is still something else concerning this scientificness. Imagine that God would deign to circulate a new doctrine of *dharma* at present; that he would transcend the science intelligible to contemporary people and, thanks to his omniscience, remain in accord with the state science will be in another three or four thousand years later. In view of the speed of science, it cannot be predicted what will be accomplished by science in another three or four thousand years. Maybe men will then create living humans by forming them with their hands, ride on the waves of ether to visit the *saptarṣimaṇḍala*[38] or the *rohiṇī nakṣatra*,[39] stand on the Himalaya and communicate or fight with grotesque beings from Mars or other planets or satellites, or every now and then go to the solar region in order to accept an invitation for a fiery meal.[40] Just imagine [what would happen if] the Lord, in His omniscience, were to proclaim a new doctrine of *dharma* in accord with this future science and in the language fitting it. If He did so, who would listen? Who would understand? Who would follow it? No-one. Therefore, the utterances of God should be circulated in the language suiting the respective times. Thereafter, together with the gradual increase of human knowledge, this language fitting the ancient times can be suitably interpreted as befits place, time and persons. It is for this reason that, notwithstanding the presence of commentaries on the *Gītā* by world-conquering pundits like Śaṅkara, etc., a stupid person like myself has had the courage to engage in creating a new commentary.

I have given these three answers to the first objection that these seven *ślokas* are tainted by scientific untruth. A second objection may be that the seven *ślokas* are contrary to the *niṣkāma dharma* proclaimed in the *Gītā*. This objection is accurate. As to why this couple of *ślokas* has come here, I have said in the commentary on *śloka* 9 how Śaṅkara and Śrīdhara have answered this question. The answer given by Madhusūdana Sarasvatī appears to be comparatively plausible. The mendicant Śrīkr̥ṣṇaprasanna Sen has explained this in a very detailed way, so I am quoting that portion from his commentary called *Gītārthasandīpanī*:

[37] ['Therein he has written down mostly the very verses uttered by Sri Krishna, composing (only) a few verses of his own to bring out the connection.' (*ŚrBhG*:2 — commentary to *BhG* 1.1)]

[38] *Great Bears* [Lat.].

[39] *Plerades* [*sic*., misprint for *Pleiades*; Lat.].

[40] [*agnibhojan* (Beng.).]

> Through that which Prajāpati has said addressing the *sahayajña*, i.e. the brahmins, kṣatriyas and vaiśyas entitled to *karman* ['sacrifice'], ritualistic action[41] has been proclaimed. But not only has ritualistic action been forbidden by the words *mā karmaphalahetur bhūḥ*, but ritualistic action too is no topic of the *Gītā*. Therefore, Brahmā's words seem to be utterly out of place in this instance; but when we look at it with consideration, this doubt will be removed. Brahmā has not said "Creatures, perform sacrifices with desire for the attainment of fruits." It is his purpose that *karman* [sacrifice] be performed for the sake of duty. But in order to proclaim the divine power that lies hidden in this accomplishment of *karman*, Brahmā said: "Perform regular sacrifices. By their supernatural influence, you will always attain no matter what you desire. Just as people plant the mango-tree for its mangoes but get its shadow and the sweet smell of its buds too without any effort, thus accomplish *karman* for the sake of duty only, but you will attain the fruits of the performance of themselves, even if you do not desire them. The fruits arise through the characteristics of the nature of the action, even without [your] desiring them.'

I think that, like Śaṅkara's and Śrīdhara's answers, this one will also leave my readers unsatisfied. But I do not feel any need for a resolution or dispute. There is a mystery in these seven *ślokas*; I shall point this out and then leave it at that.

The author of the *Gītā* says:

sahayajñāḥ prajāḥ sṛṣṭvā purovāca prajāpatiḥ.[42]

The author of the *Gītā* does not say this from himself. Such a belief was conventional in ancient India. In the *Manusaṃhitā*, there is:

karmātmanānāṃ ca devānāṃ so 'sṛjat prāṇināṃ prabhuḥ
sādhyānāṃ ca gaṇaṃ sūkṣmaṃ yajñaṃ caiva sanātanam. 1.22.[43] Etc.

The gods are satisfied and pleased by the sacrifice and grant the performer of the sacrifice the desired fruit; this is roughly what Vedic *dharma* is about. This is wordly *dharma*.

Now, how must a reformer of *dharma*[44] behave with an already current, ancient wordly *dharma*? There is not, and cannot possibly be, any wordly *dharma* which does not have any relations with superstition.[45] How should someone engaged in reform of *dharma* treat such superstition included in wordly belief?

Some say that it should be eradicated completely. Muhammad had done exactly this, but had not the force of his and the subsequent saints' sword been so great, he would not have succeeded. Jesus Christ himself built the doctrine of *dharma* propagated

[41] [*kāmya karman*.]

[42] This has been translated before.

[43] ['He, the Lord, also created the class of the Gods, who are endowed with life, and whose nature is action; and the subtile class of the Sādhyas, and the eternal Sacrifice.' (Bühler 1886:12.)]

[44] [A more adequate translation would of course be 'religious reformer', *dharma* being obviously used as an equivalent of the term 'religion' in this instance. But since a clear-cut demarcation between this modern usage of the term and its more ancient significance seems difficult to make, and for reasons of transparence, *dharma* has been kept in the translation.]

[45] [*upadharmma* (Beng.).]

by him on the Jewish *dharma*. Afterwards the Christian *dharma* completely removed the ancient superstition from the Roman Empire, the sole reason of which, however, was that the ancient *dharma* of the Roman Empire then had become absolutely lifeless. It is no difficult task to throw away the body of that which is lifeless. On the other hand, Śākyasiṃha's[46] *dharma* never engaged in a war against the ancient *dharma*.

The author of the *Gītā* does not hold a sword in the direction of Vedic *dharma*, either. He knew that the *niṣkāma karmayoga* and *jñānayoga* he spoke of would never be able to occupy the whole place of wordly *dharma*. But if the wordly *dharma* remained intact, through it [i.e. his *dharma*] the purification of that wordly *dharma* would be excellently accomplished. Therefore, he was not inclined to cut off the relationship. We have considered him to be one of those who brought forth a revolt against Vedic *dharma*. But his revolt limits itself to the point of saying that the *dharma* which there is in the Vedas is incomplete, and that is must be completed by *niṣkāma karmayoga*, etc. For this reason he called the Vedic *dharma* [associated] with desire[47] inferior. But he does not say that, being inferior, it is utterly lacking merit. I shall explain what the author of the *Gītā* says about its merits here.

Those who perform actions (everybody performs actions) can be divided into three categories. Firstly, those who perform action desirelessly, and who through *niṣkāma karmayoga* have entered the path of knowledge; they are referred to as '*ātmaratī*' or '*ātmārāma*' in *śloka* 17. Secondly, those who perform action exclusively for the pleasure of their senses; they have been designated as '*indriyārāma*' in *śloka* 16. Apart from these, there are people of the third category who perform sacrifices and eat the residues thereof, according to the conventional *dharma*. The *ślokas* 10-15 are about them. They can at least be praised for not being '*indriyārāma*'; they behave according to conventional *dharma*. Although their *dharma* is only superstition, they are worshippers of God all the same, because God is established in the sacrifice. We shall later on understand the significance of this. We shall see that Kṛṣṇa says there is no God except Himself. Those who worship any other god worship Him. He has called that worship unlawful. But still, even that is His worship, and it is He who gives its fruit, as He has said, too.

Now it is to be asked whose opinion is more generous: [that of] those who say that unlawful worship is the path to eternal hell, or [that of] those who say that any worship is acceptable for God, no matter whether it is lawful or unlawful? What is lawful and what is unlawful depends on knowledge. Whose opinion is more generous: [that of] those who say that the worshipper is abandoned by the Lord for lack of knowledge, or [that of] those who say that God does not measure knowledge but looks at the feeling in the worshipper's heart? Who shall go to heaven: he who says that eternal hell results of not worshipping the formless, or he who worships the way he understands?

The Ganges, the *Caspian Sea* [Lat.] and our Lāl'dīghi,[48] all are water. But water is neither the Ganges, nor the Caspian Sea, nor this Lāl'dīghi. Saying 'Water is extremely necessary for human life' never means that the Ganges is extremely necessary for human life, or that the Caspian Sea is extremely necessary for it, or that the

[46] [the Buddha's.]

[47] [*sakāma.*]

[48] [A lake in the Calcutta area.]

Lāl'dīghi is necessary for it. Thus the argument that, since Viṣṇu is the sacrifice because Viṣṇu is all-pervading, 'for the sake of Viṣṇu' must consequently signify 'for the sake of sacrifice', is a fallacy.

Let us see now whether any other meaning can be intended by Śaṅkara. No other intention can be found out; however, at least something is obtained in my quotation from the *Śatapathabrāhmaṇa*.[49] The significance of it is the following: Indra and the other gods performed a sacrifice on Kurukṣetra. Viṣṇu was one among these gods. In that sacrifice, he attained priority over the other gods, and therefore has come to be known as '*yajña*'. Therefore, that [i.e. the Vedic] Viṣṇu is not God. He is just one among all the other deities,[50] and initially equal to all the other deities. The interpretation made by Śaṅkarācārya runs '*yajño vai viṣṇur iti śruter yajña īśvaraḥ*'.[51] Now for those who have said that, if one accepts '*yajño vai viṣṇuḥ*', [then] the *yajña* is God — that this is said in the Vedas can by no means be accepted.

It is doubtful whether any pundit like Śaṅkara has been born in India during the last two thousand years. At present, there is no-one in India worthy of carrying his shoes. But, considering place, time and person, we must remember that he believed, or was bound to believe, that the whole *Gītā* from beginning to end has issued from the lotus of Kr̥ṣṇa's mouth. Consequently, he could not dare even to utter that there are words of others or some patchwork here. If, on the other hand, he takes the conventional meaning of *yajña*, then the Vedic rituals, i.e. action with desire, are encouraged. A contradiction is produced thereby, because so far Kr̥ṣṇa has censured action with desire and sanctioned desireless action. Therefore, it was particularly necessary here to take 'God' as the meaning of *yajña*. But even after saying so, in the following couple of *ślokas* there was no escape; in those, *yajña* had to be explained as ritualistic action. As to the reason why there are such rules of ritualistic action in the *Gītā*, Śaṅkarācārya has said that a person not knowing the *ātman* should first perform *karmayoga* in order to become worthy of the state of knowledge of the *ātman*. For this, arguments like '*na karmaṇām anārambhāt*', etc., have been used before; but it is being said that there are many faults if a person not knowing the *ātman*[52] does not perform actions.

Śrīdhara Svāmin follows Śaṅkarācārya. In the commentary on *śloka* 9, he has understood 'God' to be the meaning of *yajña*. He says that, normally, ritualistic action is superior to non-action (devoidness of action); for this reason the succeeding *ślokas* have been said.

The reader can learn below what these succeeding *ślokas* are.[53] If, before getting involved in their interpretation, anyone among us is not inclined to accept Śaṅkarācārya's interpretation of the word *yajña* in the ninth *śloka*, then it is our duty to search for another, real meaning of it.

What is the harm in taking the basic meaning of the word *yajña* here? The root

[49] [Refers to the commentary on *BhG* 1.1.]

[50] [*ār pā̃c'ṭā debatār madhye ek jan mātra* (Beng.).]

[51] [Cf. Baṅkim's commentary on *BhG* 3.9.]

[52] [*anātmajñān* (Beng.): a *bahuvrīhi* meaning 'he whose knowledge of the *ātman* is not'.]

[53] [This reference is unclear, since Śrīdhara quite obviously speaks of the *ślokas* 10-16, while Baṅkim means the *ślokas* from 17 onwards.]

yaj [is employed] in the sense of worship of a deity.[54] Thus the basic meaning of *yajña* is worship of a deity. Where the worship of many deities is accepted, there the adoration of all deities is *yajña*. But where all deities are contained in one God, as for instance:

> *'ye 'py anyadevatābhaktā yajante śraddhayānvitāḥ*
> *te 'pi mām eva kaunteya yajanty avidhipūrvakam.'* 23 (*Gītā*, Ch. 9),[55]

there the worship of God is meant by *yajña*. This is exactly what the Lord Himself has said:

> *'ahaṃ hi sarvayajñānāṃ bhoktā ca prabhur eva.'* 24 (*Gītā*, Ch. 9)[56]

In this way, the root *yaj* and the word *yajña* have again and again been used in the sense of worship of God. There are three examples [of this] in the *ślokas* quoted above. Many more can be given:

> *'bhūtāni yānti bhūtejyā yānti madyājino 'pi mām.'* (*Gītā*, 25, Ch.9)[57]
> *'yajñānāṃ japayajño 'smi sthāvarāṇāṃ himālayaḥ.'* (*Gītā*, 25, Ch.10)[58]

Many uses of the word *yajña* in the sense of worship to God can also be observed in other books, as for example in the *Mahābhārata*:

> *'vākyajñenārcito* [*sic.*] *devaḥ prīyatāṃ me janārdana.'* (*Śāntiparvan*, Chapter 47 [*Mbh* 12.47.63])[59]

Now what is there to be said against understanding the word *yajña* in this *śloka* as worship[60] of God? In doing that, the *śloka* maintains an appropriate as well as a coherent sense.

Still, there are some objections regarding the adoption of this meaning[61] of the word *yajña*. One objection is this: In a number of *ślokas* following this *śloka*, the word *yajña* has been used; there it has no such denotation as 'God'. In employments as *'sahayajñāḥ prajāḥ'*, *'yajñabhāvitāḥ devāḥ'*, *'yajñaśiṣṭāśinaḥ'*, *'yajñakarmasamudbhavaḥ'*, *'yajñe pratiṣṭhitam'*, etc., the word *yajña* cannot mean 'God' or 'Viṣṇu'. It is completely impossible that after using the word *yajña* in one sense in *śloka* 9, it should be used right afterwards in a different sense in the *ślokas* 10, 12, 13, 14, and 15. Even a mediocre writer does not do this; that the author of the *Gītā* should do so is absolutely impossible. Either the author of the *Gītā* is extremely unskilled in writing, or the interpretation of the word *yajña* by Śaṅkara and others is wrong. Neither of these two can be accepted. But if they cannot, then we must admit that either the word *yajña* is used in only one sense from *śloka* 9 to *śloka* 15, or that there is a patchwork after *śloka* 9.

Firstly, it can be seen that *yajña* is not a name of Viṣṇu. It is nowhere in the

[54] [*deb'pūjārthe* (Beng.).]

[55] ['Even all those who are devotees of other gods and worship them faithfully, etc., worship me alone, O Kaunteya, (although) without proper injunctions.']

[56] ['I am indeed the enjoyer and the Lord of all sacrifices.']

[57] ['The worshippers of the spirits go to the spirits, all my worshippers on their part go to me.' — Misprinted as *Ch.10* in *ŚBhG(a)*:755.]

[58] ['Among the *yajñas* I am *japa*, among the immovable (things) I am the Himālaya.']

[59] ['The god venerated by the *vāg-yajña* has to be pleased by me, O Janārdana.' Misprinted as *vākjajña* in *ŚBhG[a]*:756]

[60] [*ārādhanā* (Beng.)]

[61] [This obviously refers to the meaning accepted by Śaṅkara and Śrīdhara, and not to the one just proposed by Baṅkim himself.]

dictionaries that *yajña* is a name of Viṣṇu, neither is there such a use elsewhere. If I say 'O *yajña*', nobody will understand that I am calling 'O Viṣṇu'. Instead of the phrase 'the ten avatāras of Viṣṇu', it can never be said 'the ten avatāras of *yajña*'. People will laugh if one says '*yajña* is the one holding conch, discus, club and lotus, wearing a garland of wild flowers'. Why then does Śaṅkarācārya say that Viṣṇu is the meaning of *yajña*? He has told us why he says so: '*yajño vai viṣṇur iti śruteḥ*',[62] i.e. 'It is in the Vedas that *yajña* is Viṣṇu'.

It is said in the *Śatapathabrāhmaṇa*[63] that Agni, Indra, Soma, Magha, Viṣṇu and the other gods had performed a sacrifice on Kurukṣetra. At the time of the sacrifice they made a vow that the one amongst them who, by effort, austerities, faith, sacrifices and oblations, would be able to obtain the fruit of the sacrifice first, would be the best among them. Viṣṇu managed to do so first; he became the best of the gods. I am quoting from the *Śatapathabrāhmaṇa*:

> '*tad viṣṇuḥ prathamaḥ prāpa. sa devānāṃ śreṣṭho 'bhavat. tasmād āhur viṣṇur devānāṃ śreṣṭha iti. saḥ* [*sic.*] *yaḥ sa viṣṇur yajñaḥ saḥ. saḥ* [*sic.*] *yaḥ sa yajño 'sau sa ādityaḥ.*'[64]

Meaning: Viṣṇu got it first. He became the best of the gods. Therefore one says that Viṣṇu [is he] who is the best of the gods; he is Viṣṇu, he is *yajña*. He who is that *yajña* is *Āditya*.

Again in the *Taittirīyasaṃhitā*, there is such an explanation of the word *śipiviṣṇāya*: '*yajño vai viṣṇuḥ paśavaḥ śipiḥ. yajña eva paśuṣu pratitiṣṭhati.*'[65] Bhaṭṭa Bhāskara Miśra has also written '*yajño vai viṣṇuḥ paśavaḥ śipir iti śruteḥ.*'[66]

So Śaṅkara's statement is correct: The *yajña* has been called Viṣṇu in the *Śruti*. But in what sense? One meaning can be that Viṣṇu is the *yajña* because he is all-pervading. Bhaṭṭa Bhāskara Miśra has said this too. He says: '[*yajño vai*] *viṣṇuḥ paśavaḥ śipir iti śrute[ḥ] sarvaprāṇādyantaryāmitvena praviṣṭa ity arthaḥ.*'[67]

When searching in this *Gītā*, it can be found:

> '*ahaṃ kratur ahaṃ yajñaḥ svadhāham aham auṣadham*
> *mantro 'ham aham evājyam aham agnir ahaṃ hutam.*' (*Gītā*, Ch. 9, 16)

I am *Kratu*, I am the *yajña*, I am the oblation to the ancestors,[68] I am the medicine, I am the *mantra*, I am the clarified butter, I am the fire, I am that which is offered.

If this is so, then Viṣṇu is *yajña*, but the *yajña* is not Viṣṇu. Viṣṇu is all-pervading, therefore he is the *mantra*, the clarified butter, the fire; but neither is the *mantra* Viṣṇu, nor the clarified butter or the fire. Thus if it is true that Viṣṇu is the *yajña*, but the *yajña* is not Viṣṇu, then Śaṅkarācārya's interpretation does not work.

62 [Cf. *ŚBhG*, 3.9.]

63 14.1.1. [*sic.*; Muir 1868-73,IV:124 gives xiv,1,1,1ff.]

64 [Muir 1868-73,IV:124 gives xiv,1,1,5-6.]

65 I have taken this from the *Muir* [Lat.]-collection. But there is a little reason for doubt. [Muir 1868-73,IV:504 translates: '"Vishṇu" means sacrifice, and "Śipi" means victims; for sacrifice depends upon victims.']

66 [Muir 1868-73,IV:505n.: '(It is) in the *Śruti* that "Viṣṇu means sacrifice, and *śipi* means victims"'.]

67 [Fragmentary quotation from Muir 1868-73,IV:505. Translation: '*yajño vai viṣṇuḥ paśavaḥ śipir* is from the *śruti*; the meaning (of it is:) present through the all-pervasiveness in all creatures, etc.']

68 [*svadhā*.]

yas tv ātmaratir eva syād ātmatṛptaś ca mānavaḥ
ātmany eva ca santuṣṭas tasya kāryaṃ na vidyate. (17)

The human who finds pleasure in the *ātman*, who is self-contented and satisfied with the *ātman*, has no action. (17)

Humans are of two kinds: firstly those given to sensual pleasure [*indriyārāma*] (vide *śloka* 16),[69] and those contented with the Self [*ātmārāma*]. He is an *ātmārāma* who is in the state of being given to the knowledge of the *ātman*; the *sāṃkhyayoga* is for him. This *śloka* deals with him.

It has been said before that no-one can ever be without performing action even for a moment. Without action, not even one's vital functions are maintained. Now, on the other hand, it is being said that certain persons have no action. Consequently, a special kind of *karman* or *kārya* must be understood. Action with desire of the Vedas, etc., is intended here. The general intention[70] is that the knower of the doctrine of the *ātman* has no need for the sacrifices, etc., mentioned above.

naiva tasya kṛtenārtho nākṛteneha kaścana
na cāsya sarvabhūteṣu kaścid arthavyapāśrayaḥ. (18)

He has no need for action, and there is also no harm in not performing actions. He has no need to take refuge with anyone amongst all beings. (18)

tasmād asaktaḥ satataṃ kāryaṃ karma samācara
asakto hy ācaran karma[71] *param āpnoti pūruṣaḥ.* (19)

Therefore always perform action to be executed being *asakta*. If a man performs actions being *asakta*, he attains liberation. (19)

'*asakta*' means 'devoid of attachment', i.e. 'devoid of the desire for fruits'. The reader will notice that when he leaves out [the portion] after *ślokas* 8 or 9 up to 18 while reading, the word *tasmāt* (therefore) fits very well. It does [however] not seem to be especially coherent after the number of *ślokas* in between in whose interpretation so much confusion has arisen. In *śloka* 8 it has been said that if you perform no action, even your vital functions cannot be maintained. In *śloka* 9 it has been said that except in the case of worship to God, action is only a cause of bondage. Therefore, act unattachedly; by that action which is without attachment for the worship of God, man attains liberation. This right meaning results from reading *śloka* 8, then *śloka* 9, then *śloka* 19. The nine *ślokas* in between seem somewhat unconnected. But it is not so that these few intervening *ślokas* cannot be explained. I have demonstrated this above. Consequently, I do not dare to say that these nine *ślokas* are interpolated.

[69] [Erroneous indication: both editions have *śloka* 15 here.]

[70] [*bhābārtha* (Beng.).]

[71] [Error: *karma* left out in the original.]

karmaṇaiva hi saṃsiddhim āsthitā janakādayaḥ
lokasaṃgraham evāpi sampaśyan kartum arhasi. (20)

Janaka and others have attained perfection through action. You too should perform action with a view to *lokasaṃgraha*. (20)

The commentators understand this word *lokasaṃgraha* as the incitation of the people for *dharma* through an example. Śrīdhara says that *lokasaṃgraha* is the incitation of the people for *dharma*, that is, the protection of the people, namely: 'If I act, all will act; if I do not, the ignorant will follow the example of the wise and stray from the right path[72] by giving up their *svadharma*.' Śaṅkara too has explained like this. Śaṅkarācārya says that *lokasaṃgraha* is the prevention of the people's inclination for deviation [from the right path]. The author of the *Gītā* makes this clear in the following *śloka*.

yad yad ācarati śreṣṭhas tat tad evetaro janaḥ
sa yat pramāṇaṃ kurute lokas tad anuvartate. (21)

Whatever actions the best people practise, the other people also do. Whatever they regard as authoritative will be followed by the people. (21)

It has been said before that people knowing the *ātman* have no *karman*. Now it is said that even if they have no *karman*, they must perform actions [*karman*]. Because if they do not perform actions, the common people who do not know the *ātman* will follow their example and desist from action, too. If they desist from action, they will deviate from their respective *dharmas*. Thus all should perform actions.

The best personalities of India were followers of the path of knowledge. Having decided that the followers of the path of knowledge have no action, they had lost the respect for action. And it is by following this example that the whole of India, devoid of the passion for action and therefore filled with passive[73] people, has incurred this state of degeneration. If the Indians had kept in mind the harmony or unification of the doctrine of action and the doctrine of knowledge proclaimed by the Lord in the above-mentioned maxim, and had acted according to it, if both knowledge and action had equally been their goals; they would never have fallen into the present state of inferiority to more civilised nations.[74] They would not have become subjugated, dependent on others and endangered by the education given by another nation.

It is not so that Kṛṣṇa has praised the greatness of action only in the *Gītā*; He has done so also in the *Saṃjayayānaparvādhyāya* in the *Udyogaparvan* of the *Mahābhārata* [5.29.4-13]. I have quoted this in another book; I will do so here too:

> Despite the existence of the rule prescribed by the Śāstras that one should spend one's life with the study of the Vedas, being pure and the protector of one's kinsmen, the brahmins get all sorts of ideas. Some grant that they

[72] [Literally: 'become fallen'.]

[73] [*akarmā* (Beng.).]

[74] [*jāti* (Beng.).]

obtain liberation through action,[75] others that they obtain it only through the knowledge of the Vedas by renouncing action. But just as without eating satisfaction cannot be obtained, likewise liberation cannot be attained by brahmins only knowing the Vedas and not performing actions. Only the learning by which action is accomplished is fruitful; learning in which there is no rule for the performance of action, is absolutely fruitless. Therefore, as the thirst of a thirsty person is appeased as soon as he drinks, so is it a duty to perform all those actions whose fruits become manifest in the present life. O Saṃjaya, this rule has been prescribed on account of action; thus action is the most important.[76] All actions will fail of a person who considers any other thing to be superior to action.
Look, the devas have gained power through action. Through action, the wind constantly moves about; through action, the sun runs its course tirelessly by day and by night; through action, the moon, encompassed by the stars, rises during the half of a month; through action, the fire accomplishes the work[77] of the people and incessantly gives heat; through action, the earth easily carries the heaviest weight; through action, all the streams accomplish the satisfaction of the creatures by carrying masses of water. Indra, the immeasurably powerful king of the devas, performed *brahmacarya* in order to gain priority among the devas. Through the power of that action, he lets rain fall from the ten directions and the skies, and he has attained sovereignty over the devas, by reaching excellence in steadfastly immersing the desire for enjoyment and giving up all dear objects, and practising self-control, forgiveness, equanimity, truth and *dharma*. Lord Bṛhaspati, absorbed in meditation and subduing his senses, performed *brahmacarya*, and thereby obtained his position as the master of the devas. Rudra, the Ādityas, Yama, Kuvera, the Gandharvas, the Yakṣas, the Apsarās, the Viśvāvasus and the stars are resplendent through the power of action, and the Maharṣis have attained excellence through the performance of *brahmacarya* and other rites.[78]

Having said that acting is also a duty for persons knowing the *ātman*, the Lord speaks of Himself in order to further clarify the importance of attachment to action:

na me pārthāsti kartavyaṃ triṣu lokeṣu kiṃcana
nānavāptam avāptavyaṃ varta eva ca karmaṇi. (22)

yadi hy ahaṃ na varteyaṃ jātu karmaṇy atandritaḥ
mama vartmānuvartante manuṣyāḥ pārtha sarvaśaḥ. (23)

O Pārtha, there is nothing at all I am obliged to do in these three worlds. There is nothing at all unattained and nothing at all to be attained; all the same, I continuously perform actions. (22)

75 [*karmmabaśataḥ*.]

76 [*sarbapradhān* (Beng.).]

77 [*karman*.]

78 [From *Kṛṣṇacaritra* (*BR* II: 532f.)]

If I ever cease to be untiring in action and cease to act, then, O Pārtha, all humans will in every way follow my path. (23)

Here the speaker is God, the Lord of the world, Himself. The Lord has no needs, no transformations, no pleasure and pain, and thus no *karman*.[79] He has created the world, and also the laws which run the world; the world is run by the power of those laws, and there is no necessity of His interference.[80] Therefore He has no *karman*. But if He incarnates Himself in a human body in order to circulate the ideal of humanity, then, submitted to human *dharma*,[81] He also has *karman*. Although He can meet all needs by His divine power, He nevertheless has to meet them by *karman* because of the submission to human laws. He is the ideal man, and consequently also the ideal *karmin*.[82] So if He ever is overcome by idleness and does not perform *karman*, the people too, in their pursuance of the example of the ideal man, will become idle and unconcentrated in *karman*. Anyone who is idle and unconcentrated in *karman* decays. So the Lord says again:

utsīdeyur ime lokā na kuryāṃ karma ced aham
saṃkarasya ca kartā syām upahanyām imāḥ prajāḥ. (24)

If I do not act, I shall ruin all these worlds, I shall create *saṃkara* and shall be the cause of the pollution of the people. (24)

The commentators took this word *saṃkara* to mean 'mixture of *varṇas*'. The Hindus are extremely zealous in maintaining the purity of caste; for this reason, the ancient Hindus believed that the admixture of castes was a detestable social crime. Manu says that the mean mixture of castes is the reason for destruction of nation and kingdom, and it is there even in this *Gītā*:

'*saṃkaro narakāyaiva kulaghnānāṃ kulasya ca.*' [*BhG* 1.42]

But we cannot all of a sudden understand why, in the presence of so many worse evils, precisely this fear of the genesis of a mixture of castes through God's idleness should be so strong. We cannot interpret anything to the effect that God, or Kṛṣṇa, forbids the mixture of castes by grabbing brahmins and sending them to brahmin women, kṣatriyas to kṣatriya women, vaiśyas to vaiśya women, and śūdras to śūdra women. Why is Kṛṣṇa so preoccupied with the mixture of *varṇas* while remaining completely silent about famine, war, decline of population, country-wide diseases, murder, theft, and the disappearance of *dharma* [in the form of] charity, austerities, etc., through the idleness of God? It can even be proved that a majority of mixed population is favourable to modern society. Thus, if one interprets *saṃkara* as the mixture of *varṇas*, the meaning of this *śloka* does not become accessible to our simple minds.

But there is no certainty in the Sanskrit language as to whether *saṃkara* must be understood as the mixture of *varṇas*. *Saṅkara* means 'meeting', 'mixture'. Mixing [*sāṃ*-

[79] [In this instance, *karman* appears to encompass, besides 'action', the concept of accumulated *karman*. For this reason the term is left untranslated here.]

[80] [*hastakṣepaṇ* (Beng.), literally the 'throwing of the hand'.]

[81] [*manuṣyadharmin*.]

[82] ['agent'.]

the Lord first instructed him in knowledge. Then He explained the importance and compulsoriness of action. He explained that all have to act. Even if not acting otherwise, actions have to be performed to maintain the vital functions. However, the ignorant person, who has no knowledge of the *ātman*, acts with the desire for the fruits, and the knower of the *ātman* acts desirelessly; but no matter whether it be with or without desire, action to be executed [*anuṣṭheya karman*] has to be performed. And if it must be performed, then it is better to perform it desirelessly, for desireless action is the highest *dharma*. [']Thus fight desirelessly with an unperturbed mind, having abandoned the desire for fruits, not worrying whether sovereignty will be attained or not, and surrendering success and failure to God; because for a kṣatriya, war is due action.[']

ye me matam idaṃ nityam anutiṣṭhanti mānavāḥ
śraddhāvanto 'nasūyanto mucyante te 'pi karmabhiḥ. (31)

All the humans who, being respectful and devoid of jealousy, always practise this doctrine of mine, shall become free from action, i.e. free from bearing the fruits of action.

ye tv etad abhyasūyanto[86] *nānutiṣṭhanti me matam*
sarvajñānavimūḍhāṃs tān viddhi naṣṭān acetasaḥ. (32)

Know those to be totally deluded in their knowledge, corrupted and thoughtless, who, falling prey to jealousy, do not practise this doctrine of mine. (32)

sadṛśaṃ ceṣṭate svasyāḥ prakṛter jñānavān api
prakṛtiṃ yānti bhūtāni nigrahaḥ kiṃ kariṣyati. (33)

Even the wise endeavours, in a way, conform to *prakṛti*. The creatures follow the *prakṛti*. Restraint does not yield any results. (33)

indriyasyendriyasyārthe rāgadveṣau vyavasthitau
tayor na vaśam āgacchet tau hy asya paripanthinau. (34)

Attachments and aversions of the senses are fixed in the sense-objects. Do not come under their influence, for they are hindrances to the superior path. (34)

śreyān svadharmo viguṇaḥ paradharmāt svanuṣṭhitāt
svadharme nidhanaṃ śreyaḥ paradharmo bhayāvahaḥ. (35)

Even the incomplete fulfilment of *svadharma* is better than the complete fulfilment of *paradharma* [someone else's *dharma*]. Rather, even death through one's *svadharma* is better; *paradharma* is terrifying. (35)

I will now explain the significance of what has been said in the three *ślokas* 33, 34 and 35. It has been mentioned before that all are governed by their *prakṛti*. He who is wise

[86] [Misprinted as *abhyasūyantyo* in *ŚBhG(a)*:761.]

also performs actions that are in conformity with his own *svabhāva*.[87] No-one can be entrusted with or skilled in action contradicting his *svabhāva*, not even through prohibition or torment. But if a person is overpowered by the senses, then he gives up his *svadharma* and follows *paradharma*. I have explained before what *svadharma* is. It cannot be interpreted that the *svadharma* is the *varṇāśramadharma*, because then this teaching becomes inapplicable to all those societies in which there is no *varṇāśrama*. But the *dharma* of the Lord is universal, a means of protection and succour for each and every human. Therefore, *svadharma* must be understood in the following way: One's *svadharma* is that which one has accepted as one's action to be executed in this life. The difference between societies in which the *varṇāśramadharma* is conventional, and societies in which it is not, is that those following the *varṇāśramadharma* are bound by hereditary tradition to adopt one certain kind of action as their action to be executed. In other societies, people get engaged in action according to their respective liking, inclination, opportunity and capacity. The *svadharma* is in conformity with people because of its being in accord with liking and inclination, or because of its being a life-long habit. But it can often be observed that people are overcome by their senses and deluded by the greed for riches, etc., and follow *paradharma*. Often they must suffer severe misfortunes. The ancient commentators consider this misfortune to be relating to the next world. But we can see again and again that the abandonment of one's *svadharma* and adoption of *paradharma* are a cause of misfortune in this world, too. Only those men who stick to their *svadharma*, make determined efforts to perform it and accept even death for its fulfilment, are famous as heroes in this life; and if they succeed in performing their *svadharma*, they attain true happiness in this life. But it has not been observed that anyone following *paradharma*, i.e. getting involved in action that is not to be executed by him, has been able to be happy or renowned, even if succeeding in it. Therefore, even the incomplete performance of one's *svadharma* is better than the complete performance of *paradharma*. In fact, even death through one's *svadharma* is preferable; *paradharma* is even then not to be followed.

arjuna uvāca:
atha kena prayukto 'yaṃ pāpaṃ carati pūruṣaḥ
anicchann api vārṣṇeya balād iva niyojitaḥ. (36)

[Arjuna said:]
O Vārṣṇeya, what induces a man to commit sins? By whose direction is he forcibly made to commit sins[88] despite his unwillingness? (36)

Mention was made above that from sense-objects, attachment or aversion to the senses will necessarily arise. Such a statement means that a man deviates from his *svadharma* even against his will. Arjuna is asking here why it thus happens. Who makes it so?

śrībhagavān uvāca:
kāma eṣa krodha eṣa rajoguṇasamudbhavaḥ
mahāśano mahāpāpmā viddhy enam iha vairiṇam. (37)

87 ['inherent nature', 'character'.]

88 [Actually: '... what induces a man to commit sins, directed as if by force, despite...'.]

The Lord said:
It is desire [*kāma*]. It is anger. It stems from the *guṇa rajas*, is voracious and extremely fierce.[89] Consider it your enemy in this life. (37)

Let us first clarify the meanings of all the words. What the *guṇa rajas* is shall be said elsewhere. Voracious [*mahāśana*] means someone who eats too much. Desire is hard to satisfy; thus voracious.

The reader shall see that both desire and anger have been mentioned; but the singular has been used. This signifies that desire and anger are one; the subject is not two separate enemies.[90] The commentators have explained that desire, when *pratihata*, i.e. obstructed, is transformed into anger, and that, therefore, desire and anger are identical.

However, the matter is that the performance of one's *svadharma* is best, but that not all people are capable of it. Because *svabhāva* is strong; overcome by their *svabhāva*, people become unwilling, pursue others' *dharma*, and commit sins. The reason for this is the power of desire. If one does not take *kāma* to be a particular enemy but the usual desire for objects of every sense, then the true, liberal significance of all these *ślokas* can be understood.

I shall use the following three examples from national and international history as a proof of the truth and universality of the words of the Lord.

Firstly, the king's *svadharma*: governing the kingdom and preserving the subjects. He is no propagator or controller of *dharma*. I am using the word *dharma* in the sense of *Religion* [Lat.] here. But the terrifying evils that came over mankind through the adoption of control over *dharma* by the rulers in mediaeval Europe, are well-known in history. As examples, it will suffice to mention only the following three names: *St. Bartholomew*, *Sicilian Vespers* and the Spanish *Inquisition* [all Engl.]. It is said that in the country of the *Netherland*[s] [Lat.] alone, one million people had to give their lives, at the time of Charles V, merely for following a *dharma* other than the king. If today in India in the British Empire, the king had such inclinations of following another *dharma*,[91] how many Hindus would there be left?

The second example is in the initial stage of British rule in Bengal. A king's *dharma* is the *kṣatriyadharma*. Trade is the vaiśya's *dharma*. The king had then taken up the *vaiśyadharma*; the *East India Company* [Lat.] had become traders. The result of it was the destruction of Bengal's industries, trade and wealth. Bengal's cotton stuff, jute stuff, silk, brass, white brass — all went to the realm of destruction. Some [branches of] domestic trade vanished completely, some fell into the hands of others; Bengal sank into such an ocean of poverty that it has not arisen again. The Company, too, finally had to leave trade. Men give up everything except opium. Opium is the rest of that trade.

The third example is the American women's recent abandonment of their *svadharma*
and the engagement in male action. This brings about various kinds of material[92] con-

[89] [*atyugra* (Beng.); no equivalent of the Sanskrit *mahāpāpman* ('extremely sinful').]

[90] [*scil.* vices.]

[91] [*paradharma*.]

[92] [*baiṣayik* (Beng.).]

flicts among women, disorder in the home, and a national loss of happiness.[93] Remembering the woman incapable of breast-feeding the child conceived in her womb, the Hindu-woman desiring to perform *satī*[94] shall definitely say:

svadharme nidhanaṃ śreyaḥ paradharmo bhayāvahaḥ.[95]

dhūmenāvriyate vahnir yathādarśo malena ca
yatholbeṇāvṛto garbhas tathā tenedam āvṛtam. (38)

Just as fire is covered by smoke, a mirror by *mala*, and the embryo by the womb, likewise (knowledge) is covered by desire. (38)

The word 'knowledge' [*jñāna*] is not present in the original; there is 'this' [*idam*] instead of it. But in the succeeding *śloka* the word 'knowledge' is the object of covering; therefore, the translation of this *śloka* has been treated alike. It has been said in *śloka* 33 that even the one possessing knowledge endeavours according to his nature:

'sadṛśaṃ ceṣṭate svasyāḥ prakṛter jñānavān api'.

Why does one possessing knowledge do so even when knowledge is present? As an explanation of this He says that knowledge is covered by this desire; in this state, knowledge becomes inefficient.

The three comparisons are very excellent; but before explaining their device, we must say [something]. Śaṅkarācārya interprets the word *'mala'* as *'mala'*, i.e. *mal* [Beng.: 'dirt'] [*sic.*]. But Śrīdhara Svāmin says that *'malena'* means *'āgantukena'*.[96] In this case, it must be understood that the reflection in the mirror is intended by the word *'mala'*.

Let us look at the three comparisons. Both comparatus and comparandus are natural. The natural cover of fire is smoke; where there is a mirror, some image or reflection will be there, otherwise its mirrorness is not existent; and the natural cover of a foetus too is the womb. Likewise, desire as a cover of knowledge is natural. This has been said before. Both the comparandus and the comparatus[97] are characterised by exposure.[98] Fire, a mirror and a womb are all characterised by exposure; likewise, knowledge is characterised by exposure. A certain deed is necessary for exposure. The cover of smoke is destroyed by blowing, etc., that of reflexion by removal, and that of the embryo by giving birth; then fire, the mirror and the baby are exposed; in the same way, the cover of desire is destroyed by controlling the senses, and knowledge is exposed. We shall see this in *śloka* 41.

āvṛtaṃ jñānam etena jñānino nityavairiṇā
kāmarūpeṇa kaunteya duṣpūreṇānalena ca. (39)

93 [*jātīya sukhahāni* (Beng.).]

94 [I.e. offer their lives on their husbands' burning cremation pyre.]

95 [3.35.]

96 ['by that which is about to come (from outside)'.]

97 [I.e. comparatus and comparandus to the three things referred to above on the one hand, and to *jñāna* on the other.]

98 [*prakāśātmak* (Beng.).]

O Kaunteya, in the form of desire, insatiable and comparable to fire, the eternal enemy of those who possess knowledge keeps knowledge covered. (39)

Desire is the eternal enemy of those who possess knowledge. [It is] the eternal enemy because it gives pleasure at the time of enjoyment, gives pleasure as consequences and inclines one to search for that which is unnecessary even at the time of enjoyment.[99] It is insatiable, for it cannot be satiated by anything; it is a cause of agony and thus comparable to fire.

indriyāṇi mano buddhir asyādhiṣṭhānam ucyate
etair vimohayaty eṣa jñānam āvṛtya dehinam. (40)

It has been said that all the senses, *manas* and *buddhi* are its residence. Keeping knowledge covered, it (desire) deludes the *ātman* through all these. (40)

What does this desire resort to? To all the senses, the mind and the intellect. It is separate from the *ātman*. It cannot resort to the *ātman*. It keeps the *ātman* deluded.

tasmāt tvam indriyāṇy ādau niyamya bharatarṣabha
pāpmānaṃ prajahi hy enaṃ jñānavijñānanāśanam. (41)

Therefore, O Best of the *Bharatas*, first control the senses, and then destroy (or abandon) desire in the form of sin destroying *jñāna* and *vijñāna*. (41)

If the senses are the field of residence of desire, then the senses must be controlled first. By this, desire will be destroyed.

What is the difference between *jñāna* and *vijñāna*? Śrīdhara says that *jñāna* is concerned with the *ātman* and *vijñāna* derived from the Śāstras, or '*jñāna* is born from the teaching of *Śāstric* teachers, *vijñāna* from deep meditation'.[100] Śaṅkarācārya says: '*Jñāna* is the obstruction of the *ātman*, etc., obtained from the Śāstras through teachers. And a special realisation of this is *vijñāna*.' The reader will accept the explanation by Śrīdhara Svāmin as more lucid than this explanation. I think that it is enough for people such as ourselves to understand this much, namely, that desire in every way obstructs knowledge and the progress of the *ātman*.

indriyāṇi parāṇy āhur indriyebhyaḥ paraṃ manaḥ
manasas tu parā buddhir buddher yaḥ paratas tu saḥ. (42)

evaṃ buddheḥ paraṃ buddhvā saṃstabhyātmānam ātmanā
jahi śatruṃ mahābāho kāmarūpaṃ durāsadam. (43)

The senses are said to be superior; the *manas* is superior to all the senses; the *buddhi* is superior to the *manas*; and He is superior to the *buddhi*. (42)

99 The commentators speak thus.

100 [*nididhyāsajāta*.]

Thus understanding the *paramātman* by the *buddhi* and making yourself motionless, O Mighty-armed One, conquer the enemy in the shape of desire who is hard to approach [*durāsada*].[101] (43)

The reader should first concentrate on *śloka* 42. It is difficult to understand in translation.

It is being said that the senses are held[102] to be superior, the *manas* superior to the senses, etc. But to what are the senses superior? The commentators say, to the body, etc. This is the intention of the *śloka* indeed, but the modern reader might ask whether the senses are independent of the body, etc.

So we first have to understand what the senses are. Philosophy[103] says that there are five senses of knowledge [*jñānendriya*], i.e. sight, hearing, etc., five senses [organs] of action [*karmendriya*], namely, hands, feet, etc., and the *manas* as the inner sense. But in this *śloka*, the mind is described as separate from the senses. Therefore, only the senses of knowledge and action are intended here.

What is it by which they are superior to the body, etc.? The commentators say that all the senses are subtle and exposing, and that the body, etc., are perceptible by the senses. But this is only true of the senses of knowledge. And the senses of knowledge are not independent of the body. However, the commentators have clearly intended gross matter or gross elements by the term *dehādi*.[104] The statement is basically that the senses are superior to the sense-objects.

The intention of the speaker can be discovered by focusing attention on the word *āhuḥ*,[105] which is in the original. The speaker does not state that this is his own opinion, but that it has been so said. Who has said so? As soon as one recalls the *Sāṃkhya*-philosophy one can find an answer to this question. I will explain this.

In the *Sāṃkhya*-philosophy, all entities are divided into 25 *gaṇas* [groups]. In their serial order, the 25 *gaṇas* are:

1. *prakṛti*.
2. *mahat*.
3. *ahaṃkāra*.
4-19. Five *tanmātras* and eleven *indriyas*.
20-4. Five gross elements.
25. *puruṣa*.

This serial order implies that *mahat* is from [i.e. originates from] *prakṛti*, *ahaṃkāra* from *mahat*, the five *tanmātras* and eleven senses from *ahaṃkāra*, and the gross elements from the five *tanmātras*. The *puruṣa* is the *paramātman*.

According to this order, the senses are superior to the gross elements (earth, etc., thus the bodies, etc., composed of five elements). Here the mind is separate from the

[101] Śrīdhara has understood the word *durāsada* to mean 'hard to comprehend' [*durvijñeya*].

[102] [*kathita* (Beng.): 'said' has been avoided in this case because of the repetition.]

[103] [*darśan'śāstra* (Beng.).]

[104] ['the body, etc.'.]

[105] ['they say/said'.]

senses; but if, according to the doctrine of *Sāṃkhya*, the mind is a sense-organ, then it is superior to the other senses, because the others are outer senses. The second *gaṇa*, *mahat*,[106] was called *buddhi* by Vijñānabhikṣu in his *Sāṃkhyapravacanabhāṣya*. Thus, the *buddhi* is superior to the *manas*.

But it cannot be said that this *Sāṃkhya*-philosophy had come into being at the time the *Gītā* was composed. The proof is rather in the *Gītā* itself that, at the time of the composition of the *Gītā*, a different kind of *Sāṃkhya*-philosophy was current. The *Sāṃkhya* proclaimed by Kapila is only an extension of it. In *śloka* 4 of chapter 7 of the *Gītā*, the *gaṇas* are enlisted in the following way:

bhūmir āpo 'nalo vāyuḥ khaṃ mano buddhir eva ca
ahaṃkāra itīyaṃ me bhinnā prakṛtir aṣṭadhā. (4)[107]

Only eight *gaṇas* have been mentioned: the five gross elements, the *manas*, the *buddhi* and *ahaṃkāra*. Śaṅkarācārya says that by the enumeration of the five gross elements, the enumeration of the five *tanmātras* and the senses must be deemed as having been accomplished.[108] And the readers shall see too that the Lord says that these eight are his *prakṛti*. Therefore there is also an extremely important difference between this doctrine and the *Sāṃkhya* of Kapila.

Be this as it may, the sequence mentioned in the *śloka* has been somewhat understood. But there is still another meaning of *buddhi*. A determined state of the inner organ[109] can be called *buddhi*.[110] We have seen in the second chapter that the word *buddhi* has been employed in the *Gītā* in this sense. This meaning has to be recalled in order to understand the remaining part of the *śloka*. The means of subduing the senses are being related. The *paramātman* is superior to this determined state, which is superior to all other states of the inner organ.

Now we shall easily grasp the meaning of *śloka* 43. Desire must be conquered by understanding the *paramātman* with this determined *buddhi*, and by making oneself firm. I do not know whether any more excellent means for the conquest of the senses has ever anywhere been proclaimed.[111]

[106] [*ŚBhG(a)*:765 and *ŚBhG(b)*:135 have erroneously *ahaṃkāra* instead of *mahat*.]

[107] ['My *prakṛti* is of eight different kinds: earth, water, fire, air, ether, *manas*, *buddhi*, and *ahaṅkāra*.']

[108] He says also in the *ślokas* 5-6 of Chapter 13 [*BhG*]:
mahābhūtāny ahaṃkāro buddhir avyaktam eva ca / indriyāṇi daśaikañ ca pañca cendriyagocarāḥ. (5) *icchā dveṣaḥ sukhaṃ duḥkhaṃ saṃghātaś cetanā dhṛtiḥ etat kṣetraṃ samāsena savikāram udāhṛtam.* (6) ['The gross elements, *ahaṃkāra*, *buddhi*, the unmanifest, the ten senses and the one [i.e. *manas*], and the five objects of the senses (5), desire, hate, pleasure, pain, the consciousness [i.e. body], and patience — this is the *kṣetra* with its derivations [*vikāra*] declared in short. (6)']

Here there are the 13 *gaṇas* of Kapila's *Sāṃkhya*; *manas* and *ātman*, and another seven. These are not proclaimed as *gaṇas* or substances; there is no intention to divide the whole world into these few categories. Thus it is not Kapila's *Sāṃkhya*; rather it can be said that the roots of Kāpila's *Sāṃkhya* are here.

[109] [*niścayātmikā antaḥkaraṇavṛtti*.]

[110] *Vedāntasāra*, 28. [Khaṇḍa 13: '*buddhir nāma niścayātmikāntaḥkaraṇavṛtti*'.]

[111] In civilised society, it is observed that one sense is so strong that the term '*indriyadoṣa*' ['fault of the sense-organ', denoting licentiousness] is employed solely to denote the fault of that sense. Many ask about the means of controlling its might, and many, although desiring to know, cannot ask because of

iti mahābhārate śatasāhasryāṃ saṃhitāyāṃ vaiyāsikyāṃ bhīṣmaparvaṇi śrīmadbhagavadgītāsūpaniṣatsu brahmavidyāyāṃ yogaśāstre karmayogo nāma tṛtīyo 'dhyāyaḥ.[112]

---

embarrassment. Then again there are also many who are devoid of belief in God, or are incapable to realise Him with a determined *buddhi*. Therefore, I have written down all the tiny means of controlling the senses below:

(1) Bodily exercise. Thereby, both physical and mental health is acquired. In the presence of both physical and mental health, the polluting force of the senses cannot develop.

(2) Regulation of food. Give up exciting food and drink. Alcohol, etc., are especially forbidden. Fish and meat cannot totally be prohibited. Fish, especially, has many good properties; but it greatly excites the senses. Therefore, only the very moderate eating of fish and meat is good. In the Hindu Śāstras, fish and meat are prohibited for the *brahmacārin* because of this fault of theirs. Fish is prohibited for every Hindu.

(3) Abandonment of idleness. Idleness is a very important reason for faults of the sense-organs. Through idleness one gains opportunities for evil thoughts; with the lack of other thoughts, those of sensual pleasure gain strength. In the absence of any other action, the effort for satisfaction of the senses is reinforced. He who deals with worldly action [*viṣayakarman*] shall direct special attention towards his action and try for its progress even at times of leisure. Two kinds of good fruits will spring from this: the senses will be controlled, and the worldly action will be advanced. But the fault which occurs in the case of such preoccupation with worldly action is that the people become very attached to objects. This is a cause of mental decay. So those who are capable of it should read good literature or engage in scientific discussions in their leisure time. Those who are incapable to do so for their lack of education or unwillingness, shall finish their work and take on the work of others. All can spend their time with conversation in their families, looking after the learning of boys and girls, supervising their personal income and expenditures, and caring for the happiness and comfort of their neighbours. Those who dislike this can employ themselves in some important charitable work. Many have come free from many sins by dedicating themselves to the foundation or maintenance of a school or a doctor's office.

(4) A very important means is the abandonment of bad company. One should leave even the shadow of those who are overcome by the senses, obscene in their talk and given to obscene amusements. Their example, incitement and conversation can defile even *devarṣis*. This bad company is a main evil of living in a civilised society.

(5) The best means of all, subordinate only to meditating on God, is the sacred marital love. It is needless to write more on this subject.

Although not all of these statements are relevant to this commentary on the *Gītā*, they have nevertheless been written down here because they are infinitely beneficial for people.

[112] ['This is the third chapter called *Karmayoga* in the *Yogaśāstra*, with regard to the knowledge of *brahman*, in the secret teachings sung by the Lord in the *Bhīṣmaparvan* of Vyāsa's *Saṃhitā* (consisting of) 100 000 (*ślokas*), in the *Mahābhārata*.']

Fourth Chapter

śrībhagavān uvāca:
imaṃ vivasvate yogaṃ proktavān aham avyayam
vivasvān manave prāha manur ikṣvākave 'bravīt. (1)

The Lord said:
I told this indestructible *yoga* to *Sūrya*. *Sūrya* told it to *Manu*, and *Manu* told it to *Ikṣvāku*. (1)

The fruit of this *yoga* is indestructible, therefore it is called indestructible. *Ikṣvāku* is the son of *Manu* and the forefather of the rulers of the *Sūrya*-dynasty.

evaṃ paraṃparāprāptam imaṃ rājarṣayo viduḥ
sa kāleneha mahatā yogo naṣṭaḥ paraṃtapa. (2)

Thus obtained through tradition, the rājarṣis got to know this *yoga*.[1] O Paraṃtapa, that *yoga* has now been destroyed through the influence of a long time. (2)

(A commentary is unnecessary.)

sa evāyaṃ mayā te 'dya yogaḥ proktaḥ purātanaḥ
bhakto 'si me sakhā ceti rahasyaṃ hy etad uttamam. (3)

You are my devotee and friend; today I have told you that old *yoga*. This topic[2] is supreme. (3)

(A commentary is unnecessary.)

arjuna uvāca:
aparaṃ bhavato janma paraṃ janma vivasvataḥ
katham etad vijānīyāṃ tvam ādau proktavān iti. (4)

Arjuna said:
Your birth was later, that of Sūrya earlier; how am I to understand that you said this before [him]? (4)

(A commentary is unnecessary.)

śrībhagavān uvāca:
bahūni me vyatītāni janmāni tava cārjuna
tāny ahaṃ veda sarvāṇi na tvaṃ vettha paraṃtapa. (5)

[1] [*eirūp paramparāprāpta haïyā ei yog rājarṣigaṇ abagata haïyāchilen* (Beng.): The construction is ambiguous, as one could also understand it to mean that the *rājarṣis* obtained the *yoga* through tradition. The original Sanskrit, however, makes it more likely that *haïyā* and *abagata haïyāchilen* do not have the same subject.]

[2] [*prasaṅga* (Beng.): The Sanskrit original had *rahasya*, 'secret'.]

The Lord said:

I have had many births past, and you, [O Arjuna], too. I am conscious of all of them. O Paraṃtapa, you do not know. (5)

Here suddenly the doctrine of avatāras is broached. It is required for understanding the relationship between action and knowledge. At first sight, it seems from the spirit of these *ślokas* that Arjuna did not know the doctrine of avatāras. It is our duty, concerning this, to recall some things.

Firstly, it is indeed true that in the *Mahābhārata*, there is talk of Kṛṣṇa, the God Viṣṇu. But in my book *Kṛṣṇacaritra* I have tried to explain that not all parts of the *Mahābhārata* are from one time; and that all the parts on which the doctrine of Kṛṣṇa's avatāras has been imposed are comparatively modern. Secondly, the *Mahābhārata* does not merely speak of ten avatāras; a sixth avatāra, Paraśurāma, is present together with the eighth avatāra, Kṛṣṇa. Thirdly, ten avatāras are mentioned in the relatively modern Purāṇas; but there are also different sorts [of information] in the Purāṇas. In the *Bhāgavatapurāṇa* it says that there are 22 avatāras; again it is also said that there are uncountable avatāras. Kṛṣṇa too does not speak of eight, ten, or 22 avatāras. He speaks of 'many' ['*bahu*'] avatāras. There is no doubt that the words 'uncountable' of the *Bhāgavatapurāṇa* and this 'many' are synonymous.

ajo 'pi sann avyayātmā bhūtānām īśvaro 'pi san
prakṛtiṃ svām adhiṣṭhāya sambhavāmy ātmamāyayā. (6)

I am birthless [*aja*], I am He whose *ātman* is indestructible [*avyayātmā*], the Lord [*īśvara*] of all creatures; even then I subdue my *prakṛti* and get born by my power of illusion [*māyā*]. (6)

aja: birthless.
avyayātman: he whose power of knowledge does not decay (Śaṅkara).
īśvara: devoid of the dependence on *karman* (Śrīdhara).
prakṛti: the great illusion [*māyā*] characterised by the three *guṇas*, under whose domination the whole world is.

Apart from these, there is the word *adhiṣṭhāya* in the original, whose sense Śaṅkarācārya has written as '*vaśīkṛtya*';[3] Śrīdhara, however, has written '*svīkṛtya*'.[4] The interpretation given by Śaṅkara has been accepted since it is more plausible.

Briefly, the subject is the possible objection to the words of the Lord that how He, being without birth, could be born. Liberation [*mokṣa*] comes from knowledge; so why should He, whose knowledge is undecaying, be born? Birth is subjected to *karman*; why should He who is God and therefore not subjected to *karman* be born?

Śaṅkara interprets the Lord's answer to this in the following way: 'I am born by subjugating *prakṛti*, which is my own *prakṛti*, i.e. Viṣṇu's *māyā* consisting of the three *guṇas sattva*, *rajas*, *tamas*, by which the whole world is controlled, and, enchanted by

3 ['having subdued'.]

4 ['having accepted'.]

which, [no-one] can recognise me as Vāsudeva. By my power of illusion [*māyā*], as it were;[5] not like ordinary people who get born for the sake of the highest goal [*paramārtha*].'

Śrīdhara Svāmin has explained somewhat differently. According to him, the Lord is saying: 'It is by accepting my nature consisting of pure *sattva* that I incarnate myself at will by means of a pure, bright image of *sattva*.'

The explanations are quite complicated. A few things should be mentioned in order to help the reader in understanding.

'*Māyā*' is a power of God. This *māyā* has obtained a very prominent position in the theology[6] of the Hindus, especially in the Upaniṣads and the Darśanaśāstra. It is not necessary for us to research the way in which *māyā* is usually understood in the *Vedānta*. I shall explain only the way in which it is explained in this *Gītā*. The reader may remember that in the course of the commentary to *śloka* 42 of the third chapter, we quoted the following *śloka* from Chapter 7 of the *Gītā*:

> *bhūmir āpo 'nalo vāyuḥ khaṃ mano buddhir eva ca*
> *ahaṃkāra itīyaṃ me bhinnā prakṛtir aṣṭadhā*. ([*BhG* 7.]4)

My *prakṛti* is of eight different kinds: earth, water, fire, wind, ether, mind [*manas*], intellect [*buddhi*], and *ahaṃkāra*. ([7.]4)

Directly after this He says:

> *apareyam itas tv anyāṃ prakṛtiṃ viddhi me parāṃ*
> *jīvabhūtāṃ mahābāho yayedaṃ dhāryate jagat*. ([*BhG* 7.]5)

This is my *aparā* or inferior *prakṛti*; know also my *parā* or superior *prakṛti*. It is endowed with life,[7] and it holds the world. ([7.]5)

So the power of God which has the form of beings[8] and sustains the world is His higher *prakṛti* or *māyā*. Through his power over the form of beings, the Lord created the beings, and by subjugating this power He can give to his Selfness[9] the form of a creature.

[The assumption] that God cannot descend by taking a body need not be considered, for He is sovereign[10] and almighty; to say that He cannot means to point out a limit to His power. It is an independent question whether it is possible that God descends in a body or not. I have considered it as far as possible in another book,[11] so there is no need for repetition. And the Lord Himself says in the succeeding two *ślokas*

5 [*ki nā* (Beng.).]

6 [*īśvar'tattva* (Beng.).]

7 [*jīb'bhūtā* (Beng.).]

8 [*jīb'svarūpā* (Beng.).]

9 [*svatva* (Beng.).]

10 [*icchāmaẏ* (Beng.).]

11 *Kṛṣṇacaritra*, in the first part.

whether or not there is any need for Him to descend in a body.

yadā yadā hi dharmasya glānir bhavati bhārata
abhyutthānam adharmasya tadātmānaṃ sṛjāmy aham. (7)

paritrāṇāya sādhūnāṃ vināśāya ca duṣkṛtām
dharmasaṃsthāpanārthāya saṃbhavāmi yuge yuge. (8)

[O Bhārata,] I create myself whenever *dharma* becomes faint and *adharma* arises. (7)

I come into being age after age to safeguard the righteous, to destroy the doers of evil deeds and to establish *dharma.*[12] (8)

janma karma ca me divyam evaṃ yo vetti tattvataḥ
tyaktvā dehaṃ punarjanma naiti mām eti so 'rjuna. (9)

O Arjuna, my birth and deeds [*karman*] are divine. He who becomes in essence[13] knowledgeable on this is not born again, but attains me. (9)

Divya [divine] means 'supernatural', 'godly', or 'unworldly'.

Why should liberation be attained by knowing in essence the human birth and deeds of the Lord? In my book on Kṛṣṇa, I have explained that the Lord assumes a human body in order to show the ideal of humanity. No other purpose is possible. The ideal man is the ideal agent.[14] Thus it is necessary for the *karmayogin* to understand in essence the actions of the ideal agent. Without that, *karmayoga* means to throw a clod of clay into darkness. If this cannot be accepted, then there is no discernible need to take up the doctrine of avatāras while speaking on *karmayoga*. He who tries will be able to understand Kṛṣṇa's ideal agency[15] if he studies the book *Kṛṣṇacaritra* in detail. It is [however] not so that there is no other meaning. That which the philosophers call the path of knowledge is famous in this form: the knowledge of the *brahman* is the path to liberation. The *brahman* must be known; but what is the *brahman*? The *brahman* is shapeless, colourless, undivided, eternal, pure and free.[16] It is of the form of truth, knowledge and bliss. Liberation is attained by knowing this *brahman*. But the descended and embodied God cannot be called shapeless, etc. Is, therefore, the knowledge of the descended and embodied God absolutely fruitless; is there no likelihood of liberation through worship offered to Him? Such a doubt is removed in this *śloka*. There can also be attainment of liberation by knowing in essence the divine birth and actions of the descended and embodied God. But they must be known in essence. There is no such attainment by understanding just anybody to be an avatāra.

[12] All this, too, I have considered in the first part of *Kṛṣṇacaritra*. A repetition is unnecessary.

[13] [*tattvataḥ* (Beng.).]

[14] [*karmin*.]

[15] [*karmitva*.]

[16] [*śuddhamukta* (Beng.): *śuddha* and *mukta* are probably meant as single words, not as a compound.]

vītarāgabhayakrodhā manmayā mām upāśritāḥ
bahavo jñānatapasā pūtā madbhāvam āgatāḥ. (10)

Having become free from *rāga*, fear and anger, being *manmaya*, taking refuge in me, and being purified by austerity that consists in knowledge, many have attained my being. (10)

Firstly the meanings of the words: *rāga*: 'passion'. *Manmaya*: 'knowing the *brahman*, devoid of the knowledge that there are any differentiations from God.[17] Having taken refuge in me.' Śaṅkara says: 'relying only on knowledge';[18] Śrıdhara says: 'having obtained my favour, having attained my being, having attained God's being, having attained liberation.'

The commentators say that the reason for this statement being brought forward here is that 'the doctrine of devotion to me is not being newly proclaimed here. Many have attained liberation through such knowledge and austerity before also.' Quite true; but mostly it is our duty to understand this little, [namely,] that those persons are being discussed who have acted while being conscious of the significance of the ideal agent's actions. This shall become clear when reading the succeeding *śloka* 15. If you cannot understand this, no connection of all this to *karmayoga* can be seen.

As regards desireless action, there should be no passion, fear and anger; there should be knowledge of the indivisibility of God; and the character should be purified by knowledge and austerity (*Spiritual culture*) [Lat.]. If this is not so, the action will not be desireless.

Not everybody can become a desireless agent [*niṣkāmakarmin*]. Are the actions of those who act with desire totally fruitless? God ordains the fruits of every action. This is said in the subsequent two *ślokas*:

ye yathā māṃ prapadyante tāṃs tathaiva bhajāmy aham
mama vartmānuvartante manuṣyāḥ pārtha sarvaśaḥ. (11)

I satisfy everybody in the way in which he worships me. People follow my path in every sort of way. (11)

Let us first understand the initial line. Arjuna might say: 'O Master, you have still not explained what the central issue is. Is it true that through desireless actions I may attain you, whereas through actions with desire I will not attain anything? Are those vain efforts?' The Lord is dispelling these doubts. [']Not everybody worships[19] me with the same mental attitude. I bestow fruits upon each according to the way of worship he offers me. I fulfil whatever desires anyone has while worshipping me. He who does not wish anything, i.e. who is desireless, attains me. None of his wishes are fulfilled because they are completely absent; but he attains me.[']

Thereafter, the second line. At first sight, the sentence 'People follow my path in

[17] [*īśvar*ı*bhedajñān*ı*rahit* (Beng.).]

[18] [*kebal jñān*ı*niṣṭha* (Beng.).]

[19] [*upāsanā kare* (Beng.).]

every sort of way' seems to mean 'people in every sort of way follow the path I take'. But this is not the sense here; we cannot expect the '*Idiom*' [Lat.] of the author of the *Gītā* to match our '*Idiom*' exactly. This line means: 'Whatever may be the path a man adopts in his worship, he will have to come to the path on which I am.' 'No matter to which deity a man offers worship, it will be worship to me; for there is no other deity but one. I am all gods; I give the fruits of worship offered to the other gods according to the wishes accompanying them. Even if a man does not worship any god, but only serves his senses, etc., that too is my service. Because in the world there is nothing except myself; I am the senses, etc., and I bestow the fruits on the senses adequately in the form of the senses, etc. These are inferior and sorrowful fruits, no doubt, but I give the fruits according to the kind of worship and desires.'

The earth has manifold procedures of worship. Some worship the formless, others the formed. Some worship only the Lord of the world, others worship many deities. One race[20] worships those born as ghosts, another the world of the forefathers; some worship the animate, some the inanimate, some humans, some animals such as cattle, and some trees or pieces of rocks. All these are worship; although it must of course be admitted that there are differences of quality[21] in them. But these differences of quality are only [differences in] the amount of knowledge of the worshipper. He who is absolutely ignorant sees on the roadside some piece of stone on which flowers, sandal and vermilion have been put, and goes on putting flowers, sandal and vermilion on it; he who has come to know a bit is perhaps a worshipper of the formless *brahman*. But concerning the knowledge of the extension of the Lord's nature, both are almost equally blind. Both he who considers the Himalaya to be as big as a termite-hill, and he who thinks of it as big as a wall, are equally blind. Neither the *brahmavādin* nor the worshipper of a piece of stone knows the proper form[22] of God. How can it therefore be said that the worship of one of them is acceptable for God, and the other's is not? Either nobody's worship is acceptable for God, or every worship is acceptable. Basically, worship is for our mental faculties, for the accomplishment of the holiness of our lives; not for the Lord's satisfaction. He who is eternally blissful, he who is beyond satisfaction and dissatisfaction, cannot be satisfied by us. But if it be true that He is a judge — for he ordains the fruits of actions — then only such worship which is sanctioned by his pure *svabhāva* may be acceptable for Him. Hypocritical worship, being only a means for obtaining the status of being virtuous [*dhārmik*] in the eyes of people, is not acceptable for Him, since He is omniscient. And that which is sincere worship is acceptable to Him even if it be deluded. The worship of him who bangs his head [on the ground of] *Ṣaṣṭhītalā*[23] desiring good for an unfortunate son seems to be more acceptable for God than the worship of such a person who worships the *brahman* and practises austerities, if it be merely for the sake of gaining reputation among the people.

If the significance of this *śloka* is understood, there are no more differences caused by *dharma*[24] on earth; Hindus, Muslims, Christians, Jainas, worshippers of the

[20] [*jāti* (Beng.).]

[21] [*utkarṣāpakarṣa* (Beng.).]

[22] [*svarūp* (Beng.).]

[23] [Place connected with the worship of the folk goddess *Ṣaṣṭhī*.]

[24] [*dharmmagata* (Beng.).]

caused by *dharma*[24] on earth; Hindus, Muslims, Christians, Jainas, worshippers of the formless and the formed, worshippers of many gods, and of innate matter, all of them worship one God; all follow the path on which He is. The *dharma* proclaimed in this *śloka* is the world's only non-sectarian[25] *dharma*; the only *dharma* to be followed by all people. It is the genuine Hindu *dharma* too. There is no other *dharma* as generous as the Hindu *dharma*; and there is no other great utterance comparable to this *śloka*.

kāṅkṣantaḥ karmaṇāṃ siddhiṃ yajanta iha devatāḥ
kṣipraṃ hi mānuṣe loke siddhir bhavati karmajā. (12)

Those who desire the accomplishment of *karman* in this birth worship the gods. And their *karman* is quickly accomplished in this human world. (12)

In other words, men desiring the fruits of action usually worship the gods and obtain the desired fruits already in this world.

Those fruits are little. The fruits of desireless action are very great. So why do people not hope for these great fruits but try for the little ones? It is human nature that people try for the pleasure which, though it may be little, is quickly obtained.

cāturvarṇyaṃ mayā sṛṣṭaṃ guṇakarmavibhāgaśaḥ
tasya kartāram api māṃ viddhy akartāram avyayam. (13)

It is true that I have created the four *varṇas* according to the division of properties and actions, but although I am their (creative) agent, know me as not being an agent [*akartṛ*] and as unmoved. (13)

The common statement of the Hindu Śāstras is that the *brāhmaṇavarṇa* has been created from the mouth of the creator, the kṣatriyas from the arms, the vaiśyas from the thighs, and the śūdras from the feet. But it does not at first glance seem coherent with the quoted common statement of the Hindu Śāstras that the system of the four *varṇas* should have been created according to the division of qualities and actions.[26] For several reasons a detailed examination of this issue is necessary.

Firstly, it can be seen that the origin of the said common statement of the Hindu Śāstras is in the famous *sūkta* on the *puruṣa*.

The nineteenth *sūkta* of the tenth *maṇḍala* of the *Ṛgvedasaṃhitā* is called the *Puruṣasūkta*. The brahmins still use its first *ṛc* '*sahasraśīrṣā puruṣaḥ sahasrākṣaḥ*', etc.[27] [RV 10.90.1] today when performing worship[28] of Viṣṇu. The Western scholars, those who want to establish that there was no discrimination of castes in *Vedic* times, say that this *sūkta* is modern. We have no need for this consideration. It is impossible not

[24] [*dharmmagata* (Beng.).]

[25] [*asāmpradāyik* (Beng.).]

[26] [*guṇakarmavibhāgaśaḥ*.]

[27] [*sahasraśīrṣā puruṣaḥ sahasrākṣaḥ sahasrapāt*. Muir (1868-73,I:9) translates: 'Purusha has a thousand heads, a thousand eyes, a thousand feet.']

[28] [*pūjā* (Beng.).]

to accept that all of the Vedic *sūktas* are very ancient. The point I wish to make is that what is in this *sūkta* does not exactly denote that the brahmins were produced from the mouth, the kṣatriyas from the arms, etc. I am quoting those lines[29] in question:

> *brāhmaṇo 'sya mukham āsīd bāhu rājanyaḥ kṛtaḥ*
> *ūru tad asya yad vaiśyaḥ padbhyāṃ śūdro 'jāyata.* [RV 10.90.12][30]

Concerning the śūdra, '*ajāyata*' ['was born'] has in fact been said; but concerning the brahmins, it has been said that the brahmin is the mouth of that *puruṣa*, and the kṣatriya (was made from) his arms.[31] Concerning the vaiśyas, too, it has been said that his thighs are the vaiśyas.

Of all the Vedas, only in the *Taittirīya Saṃhitā* do we find that Prajāpati created the brahmins from the mouth, the kṣatriyas from the arms, the vaiśyas from the middle part (*madhyataḥ*), and the śūdras from the feet. But in the other parts of the Vedas, the creation of the system of the four *varṇas* has been described differently. In the *Śatapathabrāhmaṇa*, it has been said thus:

> *bhūr iti vai prajāpatir brahma ajanayata. bhuva iti kṣatraṃ svar iti viśam.*

[29] [*ṛk · guli* (Beng.).]

[30] [Probably taken from Muir 1868-73,I:8, who translates: 'The Brāhman was his mouth; the Rājanya was made his arms; the being (called) the Vaiśya, he was his thighs; the Śūdra sprang from his feet.' (p. 10)]

[31] Dr. Haug wrote, with regard to this *ṛc*:

'Now, according to this passage, which is the most ancient and authoritative we have on the origin of Brahmanism, and *caste in general*, the Brahmana has not come from the mouth of this primary being, the Purusha, but the mouth of the latter became the Brahmanical caste, that is to say, was transformed into it. The passage has no doubt an allegorical sense. (That is true in many *sūktas* of the Vedas [Beng.]). Mouth is the seat of speech. The allegory points out that the Brahmans are teachers and instructors of mankind. The arms are the seat of strength. If the two arms of the Purusha are said to have been made of Kshattriya (warrior), that means, then, that the Kshattriya have to carry arms to defend the empire. That the thighs of the Purusha were transformed into Vaisya, that, as the lower parts of the body are the principal repository of food taken, the Vaisya caste is destined to provide food for the others.' [Lat.; quoted from Muir 1868-73,I:14f.]

This bit requires strenuous imagination, the *ḍāl-bhāt* [rice and pulses] does not go into the thighs; but in the Hindu-Śāstras, we can also observe the use of the word 'stomach' in all these instances. As for example in the 47th Chapter of the *Śāntiparvan* of the *Mahābhārata*:

'*brahma vaktraṃ bhujau kṣatraṃ kṛtsnam ūrūdaraṃ viśaḥ.*' [*Mbh* 12.47.43. — Translation: 'Brahminhood is the face, kṣatriya-hood is the arms, the vaiśyas the entire body (thighs and stomach).'] Thereafter:

'The creation of the Sudra from the feet of the Purusha indicates that he is destined to be a servant of the others, just as the foot supports the other parts of the body as a firm support.' *Dr. Haug on the origin of Brahmanism* [1863], p. 4. [Lat.; quoted from Muir 1868-73,I:15.]

Dr. Muir [Lat.] also says:

'It is, indeed, said that the Śūdra sprang from Purusha's feet; but as regards the three superior castes and the members with which they are respectively connected, it is not quite clear which (i.e. the castes or the members) are to be taken as subjects, and which as the predicates, and consequently, whether we are to suppose verse 12, (the quoted *ṛc*) [Beng.] to declare that the three castes were the three members, or, conversely, that the three members were, or became, the three castes.' Sanskrit Texts, Vol. II, p. 15, 2nd edition [1868-73]. [Lat., deficient quotation corrected here.]

There is no mention of the śūdras.[32]

And again in the *Taittirīya Brāhmaṇa*:

ṛgbhyo jātaṃ vaiśyaṃ varṇam āhuḥ yajurvedaṃ kṣatriyasyāhur yonim.
sāmavedo brāhmaṇānāṃ prasūtiḥ.[33]

That is, the brahmins are born from the *Sāmaveda*, the kṣatriyas from the *Yajurveda*, and the vaiśyas from the *Ṛgveda*. Here again, no mention of the śūdras is made.

These opinions have been quoted as examples. There are many more of this kind. To quote all of them would be a disturbance for the readers. In general, there are various opinions in the Hindu Śāstras concerning the origin of the *varṇa*-system. Kṛṣṇa's words, too, may at first glance seem to differ from the usual opinion. He does not say: [']I have created the particular *varṇas* from particular parts of my body.['] He says [']I have [created them] according to the differences of *guṇa* and actions.['] Let us first see what *guṇa* means.

These are the three *guṇas*: *sattva*, *rajas*, and *tamas*. The commentators say that the brahmins are dominated by *sattva*, and their action is peace, sense-control, etc.; the kṣatriyas are dominated by *sattva* and *rajas*, their action is heroism, war, etc.; the vaiśyas are dominated by *rajas* and *tamas*, their action consists in agriculture, commerce, etc.; and the śūdras are dominated by *tamas*, their action is service to the other three *varṇas*. This is what the Lord intends in saying, [']I have created them according to the differences of qualities and actions.[']

Now is the nature, *sattva-*, *rajas-*, or *tamas*-dominated, etc., of one who will be born, created even before his birth, in [a mother's] womb?

He who answers that a being is born first and only then acquires its nature dominated by *sattva*, etc., must definitely admit that its brahminness, etc. is brought about not according to its lineage but according to its properties. It is not so that a person has to become a brahmin merely for being the son of a brahmin; even a śūdra's son, if having a *sattva*-dominated nature, will be a brahmin, and a brahmin's son with a *tamas*-dominated nature will become a śūdra: this is what we easily realise from the Lord's sentence.

It is not that I am making up and circulating a new doctrine[34] of my own. In ancient times, long before Śaṅkara and Śrīdhara, the ancient ṛṣis, too, circulated this doctrine. I have quoted some proof of this in *Dharmmatattva*, such as:

kṣāntaṃ dāntaṃ jitakrodhaṃ jitātmānaṃ jitendriyam
tam eva brāhmaṇaṃ manye śeṣāḥ śūdrā iti smṛtāḥ.[35]

And again:

agnihotravrataparān svādhyāyaniratān śucīn[36]
upavāsaratān dāntāṃs tān devā brāhmaṇān viduḥ.

[32] 2.1.4.11 etc. [Probably taken from Muir 1868-73,I:17, who translates: 'Saying "bhūḥ", Prajāpati generated the Brahman; (saying) "bhuvaḥ", he generated the Kshattra; (and saying) "svaḥ", he generated the Viś.']

[33] 3.12.9.2.

[34] [*mat* (Beng.): so far translated as 'opinion', which is not feasible in this instance.]

[35] [*BR* II:619. Baṅkim's translation: 'Only those who are forgiving, free from evil propensities, controlling anger, the *ātman* and the senses, are to be called brahmins; the rest are Śūdras.']

[36] [With sandhi, this should be *svādhyāyaniratāñ chucīn*.]

na jātiḥ pūjyate rājan guṇāḥ kalyāṇakārakāḥ
caṇḍālam api vṛttasthaṃ taṃ devā brāhmaṇaṃ viduḥ.
(*Gautamasaṃhitā*)[37]

[Translation:] Only he who is forgiving, restraining [his senses], who has conquered anger, is self-restrained and has conquered the senses, should be known as a brahmin; all the others are śūdras. The gods know only those as brahmins who observe the vow of maintaining the sacrificial fire, are absorbed in their studies, pure, observe the fasts, and restrain [their senses]. O king, the caste [*jāti*] is not worthy of worship, the qualities alone bring welfare; the gods know even a *caṇḍāla*, if virtuous, as a brahmin.

And again, in Chapter 215 of the *Mārkaṇḍeyasamasyāparvādhyāya* in the *Vanaparvan* of the *Mahābhārata*, there are the words by a *ṛṣi*: 'An arrogant brahmin given to evil acts resulting from degeneration, even if learned, is like a śūdra; and [on the other hand] I consider a śūdra who is true and empassioned for sense-control and *dharma* to be a brahmin. For one becomes a brahmin only by one's conduct.'[38] Again, in Chapter 180 of the *Ajagaraparvādhyāya* in the *Vanaparvan*, the Rājarṣi Nahuṣa says: 'Vedic truth, generosity, forgiveness, kindness, non-violence and mercy are observed also in śūdras. Now if the *brāhmaṇadharmas* as truth, etc., are observed also in śūdras, then also śūdras can be brahmins.' In answer to this, Yudhiṣṭhira says: 'In many śūdras, characteristics of brahmins can be observed, and in many twice-born persons characteristics of śūdras; therefore it is not so that one is a śūdra merely through descent from śūdras, and a brahmin through descent from brahmins. Instead, all those persons in whom Vedic conduct is observed are brahmins, and all those persons in whom it is not observed are śūdras.'[39]

But the matter under discussion was desireless action, action with desire and the desire for the fruits of action; why has this topic of the *varṇa*-system arisen? It was being said that some worship the gods, etc., out of the desire for quick fruits in this world, whereas others perform desireless action. Why is such dissimilar conduct seen among the people? Because of the influence of the differences in their natures. This difference of natures is the system of the four *varṇas* or the difference of *varṇas*. But why is there this difference of *varṇas*? God's will. God has made it. Does God then act? Of course He does! But even in performing such actions, He remains a non-agent.[40] For He is unmoved. If He is unmoved, then He cannot be subjected to the fruits of action; He has no pleasure or pain, increase or decrease. If He is not subjected to the fruits of action, then action performed by Him is desireless. He is a desireless agent.[41] For this reason humans also cannot merge in Him unless they be desireless. The dissolving of the *jīvātman* into the *paramātman* is liberation. But a *jīvātman* with desire cannot dissolve into the desireless *paramātman* consisting of pure *sattva*. Only the desireless agent has a right to liberation.

The pupils of modern scientists will not believe that God performs actions. They

[37] [Referred to as *Vṛddhagautamasaṃhitā* (*adhyāya* 21) in *Dharmmatattva* (*BR* II:619).]

[38] [*Mbh* 3.206.11-12.]

[39] [*Mbh* 3.177.18-21.]

[40] [*akartṛ*. There appears to be no semantical distinction between *kartṛ* and *karmin* according to the way Baṅkim employs these terms. Thus both are rendered by 'agent' (cf. below and following note).]

[41] [*niṣkāmakarmin*.]

will say that God does not act; all that happens comes about by his *niẏam (law)* [Lat.] of establishment.[42] But the establishment of this law is also an action. If those who say that all those laws are qualities of innate matter accept that this matter has been created by God, then they have accepted the agency of God. Those who deny this too are atheists, and no resolution about the agency of God can be made with them.

na māṃ karmāṇi limpanti na me karmaphale spṛhā
iti māṃ yo 'bhijānāti karmabhir na sa badhyate. (14)

Actions do not involve me.[43] And I have no desire for the fruits of action. He who knows me like this is not bound by action. (14)

Desireless action cannot be understood without knowing the desireless agency of God. If one knows it, one's actions become desireless. In that case, one can obtain release from bondage in the form of action with desire. In the commentary which has been given on the preceding *śloka*, this has been made clear.

evaṃ jñātvā kṛtaṃ karma pūrvair api mumukṣubhiḥ
kuru karmaiva tasmāt tvaṃ pūrvaiḥ pūrvatamaṃ kṛtam. (15)

Knowing thus the former seekers of liberation performed actions; perform all the actions formerly performed by the ancients. (15)

I.e., those who desired liberation in ancient times performed actions while knowing that they were non-agents, that they would not reap the fruits. You too are to act like this.

kiṃ karma kim akarmeti kavayo 'py atra mohitāḥ
tat te karma pravakṣyāmi yaj jñātvā mokṣyase 'śubhāt. (16)

Even the wise cannot understand what action and non-action are. Therefore I am telling you what action is. By knowing this you will become free from what is not good. (16)

akarman does not mean bad action here, but devoidness of action.

karmaṇo hy api boddhavyaṃ boddhavyaṃ ca vikarmaṇaḥ
akarmaṇaś ca boddhavyaṃ gahanā karmaṇo gatiḥ. (17)

It must be understood what *karman* is, it must be understood what *vikarman* is, and it must be understood what *akarman* is. The ways[44] of *karman* are difficult to know.

karman: meaning prescribed action, that which is appropriate[45] action.

[42] [*saṃsthāpan* (Beng.).]
[43] [*lipta kare nā* (Beng.): originally 'do not smear me'; figuratively 'involve', etc.]
[44] [*gati* (Beng.).]
[45] [*yathārtha* (Beng.).]

vikarman: non-prescribed action.
akarman: abandonment of action, devoidness of action.

karmaṇy akarma yaḥ paśyed akarmaṇi ca karma yaḥ
sa buddhimān manuṣyeṣu sa yuktaḥ kṛtsnakarmakṛt. (18)

He is wise among men who sees devoidness of action in action, as well as action in devoidness of action. He is endowed with *yoga* and the doer of all actions. (18)

The worship of the Lord is action; but the bondage of action does not occur in it, therefore do not consider it as of the nature of action. And unless one performs the prescribed actions, one must reap the fruits of action, and this reaping the fruits is an obstruction to liberation. Consider therefore not doing, that is devoidness of action, to be action. The essence of Śrīdhara's commentary is this. According to it, one obtains from this *śloka* that only the worship of the Lord is a duty.

Śaṅkarācārya has explained likewise. In connection with this *śloka* he has written a long and complicated essay whose rough meaning is that the *ātman* is not involved in action, action is performed by the senses, etc., but actions are erroneously attributed to the *ātman*. He who knows this sees non-action in action. And even when the senses, etc., desist from their usual performance he regards that devoidness of action, too, as action of the senses, etc.

But according to our humble intellects, we can find a simple meaning if we direct our attention to the subsequent *śloka*. Action which is free of desires and intentions[46] and is devoid of the desire for fruits, is *akarman*, devoidness of action. And he who abstains from action to be performed must of course reap the fruits of abstaining from his duty; therefore, in this case devoidness of action is also action. For it is the cause of the production of a new fruit. He who understands this is indeed wise.

yasya sarve samārambhāḥ kāmasaṃkalpavarjitāḥ
jñānāgnidagdhakarmāṇaṃ tam āhuḥ paṇḍitaṃ budhāḥ. (19)

He is called a knower by the wise whose every effort is free from desire and intentions, and whose actions are burnt by the fire of knowledge. (19)

The import of this *śloka* to a certain extent depends on the meaning of the phrase '*kāmasaṅkalpa*'. This is the explanation given by Śaṅkarācārya: '*kāmasaṅkalpavarjitāḥ*' — '*kāmais tatkāraṇaiś ca saṅkalpair varjitāḥ*'.[47] The explanation by Śrīdhara is this: '*kāmyate iti kāmaḥ. phalaṃ tatsaṅkalpena varjitāḥ*.'[48] Madhusūdana Sarasvatī says: '*kāmaḥ phalatṛṣṇā. saṅkalpo 'haṃ karomīti kartṛtvābhimānas tābhyāṃ varjitāḥ*'.[49] In

[46] [*kāmasaṅkalpavivarjita*.]

[47] ['(...) free from desires and intentions that are their causes.' (Cf. *ŚaBhG*:155)]

[48] ['Desiring is done: desire (*kāmaḥ*). The fruit (:) free from the intention (*saṅkalpa*) of it.']

[49] ['Desire is greed for fruits. (Those) whose (undertakings) are free from the erroneous belief of agency (consisting in) the imagination (*saṅkalpa*) that "I act" (...)'.]

this way, various *munis* have various opinions.[50] The meaning of the word *saṅkalpa* according to [i.e. intended by] Madhusūdana Sarasvatī is not lexicographical but very appropriate here. [According to the interpretation] made by Śaṅkarācārya, a lack of inclination to action will arise when one is devoid of both desire and its cause, intention. Why should one act who has a longing to act, but does not desire the fruits? Therefore, Śaṅkara himself has said: *'mudhaiva ceṣṭāmātram anuṣṭhīyante pravṛttena cel lokasaṃgrahārthaṃ nivṛttena jīvanayātrārthaṃ.'* That is, all the undertakings of such a person are merely senseless efforts. On the path of inclination, there is only the purpose of education of the people, and on the path of abstention, there is only the purpose of maintaining one's vital functions. My humble proposition to my readers is that even then, desire has not become devoid of intention [*saṅkalpa*].

Madhusūdana Sarasvatī, too, has kept the terms *'lokaśikṣārthaṃ'* and *'jīvanayātrārthaṃ'*, but the reader can unhesitatingly accept the interpretation he gives of the phrase *'kāmasaṅkalpavarjita'*. It is the performance of action, devoid of thirst for the fruits and *ahaṃkāra*, which is prescribed; and it is this which is devoidness of action.

Usually, people engage themselves in performing actions out of the desire for the fruits, and along with it there is the *ahaṃkāra*[51] that they are acting or have acted. The intention of the Lord is that the absence of both is an indication of action, that their absence in action is devoidness of action.

Has the objection been resolved through such an understanding? It definitely has. Usually, people do indeed engage themselves in acting out of the desire for the fruit, but it is not true that one cannot engage oneself in action without that desire. If it were so, then the word 'desireless' would not make any sense; such a thing would not exist. If it were so, then not even one line of the *Gītā* would make any sense. This has not yet been explained. Let it be explained now.

There are a number of duties[52] which are to be executed by men. They are to be executed also by him who does not desire their fruits. Without doubt there is such a person who does not desire the maintenance of his life; if he could die, all his pain would come to an end. But the maintenance of his own life is to be executed by him. It is beyond doubt that a person suffering from a colic would commit a sin in killing himself. Normally no-one wishes for the maintenance of his enemy's life, but when we see that our enemy is about to drown or almost seized by death in any other way, it is our action to be executed[53] to save him. While helping the enemy, one might think, 'It would be fair enough if my efforts were to fail'. There is no desire for the fruits here, but action.

But it also has to be mentioned that to say that there is no effort for the attainment of fruits in desireless action is impossible; this is, moreover, not the intention of the *Gītā*. either. He whose goal is liberation desires liberation and makes efforts fit for the attainment of liberation. Neither in the *Gītā* nor anywhere else is the word *kāma*[54] employed without implying the effort for the attainment of its fruits. Imagine

[50] [This is a proverbial phrase in Bengali.]

[51] [Here *ahaṃkāra* might be translated as 'ego-perception' or 'ego-consciousness'.]

[52] [here: *kāryya* (Beng.).]

[53] [*anuṣṭheya karmma* (Beng.).]

[54] ['desire'.]

that the accomplishment of one's country's or race's welfare is due action. It can never be that someone who strives for the welfare of his country does so without desiring the welfare of his country. Thus it is our duty to understand the genuine significance of the word *kāma*.

Dharma, *artha* [wealth], *kāma* and *mokṣa* [liberation]: these four sub-categories[55] are the objects of human attainment [*puruṣārtha*]. Apart from these, there is nothing else needed for human attainment.[56] *Kāma* is that which is left besides the other three, namely, *dharma*, *artha* or worldly riches, good fortune, etc., and *mokṣa*. Therefore, the endeavour for the attainment of heaven, etc., by ritualistic action can be referred to by the word *kāma*. But the enjoyment of pleasure produced through ritualistic action is one's own enjoyment. Thus the enjoyment aimed at by *kāma* is one's own pleasure, not the good of others. Action whose aim is the welfare of others, etc., is desireless action. Action whose aim is one's own welfare is not desireless.

The word *kāma* is especially explained in another place of the *Mahābhārata*:

indriyāṇāṃ ca pañcānāṃ manaso hṛdayasya ca
viṣaye vartamānānāṃ yā prītir upajāyate
sa kāma iti me buddhiḥ karmaṇāṃ phalam uttamam. [3.34.37]

The enjoyment of pleasure[57] which [takes place] when the five senses, the mind,[58] and the heart[59] are present with regard to their respective objects is, in my opinion, *kāma*. It is the highest fruit of action.

Therefore, *kāma* means pleasure of the self.

Now think of the example of that person desiring his country's welfare. If that person acts while only desiring the welfare of his own country, then his action is desireless. And if he engages in doing what is beneficial for his country while longing for his glory, honour, prestige and advancement, he is one whose actions are with desire.

55 [*apavarga*.]

56 [*puruṣārthe ihā bhinna ār kona prayojan nāi* (Beng.).]

57 [*prīti*.]

58 [*manas*.]

59 [*hṛdaya*.]

2 Analysis of *Śrīmadbhagabadgītā*

Il y a plus affaire à interpreter les interpretations qu'à interpreter les choses, et plus de livres sur les livres que sur autre subject; nous ne faisons que nous entregloser.[1]

2.1 Stocktaking and Issue

Even a cursory look at the surface structure of Baṅkim'candra's *Śrīmadbhagabadgītā* reveals some aspects of its heterogeneous nature. Its centre is the Sanskrit original text of the *Bhagavadgītā*. Baṅkim'candra proceeds *śloka* by *śloka* in his interpretation, thus following the traditional form of commentaries in India.[2] He first gives a Bengali translation of the original and then conducts his interpretation in Bengali. His text is interspersed with quotations in Sanskrit which are in most cases — but not in all[3] — translated or at least paraphrased in Bengali. By contrast, the sometimes extensive quotations from English sources are never translated. References are given either in the text or in footnotes; they are often incomplete, especially when he quotes from his own religious writings. Further, in a few instances, Baṅkim'candra uses cross-references.

In one or two places Latin and French quotations are given, but since they are marginal and negligible, the linguistic material of the commentary can be said to consist of Bengali, English and Sanskrit. In sociolinguistic terms, two among these languages are standard prestige languages: Sanskrit as the medium of classical Indian culture, and English as the rulers' language, vehicle of modern science and the primary means, in colonial India, of upward social mobility. On the other hand, Bengali at the end of the nineteenth century was still in the process of emancipation from the status of a 'vernacular' or low variety.[4] It is thus very significant to determine the role Baṅkim assigns to each of these lingual codes. While on the one hand their use mirrors the lingual capacity of the intended readership — Sanskrit quotations are translated, English quotations are not — the use of Bengali (in the commentary as well as in most of his other writings) resulted from a conscious decision on Baṅkim's part, and involved a certain amount of an educative and didactic effort.[5]

[1] 'It is more our business to interpret the interpretations than to interpret the things, and there are more books on books than on other subjects; we merely comment upon each other.' Michel de Montaigne: *Essais*; Paris, 1962; quoted from *Literaturlexikon*; ed. Walther Killy; Vol. 13: *Begriffe, Realien, Methoden*; Gütersloh/München, 1992:269.

[2] In contrast e.g. to Tilak's *Gita Rahasya* (1935).

[3] See chapter 2.3.1 for an explanation.

[4] Cf. the famous article *Diglossia* by C.A. Ferguson (1959). While the concept of diglossia as being composed of a high and low variety was originally meant to designate the relationship between a standard language and a dialect of that language, it has later been extended so as to cover any coexistence of a prestige language and a distinct popular language, whether linguistically connected or not. Bengali could, on a macro-level and with regard to the time in question, be termed a low variety in accordance with this extended meaning of diglossia; a micro-level investigation would of course have to take into consideration the relation of *sādhu* and *calit bhāṣā* ('polite' and 'usual language') within the Bengali lingual repertoire.

[5] Cf. the discussion in Chapter 2.3.1.

What, from a formal point of view, is the genre that the *Śrīmadbhagabadgītā* belongs to? Baṅkim himself calls it *ṭīkā* or (rarely) *bhāṣya*,[6] and in Bengal it is indeed commonly referred to as *Gītābhāṣya*. In Bengali, *ṭīkā* and *bhāṣya* are used synonymously in the sense of 'commentary'. In Sanskrit, however, these terms are more differentiated: *ṭīkā* (derived from Skt. *ṭīk* 'explain') means 'explanation' or 'commentary' and is especially used for commentaries on commentaries (for example Ānandagiri's *ṭīkā* on Śaṅkara's *bhāṣya* on the *Bhagavadgītā*); *bhāṣya*, on the other hand, covers a larger semantic field and has been submitted to some degree of conceptualisation. Generally, the word denotes a commentary on *sūtras* and on other texts of accepted authority, and it also occurs in the sense of a 'work written in common speech'.[7] According to Winternitz (1967,III,2:419), the *bhāṣya*-style was built upon the older *sūtra*-style and shows the influence of oral disputations by frequent insertion of similes and references to everyday events. The works of Śaṅkara, all commentaries except one, are regarded as examples of the 'fully developed *bhāṣya*-style' in Brückner (1995:239). Scharfe (1976) points out with regard to Patañjali's *Mahābhāṣya* that 'Patañjali calls his work simply *bhāṣya* '[work composed] in colloquial language' and indeed it is styled as a series of shorter or longer debates.' (p. 152) Basically, the properties of a *bhāṣya* extend to structure (proceeding verse by verse) and language (colloquial prose). There is great variety regarding the degree and kind of reference to the respective text being interpreted; there are *bhāṣyas* which are interpretative rather than analytical, i.e. where the text under discussion serves as a platform for further enquiry, not as the goal of it. In this way, independent investigations can be conducted within the limits of this form.[8] But such properties of single samples are beyond the formal frame set by the 'genre'; and it is questionable whether the term 'genre' is applicable at all. If it is, *bhāṣya* is certainly not an independent genre, but a derivative one, a 'text of secondary order' (Assmann 1995:11) as every commentary, for that matter.

These few positive characteristics of a traditional *bhāṣya* are somehow shared by Baṅkim'candra's commentary; it is indeed a commentary 'on a text of accepted authority', it is more or less written in common speech,[9] and it does not contradict those basic properties that the relation between text and commentary is not always very narrow. Moreover it is at times constructed as a debate,[10] and Baṅkim also many times gives explanations of single words in the eliptic way employed in *bhāṣyas*.

But then, it seems, there is another denomination that covers just as many characteristics of the *Śrīmadbhagabadgītā* as *bhāṣya*, i.e. the form of the essay.[11] In

[6] E.g. in the *Introduction* to *ŚBhG*.

[7] Acc. to *Encyclopedia of Indian Literature* (1987,I:469).

[8] Śaṅkara's *bhāṣya* on the *Gītā* (*ŚaBhG*) is an example of such an interpretative *bhāṣya*.

[9] Baṅkim'candra uses *sādhu bhāṣā*, the formal written variety of Bengali and the dominant language of literature until the middle of the twentieth century. Though *sādhu bhāṣā* was never used in colloquial, non-formal speech, it comes close to the 'common speech' of ancient *bhāṣyas* in view of the position it held in the common linguistic repertoire of educated Bengalis in the nineteenth century.

[10] Cf. Baṅkim's discussion of reincarnation (*ŚBhG*:49-60).

[11] The term essay was coined by Montaigne. The essay's most dominant characteristics are, according to Lukacz and Adorno, its empirical orientation as contrasted with normative approaches, its critical potential with regard to fixed systems and its exclusively mediated topics. The last point is well illustrated by the quotation from Montaigne preceding this chapter. Cf. Adorno (1990:9-33).

several instances, single *ślokas* alluding to central concepts trigger methodical expositions and discussions that arguably exceed, in extent as well as in kind, the range of possibilities of a traditional *bhāṣya*. The disproportionate length of some of these comments[12] and the general way — with only marginal reference to the respective *śloka* — in which concepts are discussed in them, make them assume a different and independent character. And apart from some stylistic features of Baṅkim'candra's commentary (e.g. his use of repeated rhetorical questions),[13] it is especially the casual nature and open-endedness of some of Baṅkim's thoughts and arguments that call to mind essayist modes of writing.

Other formal differences between a traditional *bhāṣya* and Baṅkim's are of course due to the new mode of mediation of the *Śrīmadbhagabadgītā*. Baṅkim's text is designed for reading, not for hearing; this accounts for his use of marked quotations, cross-references and footnotes for the delimitation of different types of additional information. These features are obviously due to the conventions of Western nineteenth century scientific prose. Thus we may state that Baṅkim's commentary, while appropriating several stylistic features of a traditional *bhāṣya*, nonetheless comes close to the form of the essay in many instances; accordingly, it can be said to belong to a mixed genre: an essayist *bhāṣya*, or vice versa an essay in *bhāṣya*-style.

However, as the different mode of mediation already indicates, the normative assignation to a genre on the basis of stylistic properties cannot be satisfactory and is not intended here either. Even if Baṅkim'candra's commentary had all the properties of a *bhāṣya*, the continuity of that genre could not be asserted for that reason alone. The greatest differences between traditional *bhāṣyas* and Baṅkim's *Śrīmadbhagabadgītā* lie elsewhere, namely, in their properties as communicative media in very different contexts. Baṅkim uses a journal for dissemination, a thing impossible before 'print capitalism'[14] made its way to India. Further, his readers are neither his pupils nor his adversaries in any concrete sense; his commentary is quite firmly set within certain historical parameters to which he refers again and again; his evaluations and epistemology are submitted to intercultural comparison absent in traditional commentaries.

The purpose of this enquiry is certainly not to deny Baṅkim the right to label his essayist commentary a *bhāṣya*. It is merely to show that he does not, even in these formal matters, stand in an unbroken tradition. The other nineteenth century Bengali commentaries he refers to in the introduction apparently posit to be 'traditional' — notwithstanding a new media situation. Not so Baṅkim: in attempting to write a modern *bhāṣya*, he rather *consciously* adopts a traditional Indian genre; and it is this choice which is significant in the present context.

In contrast to his other religious writings,[15] Baṅkim never revised his commentary for publication as a book. Only the first two chapters were published in his periodical *Pracār* ('Dissemination') from 1886 to 1888, and even those not continuously. After the commentary up to *BhG* 2.17, the last part of which appeared 1293 BE in the *Agrahāyaṇ*-

[12] Cf. the commentaries to *BhG* 2.12, 2.13, etc.

[13] See *ŚBhG*:39.

[14] This term was coined by Benedict Anderson (1991:39ff.), who investigated its role in the making of nationalism.

[15] Except *Letters on Hinduism*, which is also a fragment.

Pauṣ issue (Dec. 1886) of *Pracār*, the commentary's publication was interrupted for more than a year until it started again in *Baiśākh* 1395 BE (April/May 1888). These two chapters, together with the remaining part up to *Gītā* 4.19, were brought out as a book posthumously by his relative Dibyendusundar Bandyopādhyāẏ[16] in 1902, who added the rest of the *Gītā* in Kālīprasanna Siṃha's translation because, as he explains, 'every Hindu desires to keep a book on *dharma* such as the *Gītā* in his own house in complete [form], and there is also need to keep one.'[17] After this, *Śrīmadbhagabadgītā* was not edited until 1941 in the centenary edition (*ŚBhG[b]*); from then on it has been included in the *Racanābalī* editions (i.e. the Complete Works) without any alterations.

In addition to the absence of a final redaction, the modalities of publication in instalments were certainly not favourable to a systematic treatment of the *Gītā*. Baṅkim would have handed over one manuscript to the press while writing the succeeding part; he would often have to work under time pressure. Moreover there was other literary work coming in-between, apart from his professional obligations as a Deputy Collector. Some inconsistencies, reiterations and redundancies in the commentary may be caused by this situation, as well as the unsystematic, cursory use of secondary literature.[18] The commentary has to be read against the background of these modalities.

Baṅkimˈcandra uses a comparatively large number of secondary sources in his commentary. Certain though one may be that not all the sources relevant to his commentary in one way or the other are explicitly referred to, taking account of the texts that are mentioned can all the same give an idea of the range of discussion.[19] These may be grouped as follows:

— the *Bhagavadgītā* as a whole. Though being a fragment, it is nevertheless evident that the commentary takes the whole of the *Gītā* as its body of reference. Baṅkim often leaves behind the discussion of single *ślokas* and not only passes general judgements on the *Gītā* but also uses them as arguments. In a few instances, he explicitly refers to and quotes *ślokas* from the part of the *Gītā* not covered by his commentary.[20] In *Kṛṣṇacaritra* and *Dharmmatattva*, which were completed before the present fragment of his commentary, *ślokas* from later *adhyāyas* of the *Gītā* are discussed.

— ancient Sanskrit texts. Some are quoted in order to trace concepts in the *Gītā* to older sources, others for comparison. Baṅkim quotes from the *Ṛgveda-Saṃhitā*, the *Aitareyabrāhmaṇa*, the *Śatapathabrāhmaṇa*, the *Taittirīya-Upaniṣad*, the *Vṛddhagautamasaṃhitā*, the *Kaṭha-Upaniṣad*; the *Manusmṛti*; the *Vanaparvan*, *Śāntiparvan*, *Udyogaparvan* and *Karṇaparvan* of the *Mahābhārata*; the *Yogasūtra*, the *Sāṃkhyakārikās* and the *Vedāntasāra*; the *Meghadūta*; and the *Viṣṇu-* and *Bhāgavata-*

[16] The son of Rākhālˈcandra Bandyopādhyāẏ, who in turn was Baṅkim's son-in-law and supposedly the editor of *Pracār* (cf. BCJ:659f.: The editor's name was not included in *Pracār*, but Brajendranāth Bandyopādhyāẏ identified him as Rākhālˈcandra).

[17] Cf. the quotation from Dibyendusundar Bandyopādhyāẏ's preface *Saṃgrahakārer nibedan* of that first edition as given in *ŚBhG(b)*:2.

[18] A suitable example is his use of Telang's translation of the *Gītā* (1990 [1882]). Telang is quoted twice at short intervals in 2.46 and 2.47, as well as in 3.10, but hardly anywhere else. Possibly some of the books of reference he used were not constantly available.

[19] For bibliographical references of a number of the following titles, see the bibliography.

[20] e.g. *ŚBhG*:143.

Purāṇas. In some cases, Baṅkim's access to these scriptures appears to have been through editions and collections by Western Indologists.[21]

— Sanskrit commentaries on the *Gītā*. He mentions five altogether, namely, those by Śaṅkara with the *ṭīkā* by Ānandagiri, Śrīdhara, Rāmānuja, Madhusūdana Sarasvatī and Viśvanātha Cakravartin. Only Śaṅkara and Śrīdhara are quoted continuously.

— Bengali translations of the *Gītā* from the nineteenth century. In his preface, Baṅkim gives a list containing translations by Hit'lāl Miśra, Kedār'nāth Datta, Bhūdhar'candra Caṭṭopādhyāẏ and Kṛṣṇaprasanna Sen. These, however, are very rarely referred to afterwards. In addition to them, portions of Kālīprasanna Siṃha's translation of the *Mahābhārata* are given in footnotes, and it seems that Baṅkim read the epic mainly in this translation.[22]

— English translations and commentaries on the *Gītā* and other works of Indologists. The translations Baṅkim quotes and discusses are by Thomson, Davies and Telang. Other Indological works he mentions are Johnson's *Oriental Religions*, *Buddhism* by Rhys Davids, *Indian Antiquities* by Lassen, Muir's *Sanskrit Texts* and *On the Origin of Brahmanism* by Haug. It is evident that his acquaintance with Western Indology was not limited to these texts since he refers to others in his *Kṛṣṇacaritra* and other writings.[23] There is also a single quotation from Stanislas Julien's French translation of Hui-li: *Histoire de la vie de Hiouen-Thsang* (1853).

— other works of Western science, philosophy, literature, etc. In the commentary, mention is made of Tylor's *Primitive Culture*, A. v. Schlegel's *Philosophy of History*, Goethe's *Wilhelm Meister*, Kant's *Metaphysics of Ethics*, and further J.S. Mill's *Three Essays on Religion*, Comte (without direct reference to any text) and Carpenter's *Mental Physiology*.

— lastly, Baṅkim repeatedly refers to and quotes from his own writings. Besides his *Dharmmatattva* and *Kṛṣṇacaritra*, he also mentions a shorter essay, *Sāṃkhyadarśan*, and one of his novels, *Sītārām*.

This list indicates the extent of the textual material involved in Baṅkim's interpretation of the *Gītā*; the larger part of these texts are also referred to in his other religious writings. The separate listing of English, Bengali and Sanskrit commentaries or translations of the *Gītā* is justified by the different treatment Baṅkim gives to these sources, as I will demonstrate in the Chapters 2.3.2 and 2.3.3.

A significant fact demonstrated by this list is the following: almost all of the Western sources he uses are from the nineteenth century (i.e. in his own terms, 'modern'), while most of the Indian material he works with is very ancient ('traditional'). There is no reference at all to the important contemporary and preceding writings on religious topics in Bengal, e.g. to the most influential and diversified theorists of the Brāhma Samāj; the Bengali commentaries fall into the 'traditional' category. Likewise, pre-modern Western sources are totally excluded from his discussion. This inventory of texts implies a choice — whether conscious or unconscious — and, at the same time, betrays a specific orientation. It is indicative of the hermeneutical frame of the discussion in the commentary, and can itself be read as a result of a perceptive pattern

[21] e.g. John Muir's *Original Sanskrit Texts* (1858-63), and possibly also Wilson's translation of the *Viṣṇupurāṇa* (1864-77).

[22] Cf. his remarks in *Kṛṣṇacaritra* (*BR* II:542n).

[23] Especially Friedrich Max Müller, who is discussed in various of Baṅkim's writings.

on Baṅkim'candra's part, which is also detectable in the conclusions, as shall be elaborated upon.

Before beginning the analysis, I wish to give a brief survey of the current state of research regarding the commentary and Baṅkim'candra as a religious thinker, together with an outline of the procedure in the analysis. As stated in the introduction, Baṅkim'candra's commentary has not been given the same amount of attention as his other religious writings.[24] The only article entirely devoted to it, by Ajit Ray (1986, included in Minor's book on modern *Gītā* reception) is mainly descriptive and leaves many questions undiscussed. The most voluminous text about Baṅkim's commentary is included in Hīrendranāth Datta (1940-1), whose interest is exclusively religious; in giving a synopsis of *Śrīmadbhagabadgītā*, Hīrendranāth's main aim is to point out that Baṅkim did acknowledge the unification of *karma-*, *jñāna-* and *bhaktiyoga* which Hīrendranāth sees as the essence of the *Gītā*. Rather critical statements about Baṅkim's commentary are found in another book on modern *Gītā* reception by Jaẏantānuj Bandyopādhyāẏ (1994), where single topics are discussed with reference to various neo-Hindu[25] interpretations from a sociological perspective. The German theologist Huber (1991) also takes it into account in his comprehensive examination of modern commentaries on the *Gītā*. The most critical study (and the most influential on the topic, as far as German research is concerned — including the aforementioned work) of the concept of *dharma* as expounded in Baṅkim's *Śrīmadbhagabadgītā* is by Hacker (1978 [1958]). The chapter Anil'candra Bandyopādyāẏ (1989:217-28) devotes to the commentary does not go beyond a synopsis. There is no extensive study of the commentary. Compared especially to *Kṛṣṇacaritra*, the contemporary reaction to it also appears to have been very limited. The only available account is included in the first biography on Baṅkim.[26] The commentary is quoted and referred to at times, but much of the literature on his religious thinking does not take it into consideration, and sometimes it is explicitly excluded.[27] The commentary is thus a little noted text by an author — Baṅkim — who has been the object of an abundance of secondary literature ever since his lifetime.

Baṅkim'candra is mentioned in practically every book on nineteenth century Indian history, and certainly every history of modern Bengali or Indian literature. His status as the founder of the Bengali novel is asserted with overwhelming unanimity,[28] and the positive assessment of his creativity in this field prevails; there are only few

[24] I must admit, however, that, despite having collected a fair amount of secondary literature, I cannot claim completeness. The amount of articles on Baṅkim'candra spread over practically all Bengali journals, combined with the lack of comprehensive bibliographies, has made such an aspiration appear to be an exercise in futility.

[25] For a discussion of the validity of this term, see Chapter 2.4.

[26] Hīrendranāth Datta records a discussion with Baṅkim'candra about the *Gītā* and mentions the commentary (*BJ*:180-4).

[27] e.g. Tanika Sarkar (1994).

[28] Already in Dae, Ar Cy [*sic.*] (1877) and Dinesh Chandra Sen's *History of Bengali Language and Literature* (1911); again in Śrīkumār Bandyopādhyāẏ (1988) (started in 1923), Priyaranjan Sen (1932), Sukumar Sen (1965), Dušan Zbavitel (1976), etc. Cf. also Teoẏārī (1993, last chapter) about Baṅkim's influence on Hindi literature, as well as some of the essays in *BCEIP*.

unfavourable evaluations.[29] The picture is different in the case of his essayist and religious writings, which have provoked controversial opinions ever since their first appearance. It is a fact that in West Bengal and Bangladesh (as well as, to a lesser degree, in India as a whole), Baṅkim has been (and to some extent still is) perceived as a national figure, a fact that may account for many biased evaluations of his works. He is construed into the later debates on areas such as nationalism, communalism, etc., which he himself helped open up, and has in this way been instrumental in polarising opinions and standpoints.[30] As a result, much of the huge amount of writings on Baṅkim'candra is based on selective readings of his works and either decidedly appreciative or decidedly negative. The reception of Baṅkim'candra, his appropriation by later nationalism as well as his rejection, is, however, a huge separate topic; in the present context, a cursory survey — limited to the aspects of religious thinker and nationalist — must suffice.[31]

Rabīndranāth Ṭhākur's (1978 [1894])[32] assessment of Baṅkim in the year of the latter's death stresses Baṅkim's attempt to 'steer clear of factions' in interpreting tradition, and his rational approach to the Śāstras. However, in an independent essay on *Kr̥ṣṇacaritra*, Ṭhākur (1978 [1894])[33] criticises what he perceives as the artificiality of Baṅkim's conception of Kr̥ṣṇa, calling it an 'incarnate theory' and questioning the validity of the search for truth in the shape of historicity. Similar criticism was uttered by a number of Baṅkim's contemporaries.[34] Brajendranath Seal's (1903) assessment of Baṅkim as a thinker is harshly derogative, in sharp contrast to Hīrendranāth Datta's eulogy.[35] A critique of *Kr̥ṣṇacaritra* was forwarded in Surendramohan Bhaṭṭācārya's

[29] e.g. J.C. Ghosh (1948:152ff.), Manabendra Bandyopadhyay (1985); and Dāś'gupta and Bandyopādhyāẏ (1969).

[30] Baṅkim — chiefly as the author of *Bande mātaram* — continues to be appropriated by Hindu chauvinist circles (e.g. by Bal Thakeray in a TV-interview in 1993); the *Bande mātaram* is used by the RSS and VHP, and there are claims to reinstall it as India's National Anthem (cf. Klostermaier 1992:esp.178).

[31] Monographs on Baṅkim'candra without relevance to the interpretation of his religious thought are excluded from this survey but have in a few cases been listed in the bibliography. — For a list of English translations from Baṅkim'candra's works (besides those given in the bibliography), cf. Clinton B. Seely (1997:102).

[32] *Baṅkim'candra*, read 1894 and first printed in *Sādhanā* that year. Included in the *Racanābalī* edition (Vol. 9:399-410); for an English translation, see *BCEIP*:7-15.

[33] *Kr̥ṣṇacaritra*; also included in *Ādhunik sāhitya* (*Rabīndra racanābalī*, Vol. 9:446-62).

[34] Nabīn'candra Sen in *Āmār jīban* (acc. to Śaṅkarīprasād Basu, 1990: 34f.); Dvijendranāth Ṭhākur, Rāj'nārāẏaṇ Basu (cf. *BJ*:334ff.) and others. A short summary of these controversies is included in Rabīndrakumār Dāś'gupta (1988-9:42f.). — For testimonies by contemporaries, see the books *Baṅkim prasaṅga* (Sureś'candra Samāj'pati 1982 [1922]), *Purātan prasaṅga* (Bipin'bihārī Gupta 1989), *Baṅkim smārak grantha* (Kālīprasād Bandyopādhyāẏ 1972), *Kācher mānuṣ baṅkim'candra* (Somendranāth Basu 1964) and some of the articles in *BCEIP*. A contemporary polemic Muslim reaction to Baṅkim's writings is *Baṅkim duhitā* by Sheikh Mohammad Idris (according to Joarder [1977:52], unfortunately without dating). Ānisujjāmān (in *Mus'lim mānas o bāṃlā sāhitya 1757-1918*) mentions parodies of Baṅkim's 14 novels written by Ābul Hosen (acc. to Bārid'baraṇ Ghoṣ 1993:34).

[35] Hīrendranāth Datta's earliest assessment of Baṅkim's religious ideas is included in *BJ*. Later he published a monograph *Dārśanik baṅkim'candra* (1940). The English translation of an anniversary speech (without dating) is included in *BCEIP* (64-70).

Rādhākṛṣṇatattva (1906-7).[36] The crucial turn in assessing Baṅkim appears to have taken place in the hands of Bipin'candra Pāl, Aurobindo and other leaders of the *svadeśī* agitations starting in 1905: the novel *Ānandamaṭh* and especially the hymn *Bande mātaram* were perceived as revolutionary literature and the *mantra* of the nascent freedom struggle.[37] Aurobindo stylised Baṅkim into the Ṛṣi of the movement;[38] and Baṅkim also began to be noticed abroad as more than a novelist[39]. Kājī Āb'dul Odud (1936), on the other hand, is a good example of how a large part of the Muslim perception of Baṅkim limited its scope to the novelist, assigning no value at all to his social and religious writings.[40] Hīrendranāth Datta's (1940-1) mainly religious approach to Baṅkim's commentary has already been mentioned. Mohit'lāl Majum'dār's *Baṅkim baraṇ* (1949)[41] is an evaluation of Baṅkim in decidedly eulogising and nationalist terms somewhat in the Aurobindo tradition.[42] A more distanced, sympathetic evaluation — and to all appearances a very influential one as well — is Arabinda Poddār's *Baṅkim mānas* (1994 [1951]). Here, Baṅkim's writings are grouped into three phases; Baṅkim's last work phase is conceived as a defeat of the creative artist in Baṅkim or a retreat into the private, and a dichotomy in Baṅkim's personality is roughly elaborated. Baṅkim's *dharma* is seen as a synthesis of its traditional meaning with Comte's and Bentham's concepts. In 1958, Hacker's important analysis of *dharma* in neo-Hinduism appeared, followed by related studies. Baṅkim's respective argumentations are explained as non-traditional adaptations of Western thought, placed in a decidedly apologetical context, with the ultimate purpose of establishing the superiority of Hinduism. A comprehensive and rather balanced article by T.W. Clark (1961) investigates Baṅkim'candra's contribution to emerging Hindu nationalism. Bhabatoṣ Datta's *Cintānāẏak baṅkim'candra* (1961) offers a detailed study of Baṅkim's assimilation of (also religious) ideas in the frame of nineteenth century Bengal. Asit'kumār Bhaṭṭācārya (1964), in a similar vein, describes Baṅkim's religious ideas in a historical and philosophical perspective, but his critique is far more pronounced. In the part on *Dharmmatattva*, the possibility of a coordination of faculties is questioned, and incoherences as well as

[36] According to Rām'kṛṣṇa Bhaṭṭācārya (1994:44).

[37] The importance of Baṅkim's writings (especially *Ānandamaṭh* and *Bande mātaram*) for the 'extremists' is noted in most historiographies on the topic; cf. Argov (1967); Amalendu De (1974); Sumit Sarkar (1977 [1973]), Sankar Ghose (1969), Sandīp Bandyopādhyāẏ (1993); Broomfield (1968); Haithcox (1971), etc. Amales Tripathi (1967a) portrays Aurobindo's and the extremist's reception of Baṅkim as a misinterpretation (p. 15).

[38] In Aurobindo, 1940, 1955, 1986; Bipin'candra Pāl's writings on Baṅkim are collected in Bārid'baraṇ Ghoṣ (1984). This reception is dealt with in Manoj Das (1994).

[39] The *Encyclopedia Brittanica* 1910 (*BCEIP*:607-8), Farquhar (1924) — calling Baṅkim's religious thought 'a house of cards' —, Kohn (1928).

[40] Cf. the extract from a writing by Rezaul Karim in *BCEIP* (1994) which is probably taken from Rejāul Karīm (1944). Supriyā Sen Bhaṭṭācārya (1996:162, n.3) gives a quotation from Rejāul Karīm (1944) which makes clear that Karīm perceives Baṅkim's criticism as limited to specific rulers and not extending to Islam as such.

[41] Partly reprinted in a recently published collection of essays (Mohit'lāl Majum'dār:1994).

[42] Based on earlier writings (some read at Baṅkim's birth centenary), Mohit'lāl regards Baṅkim as a nationalist and pioneer of humanism, and the nineteenth century as the age of *mānab'dharma* (Beng.), i.e. 'man's *dharma* [or religion]'; *Kṛṣṇacaritra* is seen as the erection of 'the grand image of *man*' (*mānuṣeri mahimāmaẏ mūrti* [Beng.]) (p. 20).

Rabīndranāth Ṭhākur's *Religion of Man*. Kṣetra Gupta (1989) and Pārthapratim Bandyopādhyāẏ (1990) focus on literary analysis with a new theoretical outlook; in a collection of essays devoted to various aspects of Baṅkim (ed. Kṣetra Gupta 1990), Rabirañjan Caṭṭopādhyāẏ deals with Baṅkim's personal and literary treatment of Kr̥ṣṇa. Bad'rul Hāsān identifies Hindu national consciousness as the main impulse at the root of Baṅkim's writings in general. The difficulties of a balanced assessment of Baṅkim in Bangladesh are documented in different essays edited by Hak (1990), actually a record of speeches held at the occasion of the celebration of Baṅkim's 150th birthday. Ābul Kāsem Phaj'lul Hak portrays Baṅkim as a religious reformer who is yet to be understood rather than condemned (statements like this one, and the celebration in Dhaka as such, provoked violent controversy, as the editorial notes inform us). Āh'mad Śarīph, here as well as in another essay (1990b), defends Baṅkim from the allegation of being communalist, stresses however the (tragic) irrelevance of his religious writings. Bad'ruddīn Umar (1990), in his monograph on Bidyāsāgar, criticises Baṅkim as a chauvinist partly in Marxist terms. Śyāmal Rāẏ (1990-1), in his investigation of nationalism in Bengali novels, defends Baṅkim from the reproach of being communal by stressing that he did not consciously attack Muslims.

Śaṅkarīprasād Basu (1990) traces Baṅkim's religious thinking and occupation with Kr̥ṣṇa back to the times before the Hastie controversy, thus denying a clear-cut demarcation point for any new orientation on Baṅkim's part. A historical account of the nineteenth century (apparently following Sumit Sarkar) is Ghatak (1991), where the communalist pulls in Baṅkim and the 'Hindu revivalists' of his times are made explicit quite convincingly. Āh'mad Māẏ'hār (1991) displays a rather unprejudiced attitude towards Baṅkim, but skips over the religious writings. Baṅkim's commentary is treated in two studies of *Gītā* commentaries, as mentioned above: Ajit Ray (1991) and Huber (1991). Amitrasūdan Bhaṭṭācārya, a specialist on Baṅkim and author of many books on the topic (e.g. *idem* [1986] on various topics related to Baṅkim), published a detailed and well researched biography in 1991, which also contains reprints of writings not included in the *Racanābalī* edition. In a valuable assessment, Bhabatoṣ Caṭṭopādhyāẏ (1991) points out the absence of any fixed theoretical standpoint in Baṅkim's later writings. *Kr̥ṣṇacaritra* was translated into English in Pradip Bhattacharya (1991). Serge Bouez's (1992) cursory remarks — on apparently very thin factual footing — portray Baṅkim as a Hindu fundamentalist who violently opposed the Muslims. Śibājī Bandyopādhyāẏ (1993) critically analyses certain conceptual constellations in modern Hinduism, starting with an examination of *Ānandamaṭh* and drawing a line to Vivekānanda. Bārid'baraṇ Ghoṣ (1993) — who also edited Bipin'candra Pāl's writings on Baṅkim'-candra (1989) and essays by Rāj'nārāẏaṇ Basu (1995) — provides a survey of nineteenth century controversial reactions to Baṅkim'candra; the same, in a more detailed fashion, is found in Biśvanāth Mukhopādhyāẏ (1993). The use of Baṅkim's writings in early twentieth century nationalism is dealt with in Sandīp Bandyopādhyāẏ's (1993) historiographical account of that period. Amiya P. Sen (1993) furnishes a very noteworthy, methodically well-grounded enquiry into late nineteenth century 'Hindu revivalism' in which Baṅkim is amply discussed and posited in the perspective of contemporary developments; Sen argues against the compartmentalisation of Baṅkim's personality and attempts a general assessment. Alokeranjan Dasgupta (1994) inquires into the bearings of the colonial situation on Baṅkim and Māikel (Michael) Madhusūdan Datta, and focusses on Baṅkim's skill in polemics as a creative way of dealing with those circumstances while conceiving his turn towards religion as a rather deplorable event.

The influence of nineteenth century Orientalist and Christian thought on Baṅkim's (and others') cleansed image of Kṛṣṇa is the subject of an essay by David L. Haberman (1994). Nationalist and neo-Hindu *Gītā* reception is the topic of Jaẏantānuj Bandyopādhyāẏ's (1994) very critical study (from a Marxist angle); Baṅkim's religious ideas are analysed as a part of the repertoire of modern Hinduism. A significant contribution to the discussion are also Rām'kṛṣṇa Bhaṭṭācārya's essays (1994 and 1995); here a valuable attempt is made to detect and explain inconsistencies in Baṅkim's writings, and the analysis is scrutinising enough not to take recourse to simplistic stereotypes otherwise commonly alluded to instead of a genuine explanation. Again in 1994, a huge volume appeared on the occasion of the centenary of Baṅkim's death, which in large part consists of excerpts from assessments of Baṅkim ever since his lifetime (in English translation). Some (especially non-Indian) significant research is not included; the long editorial essay by Bhabatoṣ Caṭṭopādhyāẏ moves in a vein similar to *idem* (1991).[50] Tanika Sarkar (1994) — also reacting to various pre-prints of the book mentioned hereafter — argues convincingly that Baṅkim's novels and essayist writings should not be dissociated in assessments of his thinking, and demonstrates that Baṅkim's nationalist constructions are destabilised by narrative elements in his novels. Sudipta Kaviraj (1995), departing from premises similar to Partha Chatterjee's, presents a comprehensive monograph on different aspects of Baṅkim, in a broad theoretical framework informed largely by postmodernist theory. In the chapter on *Kṛṣṇacaritra*, the changes in the image of Kṛṣṇa are analysed as a classicisation, and the political purport is determined as the erection of a myth of praxis through this Kṛṣṇa.[51] Pūrṇendu Patrī (1996) has published the first volume of an extensive, strictly chronological biography of Baṅkim'candra covering the years 1838-58; the projected three more volumes will not be written because of Patrī's untimely death.[52] Finally, Supriẏā Sen Bhaṭṭācārya (1996) deals with Baṅkim'candra's patriotism on the basis of his novels and a few essays without specific focus on his religious writings.[53]

If, then, there has been a long and controversial discussion of Baṅkim's religious thinking, and also a trend towards a more distanced scholarly assessment in recent years, the commentary has not sufficiently been noticed, as this sketch makes clear. This grants the opportunity to reconsider, on its basis, some existing theses concerning Baṅkim, as well as to take up a few questions that have not yet been discussed. The present analysis will thus focus on the commentary, without however abandoning the context of Baṅkim's other writings. In a broader perspective, this analysis is intended to be a micro-study of some features of Baṅkim's modern Hindu thought.

[50] For a review, see Harder (1995).

[51] This book has provoked very different reactions. The highly appreciative review of this work by Clinton Seely (1997) is countered by Ramkrishna Bhattacharya's often polemical criticism. Bhattacharya calls Kaviraj 'so Eurocentric that he is incapable of studying any phenomenon in its own space-time context' and is annoyed about his alleged adherence to 'almost all postmodern guru-s' whose phraseology he sees 'religiously employed' (Ramkrishna Bhattacharya 1997:77).

[52] Publications later than 1996/7 could not be taken into account.

[53] Chapter 7 of this book discusses Baṅkim's 'communalism' and — in a not very convincing manner — makes a claim for innocence; Sen Bhaṭṭācārya however gives a noteworthy set of quotations from several critics of Baṅkim (among them Mahāmmad Habibur Rah'mān, Is'māil Hosen Sirājī, Munīr Caudhurī, Nārāẏaṇ Caudhurī, Rejāul Karīm, Āh'mad Śarīph).

Particular attention is accordingly given to deviations from traditional Hindu standpoints as well as to typically nineteenth century communicative strategies. The *Bhagavadgītā* is thus generally discussed only insofar as Baṅkim makes it the object of interpretation. In cases of disparities between text and commentary, the *Gītā* will be consulted for verification, and their significance will be discussed. But no encompassing attempt will be made to positively bring out the meaning of the *Bhagavadgītā* either by itself or as mediated by Baṅkim's commentary. The same applies for Baṅkim's quotations from ancient Sanskrit sources: it is not their meaning in itself which is the object of the present research, but the function and meaning they assume in the commentary. Likewise, the relationship between the *Śrīmadbhagabadgītā* and other commentaries on the *Gītā*, whether ancient or modern, will be dealt with only marginally.

It appears to be useful to distinguish between two modes in which the commentary produces meaning. The first has been called the conceptual, the second the communicative mode. The conceptual mode of meaning is dealt with in Chapter 2.2. In it, two important concepts Baṅkim'candra derives from the *Bhagavadgītā* will be examined, along with his perception of the *Gītā* as a text. In Chapter 2.3, the communicative dimension of the text will be discussed. Here the commentary is viewed as a communicative process, and the way in which Baṅkim deals with the different parties actively or passively involved in this process will be analysed. By the consideration of these relationships, it will be attempted to determine the position of the author in the commentary. The determination of shifts between normative and empirical categories, a common feature of Baṅkim's argumentations as will be shown, is of great importance in all these examinations.

In the final Chapter, the particular conclusions from the preceding Chapters are integrated into a general assessment of Baṅkim'candra's *Śrīmadbhagabadgītā*, and the historical context is regained. The commentary will be described as a text in which several different purposes or intentions (the hierarchically highest of which is cultural self-assertion) collide and impose constraints upon each other. In these terms, an attempt is made to account for the inconsistencies inherent in Baṅkim's religious thought. His religious writings are located in the frame of his entire work by showing the continuity of central issues as well as the significant shift in his orientation around 1880. Lastly, with respect to the conclusions arrived at, the terminology used to designate modern Hindu thinking will be critically examined.

Whenever relevant, Baṅkim'candra's other works are integrated into the analysis; in this way, the usual synchronic perspective of the inquiry is supported by a diachronic one. In some cases, the step-by-step development of the positions Baṅkim asserts in the commentary is relevant from a historical perspective.

2.2 The Conceptual Dimension

The aim of this chapter is to explore Baṅkim's approach to the *Bhagavadgītā* (2.2.1) and his discussion of two central topics: *dharma* and *svadharma* (2.2.2), and the plurality of worship (2.2.3). The subchapters are closely interconnected thematically; in all of them, Baṅkim's cleansing of traditional features with the aid of nineteenth century rational philosophy and philology, and their subsequent reapplication to tradition in order to assert Hinduism's superiority, becomes evident. The material of the commentary is in no way exhausted or covered by this exploration. Other topics are left for a detailed treatment, e.g. his elaboration of *niṣkāma karman* as activist ethics with nationalist potentialities,[1] his discussion of the interrelation between the *Gītā* and the Vedas, the long passages on reincarnation, the imperishability of the *ātman*, sacrifice, etc. The present choice of topics is, apart from a necessary confinement of the object of research, motivated by the examplary nature of the chosen topics with regard to Baṅkim's religious thinking. It is in the discussion of these topics that Baṅkim's hermeneutical position *between* two cultural systems, his attempts at universalisation of traditional conceptions and his specific mingling of empirical and normative categories can be most clearly perceived. In all of them, Baṅkim in fact uses the resources of argumentation from Western rationalism and traditional Hinduism to interrogate both.[2] Significantly, all three have also been treated by him outside the commentary.

2.2.1 The *Bhagavadgītā* as a Text

Before going into the interpretations Baṅkim'candra gives of certain concepts that feature in some form in the *Bhagavadgītā*, his general approach to it as a text must be discussed, especially since he regarded it as *the* central Hindu text, and it was his most important point of reference for ancient Hinduism.[3] He presents a set of premises or basic assumptions regarding the *Gītā* as the object of his investigation. It is important to clearly perceive these premises, for they delimit the discursive frame in which Baṅkim'candra wishes to operate, and serve, in fact, as criteria along which certain objections are repeatedly dismissed or disqualified. They determine the proper *locus* of the whole discussion. The premises relate to issues such as the *Gītā*'s authorship, its relation to the *Mahābhārata*, its homogeneity and, dependent upon these, its authoritative status;[4] and further, the epistemological conditions to which the *Gītā* is submitted as well as the determination of the contemporary frame within which it is

[1] This has been dealt with in Bandyopādhyāẏ, Jaẏantānuj (1994:133), where a line is drawn to Tilak's *Gītārahasya* as the most decidedly activist modern commentary. Aurobindo followed Tilak in assigning a prominent place in the *Gītā*'s teachings to *niṣkāma karman*; cf. Minor (1991:64).

[2] Cf. Tanika Sarkar 1994:2555.

[3] e.g. in the Hastie controversy, where the first text Baṅkim recommends Hastie to study in the original is the '*Bhagabat-Gita*'. *Dharmmatattva* is in large parts connected with the *Gītā*.

[4] These are dealt with by Huber (1991:38ff.) under the heading of 'Einleitungsfragen' (i.e. 'introductory issues') in accordance with the methodology of biblical studies.

relevant.[5]

The *Bhagavadgītā* is a part of the *Bhīṣmaparvan* (6.23-40)[6] of the *Mahābhārata*. Baṅkim sums up the preceding happenings, describes the narrative structure in which it stands and sketches the causal links establishing its authority, which are immanent in the epic (*ŚBhG*:21f.). The dialogue between Kṛṣṇa and Arjuna is reported simultaneously to the blind king Dhṛtarāṣṭra by Saṃjaya at Hastināpura with the aid of the 'divine eye'. Thus Kṛṣṇa and Arjuna are the speakers, Saṃjaya the narrator; the mythological author of the whole *Mahābhārata* is Ṛṣi Vyāsa (who is also an active character within the narration). The *Mahābhārata* is traditionally classified as a *smṛti* text, i.e. a conditionally authoritative text not originated in a divine revelation (as contrasted to *śruti*), but composed by a human author (*pauruṣeya*). Baṅkim disqualifies what he considers an uncritical, traditional acceptance of the epic's legitimisation of narrative authority:

> With those who say that this book, belonging to the *Mahābhārata*, was written by the Maharṣi Vyāsa, who through the force of *yoga* was omniscient and infallible, and that for this reason such doubt is out of place here, we cannot enter into discussion. I can only remark that this commentary has not been written for readers of this category. (*ŚBhG*:39)

Despite the existence of a nominal author, there are no hints in the *Mahābhārata* of any concrete authorship; the author himself, Vyāsa — even if he did not so prominently figure in the plot — clearly belongs to the world being narrated, and is integrated into the narrative structure. The actual origin of the epic, as well as its relationship to the society contemporary to its creation, is veiled. Sudipta Kaviraj puts it thus: 'In the Indian tradition, the text not only hides the individual (which it does more or less in every civilization: we know very little of Plato except his books), it erases him. Perhaps it could be put still more strongly — it was only someone who could erase himself who qualified to be a writer of such frightfully objective texts. The pretence of a collective mind in the act of inscribing is exceptionally strong. The author is not the text's creator, but its instrument. He is almost an amanuensis of a structure of ideas enriched, perfected, economized and sharpened by an impersonal tradition.'[7]

While one could certainly argue about this statement — 'erasure' appears to be too strong — it is true that authorship in epical and paurāṇic Indian texts is often veiled; and one may interpret this 'veiling' as constituting a border between the sacred and the profane. According to their narrative causality, origin and authorship are removed from human access and taken into the sacred sphere. It is this border or gap determining traditional attitudes to the text of the *Gītā* which Baṅkim'candra does not accept, and which he fills by premises in order to gain access with new tools. He does not remove the opposition with regard to the *Gītā* between sacred and profane as such; personally, he declares to believe firmly in the divinity of Kṛṣṇa and the authoritativeness of the teachings expounded in the *Gītā* (at least the greatest part of it). By touching on the issue of authorship, however, he denies it, strictly speaking, the status of a sacred and

[5] The dating of the *Gītā* and the *Mahābhārata*, which is thoroughly discussed in *Kṛṣṇacaritra*, does not play any role in the commentary. There is but one passing remark on the *Gītā* (or *Mahābhārata* as a whole?) as a book 'written three thousand years ago.' (*ŚBhG*:120)

[6] Baṅkim, who apparently used Kālīprasanna Siṃha's Bengali translation of the *Mahābhārata*, gives Chapters 25-42 (*ŚBhG*:21).

[7] Sudipta Kaviraj (1995:74f.).

thus *per se* authoritative *text*; it is rather the best, but still occasionally distorted, document of Kr̥ṣṇa's *dharma*. In *Deb'tattva o hindudharmma*, he explicitly counts himself among the group of those who hold that 'there is no adequate reason to believe that any *dharma* ['religion'] or book of *dharma* is proclaimed by God.' (*BR* II:791) As far as *dharma* is concerned, his position is withdrawn in the commentary and other later writings inasfar as he presents the acceptance of *dharma* revealed by Lord Kr̥ṣṇa as a question of personal belief. But the assertion that all *books* of *dharma* are of human origin determines his approach throughout. What happens here, in comparison with a traditional approach, is a shifting of the borderline between the divine and the human, a shifting in some respects similar to that which the Bible underwent in the biblical criticism of nineteenth century Europe.[8] The *Gītā* continues to be regarded, ultimately, as a divine utterance, but only on a level of subtextual content; as a text, by contrast, it belongs entirely to the human sphere. Baṅkim'candra transfers it into a different mode of textuality. Once conceived thus, it can be approached with new methods and tested against new criteria.

The narrative frame in which the *Gītā* is situated is in this manner taken apart. Firstly, the *Gītā* is seen as a piece of *kāvya*, and does not constitute a historical or elsewise actual speech event. Baṅkim argues that it does not 'seem very likely that, at the time when two opposite armies in battle-formation are ready to attack each other, a commander of one side should place his chariot between both armies and listen to eighteen chapters on *yoga* and *dharma*' (*ŚBhG*:38).[9] Secondly, the narration of the dialogue by Saṃjaya is dismissed as supernatural and not to be believed because of the 'divine eye' (*ŚBhG*:22). Thirdly, Vyāsa's authorship is disclaimed, and in this way the position of the *Gītā* in and its relationship to the *Mahābhārata* are opened up for consideration. The insertion of the *Gītā* into the *Mahābhārata* is in this course taken for granted and perceived as a 'device'.[10] Fourthly, the possibility of interpolations in the course of textual tradition is admitted.[11] In these determinations, especially the third and the forth, Baṅkim'candra of course merely appropriates and executes nineteenth century Western paradigms of philological research, as has often been pointed out,[12] and particularly Kashinath Trimbak Telang appears to have had a considerable impact on him.[13]

Accordingly, Baṅkim, in his portrayal of the *Mahābhārata* as basically a historical account, identifies several sources of distortions in *Kr̥ṣṇacaritra*. There is the gap (also possibly a time-gap) between the author and the events he reports, and he may uncritically rely on hear-say (*janaśruti*) in his account as well as circulate his own

[8] A famous example of this new criticism (within the older tradition of Natural Religion) and certainly a model for Baṅkim, especially for his *Kr̥ṣṇacaritra*, is Seeley's *Ecce Homo* (1869).

[9] Cf. also *Dharmmatattva* (*BR* II:633): 'I do not believe that Kr̥ṣṇa said all these words, mounted on Arjuna's chariot, on Kurukṣetra, directly before the war. There are many reasons not to believe this. It can be said that the *Gītā* is interpolated into the *Mahābhārata*, but I believe that Kr̥ṣṇa is the creator of the *dharma* proclaimed in the *Gītā*.'

[10] *kauśal* (*ŚBhG*:38; *ŚBhG[a]*:693).

[11] They can be excluded from the time of Śaṅkara's commentary onwards, as Baṅkim stresses, but for the time between the composition of the *Gītā* and Śaṅkara, no proof of accurate tradition is available.

[12] e.g. in Sisir Kumar Das (1984:173).

[13] Cf. the remarks about Telang in *Kr̥ṣṇacaritra* (*BR* II:577f.).

opinions.[14] The mode of textual tradition accounts for deviations from the historically original text and for the greater extent of such deviations in the *Mahābhārata* than in European 'books of history'; oral tradition facilitated the insertion and alteration of texts. Further, Baṅkim argues that the desire to contribute to a book of the *Mahābhārata*'s popularity must have been greater than in the case of Greek and Roman historiographical texts. And he adds a nationalist interpretation of the 'veiling' of authorship common in Indian epic texts: While authors from other countries were intent on gaining fame and therefore inserted their names into their writings, the Indian brahmins set to work without egotism and desire and therefore kept their names secret (in apparent contradiction, however, with the preceding explanation: their desire was there, merely defined differently as the wish to contribute to a popular epic).[15]

Still in *Kṛṣṇacaritra*, Baṅkim develops a larger frame to classify the different parts of the *Mahābhārata* on the basis of historicity. Starting from a set of seven criteria (inbuilt index and summary, inconsistency, stylistic characteristics, inconsistent character description, unrelatedness, redundancy), he distinguishes between three levels (*star*) of historicity.[16] At the base of these is the historical kernel: 'Firstly, an original skeleton; in it there is nothing apart from the narration of the Pāṇḍavas' lives and the related story of Kṛṣṇa.'[17] The first level, Baṅkim holds, is the narrative elaboration of this skeleton written by one author in which Kṛṣṇa is not regarded as an avatāra but simply as a human. The second consists of interpolations by other authors not long after the creation of the first; this level could be removed without doing harm to the basic chain of events, and on it Kṛṣṇa's divinity is established. The third level, finally, contains a multitude of later creations over centuries which were inserted into the *Mahābhārata* and are of varying quality.[18] Baṅkim then assigns the *Bhagavadgītā* to this third level. It cannot be called true in the sense that the situation in which it is placed has historically occurred, but it does reflect the essence of the divine Lord Kṛṣṇa's teachings. The main purpose of *Kṛṣṇacaritra* is to establish Kṛṣṇa as the 'ideal man' (*ādarśa puruṣ* [Beng.]), devoid of all supernatural elements, and to assert his historicity[19] — in

[14] Cf. *ŚBhG*:32f., e.g. 'A particular hate of the creator of the *Gītā* against the mixture of *varṇas* is apparent; he has placed the censure of *varṇa*-mixing even in the mouth of the Lord Himself.'

[15] *Kṛṣṇacaritra*, *BR* II:411f.

[16] For a discussion cf. Jaẏantānuj Bandyopādhyāẏ (1993:54).

[17] *Kṛṣṇacaritra* (*BR* II:428).

[18] Baṅkim presents this third layer as an equivalent to mass education — an assumption which, if applied to Indian epic literature in general, is substantiated by various folk traditions based on epical subjects; and particularly the *yātrā* in Bengal is a prominent pre-modern effective medium of communication. Cf. also Sudipta Kaviraj (1995:84), whose (by all appearances incorrect) allegation is that this layer, according to Baṅkim, ought 'to be discounted in any serious analysis of its [the *Mahābhārata*'s] philosophic or aesthetic truth.' In that case, Baṅkim would indeed have overlooked that 'the *Gītā*, his favourite text, would almost certainly be disqualified' (ibid.). That is not so.

[19] Cf. Amales Tripathi (1967b:479): 'He [Kṛṣṇa] was *l'uomo universale*, whom a degenerate India had forgotten for a life of ignorance and imbecility.' The denial to found religion on anything supernatural (despite his proclaimed personal belief) runs through Baṅkim's writings, and there are decisively no statements by him as the following: 'one must find out a super-natural basis for religion' (Halder 1977:93), which contains a consistently erroneous translation of *naisargik* (Beng.) — 'natural' (cf. *BR* II:791). Sudipta Kaviraj (1995:78) regards it as the basic contradiction in Baṅkim's approach to look for the historical in the mythical, since both are entirely different sorts of texts.

the course of which Kṛṣṇa is almost completely stripped of the attributes assigned to him by *Vaiṣṇava* tradition.[20] Remarkably, the claim to Kṛṣṇa's historicity is more important to Baṅkim than that to his divinity. In this frame, the authority of Kṛṣṇa as the ideal man and the *Gītā*'s authoritativeness are established in a scheme of mutual interdependence. The connection between the figure of Kṛṣṇa and the contents of the *Gītā* is set up by pointing out that there are other parts of the *Mahābhārata* containing Kṛṣṇa's ethical teachings, too:

> [...] but is there any certainty whether that *dharma* is promulgated by Kṛṣṇa or written by the author of the *Gītā*? Fortunately, we can find the teaching of *dharma* given by Kṛṣṇa also in various parts of the *Mahābhārata* apart from the *Gītāparvādhyāya*. If we see that there is unity between the new *dharma* proclaimed in the *Gītā* and the *dharma* Kṛṣṇa explained in various other parts of the *Mahābhārata*, then we can say that this *dharma* is indeed made and promulgated by Kṛṣṇa.[21]

In this way, the presumed historical layer of the epic, on which traces of Kṛṣṇa's teaching are detected, is construed as the confirmation that the *Gītā* is representative of that *dharma*. The picture of Baṅkim's historical Kṛṣṇa is, methodologically speaking, determined on the basis of the *Gītā*; the *Gītā* in turn is given ultimate authority as the teaching of the ideal man. Both are used, in a tautological circle, to determine each other and mutually establish their definite authority. Behind this endeavour is of course the confrontation with Christianity and rationalism: 'His celebration of Kṛṣṇa is not aimed against other, Indian or Hindu constructions of this ideality, but the ideality of Christ; and Christ was a *historical* figure.' (Sudipta Kaviraj 1995:81). Kṛṣṇa as a human ideal as well as the founder of a new 'religion' is decisively modelled after the picture of Jesus Christ,[22] and historicity, also on this background, becomes the major criterion for credibility. The Divine's perceptable traces, its texts and images, are to be solidly established in the human and historical sphere.

Partha Chatterjee's (1986:59) evaluation of *Kṛṣṇacaritra* is very relevant in this connection. While expressing his doubts whether 'Bankim performed this hermeneutic task with any reasonable degree of competence', he stresses: 'The more important point is that he should have felt that a discourse on ethical principles, arguing in favour of the exemplariness of the character of Krishna as an ideal for modern man, *required* a demonstration of the historicity of Krishna.' Thus, all ideal attributes of Krishna had to be included in the historical core of the *Mahābhārata*: 'History, to him, was the receptacle of rational truth; conversely, the validation of truth had to lie in a rational demonstration of its historicity.' Such an undertaking was of course bound to become a 'tour de force' (Tapan Raychaudhuri 1988:149), and Baṅkim's reaching back to the historical kernel of the *Mahābhārata* in order to establish his Kṛṣṇa is motivated by its being

[20] Cf. e.g. Giri (1988:548): 'His [Baṅkim's] ideal of Kṛṣṇa's character was totally different from the character of Kṛṣṇa of the *Vaiṣṇava* poems.' Sudipta Kaviraj (1995:88ff.) goes to some length in demonstrating Baṅkim's elimination of large parts of the *Vaiṣṇava* Kṛṣṇa and analyses it as a shift from 'the universality of eros' to 'the universality of reason'. (1995:101) Nevertheless, Baṅkim's treatment of Kṛṣṇa has found a favourable reception with some traditional *Vaiṣṇavas*; cf. Jagadīś Candra Ghoṣ (undated:47f.), where Baṅkim's conception of Kṛṣṇa is integrated as a form of *puruṣottamavāda*.

[21] *Kṛṣṇacaritra* (*BR* II:532).

[22] Cf. Amales Tripathi (1967a:13).

'both 'ancient' and 'historical', two concepts privileged by the Orientalist critics'.[23]

The ideal man Kṛṣṇa, the ancient ideal of the Hindus, which is to be re-erected,[24] is clearly developed in the perspective on Christianity and even compared to Jesus Christ: Kṛṣṇa is superior to Christ because, according to Baṅkim, he excelled in all domains of life (in the sense of the dictum elaborated in *Dharmmatattva* that perfect humanity lies in the 'unfolding and coordination of all faculties');[25] Christ, by contrast, renounced political action:

> Again, imagine if the Jews, oppressed by the Romans, had arisen for their independence and bestowed commandership on Jesus, what would Jesus have done? He had not the power nor the inclination to fight. He used to walk away after saying 'Give the emperor the emperor's due'. Kṛṣṇa too was devoid of the inclination to fight — but there is also war for the cause of *dharma*. When there was a war for the cause of *dharma*, he forcedly used to engage [in it]. Jesus was uneducated, Kṛṣṇa a knower of all Śāstras. [It was] likewise regarding other qualities. [...] The '*Hindu Ideal*' [Lat.] is better than the '*Christian Ideal*' [Lat.].[26]

In this way, the contemporary Western perception of Kṛṣṇa as an amoral folk deity is negated, but the price for that negation is a similar negation of the Kṛṣṇa of traditional Vaiṣṇavism: 'Bankim's argument tries to refute Westernism by refuting tradition' (Sudipta Kaviraj 1995:88).

Baṅkim's philological treatment of the *Gītā* must be viewed in this light. Textual criticism helps him to formulate his general theses regarding the textual situation (authorship, interpolations, etc.), but the ratio behind the uses he makes of those theses is often determined by the parameters set in the form of such an ideal. His approach utilises textual criticism for a selective reading of the *Bhagavadgītā*, the actual selection however follows other criteria. The text of the *Gītā* is therefore only the imperfect, sometimes distorted vehicle of the not necessarily divine but certainly perfect teachings on *dharma*, proclaimed by the historical ideal man, Kṛṣṇa: 'There is no doubt that the *dharma* proclaimed by the Lord has been compiled in the *Gītā*; the book called *Gītā*, however, was not written by the Lord but by some other person' (*ŚBhG*:38). But on the other hand, with regard to the *Saṃjayayānaparvādhyāya*: 'It can be accepted that He who is the speaker here, is also the genuine speaker in the *Gītā*.'[27]

Ślokas that are classified as interpolations are 2.34-37; 1.39-43 are attributed to superstitions of the *Gītā*'s author. Baṅkim further appears to have regarded the last six or seven *adhyāyas* (either following the *Viśvarūpadarśana* [11], or *Bhaktiyoga* [12]) as a later addition. Hīrendranāth Datta reports a conversation with him about the *Gītā* (in

[23] Haberman (1994:98). In this well-researched essay on primarily modern representations of Kṛṣṇa, the stylisation of Baṅkim's Kṛṣṇa is shown as crucially deliminated by both Orientalist and Christian parameters.

[24] Cf. *Kṛṣṇacaritra* (*BR* II:516, with reference to contemporary society): 'It is true, there is no [ideal]; if there was any, why should we be in such a bad state? But once there was. Then the Hindus were the best nation [*jāti*] of the world.'

[25] *Kṛṣṇacaritra* (*BR* II:516); cf. Chapter 2.2.2 of the present analysis.

[26] Ibid.; also quoted, as an example of the claim to Kṛṣṇa's superiority, in Śaṅkarīprasād Basu (1990: 32).

[27] *Kṛṣṇacaritra* (*BR* II:533).

BJ:182 ff.) where Baṅkim grounds his assumption on observations about the language style of the later *adhyāyas* and the concluding character of the *Viśvarūpadarśana*, and there is an indication in *Dharmmatattva* which seems to support that he regarded the last six *adhyāyas* as interpolated.[28] The *Viśvarūpadarśana* is praised for its poetic qualities: 'The description of the universal form in the *Gītā*'s eleventh [*adhyāya*] is the work of a poet of the first order; it is hard to find anything like it if one wanders around searching in the world of literature';[29] but according to his approach, it does not belong to the teaching of *dharma* in a strict sense.

Baṅkim'candra's approach to the *Gītā* is however not limited to a *prima facie* admission or rejection of parts according to a pre-conceived ideal. As Huber points out, Baṅkim'candra is conscious of the hermeneutical problem consisting in the time gap between the *Gītā* and his century:

> The knowledge about man and time merges in the divine word, together with the superstitious notions of the times. Baṅkim'candra refuses to subject himself to all the notions that occur in the great holy scriptures of the past, and to model the present after them. (translation; 1991:25).

Indeed he maintains the notion of an absolute truth expressed in the *Gītā* in a time-bound manner, thus juxtaposing divine truth with the changing epistemological frames of human society.

In his interpretation of 3.10-16, which describe Vedic cosmogenesis, Baṅkim takes the discussion to a more general plane. First, he dismisses these seven *ślokas* as interpolated on the ground of inconsistency with the concept of *niṣkāma karman*. But when discussing the objection about their unscientificness, he points out that the *Gītā* is not a book on science; and then, in a kind of afterthought, he proceeds hypothetically: 'But I must also say that if these are really Kr̥ṣṇa's words, then I do not believe that they should be in harmony with nineteenth century science.' (*ŚBhG*:121) This is so, he continues, because Kr̥ṣṇa as an avatāra restricted Himself to using exclusively human powers. Human knowledge being time-bound, he thus had to express Himself in terms comprehensible to his contemporaries, i.e. following 'customary belief'.[30] The implication is of course that an explanation compatible with nineteenth century science[31] would not have met this purpose.

This argument takes an epistemological turn when Baṅkim questions the validity

[28] 'The name of the twelfth *adhyāya* of the *Gītā* is *Bhaktiyoga*. But there is extremely little genuine explanation of *bhakti* in the twelfth *adhyāya*. If one does not examine all *adhyāyas* from the second to the twelfth, the true nature [*tattva*] of *bhakti* proclaimed in the *Gītā* cannot be understood.' Hīrendranāth Datta, despite indicating that Baṅkim saw the *Viśvarūpadarśana* (the eleventh *adhyāya*) as the end of the *Gītā*, speaks of Baṅkim mentioning the last *six* (13-18) *adhyāyas* as later additions (quoted in *BJ*:182; the source given is an article by Hīrendranāth in *Nārāyaṇ* 1322 [1915-16]).

[29] *Kr̥ṣṇacaritra* (*BR* II:543).

[30] *laukik biśvās* (Beng.); *ŚBhG*:117.

[31] Which he calls *bijñān* (Beng.) throughout his writings, but while stressing repeatedly that 'science' is not its original meaning. See *ŚBhG*:43n; also *Deb'tattva o hindudharmma* (*BR* II:814n): 'Those who are experienced in Hindu Śāstras know that *bijñān* [Beng.] is not [used] in the sense of *Science* [Lat.].' Baṅkim's notion of science is decidedly more sophisticated than for instance that found in the nativistic explanations of Hinduism advanced by Śaśadhar Tarkacūṛāmaṇi and Kr̥ṣṇaprasanna Sen (for a portrayal, see Sunītirañjan Rāẏ'chaudhurī 1981), to whom indeed 'scientific' meant 'technologically informed' at the most (cf. Agehananda Bharati 1971:95f.).

of modern science by comparing it to this ancient 'customary belief' if it is seen from the perspective of the science of another two or three thousand years ahead. 'Just imagine, the Lord, in His omniscience, were to proclaim a new doctrine of *dharma* in accord with this future science and in the language fitting it. If he did so, who would listen? Who would understand? Who would follow it? No-one.' (*ŚBhG*:121) Knowledge of the Absolute, according to his concept, is transmitted together with the surrounding 'customary beliefs' or science, i.e. in the epistemic frame of the respective age, and both merge in the verbal representation. The perishable, time-bound part of that representation then needs updating; the knowledge of the Absolute has to be contextualised anew. Baṅkim claims this updating to be the basic motivation of his commentary:

> Therefore, the utterances of God should be circulated in the language suiting the respective times. Thereafter, together with the gradual increase of human knowledge, this language fitting the ancient times can be suitably interpreted as befits place, time and persons. It is for this reason that, notwithstanding the presence of commentaries on the *Gītā* by world-conquering pundits like Śaṅkara, etc., a stupid person like myself has had the courage to engage in creating a new commentary. (*ŚBhG*:121)

Here again it comes down to the fundamental task of separating 'the kernel from the husks'.

Baṅkim'candra does not, at first sight, appear to maintain neutrality regarding these different representations: ancient 'customary belief' is seen as inferior to nineteenth century science. The idea of positive cultural and scientific progress is however not dominant here, Baṅkim's solution lying, as was pointed out, rather in the actualisation and re-installation of an ancient ideal. And the ironical science fiction images of future human achievements (*ŚBhG*:121) are in fact a parody of the idea of progress, with science as gigantomania.

The commentary being an attempt to explain the *Gītā* in accordance with science, the relationship between this 'science'[32] and the '*dharma* proclaimed in the *Gītā*' is perceived as a problem.

> All *dharmas* of the earth stand on one side, and they [the scientists] stand on the other; through their tremendous influence all *dharmas* on earth are about to disappear. Still, *dharma* is greater than science. On the other hand, we cannot abandon science by calling *dharma* greater. Both *dharma* and science are true. Consequently we shall have to consider in this instance how much truth there is on each side. (*ŚBhG*:43)

Science, says Baṅkim, is built on proof. Its admissible means of knowledge are direct perception (*pratyakṣa*) and inference (*anumāna*) inasfar as it is based on direct perception; in his discussion of the *pramāṇas*[33] of the classical *darśanas*, Baṅkim rejects the third means, *āptavacana* ('authoritative communication').[34] Only narrative elements admissible to validity by direct perception or inference are allowed to enter historicity. It is within this range of the scientifically possible that the human Kṛṣṇa is located, and

[32] I.e. English 'science', certainly not the *vijñāna* of the *Gītā*, as is evident from the respective passages in the commentary.

[33] 'Proofs', means of knowledge.

[34] Cf. his essay *Sāṃkhyadarśan* for his views of *pramāṇas* in *Sāṃkhya* philosophy. For an examination of his various remarks on *pramāṇas*, see Bhabatoṣ Caṭṭopādhyāẏ (1991:14ff.).

the utility of *dharma* is lastly argued out in that frame too. Science in this sense frames the area in which Baṅkim's interpretation moves. But if on the one hand side, the scientific perspective is applied to the religious, the same is done *vice versa*, and science is reduced to something of very limited importance:

> So science does not find the *ātman*. Science follows truth. Science searched as far as was possible for it, but while being genuinely in search of truth and trying as a hard as it could, it missed the *ātman* all the same. It did not find it because science lacks the power to go that far. No one can move further than [the extent of] his reach. The diver enters the ocean by tying a cord to his waist; he can go as far as the cord reaches, no further; he does not have the capacity of picking up all the jewels in the ocean. Now the cord of proof is tied to the waist of science; where should science find the *ātman* that is inaccessible to proof? Science has no right in an area where it does not reach; it is an illusion to search for any scientific proof at all at that lowest step where science sits and makes its life meaningful, while behind it there is a huge building.[35]

At this point, two of Baṅkim's premises, the divinity mediated through the *Gītā* and the authority of science, are set into hierarchical proportions by means of what one might call an *adhikārabheda*, i.e. the differentiation of qualification.[36] This concept had already previously been formulated in Baṅkim's novel *Ānandamaṭh*. In a famous passage at the end of the novel, he distinguishes between two kinds of knowledge:

> The genuine Hindu-*dharma* is cognitive [*jñānātmak*], not active [*karmmātmak*]. This knowledge [*jñān*] is of two kinds, related to outer objects [*bahirbbiṣaẏak*] and related to inner objects [*antarbbiṣaẏak*]. The knowledge related to inner objects is the main part of the *sanātana dharma*. But if the knowledge related to outer objects is not produced first, then there is no possibility of the knowledge related to inner objects to be produced. If one does not know the coarse one cannot know the subtle. Now the knowledge related to outer objects has since a long time disappeared from this country [...]. (*BR* I:643)[37]

This statement is of great importance not only within the frame of Baṅkim's thought, but also in much of later nationalist thinking as a means of asserting India's spiritual superiority (while of course removing the inbuilt causal nexus between these two kinds of knowledge); it figures prominently especially in Vivekānanda's exposition of Hinduism.[38] Baṅkim presents both kinds of knowledge side by side; he implies however a hierarchical structure among them where the knowledge related to inner objects appears to be the one requiring more refinement and is attainable only after mastering the other. This interdependence appears to contradict his other statements on the topic quoted above. According to those, Kṛṣṇa's divine teaching, which clearly forms

[35] *ŚBhG*:47; quoted in part in Huber (1991:85).

[36] Translated thus, of course in a different context, by Halbfass (1990:533n).

[37] A complete English translation of the final chapter of *Ānandamaṭh* is included in Clark (1961:442-4).

[38] The validity of this notion — the 'spiritual-materialist cliché' — is very convincingly questioned by Agehananda Bharati (1971:80ff.); cf. also Śibājī Bandyopādhyāẏ's (1993) investigation, where a line is drawn starting from Baṅkim and Vivekānanda, and the latter's outspoken statement of that cliché is regarded as most typical of contemporary Hinduism (p. 33).

part of 'knowledge related to inner objects', still retains its validity although 'false' knowledge related to outer objects is intermeshed with it. In view of the structure of Baṅkim's concepts, which of course he fully worked out only after *Ānandamaṭh* had been published, the hierarchical order of both kinds of knowledge can therefore not be held; perhaps it is not more than a rhetorical device to suggest the superiority of the subtle over the coarse and thus construct a somewhat favourable metaphor for the declined state of Indian society. The main point and something surely at work in his later writings, however, is the said distinction between two kinds of knowledge. Each of them is, according to *Ānandamaṭh*, allocated geographically — outer knowledge is Western, and inner knowledge is Indian. This state of things is nothing to be perpetuated but to be overcome and resolved through a synthesis, and Baṅkim's attempt at 'critical inquiry' is also an effort to cut a path in between the two factions of scientists and traditionalists. Nonetheless, Baṅkim does fall back upon this opposition when it suits his purposes.[39]

The *Gītā*, in these terms, represents in substance knowledge related to inner objects, something which, according to Baṅkimˈcandra, science cannot provide. The religious teaching of the *Gītā* is beyond science. But although 'the *Bhagavadgītā* is the best [*śreṣṭha*] book of the world',[40] its text represents those teachings only imperfectly and contains in fact distortions which collide with scientifically coherent representation. So science, inferior by its nature though it may be, enters his task of interpretation in several ways: Firstly, it supplies the concept of rationality which functions as Baṅkim's operational platform throughout the commentary. It also underlies his philological method. Secondly, it is the common discursive ground on which Bankim wishes to persuade his readers. Thirdly, as knowledge related to outer objects, it figures simultaneously in an opposition to the very teaching of the *Gītā* on a symbolic level along the distinction between science and spirituality, i.e. ultimately between West and East.

All this, then, is Baṅkim's methodological equipment in approaching the *Gītā*. He denies its divine authorship and invades the former gap between sacred and profane, constituted by the erasure of authorship, with a set of speculative philological criteria, which he passes in the name of science. On the other hand, he construes an opposition between outer and inner knowledge; he subjects science to relativity by means of his epistemological considerations, whereas absolute validity is claimed for the main substance of the *Gītā*, i.e. Kr̥ṣṇa's divine teachings as far as they are reflected in it. The shifts of perspective — between the 'scientific' angle and that of the 'Absolute' — which are at work in his interpretation are a very typical pattern of argumentation which is indicative of his hermeneutical position between two cultural systems. One is seen through the other respectively.[41] Such shifts shall be noticed in all the following

[39] Cf. his treatment of Western Indology (Chapter 2.3.3 of the present analysis) as well as the remarks in Chapter 2.4.

[40] *Dharmmatattva*, *BR* II:636.

[41] This typical feature of a considerable part of modern Indian thinking has been formulated most elaborately in Halbfass (1990), e.g. in the chapter on Rāmˈmohan Rāẏ (pp. 197-216); Tanika Sarkar (1994:2554f.) points out that 'he [Baṅkim] used the resources of both to interrogate both — and here lies the ineptness of the notion of hybridity that misses out on the criticality and the mutually transformative nature of this intellectual encounter [...].'

chapters of the analysis, especially in his treatment of *svadharma* and *dharma*. Evidently, this double approach promises flexibility rather than coherence. While providing Baṅkimcandra with a large repertoire of argumentations, it inevitably leads to severe ambiguities, if not tautologies and contradictions.

2.2.2 *Dharma* and *Svadharma*

One of the central traditional Indian terms that Baṅkim uses in his commentary in a variety of ways is *dharma*. Indeed it is the most conceptualised of them all and forms the very basis of his religious thinking. And it is the alteration of this *dharma* (along with *svadharma*) which has earned Baṅkim the reputation, in Indology and Religious Studies, of being the first major exponent of so-called neo-Hinduism.[42]

Before looking at Baṅkim's interpretation of the term *dharma*, it is necessary to formulate an approximate idea of its pre-modern meaning. *Dharma*, as is widely known, is derived from √*dhṛ* 'to hold, support', and thus may be interpreted as 'that which holds'.[43] Some very commonly used translations are 'law', '(world) order' as well as 'righteousness'. *Dharma* is also a set of rules regulating almost all aspects of life; as such it has again and again been codified in Dharmaśāstras, i.e. 'the teaching (or science) of righteousness',[44] etc. *Dharma* appears to be something substantial, too; according to Paul Hacker, 'The *dharma*- is, rather, a concrete, positive-salutary *behavioural model* that somehow exists even before being carried out and awaits realisation, or a collection of such models. Dharma *being carried out* is then that act corresponding to this model, Adharma that contrary to it. Finally, the dharma-substance, however, also exists *after being carried out* as the realised behavioural model. It is then something like an action congealed to supersensory effective matter, the substance of the done deed.'[45] This 'behavioural model', in the view of the ancient authors on the topic, was tightly connected with knowledge of the Vedas and could be localised in *Āryāvarta*, the country of the *Āryas*.[46] The substantial character of *dharma* counteracted a definite codification; *dharma* was not an abstract, 'objective', independent set of prescriptions, but rather the empirical value of actions performed by persons immersed in the Vedas. *Dharma* thus is endowed with qualities of a substance and localised. Further, as Rocher stresses in the course of his discussion of contradictions in the *Manusmṛti*, *dharma* is not the same for all but mirrors the diversity of society: 'The important but easily overlooked point is that it is normal, that it is a premise, in Hinduism, that what is *dharma* for one is different from what *dharma* is for another. *Dharma*, basically, is accepted custom (*ācāra*), i.e. custom accepted in a region, in a village, even in a caste or sub-caste within a village.' Hacker too points out that the concept of *dharma* is tied to the *Āryas* and, in its further

[42] See the end of Chapter 2.4 for a discussion of the term 'neo-Hinduism'.

[43] *Dharma* is built from the root √*dhṛ* with the primary suffix *-ma*; cf. Debrunner, Albert: *Die Nominalsuffixe*; in Jakob Wackernagel (1954, Vol. II,2:749), who translates it as 'Ordnung, Satzung'.

[44] Translated thus in Derrett (1976:2); 'righteousness', however, remains only one aspect of the term.

[45] Paul Hacker (1978 [1965]:506); for the translation from the German I am grateful to Prof. Rahul Peter Das. The essay is not included in the English volume Hacker (1995), edited and translated by Halbfass.

[46] Cf. Klimkeit (1981:60), who largely follows Hacker in his presentation of *dharma*.

> verbosity[63] as *good deed* [Lat.]. Fifthly, the word *dharma* means property,[64] e.g. — the magnet's *dharma* is the attraction of iron. In this case that too is *dharma* which according to other meanings would be *adharma*. For instance, 'the blame of others is the *dharma* of the narrow-minded'.[65] [...] And sixthly, the word *dharma* is then used in the sense of conduct or behaviour.[66]

The last two meanings Baṅkim presents here are supported by quotations from the *Manusmṛti*[67] and lack English equivalents.

Baṅkim was thus quite aware of the semantic complexities involved. Nevertheless, he was most attracted by the 'new' meaning of *dharma*, i.e. as the equivalent of 'religion'. In his *Dharmmajijñāsā*,[68] he considers the etymologies of both terms with the aid of F. Max Müller[69] and thereupon claims their great affinity. Further he quotes, again following F. Max Müller, several definitions of religion by German philosophers[70] and finally arrives at J.S. Mill, Seeley and Comte. His undertaking is situated on two quite different planes. One part of it is the empirical determination of the *status quo*; he isolates six different meanings of the term *dharma* and considers at least one among them ('religion') as modern, i.e. originally not intended:

> A department of thought which the people within whom it had its existence had thus failed to differentiate, has necessarily mixed itself inextricably with every other department of thought, and this is what makes it so difficult at the present day, to erect it into a separate entity.[71]

The other part then consists in the normative elaboration of the *status ad quem*, i.e. the determination of precisely that 'separate entity', religion or '*dharma*' respectively. He even acknowledges the artificiality of that *dharma* — 'a major reinterpretation' (Halbfass 1990:335) —, but does not therefore step back. And though he may still perceive this meaning of *dharma* as inauthentic, he later tries to restore to it its whole authenticity.[72]

63 [*bāgbāhulya* (Beng.).]

64 [*guṇ* (Beng.), which has been translated as 'quality' above.]

65 [*kṣudracetā* (Beng.). In *Deb'tattva o hindudharmma*, he gives another illustration of this meaning of *dharma*: 'The thief's *dharma* is to do things secretly.' (*BR* II:777)]

66 *BJC*:648; also in the appendix of *Dharmmatattva* (*BR* II:671). Cf. Halbfass (1990:338).

67 In Bengali commonly called *Manusaṃhitā*.

68 Unfortunately, this essay, which first appeared in *Pracār* in 1884, is not included in the *Racanābalī* edition. For this reason, Amitrasūdan Bhaṭṭācārya has reprinted it in full length in his *Baṅkim'candrajībanī* (BCJ:647-59).

69 Cf. *BR* II:674; the texts Baṅkim draws his material from are the so-called *Hibbert Lectures* delivered by F. Max Müller in 1878, of which two editions were printed in that same year under the title: *Lectures on the Origin and Growth of Religion as Illustrated by the Religions of India*. Müller further elaborated his ideas about religion in the *Gifford Lectures* in 1888 under the heading of *Natural Religion*.

70 Kant, Fichte, Schleiermacher, Hegel and *Mausuk*, which probably stands for Marx. Cf. Tapan Raychaudhuri (1988: 125) and Rāẏ, Jībendu (1984), esp. Chapter 1 on *ẏoroper nabya darśan* (6-16).

71 *Letters on Hinduism*, *BR* II:674.

72 It is interesting to note, in this connection, that the same perception of artificiality regarding *dharma* as the equivalent of 'religion' prompts Indranāth Bandyopādhyāẏ, a regular contributor to the journal *Baṅgabāsī* who claimed affiliation to Baṅkim and was appreciated by the latter, to take a quite different course. Indranāth argues that 'religion' is too narrow a term to cover the meaning of *dharma*, and suggests

The same constellation is at work in his *Deb'tattva o hindudharmma*. In his introduction he juxtaposes two types of Hindus. One makes it a point to live in accordance with the Śāstras; he meticulously observes all ritualistic prescriptions, regularly reads sacred literature, etc., but proves highly immoral in his dealings with his subjects. The other does not care for *śāstric* authority but is true and righteous. Baṅkim shows that both descriptions have some attributes of what is commonly understood as a *dhārmika*; the first example is presented as belonging to *ācāra* ('conduct'). Then he poses the following questions:

> Who among these two persons is a Hindu? Is none of them a Hindu? If not, then why not? If we have not found Hinduness[73] in any of them then what is *hindudharma*? One person has fallen from *dharma*, the second person has fallen from *ācāra*. Is *ācāra dharma*, or is *dharma dharma*?[74]

Obviously the second, as Baṅkim leads his readers to assume. This double-level argument is quite typical for Baṅkim's dealing with the term *dharma*. His first example illustrates the use of *dharma* in the sense of 'ritualistic conduct', the second in the sense of 'morality'. On an empirical level, *both* meanings are denoted by *dharma*, as he himself admits — *dharma* does, according to him (*Dharmmajijñāsā*), encompass the sense of *ācāra*. But Baṅkim does not argue about how things *are*; he silently switches to the normative level, the genuine level of his thinking in general, on which he is concerned with how things *should be*. *Dharma* should be 'morality' rather than 'ritualistic conduct', an interior rather than an exterior category.[75] But the decisive point in the structure of his argument is that these levels are not kept apart; his normative assumption about what *dharma* should be is projected back upon the empirical level. 'Ritualistic conduct' (*ācāra*) is extrapolated terminologically, but 'morality' (*dharma*) is not. It is thus assumed that 'morality' has greater affinities with *dharma* than 'ritualistic conduct', and by concealing this meaning under the term *dharma*, it is then presented as the obvious, true and immanent meaning of *dharma* (and, as we shall see, the one that had really been intended in some distant past). *Dharma* and *ācāra*, traditionally quite close to each other semantically,[76] are in this way conceived in opposition to each other. Another tacit assumption Baṅkim makes here is the equation of *hindu* with *dhārmika*;[77] like *dharma*, the word *hindu* too is submitted to the tension between an empirical and a normative

---

that it should be used in the sense of 'civilisation' instead of *sabhyatā* (Beng.) which he regards as an ill-suited neologism (in the article *Bhāṣāntarer biṛambanā*, published in *Baṅgabāsī* 1896; Indranāth Bandyopādhyāẏ 1925-6:769-72). In a later essay (*Dharmma-paricaẏ*, *Jāhnabī* 1907; Indranāth Bandyopādhyāẏ 1925-6:838-47), he elaborates his concept of *dharma* and especially *hindudharma*. Here, however, his use of the term is anything but unequivocal, *dharma* being semantically flexible as ever and certainly not to be rendered by 'civilisation'.

[73] [*hinduẏāni* (Beng.)].

[74] *ek byakti dharmmabhraṣṭa, dvitīya byakti ācār'bhraṣṭa. ācār dharmma, nā dharmmaï dharmma?* (Beng.) (*BR* II:707).

[75] This interiorisation of 'faith' runs through all major attempts at religious reform in nineteenth century India, including those of the Ārya Samāj, and most certainly belongs into the larger frame of Hindu reactions to Christianity. Cf. Haberman (1994:98), who detects such interiorisation in Baṅkim's treatment of Kṛṣṇa.

[76] Cf. Rocher, Ludo (1993) as quoted above, as well as Baṅkim's own sixth determination of the term in *Dharmmajijñāsā* (*vide supra*).

[77] This equation is certainly not traditional; it probably reflects the influence of Christianity.

aspect.

The first definition of *dharma* given in *Dharmmatattva* is similarly structured. *Dharma* is first taken in the sense of religion, and the guru says that 'it is not a native [*deśī*] thing.' But when the *śiṣya* asks about the meaning of religion, the guru answers: 'What for? *Religion* [Lat.] is a Western word, the Western scholars have understood it in various ways; nobody's opinion agrees with the other's.' Asked whether there is some eternal thing in all religions, the guru says 'There is, but there is no need to call that eternal substance religion; if we call it *dharma* there will be no more confusion.'[78] This, as the guru explains further, would be the *dharma* common to all religions, i.e. man's *dharma*. Now, as the magnet's *dharma* is the attraction of iron, man's *dharma* is *manuṣyatva*, Comte's '*humanité*', and the credit of having conceived such a *dharma* is given to superior Hinduism. Evidently, *dharma* in this sense is a normative category reattributed to existing, 'empirical' Hinduism, as shall be demonstrated below in this sub-chapter.

The passages discussed above are very relevant for the further discussion of Baṅkim's concept of *dharma* because they demonstrate that he was fully conscious of the complexities inherent in that term, and show the typical switch between levels he employs. And in addition to this, in *Dharmmajijñāsā*, he himself claims that the confusion of terms which is likely to arise in the case of such a huge semantic field covered by only one term, is highly undesirable: 'This mess is a very serious reason for the modern degradation of Hindu *dharma* and Hindu morality and the modern distrust in them.' (*BR* II:672)[79]

Which are, then, the meanings denoted by *dharma*, and the related *svadharma*, in his commentary? They figure prominently in a few passages, and it can be observed that Baṅkim'candra uses *dharma* in some different senses. Both *dharma* and *svadharma* are interpreted in a way that surpasses the parameters given by the *Gītā*, and they are conceived in a specific interrelation: *dharma* as an absolute ethical ideal, and *svadharma* as an imperfect, subordinated version of it due to the practical exigencies of an imperfect state of society, as shall be demonstrated.

In the *Gītā*, the term *svadharma* is not employed before 2.31, but Baṅkim takes it up as early as in 2.11, 'the real beginning' where the teaching about *dharma* starts. Why should Arjuna fight? Baṅkim presents the traditional answer — because of his being a kṣatriya — but while it was 'very easy to explain this theory' (*ŚBhG*:39) on the part of the medieval commentators, the answer is seen as irrelevant for him and his contemporary readers: 'But what has this explanation actually taught us?' (*ŚBhG*:39) *Svadharma* in this sense applies exclusively to Hindu society which is organised along the *varṇa* system and does not extend to people outside that society, i.e. is limited to Hindus.

> But what is *svadharma* for non-Hindus? The sum of all brahmins, kṣatriyas, vaiśyas and śūdras is still a very minor part of the world popu-

[78] *BR* II:530 (Chapter 3 of *Dharmmatattva*).

[79] It may be interesting to note that the terminological situation is still very much the same; cf. Jyoti Bhaṭṭācārya [1992:32] on the contemporary late-twentieth century usage: 'Many know that the word *dharma* is quite complicated [*gol'mele*]. "Water's *dharma*", "creature's *dharma*", "the *dharma* of governing [*rāj'dharma*]", "Christian *dharma*" — in these four words, *dharma* has four kinds of meaning.' Bhaṭṭācārya then indicates the current use as denoting that which is meant by 'religion'.)

lation. Most people on earth are outside the four *varṇas*; do they not have any *svadharma*? Has God not prescribed any *dharma* for them? Has He created millions and millions of people to provide only Indians with *dharma* and leave everybody else deprived of it? Is the *dharma* proclaimed by the Lord only for Hindus? Are the *mlecchas* not His children? The divine *dharma* is not as narrow-minded as this. (*ŚBhG*:39)[80]

In order to be a valid ethical category for Baṅkim, then, *svadharma* must be given such a meaning as to be universally applicable, and accordingly he continues by presenting a modern 'extension of *varṇāśramadharma*' (*ŚBhG*:42).[81] This extension is based on a sociological interpretation of the *varṇa*-system:[82] the latter is depicted as a model of labour[83] division that can, with perhaps slight alterations, be found in any existing society. Traditional Hindu society is in this way being shown as a prototype that is easily transferable to other societies. In accordance with the division of human faculties,[84] specialisation of 'actions' (*karman*) occurs: brahmins are devoted to knowledge, and the other *varṇas* to action, i.e. the kṣatriyas to protection or war, the vaiśyas to commerce and craft, and the śūdras to agriculture and service. Baṅkim is not bothered by possible objections as to whether there should be more than four categories to describe the functioning of human society. He admits himself that six categories may be more accurate, but this does not interfere with his substantial assertion that the *varṇa*-system is basically a sociological system. Caste is in this way reduced to profession, and Arjuna is a 'professional warrior' (*ŚBhG*:76) rather than a kṣatriya. This system is not specifically Indian but common to all differentiated societies including Europe.[85] What is specifically Indian is the hereditary nature of these universal 'classes' (*jāti*; *ŚBhG*:41), and Baṅkim considers this (at least in this instance) as disadvantageous because it is not compatible with demographic irregularities: once certain classes grow disproportionately, their traditional occupation is no longer sufficient. The hereditary aspect is consequently left out of his summary on *svadharma* (*ŚBhG*:40f.), and personal choice takes its place; Baṅkim's 'liberal' (*udār* [Beng.]) explanation of *svadharma*, in this instance, is summarised thus: 'Whichever one of this six-fold action someone adopts, be it as a means of livelihood or for whatever other reason, and whichever one's [i.e. 'action's'] burden one chooses to carry, that is one's action to be executed, one's "Duty" [Lat.]; that is one's *svadharma*.' (*ŚBhG*:41f.) In calling *svadharma* 'duty',[86] he conceives it as a full-fledged ethical category and seemingly tries to harmonise it with Western ethics,

[80] This passage is also quoted and discussed in Subodh candra Sen (1987:15) and Hacker (1978 [1958]:515).

[81] His interspersed general determination of *dharma* (*ŚBhG*:39f.) will be dealt with below.

[82] As observed by Śaṅkarīprasād Basu (1990:32) who points out that in his discussion of the *varṇa*-system, Baṅkim 'adopted mostly a modern sociological perspective.' Cf. also Subodh candra Sen gupta (1987:17f.) who calls it a 'new definition of *svadharma*.' David Taylor (1978:208f.) compares Vivekānanda's 'functional explanation of the emergence of caste' to Baṅkim's.

[83] The term interpreted in the sense of 'labour' or 'occupation' is still *karman*.

[84] As formulated by Comte; cf. below.

[85] Cf. the remarks in Huber (1991:361).

[86] Also in *ŚBhG*:70.

where this term was central (e.g. with Kant, Spencer, etc.).[87]

The topic of a possible choice of one's *svadharma* is dealt with in some other passages which show surprising inconsistencies and thus appear to be rather unconnected bits of argumentation. The first is the commentary on 3.33-35 and 3.37 (*ŚBhG*:133ff.). In *Gītā* 3.35, the imperfect fulfilment of *svadharma* is preferred to well-performed *paradharma*. Baṅkim argues that a universally valid interpretation must dissociate *svadharma* from *varṇāśramadharma*: 'One's *svadharma* is that which one has accepted as one's action to be executed in this life.' (*ŚBhG*:134) This 'action to be executed' is rooted in and brought about by one's *svabhāva* ('inherent nature', 'character'). This applies to a society bound by *varṇāśramadharma* as well as to other societies, the difference consisting merely in the respective determinant of *svabhāva*, namely, life-long habit or inclination. Hereditary acceptance of *svadharma* in accordance with *varṇāśrama-dharma* is depicted simply as an alternative mode of organisation; consequently the aim is not — as one might be tempted to suppose from the doubts about the utility of hereditary *svadharma* — the reformation of the *varṇa* system, but the universalisation of *svadharma*: as long as the *varṇāśramadharma* fits in, it may be kept intact.

In the next passage dealing with the choice of *svadharma* (*BhG* 3.37), the necessity of sticking to one's *svadharma* is further elaborated. This time, *svabhāva* is employed in a sense diametrically opposed to the preceding one. It is not the (in whatever way determined) basis of *svadharma*, but its opponent: 'Because *svabhāva* is strong; overcome by their *svabhāva*, people become unwilling, pursue others' *dharma*, and commit sin.' (*ŚBhG*:135) Here, *svabhāva* is used as a sort of accumulation of sensual desires.

There is a third variant on this topic where *svabhāva* is used as in the first instance and constituted by the *guṇas*: this time, caste affiliation by lineage is markedly disclaimed.

> It is not so that a person has to become a brahmin merely for being the son of a brahmin; even a śūdra's son, if having a *sattva*-dominated nature, will be a brahmin, and a brahmin's son with a *tamas*-dominated nature will become a śūdra: this is what we easily realise from the Lord's sentence. (*ŚBhG*:149)

It is however not clear whether Baṅkim wishes to support some sort of 'inter-*varṇa*' mobility. He does quote several portions from various scriptures, e.g. *Mbh* 3.177.18-21[88] (*ŚBhG*:150), that seem to admit such mobility, but does not appear to be inclined to make a well-argued point out of it; he merely states that it has been 'God's will' to make the differences of *varṇas* (*ŚBhG*:150).[89] Unlike Rāj'nārāyaṇ Basu in *Hindudharmmer*

[87] The translation of *svadharma* as 'duty' is however not always feasible even within Baṅkim's elaboration of it, for it would lead to such tautologies as 'everyone's duty (*kartabya*) is to fulfil his duty (*svadharma*)' (*ŚBhG*:39). On the overlapping semantic fields of the Hindi words *dharm* and *kartavya*, see Simon Weightman and S.M. Pandey (1978).

[88] Almost the same quotation can be found in Rāj'nārāyaṇ Basu's lecture (1995:429): 3.177.16 and 20-1. However, as the difference with regard to the *ślokas* quoted makes sufficiently clear, Baṅkim has certainly not taken his quotation directly from Rāj'nārāyaṇ.

[89] This stands in striking contradiction to earlier statements, as for example in *Debtattva o hindudharmma* (*BR* II:792): 'I do not consider any *dharma* made or sent by God.' In the commentary too, social structures based on specialisation are apparently seen as imperfect states of society (see below).

śreṣṭhatā — who claims unmistakably that *varṇa*-affiliation originally used to depend, and ought to depend, on one's personal *guṇas* — Baṅkim apparently had no unambiguous opinion regarding this topic; and despite using *svabhāva* diffusely in the sense of 'disposition' a few times, he is still far from determining *svabhāva* as 'psychological make-up' in the way Radhakrishnan does later; a psychological interpretation of *svabhāva* which was to become a current feature in modern Hinduism is absent.[90]

In the commentary on *BhG* 2.31, the interrelation between *dharma* and *svadharma* is discussed. If one's *svadharma* is determined by the affiliation to a professional group (i.e. *varṇa* in Baṅkim's interpretation), discrepancies between it and more general *dharma* are likely to arise. Kṛṣṇa reminds Arjuna that to fight in a righteous war is the best thing to do for a kṣatriya. Baṅkim asserts that on a superior ethical level, a warrior, despite fighting being his *svadharma*, does not have to engage in whatever war takes place. But there are practical exigencies due to what Baṇkim calls 'undeveloped societies':[91] '[...] because of the defects of human society, a professional warrior has to engage in it [an unrighteous war] too.' (*ŚBhG*:76)[92] The execution of one's *svadharma* is neither necessarily sanctioned by *dharma*, nor does one automatically gain *dharma* thereby:[93] the relationship between *svadharma* and *dharma* is thus more complex than that of a generality and its mere specification. If the fulfilment of *svadharma* can lead to *adharma*, then *svadharma* is also more than just a partial set of *dharma*. As Baṅkim perceives it, a part of a system counteracts the whole here. This autonomy of parts implies a compartmentalisation of ethics, where a specific action within such a compartment (*svadharma*) may have a value different from that assigned by the superstructure which is general *dharma*.[94] And such a conflict, as Baṅkim himself stresses, is not just rare coincidence but, in the case of warriors, almost stands as a rule. It is, on the contrary, the war in accordance with *dharma*, the *dharmayuddha*, which is extremely rare

[90] Cf. Hacker (1978 [1958]:517). Concerning the possibility of choosing one's *svadharma*, cf. Stevenson (1991:59) on Tilak's elaboration of individual choice, which, as Stevenson rightly argues, is not compatible with the *Gītā*. Baṅkim allows such choice in other societies for the sake of his universalisation of *svadharma*, but he is not clear about whether *svabhāva* and its constituting *guṇas* are in any way predetermined or not.

[91] Baṅkim also calls modern European societies 'undeveloped' (*ŚBhG*:40). He does not say what the characteristics of such a society are, but he seems to suggest that it is based on specialisation and therefore segmented. Consequently, *dharma* too is segmented. A developed society, it appears, would not exert such restrictions but give its members the opportunity to live up to their — more general — human *dharma* in the sense of complete humanity (see below); in such a case, it further seems, *svadharma* and *dharma* would merge in one.

[92] But cf. ŚBhG:70: 'War is nobody's duty when it can be avoided.' And, a little further: 'As an example, the most cruel and terrifying *svadharma* of all [i.e. war in general], to which every virtuous person feels *per se* uninclined, has been taken' — which seems to contradict the above-mentioned foundation of *svadharma* in *svabhāva*!

[93] ŚBhG:76f. Baṅkim indeed uses *dharma* both as something sanctioning actions, i.e. Hacker's *dharma* before execution, and as something gained, i.e. after execution, in this paragraph.

[94] Cf. also the famous discussion about lying in *Kṛṣṇacaritra*, Chapter 6 (*BR* II:562-7) — in the course of which *dharma* is mostly used in the sense of 'duty'. Such duties may come into conflict: telling the truth is an inferior duty to the accomplishment of general welfare (p. 567). Baṅkim himself points out the parallels to utilitarian thinking. The crucial point in his argumentation is, of course, that this highest *dharma* (the accomplishment of general welfare) is presented as Kṛṣṇa's teaching, and thus again as 'true Hindu *dharma*', making this latter 'religion' superior to 'narrow' Christianity (p. 565). Cf. the controversy with Rabīndranāth Ṭhākur regarding this argument (*BJ*:341-7).

and an opportunity to gain highest *dharma*. As the comparisons with European society show, *dharmayuddha* is conceived as a universally applicable term.[95] An exact, coherent delineation of the interrelation of *svadharma* and *dharma* is lacking, however.[96]

In short, by explaining *svadharma* in this way Baṅkim achieves two things, one openly and the other implicitly. Openly he takes Kṛṣṇa's teachings out of the exclusivity of traditional Hinduism. He universalises the concept of *svadharma* as an ethical category equivalent to 'duty' and describes this universalisation as 'merely an extention of *varṇāśramadharma*'. Implicitly, he furnishes an apology for the *varṇa*-system, which had been a topic of intercultural polemic dispute throughout the nineteenth century. He 'sociologises' the *varṇa*-system and takes it to a common plane with other civilised societies. He does, in one instance, seem to suggest an amendment, namely, to abolish that system's hereditary nature and substitute individual character as the criterion for *varṇa* affiliation, but he remains very vague about this topic in other places.

The elaboration of *dharma* Baṅkim presents in the commentary is built into a discussion of *svadharma*; if strictly analysed, *svadharma* too is here given a meaning different from the ones dealt with above, for what is determined here is man's *dharma* in general. The definition of *dharma* — the most conceptionalised of all the terms he uses — does not even indirectly refer to the *śloka* (2.11) that is being discussed. It is concise and runs as follows:

> The *dharma* one has is one's *svadharma*. Now what is man's *dharma*? Whatever has to do with humanity. What has to do with humanity? Man has body and mind. What is body, and what is mind? The body is a conglomerate of a number of substances and has a number of powers. When these powers disappear from the body, humanity does not remain; for one can hardly say that there is humanity in a man's corpse. Therefore one has to leave out the substances — those physical powers alone are the true constituents of the human body. Elsewhere[97] I have called them 'physical faculties'. The human mind too is such an aggregate of powers or faculties. Let these be called 'mental faculties'. Now it can be seen that man, or the humanity of man, consists in these physical and mental faculties. If that be so, then the prescribed cultivation of all these faculties is man's *dharma*. (*ŚBhG*:39f.)

This formulation comes close to the well-known final passage from *Dharmmatattva* where the pupil summarises what he has heard about *dharma*.[98] The heteroge-

[95] In the case of an *adharmayuddha* however, he is not clear about how a member of a non-Hindu society should behave: his *svadharma* is based on his not necessarily life-long inclinations, and these are particularly likely to change in 'crucial' situations. And it is not clear either whether the constraints tying one to one's *svadharma* are then of an ethical or simply conventional nature. The present passage rather suggests the latter.

[96] The discrepancies between these categories have other potentialities in the light of (Western) ethics: as ethical categories *dharma* and *svadharma* could be elaborated as to encompass, for example, the tension between the limited individual perspective versus general welfare or the like. Baṅkim does not elaborate this point.

[97] [In *Dharmmatattva*.]

[98] '1. Man has a number of powers. You have called them *vṛttis* ['faculties']. *Manuṣyatva* ['humanity'] is in their *anuśīlana* ['cultivation'], development and gratification.

2. This is man's *dharma*.

neous nature of this definition of *dharma* is evident. Baṅkim does not claim to take it directly from the *Bhagavadgītā*. In this definition, three direct borrowings from Western sources can be distinguished. The first is the idea that religion — for it is obviously this meaning of *dharma* which is elaborated here — is in substance culture.[99] Baṅkim takes this idea from Seeley's *Natural Religion*,[100] overlooking however that the notion of culture is not Seeley's own but only a reference.[101] In *Natural Religion*, in any case, religion is presented not as an isolated sphere among others but as the main system of mediation governing the relation between the individual, society and the Absolute. This matches Baṅkim's notion of Hinduism, which evades the fragmentary label of 'religion' because it pervades 'all aspects of life'.

The second borrowing is the term *manuṣyatva* which obviously represents Auguste Comte's *humanité*. Positivist ideas were very important in Bengal at that time, as the existence of a Positivist Society clearly demonstrates.[102] In his late years Comte founded the *religion de l'humanité*, an antimetaphysical cult of man based on the harmony of positive[103] human qualities. This too is a new way of using 'religion' which certainly influenced Baṅkim. Comte was a very important thinker for Baṅkim as the frequent mention in many of his writings shows. *Manuṣyatva* then is the *dharma* of man.[104] The idea adapts itself smoothly to the Bengali language because *dharma*, as was observed, also means 'property': a magnet's *dharma* is magnetism. Humanity, however, is not just one but a whole set of properties, and the values ascribed to each of them differs considerably.

The third borrowing is closely related to the second. Man has a set of faculties (rather than properties), all of which exist legitimately, some more and some less.

---

3. The limit of this cultivation is the harmony of these faculties with one another.
4. This is happiness.
5. In case of proper cultivation of all these faculties, they are all directed towards God. Directing them towards God [*īśvar'mukhatā*] is proper cultivation. This state is *bhakti* ['devotion'].
6. God is in all beings; therefore love [*prīti*] for all beings is contained in *bhakti* and is a very necessary part [of it]. Without love for all beings, there is no *bhakti* for God, no humanity, no *dharma*.
7. Self-love, love of one's relatives, love of one's country, love of animals, compassion are contained in this love. Among these, when considering man's position, the love of one's country should be called the highest *dharma* of all.' *BR* II:671.

99 Cf. an English quotation in the original edition of his novel *Debīcaudhurāṇī* (April-May 1884): 'The Substance of Religion is Culture — "The Fruit of it The Higher Life"'. According to Rām'kṛṣṇa Bhaṭṭācārya (1994:30).

100 Cf. J.R. Seeley (1895 [1882]), in particular the chapter entitled *Religion and Culture* (159-81, esp. p. 167): '[...] instead of saying that the substance of religion is morality and the effect of it moral goodness, we may lay down that the substance of religion is culture, and the fruit of it the higher life.' Seeley refers to culture in the conceptualisation of Goethe and Schiller (169): 'But their [i.e. Goethe and Schiller's] fundamental conception, to which they gave the name of Culture, is of a threefold religion such as has been set forth here', and that religion is directed towards 'Beauty, Truth and Goodness'. Seeley conceives this as in opposition to puritanism (ibid.).

101 Cf. Rām'kṛṣṇa Bhaṭṭācārya (1994:30ff.) who calls Baṅkim's mistake a 'faux pas': 'In Seeley's opinion, the word "culture" [*anuśīlan* (Beng.)] is not good. It is unfortunate that those who speak about culture now, do not speak about religion.'

102 Cf. the monograph by Forbes (1975).

103 'Positive' in the sense of accessible to perception, not speculative.

104 Cf. *Dharmmatattva*, Chapter 4.

Baṅkim uses *vṛtti* as equivalent for 'faculty' and admits in his *Dharmmatattva* that the original meaning of *vṛtti* is different. He legitimises his choice by giving other examples of current neologisms and pointing out that other Bengali writers before him have used it in this sense.[105] None of these faculties should be eliminated;[106] they should be cultivated in a balanced way. This concept of faculties figures prominently in utilitarian and positivist ethics (Bentham, Mill, Spencer, Comte) and, probably through their influence, in many scientific writings of the period, among them some of the works Baṅkim quotes in the commentary (e.g. Tylor's *Primitive Culture*).

Baṅkim's choice of these borrowings is certainly not motivated by the content of the *Gītā* in any way, but it is not just haphazard. Utilitarian and positivist thought had much in common, especially since Mill, who was one of the most important receptants of Comte's positivism in England.[107] Neither do they indicate a total identification with those doctrines on Baṅkim's part; their controversial discussion runs through quite a few of his essays.[108] There are substantial differences too, as for example the question of the existence of God: Baṅkim's decidedly theistic position was neither Comte's nor Mill's.[109] It would therefore certainly be too superficial to speak of a mere adaption of two closely related Western systems of philosophy. Rationalist Natural Religion, the name of the exegetical and theological movement[110] to which Seeley belonged andd which also influenced Baṅkim, shared a part of Mill's premises (e.g. in *The Utility of Religion* included in his *Three Essays on Religion*).

Another point to be made is that in the context of nineteenth century Bengal, these borrowings are not very new or far-fetched in any way. The reception of utilitarian, and later positivist, thought in India had been underway for almost a century.[111] In view of the great impact of utilitarian thinking on nineteenth century England and, as a

[105] Cf. *BR* II:588: The guru searches for a terminological alternative to *śakti*, and the *śiṣya* replies that 'faculty' would be adequate and has been translated as *vṛtti* by 'many Bengali writers'. Then the guru objects that *vṛtti* was used in a different sense by Patañjali; the *śiṣya* calls this sense obsolete. And the teacher gives in: 'Then circulate *vṛtti*. If only it is understood it is fine. When you have circulated the word *nīti* in the sense of "morals" and *vijñāna* / Beng. *bijñān* in the sense of "science", then I will not take it as a sin if you circulate *vṛtti* for "faculty".' — This 'you' is very interesting. Concerning *Dharmmatattva*, the current interpretation sees Baṅkim in the guru. This instance however is at least ambiguous; and there are in fact many passages where the guru is anything but a superior teacher and the *śiṣya* anything but an obedient pupil. It is possible to read *Dharmmatattva* in another way, i.e. to interpret the dialogical structure of the instruction (which often evolves into a discussion) as a mode of exteriorisation. Baṅkim thus does not have to pose exclusively as a teacher, but by inventing a narrative level between himself and the reader as a sort of refraction, he dissimulates his presence.

[106] Asceticism is regarded as a fault; cf. *ŚBhG*:105, 108f.

[107] On the close relationship between Comte and Mill — personally as well as philosophically — see Mary Pickering (1993), Chapter 12 on *The Encounter between two Luminaries: Comte and Mill* (505-38).

[108] e.g. *Kamalākānta* and *Dharmmatattva*.

[109] Cf. Amales Tripathi (1967a:10). Comte, however, while rejecting theism, has strong links with catholicism; he conceives his positivism as a necessary successor of it (cf. Kofman 1978:293-7).

[110] Cf. Rām׀kṛṣṇa Bhaṭṭācārya (1994:34-6) for an outline of the movement of Natural Religion.

[111] The line can be drawn back to Rām׀mohan Rāy̐, whose correspondence with Jeremy Bentham is famous.

consequence, on education in India, this reception was only natural.[112] In 1851 and 1853, the rationalist Akṣaẏ'kumār Datta had published his *Bāhyabastur sahit mānab'-prakṛtir sambandhabicār*, a Bengali version of the utilitarian George Cumbe's *Constitution of Man*. Bhabatoṣ Datta points out the striking similarities between that book and Baṅkim's interpretation of *dharma*: body and mind have to be exercised for attaining happiness, and the 'mental faculties' (*manovṛtti*) have to be brought to their destination in a completely harmonised way.[113] A similar ideal of education is incidentally expressed shortly after in the attempted novel *Ālāler gharer dulāl* (1855-7)[114] by Pyārīcā̃d Mitra: 'The main significance of education is that all the powers and moods[115] are exercised in accordance with the students' age', and even with a theistic bent: '[...] the root of the exercise of the moods, etc., of the mind is devotion towards God [...]'.[116] If then similar thoughts had been common knowledge more than thirty years before Baṅkim wrote his commentary, it can be concluded with certainty that these were as much an influence on Baṅkim as the original English works and authors he refers to. Moreover, his personal acquaintance and friendship with Yogendracandra Ghoṣ,[117] member of the Positivist Society of Bengal, bears testimony to the fact that the material he worked with was not very new to him or his contemporaries. The contagion of the term *dharma* with 'religion' had been a fact long before Baṅkim; the same is true for the educational ideal of developing all one's faculties in harmony. What seems to be new, and may thus be regarded as Baṅkim's invention, is the combination of these ideas within the term *dharma* with the aid of another — Seeley's — contention that religion is culture.

The most pointed critique of Baṅkim's interpretation and use of *dharma* has been put forward by Hacker,[118] and it will now have to be discussed in some length. The basic reproach is that Baṅkim twice confuses different meanings of *dharma* and thereby tries to find Western ideas on an Indian ground. The first confusion is stated for *Dharmmatattva* (Chapter 3, see above): While *dharma* is initially taken in the sense of 'religion', Baṅkim changes it to 'property'[119] in order to establish 'humanity' as the *dharma* of man. Secondly, Hacker holds that Baṅkim arrives at his idea of the universality of Hindu *dharma* by intermixing the meanings of 'religion' and 'caste-bound duty'.[120] Thirdly, Baṅkim's concept of *dharma*, according to Hacker, is individualistic and thus directly opposed to the meaning of the *Gītā* which he claims to interpret. *Dharma* is thus totally alienated from the old concept denoted by it: 'Like a container it has been emptied and then filled with a new content.'[121] Baṅkim's concept, as

[112] Cf. Bhabatoṣ Datta (1987-8). For a detailed study of the impact of Utilitarian thought on India, see Stokes (1963).

[113] Cf. Bhabatoṣ Datta (1987-8:41). The influence of Akṣaẏ'kumār's work on Baṅkim is also dealt with in Asit'kumār Bhaṭṭācārya (1964:131).

[114] Cf. Introduction, p. 7 of this book.

[115] [*bhāb* (Beng.).]

[116] Pyārīcā̃d Mitra (n.d. [1855-7]:161).

[117] Yogendracandra was the original addressee of Baṅkim's *Letters on Hinduism*.

[118] Paul Hacker (1978 [1958]), also (1978 [1970]).

[119] 'Wesentliche Eigenschaft', or 'essential quality', as translated by Paul Hacker (1978 [1970]).

[120] Hacker (1978 [1970]:515).

[121] Ibid.

Hacker emphasises, is so important because he is the first in a whole line (Aurobindo, Radhakrishnan, etc.) of thinkers belonging to what he calls neo-Hinduism and exposing similar concepts.

Hacker's analysis of the changes *dharma* undergoes in Baṅkim's hands is sharp and mostly accurate. He is to all appearance the first author on modern Hinduism to precisely state the three aspects of the changes *dharma* undergoes in modern Hinduism: *dharma* is universalised, personalised and psychologised. In the case of Baṅkim, however, the latter two are not fully discernible. Hacker relies on Baṅkim's interpretation of *dharma* as humanity in his conclusion that Baṅkim relates *svadharma* to individual inclination; but a closer look at other parts of the commentary reveals that Baṅkim's interpretation is not coherently individualistic, and not at all psychological.[122] In one instance, Hacker's insinuation of a confusion of meanings within the term *dharma* on Baṅkim's part appears to be due to a slight mistake in his German translation.[123]

Nevertheless, notwithstanding some inaccuracies and omissions, Hacker's objections are relevant, even if his references to 'surviving traditional Hinduism' are problematic.[124] What has to be reconsidered is his evaluation. His point is to show that Baṅkim and other 'neo-Hindus' are more indebted to nineteenth century Western philosophy and Christianity than to traditional Hinduism, and this contrary to their declaration. They circulate various borrowings in the garb of authentic Hinduism in a way which, to judge from the tenor of Hacker's writings, almost amounts to deception. Hacker's bias — a decidedly Christian bias — reveals itself most clearly in his discussion of Baṅkim's passing blow at Christianity, reinforced by a misunderstanding. The passage in question is from Baṅkim's interpretation of *Gītā* 2.11 (*ŚBhG[a]*:694): 'Whoever believes in this sort of fall from *dharma* by the Lord is comparable to the Christians' and the footnote: 'The Christians believe that God throws him who does not honour Jesus

[122] See the above discussion of *svadharma*: *Dharma* is personalised only to some extent, as worked out above, namely, as far as non-Hindu societies are concerned. For Hindu society, the *varṇāśramadharma* is kept intact in at least one instance of the commentary. It was further argued that a psychologisation in the proper sense of the term is still absent from Baṅkim's conception.

[123] Hacker (1978 [1958]:515); in his reading of the passage where Baṅkim asks what *svadharma* is for non-Hindus. While the old pundits had no problems in defining *svadharma*, Baṅkim claims, modern readers do. 'We seem to have understood [*ihā yena bujhilām*] that the *svadharma* of the Hindu religion, which depends upon the *varṇa*-system, can be determined according to the divisions of the *varṇas*. But what is *svadharma* for non-Hindus?' (*ŚBhG*:39) This 'seem', which represents *yena* (Beng.), is wrongly translated by Hacker as '*das haben wir wohl verstanden*', i.e. 'we have certainly understood' (rendered as 'we have understood that' by Halbfass' English translation [Hacker 1995:261]), and this is significant for the interpretation of what Baṅkim implies. *yena* (Beng.) may be read as a distance marker in this instance, implying that something has maybe been understood, but not in its full extension. And in fact, the sentence in question is nothing but a paraphrase of the 'easy' explanation of the 'old pundits'. It would therefore make more sense to interpret the passage in question as a polemical utterance: it may be easy to explain in narrow traditional ways, but that does not satisfy modern readers (and contemporaries who accept the traditional explanation are therefore narrow-minded). Modern readers search for another meaning of *svadharma*, i.e. as the individual specification of the general *dharma* of man, humanity. In this passage then there is, contrary to Hacker' opinion, no confusion of *varṇāśramadharma* and Baṅkim's new interpretation; one could rather say that he plays out one against the other. The confusion does however occur at other places.

[124] Hacker sees the publications of the Gītā Press at Gorakhpur as an indication for the survival of traditional Hinduism; according to Monika Horstmann (1995), this assumption does not stand proof since neo-Hindu attitudes are detectable in those publications too.

Christ into hell for eternity.'[125] Provoked by Baṅkim's polemical statement, Hacker then hurries to state that Baṅkim willingly overlooks the exclusivity (of birth) of traditional Hinduism as well as the different character of Christian exclusivity, namely, one of 'spirit and faith'.[126] It is true that Baṅkim applies double standards to Christianity and Hinduism: Hinduism is judged as a potential religion in the process of reformation, whereas Christianity is judged empirically and without taking into account the changes underway within it at that time.[127] Irritated by the polemics against Christianity, Hacker takes Baṅkim literally and misses the strategy behind his words: The readers are invited by Baṅkim to leave behind narrow-minded traditionalist notions of exclusivity and proceed to a new and more universal plane; those who hesitate are provoked by the comparison with their opponents, i.e. the Christians. Hacker is in this way trapped by a rhetorical device.

Furthermore, Hacker's critique remains silent about the reasons and circumstances of religious reform in nineteenth century India, and he implicitly claims that any reform of Hinduism ought to be entirely 'Indian'. Baṅkim꞉candra's interpretation of *dharma* is unacceptable to him in as far as it is incompatible with the traditional meaning of that term and contaminated by Western concepts. Hacker takes offence at Baṅkim's arguments, and maybe this partly motivates his dissecting and thorough analysis; but thereby he enters the field of inter-religious attack and counter-attack. Hacker certainly 'is not merely an objective "Indologist and Historian", or a neutral observer, but also an advocate of specific cultural and religious premises.' (Halbfass 1995:222) In ignoring the foregoing discussion in Bengal, Hacker follows Baṅkim in so far as Baṅkim himself does not refer to it, placing his discussion entirely between ancient Indian and contemporary Western texts. But that foregoing discussion is necessary to understand that Baṅkim's elaboration of *dharma* is not a *deus ex machina*-jugglery but an attempt at a synthesis.[128] As a matter of fact, Baṅkim did avow the Western influence on his thinking.[129] That attempt at a synthesis is certainly not within the range of traditional Hinduism, but this is not enough to reject it. A synthesis between Western and Eastern concepts, according to the tenor of Hacker's writings, is something hardly achievable at all. So while furnishing a very valuable analysis of the difference between traditional and modern *dharma*, Hacker's writings present an evaluation thereof which is fragmentary, and bears characteristics of an Indologist's dream of a 'pure' India uncontamined by the West. The perception of hybridity demands synthesis, and as far as Baṅkim's attempts answer to that need, they in turn do not allow of such a treatment. It is true that Baṅkim goes beyond a synthesis in claiming his refined *dharma* as an achievement of Hinduism; but Hacker fails to recognise the reasons why

[125] *ŚBhG*:39. The Bengali original is: *yini svaẏaṃ jagadīśvarer eirūp dharmmacyutite biśvās꞉bān, tini khrīṣṭāner* (Footnote: *khrīṣṭān꞉diger biśvās ye, ye yīśukhrīṣṭa nā bhaje, jagadīśvar tāhāke anantakāl janya narake nikṣep karen*) *tulya*.

[126] Hacker (1958 [1978]:516).

[127] Cf. Harder (1996:500f.) on Brahmabāndhab Upādhyāẏ, whose polemic articles employ the same structure of argument.

[128] Asit꞉kumār Bhaṭṭācārya (1964:149), however, claims convincingly that Baṅkim's approach is inept to integrate theses and counter-theses into a synthesis. Nonetheless, the failure does not, in this case, negate the attempt.

[129] Cf. also Amiya P. Sen (1993:112).

Baṅkim, caught up in a specific historical context, could not simply adopt Mill or Kant.[130]

A different approach can be found in the already mentioned book *Cintānāẏak baṅkim'candra* by Bhabatoṣ Datta. Datta's aim is not to compare the traditional and modern use of the term *dharma*, but to understand Baṅkim's thinking in the context of the nineteenth century and thereby determine the genesis and novelty of Baṅkim's ideas. Datta, unlike Hacker, lets us miss a precise formulation of the alteration of *dharma*; he does not seem to be intent on finding it; it rather seems to stand as a rule in that century. Neither does he analyse the inconsistent way in which Baṅkim uses the term. But his book demonstrates very well that at Baṅkim'candra's time there were manifold possible influences within Bengal prompting such a reformulation of *dharma*. What in Hacker's description appears as an individual's skilful cheating is here presented as something of relevance in a rather long period of history — as something whose synthetic character is nothing to be astonished about.

But nonetheless, even a sympathetic reading of Baṅkim'candra's elaboration of *dharma* cannot leave the reader altogether satisfied with the 'synthesis' in the garb of *dharma* offered by Baṅkim. And once cleansed of its excesses in counter-polemics, Hacker's critique of it is quite accurate. Discontent with that synthesis is also shared by a number of Bengali authors on the subject, e.g. Asit'kumār Bandyopādhyāẏ (1964) and Rām'kṛṣṇa Bhaṭṭācārya (1994). The latter, in a convincing and critical article, elaborates thoroughly that Baṅkim's approach to *dharma* suffers heavily from the intermingling of a refined 'Hindu version' (p. 36) of Natural Religion and Hindu *dharma*, and points out that the main inconsistency on Baṅkim's part is found in the attempt to reconcile these two. After a quotation in which Baṅkim calls the discussion of antiquated Hindu practices a necessary irony, Bhaṭṭācārya rightly states: 'If one places one's feet simultaneously into two boats — that of Natural religion and that of Hinduism [*hindutva* (Beng.)] — such irony is unavoidable.' (p. 46) The additional problems created by the term *dharma* are however not examined, *dharma* being used in the sense of religion throughout the article.

Baṅkim certainly does not remove the confusion regarding *dharma* as he claims to do, but increases it by elaborating a new meaning of it and simultaneously continuing to use all the other meanings. What results is a slender and a broad version of it — his newly formulated *dharma* and empirical, manifold *dharma* — as well as a thin and a thick version of Hinduism. The following chapter will show that the elasticity of these terms is crucial to the structuring of his arguments and the substance upon which the claim to Hinduism's superiority is built. Some of the inconsistencies discovered in the course of the present chapter (mainly those concerning the admission of individual choice of *svadharma*) seem to be due to unfinished thinking on Baṅkim's part. Others are strategic and shall be discussed on a general level in Chapters 2.3 and 2.4.

130 Hacker (1978 [1958]:517).

2.2.3 The Plurality of Worship

> 'If the English do not become the rulers, there is no possibility of the survival of *sanātanadharma*. Let me explain this to you the way the great men have understood it. Listen with concentration. The worship of 330 milion gods is not *sanātanadharma*; it is a worldly, inferior *dharma*; through its impact the genuine *sanātanadharma* — that which the *mlecchas* call *hindudharma* — has disappeared. The genuine *hindudharma* is concerned with knowledge, not with action.'[131]

Idolatry, combined with polytheism, was probably the most common ground on which traditional 'Hinduism' was attacked ever since it had been noticed by the West. The contempt of these practices was not only voiced by Christian missionaries, but also by philosophers, writers and theoreticians of religion; and at the outset of the nineteenth century, a strong critique of it from within Hindu society was initiated by Rām'mohan Rāẏ. The pattern of apologetics this attack produced, namely, as pronounced in Mr̥tyuñjaẏ Bidyālaṅkār's *Bedānta candrikā* (1817), was apparently very ancient. Bidyālaṅkār presents idolatry as a mechanism of mediation between humans and the absolute, not as a purpose in itself. The worshipped idol is nothing substantial, but merely a symbol: '[...] the king is adored through the adoration of his disguised form, and God is worshipped through the worship of his image.'[132] This indeed seems to have been the 'popular view', as Sisir Kumar Das calls it.[133] Richard F. Young presents a somewhat similar view from the Ziegenbalg papers, written as early as in 1709 by 'Malabarian priests':

> We teach the People to worship One only, and not many Gods; and the Notion of a plurality comes hence, viz. because God is variously presented under different Attributes and forms; yet he is still but One God, as God is but one, as to its kind, tho' wrought into a Thousand different Figures.[134]

Rām'mohan and the critics to come did not however accept the basic claim of this argument, that idol worship was de facto executed as a symbolic action. In defying such an interpretation, he states that

> the truth is, the Hindoos of the present day have no such views on the subject, but firmly believe in the real existence of innumerable gods and goddesses, who possess, in their own departments, full and independent power; and to propitiate them, and not the true God, are temples erected and ceremonies performed.[135]

This was the status quo of his contemporary Hindu society in Rām'mohan's view, which differed a lot from what he saw as the *true* essence of 'Hindu' religion:

> There can be no doubt, however, and it is my whole design to prove, that

131 *Ānandamaṭh* (*BR* I:643).

132 *Bedānta candrikā*; quoted from, and as translated by, Sisir Kumar Das (1974:22).

133 Ibid.

134 Young (1981:24).

135 From the *Introduction* of his English *Translation of an Abridgment of the Vedant, or the Resolution of all the Veds* [1816]; in Rammohun Roy (1901, Vol. I, 1-24:5).

> every rite has its derivation from the allegorical adoration of the true deity; but at the present day all this is forgotten, and among many it is even heresy to mention it.[136]

The discussion of the appropriate form of worship remained a major concern throughout the nineteenth century. Young documents the extensive controversy started by the missionary John Muir, which took place in the fifties.[137] Rāj'nārāyaṇ Basu (1995) in his lecture in 1872 conceives of the toleration of idolatry in Hinduism as a positive characteristic. One of the criteria of the superiority of Hinduism, for him, is its liberality (1995:435f.): all religions are accepted by Hinduism, and idolatry is one of the steps on the ascending ladder of worship. While according to Rāj'nārāyaṇ, it is assuredly wrong to worship idols, and just as wrong to suppose that Hindu *dharma* is based on it, those who are not able to progress beyond this initial step are not disowned by their religion.[138] The topic is raised again in the eighties in the controversy between Reverend Hastie and Baṅkim'candra. The Hastie controversy is in fact a convenient point to start the analysis of Baṅkim's concepts regarding worship; in drawing a line from there to the commentary, a significant shift from an apologetical to a more offensive attitude can be observed.

Hastie's attack starts off with a critique of idolatry, but it would be wrong to assume that this was the topic which prompted Baṅkim's reply. Hastie's first letter which, in contrast to the following ones, is mostly limited to this topic, is still of a fairly moderate tenor. It criticises the habitual Hindu apologetics of idolatry that postulate idolatry as an 'intellectual necessity' (*BR* III:187) for less cultivated minds, and in this context quotes Rādhākānta Deb as an example:

> 'As you Europeans give *dolls* to *your* children, so do we Hindoos give these *idols* to *our* children, to our uneducated women and common people, who cannot do without them, but' — adding with an expressive smile — 'we do not really worship them ourselves.' (*BR* III:187).

Hastie further claims that idolatry is refuted also from within the system of Hindu belief, i.e. by the 'etherial and incorporeal [...] abstractions of the Brahmanic doctrine' (*BR* III:188). In the second letter, preaching fervour makes its way into Hastie's representation of Hinduism, and his arguments start to deteriorate into gross generalisations: 'Hinduism with all its apparent humanism is but a disguised Nature-worship' (*BR* III:192). This leads to the third where he asserts that none of 'the problems of human life or thought' have been solved by Brahmanic theology, and that therefore Christianity is the only hope for India.

Idolatry and polytheistic worship were, at that time, nothing Baṅkim had shown much interest in, and a defence of them was apparently still outside his concerns; this is evidenced by the introductory quotation from *Ānandamaṭh* in this subchapter. It is quite likely that Baṅkim would not have entered the controversy at all had Hastie confined

[136] Ibid.

[137] Provoked by Muir's *Mataparīkṣā* [1839], written in what Young calls 'church Sanskrit' and designed to establish the superiority of Christianity as the true religion, three apologists published tracts in Sanskrit against Muir's theses. Cf. Young (1981:126f.); especially the response by Nīlakaṇṭha Gore (p. 127) in the present context.

[138] Ibid. (*Hindudharmmer śreṣṭhatā*). An English synopsis of the lecture is included in Kamal Kumar Ghatak (1991:43).

himself to a critique of idolatry. Baṅkim reacts exclusively to Hastie's other assumptions until his third letter, where he is compelled to give a short systematic exposition of Hinduism. His argument is developed by using the metaphor of the 'kernel' and the 'husks':[139] idolatry belongs to the husks, being a ritualistic convention without much connection to the true doctrinal basis of Hindu religion; nowhere in the scriptures, Baṅkim claims, is it indicated as a compulsory practice.[140] He dismisses Rādhākānta Deb's explanation as 'simply childish' (*BR* III:215) and furnishes an aesthetical explanation instead, reducing idolatry to mere imaginative creativity common to all arts, literature and practically any field of human activity.[141] The fundamental point in this argument is his assertion that idols are — empirically — *never* equated with God, but perceived exclusively as symbols.[142] Idols have no separate sanctity of their own, as is evident, he argues, from the practice of *visarjana*, the immersion into the water of images after *Durgā pūjā* (and the other great *pūjās* in Bengal). As for the idols commonly used, he concludes, they truly are hideous from an artistic point of view, and gives the advice that 'wealthy Hindus should get their Krishnas and Radhas made in Europe.' (*BR* III:216)

In his *Deb'tattva o hindudharmma*, written not long after the controversy, Baṅkim rejects the notion of Hindu polytheism. He argues that Vedic religion alone, in its development until the Upaniṣads, had three historically subsequent theologies to offer,

> three stages [*abasthā* (Beng.)] of Vedic *dharma*: (1) Firstly, the worship of the devas — i.e. the imposition of consciousness on innate matter, and its worship. (2) Worship of God, and worship of the devas along with it. (3) Worship of God, and the devas merging into God. (*BR* II:816)

These stages correspond very well to the concept of stage-wise religious evolution so common in nineteenth century Europe;[143] even Vedic literature has, according to Baṅkim, trodden on the ladder of progress.

What lacks to render Vedic religion, including *Vedānta* thought, complete is the concept of *bhakti*,[144] the contribution of purānic Hinduism as stated in *Dharmmatattva*:

[139] This is a recurring motif in his writings around this period. To my knowledge, this metaphor is first used in *Baṛa bājār*, one of the essays of *Kamalākānta* (cf. Chapter 2.3.3 for a quotation), and significantly in a reverse constellation: There, contemporary Indian pundits are experts in husk-chewing, whereas the Europeans get directly at the kernel of Indian religious tradition.

[140] Cf. Ajit Ray (1986:37).

[141] Cf. Sisir Kumar Das (1974:102): Baṅkim'candra 'defended idolatry not from any religious standpoint but from a purely aesthetic standpoint.' Also Ajit Ray (1986:37), who speaks of a 'philosophical justification for the use of images in worship'. Amales Tripathi (1967:480), with reference to Baṅkim's essay *Hindu dharmma sambandhe kayek'ṭi sthūl kathā*: 'He was aware of the unscientific character of image-worship and afraid that it would hamper realisation of truth by confining man's mind within a narrow orbit. But he stressed its aesthetic aspect which the Brahmos had missed'. By contrast, M.K. Halder (1977:99), while not taking into account Baṅkim's apologetical situation, expresses his discontent with Baṅkim's argumentation by calling it a 'pseudo-philosophical rigmarole'.

[142] In contrast e.g. to Rām'mohan's above-quoted assumption.

[143] Cf. the books quoted in the commentary, e.g. Mill's *Three Essays on Religion*, Tylor's *Primitive Culture*, etc.

[144] Cf. Amales Tripathi (1967a:11f.) as well as *idem* (1967b:478): 'Baṅkim regarded Upanishadic monotheism as the fourth and highest stage in the evolution of Vedic religion but still incomplete [...] The final touch was given by *Bhaktishastras* like the *Gita*.' Minor (1991:82) is wrong in stating that Baṅkim sees the

> The *Sāhebs* and native pundits like Dayānand Sarasvatī, etc., call the Vedic *dharma* the best *dharma*, and the paurāṇic or modern *dharma* an inferior *dharma*. But now I see that this is highly untrue. A *dharma* without *bhakti* is an incomplete and inferior *dharma* — so when there is no *bhakti* in Vedic *dharma*, then Vedic *dharma* is inferior. (*BR* II:624)

Vedic ritualistic religion is however not to be abolished, but rather to remain on a subordinate level. As Baṅkim points out in his discussion of Vedic *sakāma karman* in the commentary,

> The author of the *Gītā* does not hold a sword in the direction of Vedic *dharma*, either. He knew that the *niṣkāma karmayoga* and *jñānayoga* he spoke of would never be able to occupy the whole place of wordly *dharma*. But if the wordly *dharma* remained intact, through it [his *dharma*] the purification of that wordly *dharma* would be exellently accomplished. Therefore, he was not inclined to cut off the relationship. We have considered him to be one of those who brought forth a revolt against Vedic *dharma*. But his revolt limits itself to the point of saying that the *dharma* which there is in the Vedas is incomplete, and that it must be completed by *niṣkāma karmayoga*, etc. For this reason he called the Vedic *dharma* [associated] with desire [*sakāma*] inferior. But he does not say that, being inferior, it is utterly lacking merit. (*ŚBhG*:123)

The relation between the new and the old *dharma* is conceived as historical and additive.

Baṅkim stresses that there are various paths to God:

> A few strong [people] take the straight [*sojā* (Beng.)] path there is to ascend the top of the mountain. For usual people, a curved path moving to and fro has been prescribed.[145]

There are different means of attaining God to be employed by the householder and the *saṃnyāsin*, the *jñānin* and *bhakta*, etc. Ultimately, all these paths are presented as aspects of *bhakti*; the 'merciful' Lord of the world has made them for all possible kinds of humans: 'It is His goal [to render] the *dharma* easy [*sojā* (Beng.)] for all.' The straightest path is determined, in accordance with *BhG* 12.5-7, as worship to the *īśvara*, i.e. Kṛṣṇa (*BR* II:635).

The formulation of a *bhakti*-oriented theism — which Asit Kumar Bandyopadhyay (1994) calls 'neo-Puranism' — with Kṛṣṇa as the personal God is the main purpose of *Dharmmatattva* and *Kṛṣṇacaritra*. Only a personal God is apt to become the object of worship because he can serve as an ideal to mankind.[146] The worship of this personal God is described in some length in *Dharmmatattva*:

> We cannot see God. There is no possibility of moving while constantly watching Him. We can only think Him in our minds. That thinking is worship. [...] We will have to take the vow firmly on our minds that our nature [*svabhāb* (Beng.)] should be built by the ideal of His nature; only then will the stainless light of that holy character [*pabitra caritra* (Beng.)]

Gītā as subjugating *jñāna* and *bhakti* to *karman*; *bhakti* is the hierarchically highest of these categories for Baṅkim.

[145] *Dharmmatattva* (*BR* II:635).

[146] This is one of his major differences with the Brāhma faith.

> fall on our character. [...] (*BR* II:593).

This conception is fairly removed from traditional idol worship; but in giving *saguṇa bhakti* priority over *nirguṇa bhakti*, it furnishes at least an implicit justification for it. This justification is finally made explicit in the commentary as will be shown.

The topic of worship is dealt with in detail in two passages of the commentary. It comes up first in *Gītā* 2.17 where the all-pervading principle is described as imperishable and immutable. Baṅkim takes this as a proof of God's shapelessness. He proceeds to claim that the Purāṇas, too, hold that God is shapeless. If this seems, at first sight, to be to the contrary, such appearance is ascribed to the need for external representation:

> It is true, of course, that in the Purāṇas and Itihāsas, Brahmā, Viṣṇu and Śiva have been imagined as consciousness having a form and in many cases worshipped as God.[147] It is not necessary here to investigate for which reasons the need for or origin of imagining such images of God had come about. It must only be said that the authors of the Purāṇas and Itihāsas do not want to establish the formedness of God, even when Śiva, etc., have been described as having shape; they never forget that God is formless.

Baṅkim admits that 'India is full of the veneration of idols', but he denies, if less categorically than in the Hastie controversy, that the idols are identified with God: '[...] the Hindu who venerates an idol will unless he is utterly ignorant or uneducated, never imagine the idol to be God, or that God is shaped like this and that this is God's genuine image.'[148] The example he chooses to illustrate this assertion is, however, problematic and leaves much space for doubt: an actual worshipper in front of a '*Kālī* made of a lump of clay' (*ŚBhG*:68) would in fact probably rarely call upon the 'world-pervading, omnipresent primordial energy' (ibid.) to manifest itself in that image in order to help him to make up his mind where to put the sandal paste.

The alleged degradation of India because of the practice of idolatry is then negated by submitting the discussion to a new criterion. Not the accuracy of the worship one has chosen matters, but 'the essence of adoration' (*ŚBhG*:68), i.e. devotion, *bhakti*. The question of superiority or inferiority is dismissed as irrelevant by setting all worship in opposition to the Absolute. God cannot be known, neither by the worshipper of the unmanifest nor by the worshipper of the manifest. So there is only a difference of degree, and these subtleties of the relative become meaningless in the perspective of the Absolute. The position Baṅkim takes here is dominated by *bhakti* and reduces *jñāna*, praised as the genuine nature of Hindu *dharma* in *Ānandamaṭh* as quoted above, to an unspecified, but certainly inferior component. The attainment of *mokṣa* by merging into the Absolute is, however, precluded in his approach, and his notion of *bhakti* as persisting separation seems, at least at this instance, influenced by Christian devotion, since traditionally, *bhakti* is conceived as the state of separation from the divine, a state

[147] [*īśvara*.]

[148] *ŚBhG*:67. Cf. Nabīncandra Sen: 'Ask a usual, ignorant peasant: even he will say that there are not so many Lords. The Lord is one. The images are merely images of gods [*debatā* (Beng.)] or divine powers.' (Harder 1994:99)

which can be overcome.[149] He stresses however that a *sākāravāda*, a *doctrine* of the corporeal, is to be abolished; worship of the manifest is an equivalent mode only when performed with the awareness of the non-identity of God and the image.

The argument is taken further in a passage of central importance to Baṅkim's commentary, the interpretation of *Gītā* 4.11.[150] The relativistic approach is radicalised here. A list of different kinds of worship is given, from fetishism to worship of the formless *brahman*, and Baṅkim'candra admits that there are 'differences of quality' (*ŚBhG*:146) in them. But these are merely differences of *knowledge*:

> He who is absolutely ignorant sees on the roadside some piece of stone on which flowers, sandal and vermilion have been put, and goes on putting flowers, sandal and vermilion on it; he who has come to know a bit is perhaps a worshipper of the formless *brahman*. But concerning the knowledge of the extension of the Lord's nature, both are almost equally blind.[151]

Firstly, this gives rise to doubt concerning the assertion formerly made that the worship in front of a lump of clay is, in the worshipper's mind, actually worship of the Absolute by using a mediating symbol. But it becomes also problematic theoretically insofar as the result of such variegated worship is no longer the approach of God at all, as the paraphrase of the *śloka* in question clearly demonstrates: 'Even if a man does not worship any god, but only serves his senses, etc., that too is my service.' (*ŚBhG*:146). By this step, the meaning of *upāsanā* is enlarged as nowhere else in the commentary, and even more than the term *yajña* which on p. 125 was defined as 'worship [*pūjā*] of a deity'. *Upāsanā* is, in this sense, no longer a conscious act on the devotee's part, not an intentional, specific kind of action; it is — seen from Kṛṣṇa's, as the personal God's, perspective — just any possible sort of activity, i.e. anything one does. Therefore, according to Baṅkim, if 'worship' of the senses be performed with devotion, it becomes acceptable to God. But devotion to whom or what? It is extremely unlikely that Baṅkim suggests here that even when serving one's senses the intentional target of this 'worship' is God. His argument starts from the Absolute: '[...] in the world there is nothing except myself; I am the senses, etc., and I bestow the fruits on the senses adequately in the form of the senses, etc.' When, in this way, any sort of action is bound to be directed to the all-pervading God, then the bestowal of the results thereof does *not* depend on the acceptibility of this *upāsanā* on God's part. On this absolute level, just *anything* is *upāsanā*, no matter whether the fruits are salutory or 'inferior and sorrowful' (*ŚBhG*:146). Kṛṣṇa is in this case a karmic agent, i.e. the personalised divine enacter and implementer of *karman*.[152]

149 Tilak, by contrast, points out that *bhakti* ('separation'; from √*bhaj* 'to divide, grant, adore') ceases when the goal is reached, i.e. when *mokṣa* is attained; cf. Stevenson (1991:55). Tripathi (1967[b]:480) points out, with reference to Brāhma and modern Hindu positions: 'In fact, both the streams of idealism yearned after an equivalence with God (*svādharmya*) and not after an identity (*sāyujya*).'

150 See *ŚBhG*:145ff.: *ye yathā māṃ prapadyante tāṃs tathaiva bhajāmy aham / mama vartmānuvartante manuṣyāḥ pārtha sarvaśaḥ*. Baṅkim's translation: 'I satisfy everybody the way in which he worships me. People follow my path in every sort of way.'

151 Ibid. It is evident that this part formally belongs to the interpretation as opposed to the preceding paraphrase of the *Gītā*.

152 *karman* not simply as 'action', but in its conceptualised meaning.

It is worthy of consideration whether this interpretation of *Gītā* 4.11 is compatible with the semantic frame set by the original. *manuṣyāḥ* does not mean 'all people', but simply 'people', and Baṅkim translates correctly, too. The 'people' of this *śloka* are to all appearance not the whole of mankind, but only worshippers of different kinds, as is indicated by the preceding line: *pra-√pad* means 'to arrive at', 'to reach', also 'to prostrate oneself', all of which imply intentionality; worship thus appears to mean not just any human action, as interpreted by Baṅkim, but an action meant to be such. The only way to interpret *manuṣyāḥ* as 'all people' would be by dissociation of the two lines of the *śloka*, in which case *anuvartante* would not necessarily relate to *prapadyante*, i.e. *upāsanā*. A further indication that *Gītā* 4.11 does not speak of an inborn necessity *per definitionem* to worship Kr̥ṣṇa is the mention of *duṣkr̥t* ('doers of evil deeds') in *Gītā* 4.8, who are to be destroyed by Kr̥ṣṇa. Consequently, it is rather evident that Kr̥ṣṇa in 4.11 is the receiver of intentional worship, and *not* simply the bestower of all results. The most probable groups of reference would then be the different religious groups in *the Gītā's* contemporary society and their respective modes of worship; Baṅkim's implicit assertion that any action is *upāsanā* is not implied in the original.

But the aspect of Kr̥ṣṇa as a karmic agent is not important to the conclusion Baṅkim draws from his interpretation of *Gītā* 4.11. Basically, his argument is two-fold: (a) there are various forms of worship of differing quality, at an empirical level; (b) there is, on the other end, Kr̥ṣṇa, the personal Absolute Being who in this *Gītā* sanctions all those forms. In *Deb'tattva o hindudharmma*, this topic is dealt with on the basis of *Gītā* 9.23,[153] and Baṅkim's contention is merely that worship of various Hindu gods is ultimately worship of the *Jagadīśvara*, of God.[154] Here in the commentary, the argument is taken one significant step further: Baṅkim's conclusion is that he, Kr̥ṣṇa, *mediated as his voice is through a central text of the Hindu religion*, is beyond all sectarian and religious boundaries and therefore the common ultimate goal of all religions, while it is of course Hindu tradition, as his medium, which can claim him as part of itself:

> If the significance of this *śloka* is understood, there are no more differences caused by *dharma* [*dharmmagata* (Beng.)] on earth; Hindus, Muslims, Christians, Jainas, worshippers of the formless and the formed, worshippers of many gods, and of innate matter, all of them worship that one God; all follow the path on which he is. The *dharma* proclaimed in this *śloka* is the world's only non-sectarian[155] *dharma*; the only *dharma* to be followed by all people. It is the genuine Hindu *dharma* too. There is no other *dharma* as generous as the Hindu *dharma*; and there is no

[153] Cf. the quotation from Chapter 9 of the *Gītā* in *ŚBhG*:125.

[154] Cf. *BR* II:819: 'Thus in very ancient time, the *vaidikas* arrived gradually from worship to innate matter at the worship of one God. For some time, the worship of the many Gods Indra, etc., remained. We shall see in due course that those Indra, etc., also merged in the *paramātman*. We shall see that the genuine significance of Hindu *dharma* is only the worship to the Lord of the world. All others are only his different names. *ye 'py anyadevatābhaktā yajante śraddhayānvitāḥ / te 'pi mām eva kaunteya yajanty avidhipūrvakam*. (9.23) [Those worshippers of other gods who worship with reverence, O Kaunteya, worship me, (but) not according to (scriptural) instructions.]' The same *śloka* is again quoted at the very end of the essay (p. 822).

[155] [*asāmpradāẏik* (Beng.).] The same term was used by Rāj'nārāẏaṇ Basu (1995:446). *Asāmpradāẏik* is the modern Bengali equivalent to 'secular' or 'non-communal'; this instance, however, makes clear that the connotations of both terms are quite different. 'Secular' could hardly be considered a viable translation of *asāmpradāẏik* here.

other great utterance comparable to this *śloka*. (*ŚBhG*:146f.).

The inclusivistic[156] harmonisation of different *sectarian* (*sāmpradāyik* [Beng.]) beliefs intended by the *Gītā* is generalised by Baṅkim so as to encompass all *religious* beliefs; this type of generalisation, as Agehananda Bharati (1971) rightly stresses, goes beyond the possible limits of a traditional harmonisation.[157] And the merit of this 'meta-religion' is swiftly taken home to India. Baṅkim does speak of 'that one God' and not of Kr̥ṣṇa; but this dissolution of sectarian differences is 'the genuine Hindu *dharma* too', and consequently 'there is no other *dharma* as generous as the Hindu *dharma*'. And anyhow, the still more explicit formulation in *Dharmmatattva* leaves no doubts regarding who is 'that one God': 'Whether we say God, Allah or Brahmā, it is that one Lord of the world, Viṣṇu, whom we call upon.' (*BR* II:643)[158] In this way, a very thin definition of *dharma* is as a *pars pro toto* reapplied to Hindu *dharma* in order to assert the latter's superiority.[159]

There are striking similarities between this argument structure and the earlier claim to Hinduism's superiority by Rāj'nārāẏaṇ Basu (*Hindudharmmer śreṣṭhatā* [1872]; in Rāj'nārāẏaṇ Basu 1995). Here, it is *Brāhma dharma* which is universal and 'non-sectarian' (*asāmpradāyik* [Beng.]), and which is in fact the highest branch of *Hindu dharma* as well. At the same time, it constitutes the highest form of any religion:

> As much right as a Christian *brahmavādin* has to call the *Brāhma dharma* the pure and fully developed form of Christian religion, and a Muslim *brahmavādin* to call it the pure and fully developed form of Muslim *dharma*, so much right has a Hindu *brahmavādin* to call it the pure and fully developed form of Hindu *dharma*. (Rāj'nārāẏaṇ Basu 1995:447)

Here too, the merit of having developed this superior religion goes indirectly to the Hindus, since Rāj'nārāẏaṇ's *Brāhma dharma* claims to be an integral part of Hinduism, as it were.[160] Baṅkim makes the claim more direct by shifting the emphasis to what he perceives as the core of Hinduism, i.e. its most central and simultaneously most superior

[156] For a definition of the term 'inclusivism', coined by Hacker, see his essay *Zur Geschichte und Beurteilung des Hinduismus* (1978 [1964]). Another significant book is Oberhammer (ed.) (1983). Cf. also Mahaffey (1994).

[157] Bharati refers to *samanvaya* as 'a traditional though not canonical injunction for pandits to find a basic agreement among themselves in the process of *śāstrārtha*' and points out that '*samanvaya* never meant what the more learned modern eclectics think it did. It did not include Islam, Christianity, Buddhism, communism, nationalism, or "science" [...]. [...] Typically a modern Hindu would say that Hinduism is all-tolerant, that it embraces every religion. But *samanvaya* is something quite different, and those scholars within the Renaissance who know about *samanvaya* consistently confuse it with "tolerance" in order to legitimize their universalistic claims.' (1971:83).

[158] Also quoted in Śāntanu Kāẏ'sār (1982:52).

[159] The same mechanism is at work in the following passage from *Dharmmatattva* where the ideal (that is 'thin', i.e. selectively interpreted) Kr̥ṣṇa is made to encompass all other religious ideal figures: 'I bow to Him who is Śākyasiṃha [Buddha], Jesus Christ, Mohammad and *Rāmacandra* in one; who is the base of all powers and the base of all qualities [*sarbbaguṇādhār* (Beng.)], the knower of all *dharmas*, everywhere full of love, be He God or not.' (*BR* II:594).

[160] Cf. also Kamal Kumar Ghatak 1991:43f. For a later Hindu response to such claims by Brahmoism, cf. Nabīn'candra Sen's novel *Bhānumati* (Hans Harder 1994:98): 'The highest branch of Hindu *dharma* is the *Brahma dharma*. But the Brāhmas want to jump on that branch with one leap. [...] The Hindus hold that one has to ascend to the top by starting from the root.'

part; he applies the same argument as Rāj'nārāẏaṇ to Kr̥ṣṇa and the *Gītā*.

It is quite a long way from the defensive, apologetic remarks in the Hastie controversy to this claim to religious superiority over other 'narrow' religions like Christianity. The claim is of course not built upon idolatry as such, but on the generous sanction of all kinds of religious practices in *Gītā* 4.11. The thing Baṅkim misses is that what he calls Kr̥ṣṇa's *dharma* on the basis of this *śloka* is not a 'religion' at all in any concrete sense, and does not correspond to any of the other meanings of *dharma* he mentions. It is rather a harmonising 'meta-religious' statement, and in any case nothing so concrete as being possibly apt to become 'the only *dharma* to be followed by all people'. The *śloka* is a metaphysical claim for Kr̥ṣṇa as the ultimate Godhead, combined with the assignment of legitimacy to different forms of worship *under that heading*, and its inclusivism extends to such forms of worship as are mentioned in the *Gītā*. In Baṅkim's interpretation, the *śloka* is, on the one hand, generalised so as to apply to all 'religions'; on the other, the claim to the ultimate position is also universalised. In this sense, Baṅkim's interpretation becomes an ethnocentric cultural self-assertion which results in a *primus inter pares* type of situation: 'Hindu Dharma is more equal than other Dharmas',[161] because it has developed the notion of equality in worship.

In this constellation, the most refined elaboration of *dharma* reverberates glory on the term *Hindu dharma*; there is still another, however, in which *dharma* in Baṅkim's positivist sense is *applied* to 'thick' (i.e. traditionally agglomerated) Hindu *dharma* and implicitly makes precisely the diversification inherent in Hindu modes of worship the criterion for superiority. Seeley, in his contention that lower and higher forms of religion ought to coexist,[162] conceives the model of a superior religion; and Baṅkim's *Hindu dharma* readily complies with this model:

> [...] a religion which excludes nature-worship is an imperfect religion. Experience has shown that the absence of this element from a religion, as in Christianity and Mohammedanism, serves to develop narrowness and bigotry, and to harden the sterner virtues into cruelty and fanaticism. Hinduism alone contains within it all these elements of worship, Hinduism alone therefore is a perfect religion.[163]

[161] M.K. Halder (1977:93).

[162] Cf. Seeley (1895 [1882]:86f.): 'The words religion and worship are commonly and conveniently appropriated to the feelings with which we regard God. But those feelings — love, awe, admiration, which together make up worship — are felt in various combinations for human beings, and even for inanimate objects. It is not exclusively but only *par excellence* that religion is directed towards God. When feelings of admiration are very strong they find vent in some act; when they are strong and at the same time serious and permanent, they express themselves in recurring acts, and hence arise ritual, liturgy, and whatever the multitude identifies with religion. But without ritual, religion may exist in its elementary state, and this elementary state of religion is what may be described as *habitual and permanent admiration*. Now it is surely not to be supposed that every higher form of religion ought to supersede and drive out the lower forms.'

[163] *Letters on Hinduism* (*BR* III:265).

2.3 The Communicative Dimension

In this chapter, the commentary will be analysed as a communicative process. All three sub-chapters will deal with the strategies Baṅkim'candra employs in order to form a coherent picture of the *Gītā* and Hinduism, and to persuade his readers to accept his interpretations. It is on this level that his construction, sometimes consciously, sometimes despite himself, of an in- and outside is at work, that is, the demarcation between identity and non-identity with regard to his readers as well as to the topics under discussion. Baṅkim's treatment of his readers (2.3.1), of the ancient commentators (2.3.2) and of Western Indologists (2.3.3) is dealt with from this perspective. In analysing his creation of and moves through a complex set of oppositions, an accurate representation of Baṅkim's self-perception and position (argumentative as well as social) will be the main aim.

2.3.1 Baṅkim'candra and His Readers

As an educationist, Baṅkim'candra did not believe in vertical diffusion of knowledge or the theory of 'filtering down education' as proclaimed by Macaulay;[1] 'Knowledge [*bidyā* (Beng.)] is not water or milk that if you pour it on the top it is absorbed at the bottom.'[2] In both his inaugural editorial articles to *Baṅgadarśan* (1872) and *Pracār* (1884), he stresses that he chooses Bengali as the medium of those periodicals in order to reach the *general* Bengali public. One purpose being of course to furnish readable literature to well-educated Bengalis, he argues that this does not contradict his main purpose of general public education:

> That which is not suited for the lecture of a well-educated person will be read by nobody. [But] everyone wants to read that which is excellent; he who cannot understand it will make an effort to do so. This effort is the root of general education.[3]

A passage similar to this one from the editorial of *Baṅgadarśan* is found in that of *Pracār* (where *adhyāyas* 1 and 2 of his commentary were to appear):

> When we are disseminating a periodical for the general public,[4] then it will of course be our aim that the articles of *Pracār* are intelligible to the general public. [...] The work is difficult, and there is very little hope that we can achieve it. But we will not present in it children's articles as generally readable. We hope that both pundits and non-pundits will be able to discuss that which will be published in *Pracār*. Many believe that that which persons of unaccomplished learning wish to read or understand or hear, is not worthy of the pundits' reading, understanding or hearing. We have many doubts regarding this.[5]

English as the rulers' language is not rejected as such by Baṅkim, but it is of

[1] Cf. Tapan Raychaudhuri (1988:3).

[2] From *Baṅgadarśaner patrasūcanā* (*BR* II:282); also quoted in Tapobijaẏ Ghoṣ (1989:49).

[3] *Baṅgadarśaner patrasūcanā* (*BR* II:284).

[4] [*sarbbasādhāraṇ* (Beng.).]

[5] From *Sūcanā* (*BR* II:912).

limited use for Bengalis. Again and again he mocks most effectively the artificiality of his educated contemporaries' use of English in practically every domain of life, and points out the unlikelihood of English ever becoming a commonly understood language in Bengal. Nonetheless English is of great importance as 'the rulers' language, the language for the acquisition of wealth; moreover it is the base of many [branches of] learning [*bidyā* (Beng.)], at this moment it is our only step to the acquisition of knowledge [*jñān* (Beng.)].'[6] English, then, is clearly perceived as an élite language unsuited for communication with the general public of Bengal, and thus cannot be the medium for bridging the gap between the educated and the uneducated which was Baṅkim's aim in bringing out his periodicals.[7]

In an English paper read before the Bengal Social Science Association in 1870, Baṅkim specifies what he means by a general public:

> But it is not altogether true to entertain the idea that the absolute number of purely Bengali readers are in reality so few. The artizan and the shopkeeper who keep their own accounts, the village zemindar and the mofussil lawyer, the humbler official employé whose English carries him no further than the duties of his office, and the small proprietor who has as little to do with English as with office, all these classes read Bengali and Bengali only; all in fact between the ignorant peasant and the really well-educated classes. And if to these be added the vast numbers who are likely to benefit by a system of vernacular education, extended and developed so as to suit the requirements of the country, we may be in a position to appreciate fully the importance of a literature for the *people* of Bengal; for these classes constitute *the people*.[8]

At the same time, Baṅkim was, however, fully aware of how limited the reading public actually was, and that his proposition was more problematic than it may seem. In his article *Lok'śikṣā* (1878), he states that 'in this country, there are in every language some ten or fifteen periodicals; some has 200, another 500 buyers, [so] five or seven thousand people read [them].' (*BR* II:376)[9] In relation to the total number of inhabitants of the province of Bengal, which was 66 million according to a census to which Baṅkim refers, this is a small number indeed.

At this point, the question may arise whether the actual readership was in fact representative of the intended readership at all, i.e. whether the different layers of society did form a part of this limited readership in some relevant proportion. Amiya P. Sen (1993:95) gives some details about the publication of *Baṅgadarśan*, stating that it had a rising number of regular subscribers from 1872 (1000) to 1876 (1600). I have not been able to trace any records of the actual dissemination of *Pracār*, so a solid empirical answer cannot be given. But there are some clues in Baṅkim's writings which suggest a tentative answer. *Baṅgadarśan* was started in the spirit of an educative mission, as the *Patra-sūcanā* shows. The inclusion of writings like *Bijñān-rahasya*, which more than any other of Baṅkim's works is purely designed for the mediation of modern scientific

[6] *Baṅgadarśaner patra-sūcanā* (*BR* II:281).

[7] Cf. Tapobijaẏ Ghoṣ (1989:36f.).

[8] *A Popular Literature for Bengal* (*BR* III:97).

[9] This is contrasted to the great impact of newspapers in Europe, as again in the *Sūcanā* to *Pracār* where the European newspapers are in size and depth compared to Purāṇas (*BR* II:911).

knowledge (largely cosmology) in Bengali, substantiates that this was more than mere rhetoric. *Pracār* was announced as a smaller magazine, but still the educationist orientation was there, if with a new touch of pessimism. There is a remark on the periodicals' prices as well: *Pracār* cost 3 Rs. per year. Baṅkim'candra reports that this moderate price was still regarded as too much, and seems to suggest (in the *Sūcanā* to *Pracār*) that exceptions be made in the case of people unable to pay it:

> [...] I have concluded that even Rs. 3 are beyond the capability of the common Bengali reader. Not all can avail Rs. 3, therefore they do not give [them], they do not give [them] simply because they do not have them. With the consideration that those who cannot afford Rs. 3 can afford Rs. 1 1/2, we are publishing this new periodical. (*BR* II:912)

Later, as his nephew and biographer Śrīś'candra Caṭṭopādhyāẏ reports, he refers to his experiences when advising Sureś'candra Samāj'pati not to lower the price of the newspaper he is bringing out below Rs. 3:

> Those who are able to pay Rs. 2 can also pay Rs. 3; those who can give neither Rs. 3 nor 2, do not buy anything. I have noticed in the case of *Baṅgadarśan* as well as in the case of *Pracār*: to the class of people who become customers, Rs. 2 or 3 do not matter. [...] The number of people who are very poor, but are able to read and want to read, is still extremely small in this country. In our country there is no education system for the common people, so the number of the educated is very small.[10]

This sounds disillusioned. But this experience made itself felt earlier in a tacit change of the communicative direction of Baṅkim's essays; and in the commentary, Baṅkim openly states several times that it is written for the 'educated class'. It would be stretching it too far if one called this an exclusion of the 'common reader'; nonetheless, a formerly absent communicative decision is made here.

Despite the lack of data about the distribution of *Pracār*, it is still possible to name those readers who have left accounts of their reading it. Among them were two prominent Brāhma Samāj members, Dvijendranāth Ṭhākur and Rāj'nārāẏaṇ Basu, who both reacted strongly to certain of Baṅkim's theses.[11] Rabīndranāth Ṭhākur (Dvijendranāth's son) too read *Pracār* and attacked Baṅkim'candra for sanctioning lies for good causes.[12] Śacīś'candra Caṭṭopādhyāẏ also names Kailās'candra Siṃha.[13] Nabīn'candra Sen, a younger writer with whom Baṅkim was on intimate terms, criticises *Kṛṣṇacaritra* in his autobiography.[14] Bhūdeb Mukhopādhyāẏ also probably took notice

[10] *BJ*:280; the encounter with Sureś'candra Samāj'pati probably took place after 1890.

[11] This led to the controversies Śacīś'candra Caṭṭopādhyāẏ summarises in his biography: *BJ*:336-7 and 337-9 respectively.

[12] Cf. *BJ*:341-7. In his *Reminiscences*, Rabīndranāth attributes the struggle to the 'coming out of the seclusion of my corner' at that time, and makes clear that Baṅkim had nothing to do with the 'curious attempt made by Hindu orthodoxy', i.e. Śaśadhar Tarkacūṛāmaṇi (R. Ṭhākur 1961:251f.). For a discussion of the controversy between Baṅkim and Rabīndranāth, cf. Bimal'kṛṣṇa Matilāl (1988:52ff.) and Biśvanāth Mukhopādhyāẏ (1993:66-83).

[13] The Assistant Secretary of the Brāhma Samāj, according to Dhar (1977:179).

[14] In *Āmār jīban*; cf. Śaṅkarīprasād Basu (1990:34f.).

of *Pracār*, although he was certainly not a subscriber.[15] Rameś'candra Datta published a book called *Hindu śāstra* after Baṅkim's death in which the first two chapters of Baṅkim'candra's translation (without the commentary) of the *Gītā* were incorporated, i.e. exactly the portion which had by then appeared.[16] Haraprasād Śāstrī too appears to belong to the readers because he published a review of *Kṛṣṇacaritra* in 1892.[17] Obvious additions to this short list are the names of Baṅkim's collaborators at *Pracār*: Candranāth Basu, Indranāth Bandyopādhyāẏ, etc.,[18] and probably also some younger writers with whom Baṅkim had contact, e.g. Sureś'candra Samāj'pati, Śib'nāth Śāstrī and Yogendracandra Basu (the *Baṅgabāsī* editor).[19] Śacīś'candra further gives a number of names of participants in *āḍḍās* (i.e. informal gatherings) at Baṅkim's home during the eighties: Candranāth Basu, Hem'candra Bandyopādhyāẏ, Rāj'kṛṣṇa Mukhopādhyāẏ, Yogendracandra Ghoṣ (Chairman of the Positivist Society from 1890), Akṣaẏ'candra Sar'kār, Kṛṣṇabihārī Sen, Muralīdhar Sen, Nīl'kaṇṭha Majum'dār and Dāmodar Mukhopādhyāẏ as regular visitors, and Tārāprasād Caṭṭopādhyāẏ, Indranāth Bandyopādhyāẏ, Kālīprasanna Ghoṣ and one Gobindadās as occasional visitors.[20] This list of mostly late nineteenth century celebrities is however quite unsatisfactory in the present context, because it consists, so to speak, of co-actors on the stage while remaining silent about the audience. None of these personalities appears to be a typical representative of the 'educated class' for whom, in his commentary, Baṅkim finds it necessary to translate Sanskrit passages in order to make them intelligible.

Who then are those 'members of the educated class' Baṅkim addresses in his commentary? In accordance with Baṅkim's contention, they were limited in number, as Tapobijaẏ Ghoṣ (1989:44, with reference to Binaẏ Ghoṣ) points out:

> By the end of the nineteenth century, the number of Bengalis who had passed their entrance examinations was about 30 thousand. The number of those who had passed their B.A. exams was only 1712 from 1858 to 1881. At the time they were considered 'highly educated of high value'.[21]

But this education, Ghoṣ continues, produced undesired results as well, so much that the *Tattvabodhinī Patrikā* (in 1880) doubts of the use of having female Bengali title-holders, because 'we have seen the beneficial results of higher learning as taught at University by the example of the Bengali youths', those being 'blind to the uplift of their country and guilty of a number of despicable vices such as drinking of alcohol, etc.'. From the times of the Hindu College, then, 'it can be very easily proved by figures that

[15] This is evident from a letter (1888) written in Bengali by Baṅkim'candra to Bhūdeb where it says: 'The *Gītā* is again being published in *Pracār*. If you feel like taking a look at it, I can send it. It goes without saying that there is nothing in it worthy of your attention [*dekhibār yogya* (Beng.)]. But it seems that you may feel like seeing what we think and what we do.' (*BR* II:925) On the relationship between Bhūdeb and Baṅkim, cf. Tapan Raychaudhuri (1988). Some remarks are found in Āśālatā Rāẏ (1984:70-5).

[16] Rameś'candra Datta (1994 [1893-4]).

[17] Cf. Haraprasād Śāstrī (1981:805-6).

[18] For further information about these two cf. Amiya P. Sen (1993), Karuṇāmaẏ Majum'dār's (1984) monograph about Candranāth Basu, and Sunītirañjan Rāẏ'caudhurī (1981).

[19] On Yogendracandra Basu, see Amiya P. Sen (1988) as well as Brajendranāth Bandyopādhyāẏ (1974).

[20] *BJ*:283.

[21] Cf. also the figures in Tapan Raychaudhuri (1988:17).

the number of these [worthless absolvents] was a hundred times higher [than that of creative minds]. It was these who came sprouting in thousands from Calcutta University.'[22]

Baṅkim, however, was himself a B.A. of Calcutta University; he was conscious of himself belonging to the *śikṣita sampradāẏ* (Beng., 'educated class'). And he clearly identifies with it at certain times and shows it in a positive light, e.g. in *Larḍ ripaṇer utsaber jamā-kharac*:

> Our fourth gain — and this is only Bengal's gain — [:] the agency of society has for the first time come from the hands of the landowners to those of the middle-class people.[23] That is, the agency has come from the hands of wealth to those of intellect and learning.[24] From now on, the wealthy of Bengal are nobody anymore, only the educated class[25] are the agents. This is especially beneficial for society, it is a sign of uplift and a step [on the ladder] of uplift. (*BR* II:919)

Much more numerous, however, are instances of the problematic aspect of his relationship to his own class. And his critique of that class is not limited to a special period, but runs through his writings from the beginning of *Baṅgadarśan* (1872) until the end.

A good example of how Baṅkim portrayed the 'highly educated Bengali Bābu' is the dramatical sketch *Bāṅgālā sāhityer ādar* included in *Lok'rahasya*. In this satirical piece, an *uccaśikṣita* ('highly educated') Bābu and his rather traditional Bengali wife talk about Bengali literature. The Babu expresses his prejudices against it in English words (*immoral, obscene, filthy* and the like)[26] and gets into trouble each time his wife asks him to explain the meaning of these words in Bengali. He declines to believe that a Bengali book (*Biṣ'bṛkṣa*, Baṅkim's novel) is appreciated and translated by the English. When his wife persuades him to read a Bengali book, he declares to do so only for her sake. The wife then chooses not *Biṣ'bṛkṣa*, but some truly 'immoral' and 'filthy' book which he enjoys greatly: 'Great. I did not know that such books are written in Bengali.'[27] Baṅkim's satirical writings contain many similar denunciations of the English-educated Bābu. Interestingly, in this sketch, the platform from which his critique is developed is the wife as the voice of traditional common sense. It is by her agency that the final compromise of the Bābu is achieved. Such shifts of identification are a common operative tool wherever Baṅkim is concerned with subversive, satirical critique. They also play a role in his discursive prose and are at work in his commentary, as will be argued below.

The literary dealings with the (Western-educated) Bābu are however much older than Baṅkim. The first who took up this figure for caricature was Bhabānīcaraṇ

[22] Tapobijaẏ Ghoṣ (1981:45).

[23] [*madhyabitta lok* (Beng.).]

[24] [*buddhibidyā* (Beng.).]

[25] [*śikṣita sampradāẏ* (Beng.).]

[26] *BR* II:45.

[27] Ibid.:47.

Bandyopādhyāẏ in 1823,[28] and the *naksā* ('sketch') on the Bengali Bābu soon became a genre. Pyārīcā̃d Mitra's *Ālāler gharer dulāl* for instance, while not being a *naksā* itself, is heavily influenced by it.[29] By Baṅkim's time, then, the lecherous, alcoholic, imitative, pompous, pretentious and anti-traditional Bābu, a cultural stereotype of nineteenth century Bengal, had already been codified to a certain extent. He had therefore arguably become a piece of exaggerated literary imagination which was perceived as such, rather than any kind of description of some concrete human being. It is a fact that, in many of Baṅkim's writings, the terms *śikṣita sampradāẏ* and *bābu* overlap. If the above assumption is right, their original relationship could tentatively be defined as that between a social class and its typologised literary representation; of course this is not to deny, however, that *bābu* also denoted a member of a specific social class. *Śikṣita sampradāẏ*, on the other hand, is not a class of literary types; but contagions with the content of *bābu* are frequent in Baṅkim's later writings.[30] They are effectively applied in the communicative strategies Baṅkim uses with his readers in the commentary.

The intended readership of *Śrīmadbhagabadgītā* consists, as it were, of members of the educated class. The readers' opinions may vary a lot (there are e.g. atheists and believers in heaven and hell), but still, as was argued in 2.2.1, they are required to agree on a certain set of assumptions regarding life, faith, etc.; their approach must stay within certain parameters. Baṅkim is intent on keeping the discussion at a distinct level, and he repeatedly defines the area within which it must remain. Sometimes, this definition process takes the form of disqualifications of certain factions of possible readers. The first is there right in the introduction where important reading instructions are given:

> I have no sympathy whatsoever with those people who think that all the native ancient pundits said is true, and all what Westerners say about material principles is wrong. (*ŚBhG*:20).

Another, similar disqualification features in Baṅkim'candra's first elaborate exposition of his approach, the commentary on 2.11:

> With those who say that this book, belonging to the *Mahābhārata*, was written by the Maharṣi Vyāsa, who through the force of *yoga* was omniscient and infallible, and that for this reason such doubt is out of place here, we cannot enter into discussion. I can only remark that this commentary has not been written for readers of this category. (*ŚBhG*:39)

These statements are not neutral, but decidedly derogatory. On the other hand, there are places where the traditional *bhakta*'s position is presented as superior to that of a nineteenth century educated person:

> A devotee has no need of all these quarrels. A devotee of God does not

[28] When his *Kalikātā kamalālaẏ* appeared; this critique took full shape in *Nababābubilās* and *Nababibibilās*.

[29] Pyārīcā̃d Mitra (n.d. [1855-7]); *naksās* of some more authors before Baṅkim feature in Pradyot Sen'gupta (1982).

[30] Baṅkim'candra can in fact be found to justify some of the constituents of the Bābu as a literary figure, e.g. imitation (cf. his essay *Anukaraṇ*, *BR* II:200-4). This shows that abundant nineteenth century mockery at the Bābu was not at all synonymous with the rejection of each of his ingredients. He was rather projected as the prototype image of an unsuccessful synthesis of different cultural influences, while his opposite stood as the true *desideratum*, i.e. a *successful* synthesis. Arguably even in the most conservative writings on this topic (e.g. Bhabānīcaraṇ Bandyopādhyāẏ), the Bābu was not simply conceived as the symbol of modernity as opposed to tradition.

> depend on miserable philosophy to accept the independence and indestructibility of the *ātman*. For the devotee it is sufficient that God exists and that He has proclaimed Himself to be the *paramātman* and to have descended among all living beings. (*ŚBhG*:49)

And again after the long discussion of reincarnation:

> All these discussions are unnecessary for a devotee; when this *śloka* represents the sense of divine speech then that is sufficient reason for his belief. (*ŚBhG*:60)

It cannot be determined to which degree the groups referred to in these two kinds of statements are identical. In any case, both are conceived as traditional groups as opposed to the Western-educated class. Rather than assume that Baṅkim differentiates between two formulated positions, it seems more adequate to interpret both 'positions' as facets of a diffuse and ambivalent traditional view. This view is very marginal to Baṅkim's interpretation of the *Gītā*, and his treatment of these traditional Hindus is indeed somewhat similar to his treatment of the ancient commentators.[31]

With the aid of such disqualifications, then, the main part of the readership is circumscribed. The Western-educated Bengalis are explicitly characterised in a few passages of the commentary. In the introduction, the epistemological gap between ancient Indian and Western thinking is stressed, which makes them unable to understand the former even in translation. Many do not know sufficient Sanskrit. Next to such indications, there are other characterisations which are apparently polemic and much in keeping with his earlier critique of educated society, e.g. when it comes to idol worship:

> The educated Indians are angry because the English are angry. What the English blame must of course be blamed by 'us'. [etc.] (*ŚBhG*:68).

There is, on the basis of this and similar utterances, reason to believe that his statements about the educated class oscillate between his intended readership and the literary stereotype of Bābu society, and furthermore, that Baṅkim himself oscillates between identification and opposition with regard to the educated class. In order to make this point clear, it is necessary to examine closely the communicative structure of the commentary. While the treatment and addressing of 'the reader' in Baṅkim's novels has been dealt with before (Bikāś Basu 1987:63-73), this remains to be done for his discursive writings.

An analysis of the rhetorical set-up of Baṅkim's *Śrīmadbhagabadgītā* reveals quite a large number of communicative patterns with regard to the categories of address and reference. For the sake of this analysis it is convenient for the moment to distinguish between a narrator and the author, as is common when dealing with fictional prose. Usually Baṅkim reserves the first person singular for the 'narrator', but the first person plural is also used frequently. A second person *tumi* form is occasionally found as the narrator's counterpart (*ŚBhG*:51ff., 57, 73). The readers are in a few instances addressed in the polite *āp'nārā* form (e.g. *ŚBhG*:46); more often, however, they are referred to in the third person (directly as *pāṭhak* ['readers'], more generally as *āj'ker pāṭhak* ['today's readers'], or indirectly as *āj'ker śikṣita sampradāẏ* ['today's educated class']); the likes, dislikes or objections of these fictive readers are sometimes given in the first person singular with or without quotation marks. Then again the readers are often included in

[31] Cf. Chapter 2.3.2; except that his contemporary expounders of 'traditional' views are not entitled to the same amount of respect, and his occasional dismissal of them is not at all polite.

the narrator's first person plural. Different types of rhetorical situations can be found in the combination of the narrator's and readers' forms included in the above repertoire; their handling by Baṅkim is strategic and very relevant in the context of in-group formation, as we shall see.

The first pattern usually features two adversaries, or, more precisely, one expounder and one objector. The objector's contributions are mostly introduced by the formula-like *yadi bala* ('If you say') and given in the form of direct speech. The expounder remains mostly unnamed and invisible. An example of this infrequent pattern is a part of the discussion on reincarnation (*ŚBhG*:51ff.). It seems to be modelled on the way in which Śaṅkara quotes objections and then resolves them; the translation quoted by Baṅkim uses the same form.[32] Since Baṅkim usually takes the respectful form *tā̃hārā* for his readers, the objector is not identical with the reader. There is only one exception (*ŚBhG*:73), where the objector is referred to the subsequent *śloka* for an answer, i.e. equated with the reader.

In a related pattern, there is a first person singular and a second person *tumi*, too, but the relationship is one between a guru and a *śiṣya*. This is found only twice; once in a quotation from *Sāṃkhyadarśan* (*ŚBhG*:43f.), then again in its direct vicinity, suggesting that the latter is in fact a rhetorical contagion. What is significant here is that — in a much more obvious way than in the first pattern — the first person singular is definitely *not* the author Baṅkim'candra, but a narrator. As already pointed out above, this is very commonly overlooked in secondary literature on *Dharmmatattva* which has the same structure. Usually the guru is simply taken for Baṅkim'candra; the dialogical set-up of that essay is completely ignored. It is true that Baṅkim's late writings are decidedly pedagogical, but that does not necessarily imply that he can simply be equated with his own portrayal of a teacher.[33]

A third pattern is the first person narrator (this time merging into the author) addressing his readers in the second person *āp'nārā* form. This pattern, however, even more than the preceding ones, is peripheral to the commentary. Direct address, i.e. the occurrence of either *tumi* or *āp'ni* forms, is rarely used.

The dominant, and from the present perspective most interesting, patterns are the combinations of first and third person forms. Both first person singular and plural forms are used throughout the commentary, and most of the time they have implicit or explicit third person counterparts of quite varying semantic extension. Both 'we' and 'I' are agency markers with regard to the process of interpretation underway. The examination of how they are employed each by itself and then in combination reveals Baṅkim's communicative strategies on the one hand, and allows conclusions to be drawn about his self-perception within nineteenth century educated society on the other. There is of course also a casual, non-intentional use on his part of alternating 'agency markers', and in a number of instances the first person singular could be substituted by the plural without producing semantic changes of any significance. In another good number of places, however, they could not, as will be demonstrated in the following.

The first person singular is mostly the voice of the author. The 'I' addressing 'my readers' or 'those who ...' indirectly in the third person is Baṅkim'candra, just as much as the 'I' in the introduction; the author guides his readers through the commentary.

[32] See *ŚBhG*:64f.

[33] See, in this context, the note on p. 191 of this book.

Baṅkim determines the purpose of his project in the introduction: 'The motive of this commentary of mine is thus to teach these people the meaning of the *Gītā* according to Western methods and with the help of Western ideas' (*ŚBhG*:20); in the same vein he remarks in the course of the commentary that

> This matter of the divine eye is something supernatural; I do not tell the readers to believe in it. It has got nothing to do with the *dharma* exposed in the *Gītā*. (*ŚBhG*:22).

He gives reading instructions, references, remarks (*ŚBhG*:47n), terminological explanations (e.g. *ŚBhG*:40n [*man* (Beng.)], 43n), etc., by using the first person. As in the introduction, and especially in the passage quoted above, his attitude is often that of a teacher. Then again, he uses it where he states markedly personal opinions or beliefs, the acceptance of which does not necessarily have to be the readers':

> But I feel obliged here to say what according to my knowledge and belief is true: I believe that when all the faculties of the mind are adequately purified, this knowledge regarding the *ātman* is proved *per se*. (*ŚBhG*:49)

In many cases the first person singular is used in a rather unqualified way as an agency marker of the interpretative process. Here, the stress is generally on the 'active' aspect of interpreting, i.e. anything that involves intellectual initiative. It is quite regularly found with verbs such as *dekhāna* ('to show, to demonstrate'), *bojhāna* ('to explain'), etc. The first person plural is more integrative; the readership is so-to-speak pulled into the interpretative process. Even when used as an apparently formula-like, hardly qualified agency marker,[34] it has, however, a slightly different function than the singular. It is preferred when the rather passive, i.e. receptive, aspect of the interpretative process is emphasised. The verbs commonly found with it are *dekhā* ('to see'), *bojhā* ('to understand') and the like, although there are admittedly quite a few exceptions;[35] singular and plural forms overlap to some extent.

Both forms, in this function, are combined in several places. A good example is the discussion on *svadharma* (*ŚBhG*:39ff.): Baṅkimcandra introduces what 'to my understanding is the liberal interpretation of *svadharma* exposed in the *Gītā*' (*ŚBhG*:42); when the exposition is complete, the readers are reintegrated into the process:

> If we have understood at least in some way or the other what *svadharma* is, then we shall now have to understand why we should observe *svadharma*. (*ŚBhG*:42)

Baṅkim's new interpretation is presented and thus 'shared' — it is transformed into the common property of the readership.

The integrative function of the plural is fully played out at a crucial instance shortly before the place just mentioned: in the universalisation of *svadharma*. 'We' are left unsatisfied with the traditional exposition of *svadharma*; regarding this many questions arise. Baṅkim gives a list of rhetorical questions, implying that they are 'our', the readers', questions, and furnishes 'our' desired answer: 'The divine *dharma* is not as narrow-minded as this.' Here the interpretative agency is fully Baṅkim's, but he skilfully tries to make his argument the reader's by giving him the opportunity to identify

[34] In this function, 'we' is commonly used in Western discursive literature, which has probably influenced Baṅkim's use of it.

[35] e.g. *ŚBhG*:103: 'The foreign opinion matches more coherently than the native Kṛṣṇa's opinion concerning the Vedas as we have understood or explained it.'

effortlessly with a most important line of argumentation. In a further step, dissenters are grammatically banned from the collective movement towards new conclusions: 'Whoever believes in this sort of fall from *dharma* by the Lord of the world is comparable to the Christians.' (*ŚBhG*:39).[36]

The readers' integrative 'we' thus often alters its semantic extension when third person counterparts to this in-group are given, or when it is further qualified. Talking about reincarnation, 'we' stresses the readers' Hindu identity — 'We have heard it [the doctrine of reincarnation] from our childhood, it belonged to our socialisation' — as opposed to 'pensive pundits from other countries' (*ŚBhG*:51).[37] When discussing action and non-action, 'we' takes on the meaning of 'man' (*ŚBhG*:98). Such alterations are nothing exceptional as such. But in Baṅkim's commentary, they take on a peculiar form which is of great significance.

On the one hand, the first person plural usually refers to the educated class. 'We, influenced as we are by the moral code of the nineteenth century' (*ŚBhG*:39) is opposed to the traditional view; likewise when dealing with 'the difference between the point of view our ancestors had of all these topics and the one we have now' (*ŚBhG*:62).[38] But there are other places where precisely this identification is categorically denied — not only with a part of Bengali educated society, but with the whole of it. For example, when determining the relation between science and religion, 'we' marks a middle position which is *not* the educated Bengali's:

> [...] we shall have to consider in this instance how much truth there is on each side. Especially the educated Bengalis, whether they know about science or not, are stricken with unshakeable devotion towards it. [...] Since this commentary is being written for educated Bengalis, it is fair to consider the counter-arguments of science against the theory of *ātman*. (*ŚBhG*:43)

A similar case is *ŚBhG*:50. So while usually being applied to the 'educated class', the first person plural is at some places shifted in such a way as to contradict this common meaning.

Somewhat in between these different cases, there is another variant when it comes to idol-worship. This is the most interesting of all:

> For this idol-worship the English, our teachers, are very angry with *us*, and their pupils, the new Indians, as well. The reason for the anger of the English is that the Bible forbids it. The educated Indians are angry because the English are angry. What the English blame must of course be blamed by *'us'*. The English blame idol-worship, thus it must be blamed by *'us'*; there is no need of [independent] investigation. The English say that India has been ruined because of this idol-worship, and shall be utterly

[36] Cf. the discussion of this quotation and its critique by Hacker on p. 193f.

[37] Cf. also *ŚBhG*:96: 'But although the *Hindus* have obtained it [a holy religious doctrine], it has not been particularly fruitful for them. This is because even in the case of such things, much confusion has occured due to *our* errancy of intellect. Even today *we* have not yet been able to understand it well.' [italics mine]

[38] Cf. also *ŚBhG*:93: 'Now we, disciples of the English in the nineteenth century, can maybe daringly utter that there is no need for the Vedas; but could Śaṅkarācārya or Śrīdhara Svāmin have said such words?'

ruined if it is not abolished; thus *we*, too, are bound to believe this; there is no need of further [independent] investigation any more. It is true that ancient states like Rome, Greece etc. had developed despite their worshipping idols; but the English maintain that India will be ruined through idol-worship, so India will definitely be ruined by idol-worship; considerations on this topic are unnecessary. *Many members of the educated class* think like this. Judging differently is, to them, the result of wrong education, perverted intelligence and depravedness. *We* cannot approve of such utterances. (italics H.H.) (*ŚBhG*:68)

Here the 'we' shifts its meaning to a formerly unknown place. While still integrating the readership — *members of the educated class*, as it were — it moves into opposition of — again — the 'educated Indians'.[39] That is, the empirical in-group, the educated class as a synonym here of emulating Bābu society, is negated. This certainly has to be read as an attempt to form a new sort of collective identity among the readers; instead of a given 'we', this is a new, projected 'we' at the moment of its formation.

This fragile new in-group, then, is a claim and not a given fact; it is very unstable in the frame of Baṅkim's rhetoric in the commentary, or even hardly ever reached. The usual case is rather, as demonstrated above, a constant shift of identity in the course of which the traditional side is criticised from the modern and *vice versa*. A stable *third* position is absent, rhetorically as well as conceptually.

2.3.2 Baṅkim'candra and the *Mahāmahopādhyāys*

The greatest number of quotations in the commentary, about one hundred, are from earlier, mostly Sanskrit commentaries on the *Bhagavadgītā*. Śaṅkara's commentary (*ŚaBhG*) is most frequently referred to, followed by Śrīdhara's (*ŚrBhG*). Ānandagiri, Madhusūdana Sarasvatī, Rāmānuja and Viśvanātha Cakravartin as well as the Bengali commentaries hold a comparatively minor position. Baṅkim's treatment of this category of interpretations is no less interesting than that of Western Indology, for it is here that the clash between what Baṅkim conceives as a traditional and a modern outlook on the text of the *Gītā* is most clearly articulated.

There is at least one reference to Sanskrit *Gītā* commentaries in Baṅkim's writings prior to the commentary, namely, in *Dharmmatattva* (*BR* II:665). The topic under discussion is *dāna*, 'donation', the scriptural basis *BhG* 17.20-22. The *Gītā* distinguishes between three kinds of donations: *sāttvika*, given at the right place and time for the sake of charity; *rājasika*, given out of some interest or unwillingly, and *tāmasika*, given at the wrong place and time to the wrong person improperly or insultingly. Baṅkim quotes Śaṅkara's and Śrīdhara's interpretations of the terms place (*deśa*), time (*kāla*) and recipient (*pātra*); Śaṅkara, for instance, explains *deśa* as 'places like Kurukṣetra, etc.', *kāla* as 'the junction of months [*saṃkrānti*] and the like', and *pātra* as 'a Vedic scholar [...]'.[40] Baṅkim's reaction to this explanation is decidedly negative. In Ghosh's (1977) translation:

How dangerous! If I give anything to a very distressed cobbler or to a

[39] It is certainly not intended here to build up any sort of dichotomy between Bengalis and Indians.

[40] Cf. *ŚaBhG*:542.

> Dom within the first and thirtieth date of any month, that will not be the kind of giving approved of by God. Due to this kind of interpretation by the commentators the very high and liberal *dharma* of the Hindus has become very narrow, illiberal and perverted.[41] What Śaṅkarācārya, and Śrīdhara say on these points are not words of Krishna, but of the Smṛtis. Just to find out a sanction for words of Krishna in the Smṛitis, they have turned the liberal *dharma* into illiberal [*sic.*].[42]

This sharp critique, more pronounced in fact than any similar passage in the commentary, is then immediately attenuated by a most typical rhetorical gesture:

> Compared with these *mahāmahopādhyāys* who had great genius and who were proficient in all the Śāstras, humble people like us are like corns of sand (*BR* II:665, transl. H.H.).

This does not, however, alter Baṅkim's position in any way:

> but it has also been said that *kevalaṃ śāstram āśritya na kartavyo vinirṇayaḥ / yuktihīnavicāre tu dharmahāniḥ prajāyate.*[43] ([Baṅkim's footnote:] Utterance of Bṛhaspati, quoted by Kullūkabhaṭṭa in the commentary to Manu 12.113.) It is by carrying all the sentences of the *Ṛṣis* on our heads without consideration that we have arrived in this disorder, *adharma* and bad condition. It is no longer a duty now to carry them without consideration. All should consider according to their intellects. (*BR* II:665)

When the *śiṣya* assumes that it is thus a duty to save the *dharma* from the commentators, the guru stresses that they are worthy of special devotion; but when they go against God's intention, the latter must be followed.

A similar pattern of dealing with the commentators is at work in *Śrīmadbhagabadgītā*. There, the *prācīn paṇḍiterā* (Beng., 'ancient pundits') or *mahāmahopādhyāys* (Beng., 'very great preceptor', a title awarded to eminent Sanskrit scholars), as they are alternatingly called, are in fact treated as a relatively homogeneous class by themselves. Baṅkim is doubtlessly aware that there are quite different opinions in those commentaries, and often he juxtaposes them: 'Various *munis* have various opinions.' (*ŚBhG*:153) But those differences are beyond the scope of his investigation. He merely states in a few instances that such and such commentators have followed either Śaṅkara or Śrīdhara. He is apparently not interested in the various philosophical positions taken by the commentators and their relation to each other, except one cursory remark in *Dharmmatattva* where he categorises Śaṅkara as a *jñānavādin* and Śrīdhara as a *bhaktivādin*. (*BR* II:631) One would in vain go through his commentary for a mention of, say *Advaita Vedānta*.[44] Śaṅkara does get a slightly special treatment from Baṅkim, but hardly because of his philosophical and theological positions.[45] As a matter of fact, the

[41] Here the original (*BR* II:665) has *upadharmma* (Beng.).

[42] Quoted from the translation by Manomohan Ghosh (1977:169).

[43] ['A full decision (*vinirṇaya*) is not to be made by exclusively relying on the Śāstra; a loss of *dharma* is produced by a decision devoid of reasoning.']

[44] It is also worth considering whether Baṅkimcandra knew the commentaries well at all. The absence of any discussion of their philosophical positions seems to suggest this. He probably did not study them one by one, but rather used them as cursory reference while writing the commentary.

[45] Cf. below in this chapter.

commentators are seen as exponents of traditional positions — the plural being of secondary importance — as opposed to a modern, Western understanding of the *Gītā*.

This is laid down as early as in his introduction. A mere translation of those commentaries would be an effort lost on the educated class who 'do not understand easily the sentences of their ancient Eastern pundits' (*ŚBhG*:19); and 'the Western way of thinking is so different from the ancient Indian way of thinking that the ideas cannot be conveyed to them by a transformation of language.' (*ŚBhG*:19) Baṅkim's field is accordingly the rendering of the *Gītā*'s meaning in Western terms; all the same he claims to follow the ancients as far as he can. But, as he admits, he disagrees with them at times and does not consider them his only authorities. With persons who do so he declares to have no 'sympathy whatsoever' (*ŚBhG*:20).

In view of their frequency, the quoted commentaries are of astonishingly little importance to Baṅkim's interpretation. There are a few instances where they seem to contribute to the process of understanding the *Gītā*, e.g. in the course of determinating the meaning of *mātrāsparśāḥ* (*Gītā* 2.14; *ŚBhG*:61n). Most, however, deal with trifling matters, e.g. the resolution of compounds.[46] Baṅkim's way of inserting quotations from the ancient commentators leaves the impression of being 'dutiful', and he indeed uses the word *karttabya* (Beng., 'duty') with regard to the readers' consideration of a passage from Śaṅkara (*ŚBhG*:62). Often, again, they are quoted in contexts where no dissent is likely to arise, i.e. where the meaning of the *Gītā* is quite evident — in contrast to his treatment of Western interpretations where such cases are rare. It appears that consent with the ancients is very welcome in general.

The more interesting places, however, are those where Baṅkim cannot follow them. The first of these has already been mentioned in the analysis of his elaboration of *dharma* and *svadharma* (*Gītā* 2.11):[47]

> For Śaṅkara and the other old pundits it had been very easy to explain this theory. Arjuna is a kṣatriya, consequently his *svadharma* is the *dharma* of the kṣatriyas, i.e. war. His saying that rather than making war he would depend on alms shows his desire for others' *dharma*; for begging is the *dharma* of the brahmins. But what has this explanation actually taught us? (*ŚBhG*:39)

In a footnote, the quotation from Śaṅkara is given in the original. The explanation is not acceptable for Baṅkim, because it is restricted to Hindu society, i.e. the society organised by *varṇas* and *āśramas*. The complexities Baṅkim has to deal with, as opposed to the 'easy' ancient interpretation, arise from the necessity of claiming intercultural validity. And in fact, if *dharma* remained confined to this 'narrow' meaning, it would run the risk of resting entirely on the *varṇāśrama*, which was anything but a strong footing already in Baṅkim's time. Baṅkim presents *svadharma* and *dharma* as universal concepts independent of particular religions; in order to do so, he unties *dharma* from the *varṇāśrama*, as was shown.

But why, in fact, should it have been so 'easy' for the ancient commentators to explain *svadharma*? Baṅkimcandra's formulation suggests an almost nostalgic picture of the 'ancient' (actually medieval) period, and it seems legitimate to say that he attributes great cultural homogeneity to it. The social system, he seems to imply, was simply given

[46] Cf. *ŚBhG*:84 (*janmakarmaphaladā*).

[47] See Subchapter 2.2.2.

and thus the natural frame within which concepts were to be discussed. But such a picture of the Indian Middle Ages does not correspond to the facts; Śaṅkara's writings, for example, are decidedly placed in the controversy with Buddhism, Madhusūdana Sarasvatī's in the context of Gauḍīya Vaiṣnavism. Only, the plurality, with its ruptures and heterogenities, of medieval society was evidently not a topic of interest for medieval commentators on the *Gītā*. However, the frame of validity they claimed was definitely more limited than his — he felt that in order to give national importance to the *Gītā*'s *dharma*, its universal validity had to be established. Baṅkim certainly knew that the Middle Ages did not belong to any homogeneous 'Golden Age'; he himself was among those who propagated the notion of the Middle Ages as an epoch of Hindu suppression. Evidently, then, he refers not to medieval society as such but rather to the different hermeneutical situation the medieval commentators set down for themselves, i.e. to their more exclusivist argumentative strategies as compared to his own. They operated within a cultural system which was largely exclusive, and felt no particular need of mediating ideas other than within their cultural context. Baṅkim's position is very different. He works in a situation of rapid social change which puts into question that very cultural system as such. So his nostalgia, if it really can be read into his statement, relates to the self-perception of the medieval commentators who had no reason for being openly apologetic; on their part, Baṅkim seems to suggest, an invocation of the system was sufficient for explanation.

The second instance of dissent occurs in the course of the interpretation of *śloka* 2.16. The question is of the meaning of *sat* and *asat*. Baṅkim quotes nearly the whole of Śaṅkara's quite extensive commentary in order to demonstrate the different point of view taken by 'our ancestors'. The relevant portion from Śaṅkara does indeed touch central issues of his philosophy based upon ideas of the *Sāṃkhya*'s *Satkāryavāda*.

Cold, heat and the like, as qualities, are *asat*, 'unreal' because they are mere transformations (*vikāra*) reducible to their causes. Hence *satkāryavāda*, the 'doctrine that the products exist (already in their causes)'. Taking a vessel (made of clay) as his example, Śaṅkara introduces two kinds of cognition (*buddhi*), the cognition of the real (*sadbuddhi*) and the cognition of the unreal (*asadbuddhi*). *Asadbuddhi* is the cognition of mutable, perishable objects (=vessels), whereas *sadbuddhi* is the cognition of being as such (=clay). Both merge in the cognition of objects. The *ātman* is purely *sat*, and outer objects appear as *sat* from the perspective of this doctrine; as compared to the *ātman*, however, they are completely *asat*. Śaṅkara defends this concept against several objections by using both grammatical and metaphysical categories.

In a footnote, Baṅkim notifies that he got the (not always accurate) Bengali translation from a friend. But then Baṅkim appears to be at a loss of words to deal with his long quotation. He pays his certainly slightly ironical reverence to Śaṅkara ('As world-conquering a pundit as Śaṅkarācārya was, this philosophical argument is indeed suitable for him') and then declares that his explanation does not match nineteenth century Western education. All he adds is a common-sense judgement — back from the ivory tower, one is tempted to say: pleasure and pain do exist. A serious discussion of Śaṅkara's commentary is lacking. What is there is a polite dismissal, in which the politeness borders on irony. But strikingly, the interpretation Baṅkim himself presents of the *śloka* in question is not contradictory to Śaṅkara's. He accepts Śrīdhara's explanation which maintains, like Śaṅkara's,[48] the *asat* nature of heat, cold, etc. Then he furnishes an explanation of the relation between the transitory and the lasting according to *Sāṃkhya* philosophy, substituting *puruṣa* for *ātman*. The objection to Śaṅkara that pleasure and pain do exist could similarly be applied to Śrīdhara and the *Sāṃkhya* position as Baṅkim sketches it. Śaṅkara's text, according to the way Baṅkim presents it in his commentary, can thus only be read as an instance of sophistic and futile verbosity, which moreover bears all characteristics of an unnecessarily complicating philosophical jargon.

When dealing with *śloka* 2.46, the discussion of interpretations is taken to an epistemological level. Here, Śaṅkara and Śrīdhara, together with their followers, are ranked as belonging to one out of three groups of interpreters. First, a Bengali translation of this interpretation by Hit'lāl Miśra is given, then Śrīdhara's interpretation in the Sanskrit original with a 'rough' translation thereof by Baṅkim. The discussion which ensues is introduced by the following statement:

> We are of humble intellect, and so I am setting forth the confusion we had to undergo when trying to understand this interpretation, paying reverence to the lotus-feet of the ancient masters. He who does not dare express his doubts cannot acquire any knowledge; neither is there any possibility of such an acquisition. (*ŚBhG*:90f.)

Another polite dismissal of the ancient commentators is intimated here, and indeed the subsequent lengthy, step-by-step argumentation proves that their interpretation is based on the illegitimate insertion of a second pair of the correlatives *yāvān* and *tāvān*. This evidently happens, as Baṅkim stresses, because a straightforward interpretation of *śloka* 2.46 would belittle the authority of the Vedas.

Baṅkim explains the rejection of this 'simple meaning' on the mediaeval pundits' part by pointing out the enormous authority attributed to the Vedas as revealed *śruti* literature in traditional Indian society, presenting it as an impossibility to criticise the Vedas. Thus an interpretation had to be found which would keep intact the status of the Vedas. Baṅkim alleges that Śaṅkara and Śrīdhara were aware of the presence of a 'simple meaning', but chose to interpret otherwise for the reason mentioned. What he does not ask is whether Śaṅkara perhaps made a concious effort to dissimulate the critique of the Vedas in the *Gītā* in order to present a homogeneous picture. The ancients are seen almost as 'victims' of their contemporary epistemological frame; a possible agency on their part is precluded. And even after this more than thorough demonstration of how the ancients have distorted the meaning, Baṅkim wipes it all away by presenting both interpretations, theirs and his own, side by side as valid, and leaving the choice as to which one is preferable to his readers.

One more instance deserves mention in the present context. The interpretation of 3.10-16, is concerned with cosmology. 'Here none of the ancient, maharṣi-like commentators comes to our aid; they have set the sails of belief and passed over easily.' (*ŚBhG*:120). The problem is that the cosmology of the *Gītā* does not match nineteenth century science; the way Baṅkim resolves this divergency has been dealt with before.[49] Śaṅkara however, according to Baṅkim, was 'bound to believe, that the whole *Gītā* from

[48] Śrīdhara: *asato 'nātmadharmatvād avidyamānasya śītoṣṇāder ātmani na bhāvaḥ*; Śaṅkara: *na asataḥ avidyamāṇasya śītośṇādeḥ sakāraṇasya vidyate nāsti bhāvo bhavanaṃ astitā*.

[49] In Chapter 2.2.1.

beginning to end has issued from the lotus of Kṛṣṇa's mouth' and thus had no opportunity of gaining distance from the text. It is questionable whether the *Gītā* as a *smṛti* text really required such a reading; and Baṅkim himself furnishes a quotation from Śrīdhara (*ŚrBhG* 1.1 — *ŚBhG*:3.16) proving that Śrīdhara admits the interference of the *Gītā*'s author. Baṅkim thus again points at the obligatory epistemological frame of past times for an explanation of divergencies; it becomes clear, however, that he was not too conscious about the exact deliminations of that frame.

Apart from a few low-voiced doubts, these are the only major cases of disagreement in the commentary. None of them comes near anything one could call sharp criticism. The only exception is *Gītā* 2.46; but even there Baṅkimcandra does his best to smooth it down. In most of these and some other cases, the expression of doubt, as already in *Dharmmatattva*, is accompanied by the word *kṣudra*, 'humble', and by something which comes close to a traditional *guruvandanā*. The very first sentence of the introduction in fact declares Śaṅkara's ultimate authority in interpreting the *Gītā*, making new attempts unnecessary. After explaining the specific situation which all the same induces Baṅkim to venture a new commentary, he hastens to assert that

> I do not compete with all the pundits who have circulated or circulate explanations of the *Gītā* in Bengali [by following the ancients]; my humble ambition is no more than to assist them as much as possible. (*ŚBhG*:20)

It occurs again in the course of *Gītā* 2.46; Baṅkim, about to express his doubts concerning the traditional interpretation of that *śloka*, first points out his (and his readers' or contemporaries') 'humble intellect' (*ŚBhG*:93). In 3.10-16 he shows Śaṅkara's epistemological limitations, but not without stating before that

> It is doubtful whether any pundit like Śaṅkara has been born in India during the last two thousand years. At present, there is no-one in India worthy of carrying his shoes. (*ŚBhG*:124)

Likewise in another place on the *Gītā*'s cosmology, where he justifies his undertaking:

> It is for this reason that, notwithstanding the presence of commentaries on the *Gītā* by world-conquering pundits like Śaṅkara, etc., a stupid person like myself has had the courage to engage in creating a new commentary. (*ŚBhG*:121)

And again at the end of the commentary (4.18), where a 'simple meaning' can be discovered 'according to our humble intellects', and where an expression of doubt appears in the form of a 'humble proposition' (*ŚBhG*:153).

It is evident that these statements are a rhetorical device employed in hierarchical relationships. But considering its implications may be worthwhile. Firstly, it is significant that Baṅkim obviously seems to be obliged to perform such obeisances; as was stated above, as expressions of politeness some of them (but not all) border on irony. It can be noted that Śaṅkara is most frequently their addressee. And there are other instances which substantiate the hypothesis that Śaṅkara is treated in a peculiar way; Baṅkim apparently regards Śaṅkara's commentary as especially dignified (also for being the most ancient one) and brilliant, but abstract and metaphysical to the extent of incompatibility with real life.[50] Śaṅkara stands for the properties mediaeval

[50] Cf. *ŚBhG*:102: 'Śaṅkarācārya says the same, the greater part, however, consisting in the brilliance of the words of his polished pen.' Also *ŚBhG*:137 (Śrīdhara 'more lucid' than Śaṅkara) and p. 152, where Śaṅkara's commentary is called 'a long and complicated essay [*prabandha*]'.

commentaries in general had in Baṅkim's eyes: worthy of great respect as authorities within traditional 'Hinduism', i.e. within the nationalist context of Baṅkim's religious writings, parts of the cultural 'in-group';[51] but irrelevant to either modern life or simply common life.[52] So Baṅkim's position is ambivalent: He (a) honours tradition in the traditional way, i.e. by reducing his own importance and declaring his humbleness; but (b) he cannot hide that most traditional explanations are not very relevant to his own. Apart from this, of course, his humbleness may also have a demonstrative aspect with regard to the more orthodox section of his readership.

Secondly, it is interesting to look at the structure of this rhetorical device: by reducing his own status, Baṅkim establishes two separate planes of authority; the greater the respect and gestures of humbleness, the greater the distance und fundamental difference between those planes. The upper plane, seen from the lower, is presented as unattainable (as recurrent in Baṅkim's finding of 'simple meanings'); and such an unattainability of course implies two aspects both present in Baṅkim's commentary, namely, a kind of elevation and sacralisation on the one hand, and elimination on the other. Once thus eliminated, there is no need anymore to consider these commentaries seriously. This 'polite dismissal' rejects the ancient interpretations by keeping formally intact the authority of their authors. It is the communicative strategy Baṅkim chooses to smoothen dissent with the ancient commentators, i.e. members of the 'in-group' in the context of his nationalist endeavour, whenever it arises. His strategies when dealing with Western Indologists, who largely constitute the respective 'out-group', are significantly different, as we shall see in the following.

2.3.3 Baṅkim'candra and Western Indology

One peculiarity of Baṅkim'candra's religious writings in general, and especially of *Kr̥ṣṇacaritra* and *Śrīmadbhagabadgītā*, is their examination of contemporary Western Indology. This aspect has been dealt with by a number of authors.[53] The critical use of

[51] Cf. Baṅkim's treatment of Davies in the rhetorical shift to this in-group as analysed in 2.3.3, and the semantical change the word *kṣudra* (Beng.) undergoes when employed for Davies.

[52] Here one aspect of the Bengal Renaissance, the dissemination of general education, further accentuates the differences in the approaches of Baṅkim and the older commentators.

[53] Partha Chatterjee's (1986) comments will be dealt with in the following discussion. Sunil Bandyopadhyay (1994) gives a condensed survey over late nineteenth and twentieth century Western Indology and claims that Baṅkim'candra did not intimately know those writings (p. 269). Baṅkim's uncharitable comments on Indology are mainly explained by his belonging to 'the veritable race of neo-Hindu revivalists'. Jībendu Rāẏ (1984:34-8), after quoting a passage from *Kamalākānta* (see below), proceeds by furnishing unfortunately very vague paragraphs on Jones, Colebrooke, Müller and the genesis of the 'Aryan myth'; the connection of these paragraphs with Baṅkim's writings remains unclear. A detailed study is found in Biṣṇupada Bhaṭṭācārya (1987:72-128); most of the relevant material is included. What is lacking, however, is an attempt to bring to the point and explain the ambivalence in Baṅkim's attitude towards Indology. There is a passing, uncritical reference in Śaṅkarīprasād Basu (1990:32). Tapan Ray-chaudhuri (1988:176), in his valuable outline of Baṅkim's attitude, states that 'his assessment ranged from sardonic rejection to strictly qualified admiration'. Alokeranjan Dasgupta (1994) highlights the polemical aspect of Baṅkim's encounter with Western Indology in the context of his satirical writings. Baṅkim's originally creative way of dealing with this encounter is conceived as withering away along with the increase of his 'conservatism': when Baṅkim chose the 'narrow-minded logic of antiquities', 'his axis of creativity

Indological literature was a novelty in Bengali attempts at normative ethics, and was apparently rarely pursued afterwards in this somewhat detailed form.[54] As we have seen in the chapter on Baṅkim's readership, the critical examination of sources and interpretations irrespective of their origin was of crucial importance to his approach. 'Freedom of enquiry' (*ŚBhG*:103), so far lacking in India, was to be achieved at any cost. In 1894, in an address read to students of the Society for the Higher Training of Young Men in his function as President of the literary section, Baṅkim would put forward what determined the attitude he claimed to cling to in the commentary and related texts. The programmatic character of that well-known passage may justify a lengthy quotation:

> One of the dangers against which I must warn the students of Vedic literature is the tendency to accept unquestioned the dicta of foreign orientalists. Let us give them the honour which is unquestionably their due, but let us also exercise our judgement as to what is true and what is false. The study of no literature — however patient the study and however valuable the literature, — is of any worth, unless you bring to that study a critical spirit. Approach the Vedas in the spirit of reverence due to them from a Hindu, but study them in the spirit of a respectful and appreciative critic. If they are a Divine revelation, you can convince yourselves that they are such only by a thoroughly critical and appreciative study. If a great Pandit should tell you that the Vedas are eternal, do not believe him unless you can find reasonable evidence in the Vedas themselves of their eternal existence; and if Professor Max Müller should tell you that the Vedic mythology is nothing but a series of Solar myths, never believe him unless you find, according to your own lights, that that is the only rational explanation which it admits of. Never surrender your judgment to authority in matters like these. (*BR* III:161).

Baṅkim'candra's argument in these matters is in general with those Westernised members of his own class who tend to accept everything uttered by Westerners, that is, members of the 'educated class', and the emphasis is laid on Western research work which should be read critically. 'Critical' is meant to denote exactly the abolition of polarised judgement by substituting rational criteria. The fixed patterns of adoption or rejection Baṅkim sees at work with many of his contemporaries are to be done away with; statements should be judged irrespective of the cultural background of their author.

It would, however, be wrong to assume that Baṅkim'candra's relationship to Western Indology was simply an implementation of this general rule. While claiming, on a general plane, this neutrality of judgement and professing his own indebtedness to that discipline, he all the same saw the Western academic treatment of India from a specific angle. His bias is perhaps best demonstrated in the satire *Baṛa bājār* from his *Kamalākānta* (1875). The opium-eater Kamalākānta, during a walk in the market, sees brahmins in a coconut store who are engaged in eloquent discussion:

> When I saw the foreheads smeared with sweat from the acute heat and the rain of nectar from their lower lips produced by sophistic discussions,

strangely decayed'. (p. 94).

[54] Cf. however Aurobindo's treatment of F. Max Müller; it would be interesting to examine the reception of Indological research in modern Hindu / neo-Hindu literature in general.

> I had mercy, and I asked: 'Hey Bhaṭṭācārya *Mahāśaẏ*! I have no objection to purchase a ripe coconut, but do you have a chopper in the shop? How will you peel them?' 'No, dear, we don't keep choppers.' 'So how do you peel coconuts?' 'We don't peel them. We eat them by biting into the husks.' When I had heard this I greeted the brahmins and went to the neighbouring shop. [(...) — an English shop; on the signboard it says in English:] established 1757 on the Field of Plassey. Messrs Brown and Robinson offer to the Indian Public A Large Assortment of Nuts. Physical, Metaphysical, Logical, Illogical and Sufficient to Break the Jaws And Dislocate the Teeth Of All Indian Youths [...]. While I was watching and listening to all this, I suddenly saw that the English shopkeepers, with sticks in their hands, fell fast upon the heaps of ripe coconuts of the brahmins, and the brahmins, on seeing this, threw away their *nāmāvalī*-shawls and escaped breathlessly with untied *dhotis*. Then the Sāhebs took all those abandoned coconuts to their shop, and after splitting them with foreign weapons they began to eat them happily. I asked: 'What is this?' The Sāhebs replied: 'This is called *Asiatic Researches* [Lat.].' Frightened and with the misgiving of some sort of *Anatomical Researches* [Lat.] on my own body, I escaped from there. (*BR* II:69f.)[55]

Indology, then, does get somewhere, farther at least than the contemporary pundits. But its approach is compared to an assault and a dissection; it is the fear of being taken *apart* that drives Kamalākānta away.[56] Such an understanding of India is of course anything but complete and remains incompetent to pass valid judgements on it.[57] This attitude is situated on a different level than the plea for critical, unprejudiced inquiry. It is no less programmatic in Baṅkim's religious writings than the latter, and stands as a second determinator of his treatment of Western Indology. This attitude is obviously closely connected with control and power,[58] and the question of what legitimises the access to Indian tradition and culture is bound to come up in a more explicit fashion.

> Later in his life, he formulated the problem as one of an irreconcilable difference in points of view, arising out of the fact that Hindu scriptures

[55] The same passage is dealt with or quoted by most writers on this or connected topics (Biṣṇupada Bhaṭṭācārya 1987, Jībendu Rāẏ 1984, Tapan Raychaudhuri 1988 and Śibājī Bandyopādhyāẏ 1991).

[56] Cf. Rāmendrasundar Tribedī who describes the gain of medical knowledge by dissection and then continues: 'Unfortunately, the work of many of those among Western pundits who discuss the ancient literature and ancient history of India can, to some extent, be compared to such a dissection of dead bodies. By dissecting the dead body of this dead race and by discovering various principles [*tattva*] through this exercise, they experience a fair amount of joy or curiosity; but I cannot say whether the touch of that dead body is very pleasent.' *Carit'kathā: adhyāpak makṣamūlar*; *Rāmendrasundar racanāsamagra* Vol. 1; quoted from Biṣṇupada Bhaṭṭācārya (1987:114f.).

[57] Incompetence to understand India is a recurring accusal in Baṅkim's writings: 'In his opinion, the English especially had failed to understand anything of India despite their close contact with the country for some hundred fifty years.' Tapan Raychaudhuri (1988:176), who then recounts the satire *Byāghrācārya bṛhallāṅgul* (*BR* II:1-9). The same piece is quoted in length in Śaśibhūṣaṇ Dāś'gupta (1993 [1944]:103f.). Cf. also Nabīn'candra Sen: the English 'cannot grasp the high spiritual feeling of our eternal *dharma* and the subtle complexity of our philosophy' (Hans Harder 1994:95).

[58] Jībendu Rāẏ (1984:34) expresses it thus: 'i.e. also science [*bidyā*] is subject to power. Due to the lack of power, Indology has slipped from our hands.'

> or religious practices had a significance for European scholars that was fundamentally different from its significance for Indians. (Partha Chatterjee 1986:60).

The question of these points of view, in close connection with that about the legitimacy of access, is raised in a new explicitness in the controversy with Reverend Hastie, from then on remaining a discernible factor in his religious writings:

> I did mean to say that the fundamental doctrines of the Hindu religion and its vast details are what no European scholar understands and what no European scholar is competent to teach. This I did mean to say, and this I again positively assert. I will add, that there are many other things in Indian literature and Indian philosophy — other things than the religious doctrines — which no European scholar understands, and no European scholar is competent to teach. [...] (*BR* III:206)

This emphatical statement does not of course arise out of a vacuum, but is provoked by the dynamics of the controversy. It is directly prompted by Hastie's claim that 'both the Sanskrit language and the Sanskrit literature are much better understood at this moment in Europe and America than they are in India'. (*BR* III:201ff.) Baṅkim answers this 'monstrous assertion' by introducing a most significant division: he distinguishes between an inside and an outside perspective on culture. The person on the inside, having been 'nurtured in them [Indian ideas and conceptions] from his infancy' (*BR* III:205.), is more qualified to expound them than the outsider, for such ideas are not conveyable by mere translation:

> The English or the German language can possess no words or expressions to denote ideas or conceptions which have never entered a Teutonic brain. (*BR* III:204)[59]

Baṅkim recommends Hastie to take lessons from a brahmin who believes in those ideas and conceptions, suggesting that hereditary acquaintance with a set of cultural ideas plus belief in them mark the superior access to their significance. The distinction between inside and outside is seen as a hermeneutical boundary; the cultural otherness of Westerners inhibits an accurate understanding of Indian phenomena on their part. The Indian tradition must be studied in the original, but even then the hermeneutical wall does not come down.

If these formulations do arise out of the polemic tenor of the controversy, they do not vanish afterwards but run through all of his later religious writings including the commentary. On the other hand, there is also — right by their side — not a small amount of appreciative and even enthusiastic statements about Western Indology.[60] And it is exactly this strong, emotionally loaded ambivalence which strikes one most. This ambivalence substantiates the assumption that also in the religious writings after the dispute with Hastie, despite the absence of any direct opponent, the intellectual climate in which Baṅkim moves is packed with hardly concealed controversy.

Baṅkim does not intend, either in his Bengali or in his English writings, to enter into discussion with the Indologists he quotes. His addressees are the members of the 'educated class'. And it is in this context that his quotations must be read, as he makes clear in *Kṛṣṇacaritra* when dealing with opinions of Indologists:

[59] Cf. *ŚBhG*:19f. concerning Baṅkim's view regarding the translation of concepts.

[60] See Tapan Raychaudhuri (1988:178) for examples.

> I had no need for the critique of all these great men.[61] For I write for native readers, not for the haters of the Hindus. But unfortunately many in the educated class of my country follow their opinions. Many follow all those opinions without any own considerations, just because they are opinions of European pundits. (*BR* II:410)[62]

Baṅkim's religious writings have some characteristics of a scholarly dispute, but the controversial discussion *with* Western Indology is beyond their scope. Intended is rather a discussion *of* Indology. And in any case, his Bengali writings lack a major criterion for really becoming an international scholarly dispute, i.e. communicability beyond Bengal. The discussion is never direct, but demonstrative.

In the commentary there are about 25 instances where Indological writings in the larger sense, including English translations of the *Gītā*, are referred to.[63] In a number of cases, Baṅkim's access to the primary Sanskrit sources he quotes is through Indological works: Muir's *Sanskrit Texts* are mentioned only twice, but seem to underlie quite a few more of his quotations especially from Vedic literature.[64] Most of Baṅkim's references to Western Indological writings (including those to Muir) are made affirmatively; only nine among them provoke Baṅkim'candra's criticism. Of what kind are those quotations? What is the environment into which they are inserted; which are the places assigned to them in his arguments, and to what degree do they function as authoritative voices?

Firstly, the quotations are different in length as well as in topic and nature: Some are concerned with the translation of the Sanskrit text of the *Gītā* merely with regard to terminology.[65] Others belong rather to the domain of philological interpretation, being concerned more with the semantic than the merely lexical dimension of the *Gītā*.[66] The third, largest group of quotations is not directly related to the *Gītā*, but of a more general kind.[67]

Secondly, another set of three distinctions can be made with regard to the position assigned to these quotations within Baṅkim'candra's arguments. In a first category, the quotations are merely attached to a usually finished line of argument. They do not affect Baṅkim's position in any way. Many of these are given in the form of footnotes, although Baṅkim's use of footnotes is not the same throughout the commentary and thus not necessarily indicative of the respective content. The quotations of this category are usually in support of Baṅkim's arguments. The quotations of the second category do not alter Baṅkim's conclusions either, but they enter his text more massively. This second group consists mainly of the quotations in the course of his discussion of reincarnation (*ŚBhG*:49-61). The third category, lastly, consists of such

[61] [*mahāpuruṣ'gaṇer* (Beng.).]

[62] Also quoted by Biṣṇupada Bhaṭṭācārya (1987:103).

[63] Kashinath Trimbak Telang is grouped with Western Indologists by Baṅkim insofar as he participated in F. Max Müller's *Sacred Books of the East* project, although his ethnically belonging to India leads to an ambivalent position. See below.

[64] This has not found the attention of many writers on Baṅkim, and Baṅkim's scholarly achievements thus tend to be overrated; cf. e.g. Rākhāl'candra Nāth (1988:108ff.).

[65] e.g. those from Julien (*ŚBhG*:23) and Telang (*ŚBhG*:36).

[66] e.g. Thomson (*ŚBhG*:94) and Davies (*ŚBhG*:102f.).

[67] e.g. Thomson and Davies (*ŚBhG*:33n), Thomson (*ŚBhG*:33n), Johnson (*ŚBhG*:54f.n), etc.

quotations as are markedly commented upon and thus become objects of his examination in themselves. The quotations of this category are heavily criticised by Baṅkim.

If these two sets of criteria are combined, and the value Baṅkim assigns to the respective quotations is added, one regularity can be observed. All of Baṅkim's sometimes very harsh criticisms are directed to quotations concerned with what was called philological interpretation of the *Gītā*; these quotations become objects of his examination. The general evaluative statements without direct reference to the *Gītā* are, by contrast, nowhere criticised, and the general tenor in their environment is, rather, praise. It is almost exclusively on the mere lexical level of interpretation that some neutral quotations can be found, and their position is so marginal to Baṅkim's text that they are hardly worth a separate discussion. Most of the quotations are quite decisively value-loaded. Which function is assigned to them in the communicative process the commentary represents?

As is clear from the above-cited passage from *Kṛṣṇacaritra* and substantiated by the commentary, Baṅkim's main aim was not a scholarly dispute, but to bring his readers, Western-educated *bhadraloks*, closer to what he sees as their cultural and ethnical identity. In order to do so, he employs two quite different communicative strategies, playing, to put it generally, on the ambiguous character of the West. These, however, are not merely rhetorical tools but bear close connections with underlying diverging attitudes that were germane to Baṅkim's hermeneutical position.

The first strategy is best illustrated in his discussion of reincarnation, the longest of what was described as interspersed essays in the commentary (*ŚBhG*:49-60).[68] This essay is set against a specific apologetical background: reincarnation not being accepted by Christianity and Islam, it is, says Baṅkim, rejected by the educated who instead believe in heaven and hell. Then a survey is given of four different possibilities of life after death, and Hinduism is presented as a combination of three of them. Then, anticipating the prejudiced contempt of his readers, Baṅkim juxtaposes what he presents as a more neutral assessment:

> But *pensive* pundits from other countries and other religious faiths have, *by freeing themselves from prejudice*, been overcome with astonishment when discussing it [italics mine]. (*ŚBhG*:51)

The two quotations from Thomson (1855) and Tylor (1913 [1871]) that ensue prove the weight of the issue at question, as the sentence following them suggests:

> 'If the topic is as important as this, then let us make an attempt at understanding it a little better.' (*ŚBhG*:51)

The assessment of Tylor and Thomson is construed as a sort of importance-marker; their works are relevant insofar as they motivate a long discussion to follow.

After this, a list of commonly forwarded proofs for reincarnation is given; the conclusion is reached that for a person who accepts the *ātman* to be eternal, belief in reincarnation follows necessarily. Then Baṅkim takes up the discussion with the (formerly excluded) non-believers in the *ātman* and argues that reincarnation should not be contemptible to them. In order to make his point, he groups them together with the European pundits and quotes appreciative passages from Rhys Davids (1877) and Tylor. Especially Tylor's quotation comes to bear upon Baṅkim's text: Baṅkim assigns it a 'deeper meaning' and, in elaborating this, brings out the notion that reincarnation has

[68] Cf. Chapter 2.1.

all traits of a natural law and thus makes superfluous (Christian) 'miracles'. Thereafter, two more appreciative quotations from Schlegel (1846) and Johnson (1885) are enlisted. All these quotations have authority and, in this instance, speak almost entirely for themselves; with the exception of his elaboration of Tylor's remarks, Baṅkim does not do more than prefix laudative preambles to the respective quotations.

In all these instances, and a few more in the commentary, Baṅkim takes his support from Western Indology. By all appearances, he regards them as authoritative himself. In any case he construes the quotations as authority markers to solidify his positions. His strategy is to confront his readers with the acclaim reincarnation has found in the West; he counts on the effect of its symbolic weight on his readers: the authority of 'the West' is used to reinforce his readers' (and probably his own) identification with their own culture.

The second strategy is at work mainly in two passages of the commentary, namely, in the interpretations of *Gītā* 2.46 (*ŚBhG*:89-95) and 2.53 (*ŚBhG*:102f.). Here, nothing is enforced by the authority of Western Indology; on the contrary, it is exactly this authority which is put up for trial.

In his interpretation of *Gītā* 2.46, Baṅkim takes great pains — about six pages — meticulously to discuss different translations and find the semantically accurate understanding of that *śloka*. The importance of that verse lies in its determination of the status of the Vedas for a knowing brahmin. As discussed in the preceding chapter, the interpretation by the ancient commentators is taken *ad absurdum* by a thorough grammatical analysis, but the resolution is hardly uttered when Baṅkim already withdraws and makes great efforts to attenuate the implications.[69] The English translators, whose turn comes next, are treated less mildly, although unlike the traditional interpretation, their interpretation is grammatically possible. Fair enough still is the treatment of Telang (1990 [1882]). His translation and commentary are quoted, and Baṅkim simply states that they do not make sense. Significantly, in this instance, Telang — obviously on the ground of his ethnic identity — seems to be seen as belonging to the cultural inside and thereby entitled to claim greater legitimacy than the other translators: 'Whether the readers have respect for the other English translators or not, Kashinath Trimbak Telang may be respected.' (*ŚBhG*:93)

When it comes to Thomson, the tenor changes; an example is to be made of him. Thomson and Davies translate like Telang, i.e. wrongly. 'But there is even more flavour in the small glosses they have attached to those translations.' (*ŚBhG*:94) The gloss is cited for ridicule, and after the quotation Baṅkim uses a curious rhetorical device to make his point. He does not at all comment upon the content of Thomson's sentences, suggesting that this would be below the dignity of any competent reader. Thomson's comments, according to Baṅkim, are almost outrageously absurd. Instead of taking them apart, Baṅkim silently switches his frame of authority, taking it back to the cultural inside. Outwardly he pseudo-humbly confesses his own incompetence to explain the *Gītā* (but — *nota bene* — by implying his superiority over Thomson) and hopes that at least his quotations from the ancient commentators may be of some help (which is certainly hard to believe in the light of Baṅkim's own assessment of their relevance). But whether successfully or not, this is the hermeneutical path to be followed in order to have some chance of understanding the *Gītā*, whereas it is totally absurd to 'go to the English to

[69] Cf. preceding chapter.

understand the meaning of the *Gītā*' (*ŚBhG*:94).

In a second passage in the course of the interpretation of 2.53, Baṅkim continues in this vein and drives it further to explicitness. Here again, a question of translation is being discussed, namely, the meaning of *śruti*. After giving the interpretations of the ancient commentators, Baṅkim proceeds with a quotation from Davies (1882). The ignorance of English interpretations is now referred to as an already established fact:

> The English do not understand anything of the *Gītā*, and there is no possibility for such an understanding. But often, the pundit does not see any harm in listening to the words of the ignorant. (*ŚBhG*:102)

Introduced by this preamble, Davies is then exposed to utter ridicule. Baṅkim even inserts comments in brackets into the quoted text to express his doubts about the truth of the scholarliness the *Sāheb* 'boasts' of. The authoritativeness of Western scholarship on the *Gītā* (and, as is to be inferred, on large parts of Indian literature except Vedic texts) is thus categorically denied.

This second strategy, then, stresses the otherness, the outsider's position of Western Indologists. Due to it, their Indology cannot claim authoritativeness. The goal is the same here as regarding the first strategy: to bring the educated back to their own culture. But whereas in the latter he uses the approval from the West, including all the authority it possesses in the minds of his readers for his purpose, he denies precisely this authority in the course of his second strategy. This is a contradiction indeed; and this contradiction becomes evident in Baṅkim's treatment of Thomson, where both strategies collide. In his first strategy, Thomson figures as a 'pensive' pundit who has managed to rid himself of prejudices in his assessment of reincarnation (*ŚBhG*:51); in the second, he is portrayed as an object of mockery (*ŚBhG*:94).

At one point, however, the notion of different strategies, in the sense of exteriorised rhetorical techniques, apparently becomes inadequate to account for such inconsistencies. Only a few lines after Davies has been torn to pieces (as quoted above, *ŚBhG*:102), we find Baṅkim accepting precisely the opinion held by Davies (as a follower of Lassen [1846]): 'The foreign opinion matches more coherently than the native Kṛṣṇa's opinion concerning the Vedas as we have understood or explained it.' (ibid.) The occurrence of such an obvious inconsistency proves that there are mechanisms at work other than those to be expected in a usual polemical argumentation with the ultimate aim of establishing a viable interpretation: it is impossible to explain this in terms of strategies, unless of course one puts up with the contention that Baṅkim was indeed a poor thinker and rhetorician.[70] What collides here are not strategies but basic intentions which are, however, situated on very different levels of context. The contradiction is due to considerable strain from two opposite sides that acted upon Baṅkim's thinking; two different attitudes make their influence felt. One is the claim for critical inquiry within rational bounds, which ultimately forces Baṅkim to accept the more coherent (and, in this instance, Western) explanation. The second is the impulse to deny access to the intruders in the form of Western Indologists; hence the ascription of otherness to Western Indology, i.e. the constitution of a hermeneutical boundary. The first attitude is rational and scholarly, the second affective and political in nature. This opposition will still be dealt with.

[70] It would, in that case, suffice to apply the standard he himself lays down for the analysis of consistency regarding traditional texts in *Kṛṣṇacaritra* and also in the commentary.

Baṅkim's treatment of Western Indology can be decoded only if the quotations are read not merely as semantic units employed in a process of truth-finding, but as symbolic signs. They stand for the attributes of the West in colonial Bengal: they derive their strength of conviction from the authority and power of the West, and this quality is made use of for persuasion; on the other hand, they are intruders and extraneous elements to whom access should be denied whenever possible.[71]

Inherent in Baṅkim's procedure is something that may tentatively be called a closure. Most of his religious writings are entirely domestic affairs. His addressees are invariably the educated Bengalis of his own class. With the exception of his letters in the course of his controversy with Hastie, this applies also to his English writings; it is obvious in the Bengali texts where the language marks the boundary. 'Foreign' thought is taken into this domestic frame, but without therefore widening the frame or changing the communicative direction. Despite their 'international' appearance, Baṅkim's texts are exclusively designed for Bengal. Rather than breaking this frame, this internationality becomes a sign within it. The closure is especially evident in the denial of authoritativeness which follows from the essentialist ascription of otherness to Western Indology. It is indicative of a process of separation from the rulers' culture and an attempt at in-group formation.

This closure, however, was not of Baṅkim's own making; and this is especially strong evidence for the very common notion that his thinking is inseparably tied up with the constellation of power in nineteenth century colonised India. The communicative blind alley which he set up with regard to Indology — taking its messages in and occasionally apart in a demonstrative way, without transferring the results back to the senders — was an inherent feature of a situation of asymmetrical cultural contact. It was indeed paralleled by the framing of Indologists' talk about India which was from the start anything but a (in whichever way conceived) dialogue with that country. And the narrow circle of readers he defines as the recipients of his late writings did in fact correspond more or less to the actual Bengali readership he could expect; if Indologists did not take part in his discussion, it must be counted among the minor reasons for this that he did not ask them in. Allegations as Hastie's that India was understood better in Europe than in India itself certainly did not facilitate matters — nor did the disparaging views about India held and expressed by many nineteenth century Indologists.[72] The sight of Indology monopolising the 'right' access to Indian tradition must in these circumstances indeed have been unbearable. The communicative closure, which augments the reification of the Indological statements and accounts for the occasional show trial, does betray a non-cooperation decision in matters of Indological knowledge. And no matter how extensively Baṅkim remains informed by Indology, this does imply the acute awareness of a significant difference of perspective in his own and the Indologists'

[71] This bias of Baṅkim's religious writings was detected and comdemned by Rabīndranāth Ṭhākur (1978 [1984]), whose assessment regarding this aspect of *Kṛṣṇacaritra* runs thus: 'The writer [Baṅkim] showered innumerable insults on the "Western ignorants", i.e. the European pundits. Firstly, this is detestable as such; secondly, it has resulted highly unseemly in a book of this kind. Unsuitable ill-behaviour in front of respectable people is not only ill-behaviour, it is also ill-manneredness towards the respectable persons. In the place where His character is being established whom Baṅkim knows as the best among men [...], it is an insult of that ideal to show impudence at the occasion of disagreement, while having seated oneself in front of His ideal.' (p. 458)

[72] Cf. Haberman (1994:90ff.) for examples.

speaking about India.

Baṅkim's 'closure' is however certainly not equivalent to the 'reversal of Orientalism' that Sudipta Kaviraj (1995) detects in Bhūdeb Mukhopādhyāẏ's writings. As Partha Chatterjee (1986:61) rightly points out, 'Bankim's critique of Orientalist knowledge is not epistemological, or even methodical'; in *Kṛṣṇacaritra*, he criticises the Indologists for their prejudices, and in the commentary he pays them back by alleging the impossibility of any real understanding from an outsider's perspective. The reasons he gives for this impossibility of understanding are not sufficient. And the ground upon which this statement is validated, in the commentary, is philology, i.e. a terrain framed and represented by exactly those whom he apparently wants to drive out of it, or at least its extension to India. Baṅkim's determination to drive them out of what he conceives as *Indian* property cannot cover the fact that he is fighting almost exclusively with *their* weapons: he uses their criteria and partly even material mediated by them. In this course, the quotations only partly retain the status of own, sovereign voices. It seems that the plurality of opinions almost completely vanishes; they are very much reduced to instruments in his attempt to establish a discourse of power. Baṅkim even struggles by using strategies which, in strict analysis, contradict each other. In spite of all this, the basic impulse — to keep at least that last area, Indian tradition, away from what he must have perceived as an aspect of colonialism, and under Indian control — is very understandable. And in this perspective, Baṅkim's constant attempts at critical inquiry and coherent reasoning, which *are* after all at work in considerable parts of the commentary, must be appreciated; their occasional repression is indicative of his acute and massive irritations, and the great pressure from various sides acting on his thinking.

2.4 Summing Up

In the introduction, heterogeneity was referred to as a typical feature of nineteenth century Bengal and later shown as a characteristic trait of the commentary. In the course of the analysis, some inconsistencies and contradictions have been demonstrated both in the conceptual and the communicative dimensions of the commentary. This may be of some importance for the interpretation of Baṅkim's writings, but if it were all *quod erat demonstrandum*, the analysis would rightly bear appearances, to some extent, of an exercise of scholarly pedantism. What remains to be made, then, is an attempt to regain a larger perspective on the commentary and to explain these 'waverings'. Here it will not do to content oneself by simply attributing all inconsistencies to some deficiency in Baṅkim's capacity of reasoning and calling him a 'mediocre thinker',[1] or pointing to his alleged 'practice of adapting his views to support the argument of the moment'.[2] Neither will it suffice to merely state that his contradictions correspond to or mirror the contradictions of the Western educated élite as a class, because this would not be much more than a tautology.[3] Such a correspondence (and certainly not an equation), if it can be reasonably demonstrated, is bound to consist in a rather complex set of notions, concepts and intentions situated on different levels of context. In order to put the commentary into perspective, this set will have to be examined closely.

In his *Śrīmadbhagabadgītā*, quite a variety of purposes, intentions and motivations merge into the intentional basis of the text. What are Baṅkim's intentions in the commentary? Generally, a commentary's aim may be expected to primarily consist of an attempt to bring out the genuine intention of the text which is being interpreted. Accordingly, Baṅkim in his introduction declares his intention as follows:

> The motive of this commentary of mine is thus to teach these people [Bengalis with Western education] the meaning of the *Gītā* according to Western methods and with the help of Western ideas. (*ŚBhG*:20)

But as demonstrated in Chapter 2, in Baṅkim's commentary there are central concepts taken beyond the semantical confines set by the *Gītā*, or, to put it differently, forced interpretations; and such obviously forced interpretations indicate precisely the difference of intentions inherent in the commentary. Therefore, the commentary's intentions may be determined independently and grouped hierarchically; and the very choice of the *Gītā* by Baṅkim is one of the questions to be dealt with in this context.

Baṅkim's main intention is certainly not of a philological kind. He uses philological methods, but his approach is not philological. He merely employs some basic assumptions of modern textual criticism for his other intentions. The evidence he produces in cases of assumed interpolations is not based on philological criteria.[4]

[1] J.C. Ghosh (1976:130).

[2] Van M. Baumer (1969:66); cf. also similar statements in her dissertation (1964:249ff.).

[3] Cf. Rām।kṛṣṇa Bhaṭṭācārya (1995:87), who quotes from Asit।kumār Bhaṭṭācārya (1964:150 — 'Basically, Baṅkim's self-contradiction was merely a reflection of the inherent self-contradiction of the educated Hindu class of that time.') and states that is has become very common to explain by equating personal to class contradiction. He dismisses the explanation as not taking into account personal angularities, and adduces Baṅkim's contemporary Kṛṣṇakamal Bhaṭṭācārya as an example of non-eclecticism. This objection is very accurate — although maybe not suitable with regard to Asit।kumār Bhaṭṭācārya's inquisitive and critical book, where this question is not answered as summarily as the quotation suggests.

[4] Except when dealing with the parallels between the *Gītā* and the *Kaṭha-Upaniṣad* (*ŚBhG*:71f.).

Philology merely furnishes him the basic premise that the *Gītā* probably consists of different layers, i.e. the means of fragmentising it. The ratio behind his qualification of certain portions as interpolations is not philological considerations, but compatibility with certain presuppositions: Kṛṣṇa is both personal God and ideal man, and the *Gītā* the mediated account of his teachings. The text Baṅkim is looking for is not the *Gītā*'s most ancient, 'authentic' version, but the most coherent textual representation of that divine teaching. The use of philological arguments is not more than an outer justification of an eclectic reading,[5] and when Sisir Kumar Das claims that Baṅkim applied 'the methods of higher criticism'[6] 'with great measure of success',[7] it must be stated that this success is certainly not a philological one.[8] If a further indication for the minor role of philological inquiry in the commentary is necessary, one may look at his treatment of the philological errors he detects in Western translations of the *Gītā*. Once found, these errors are immediately transferred to a different plane where they function as proof of the Westerners' incompetence. It is thus evident that Baṅkim's philological inquiries are instrumental to other, more basic intentions.

Is the main intention 'religious'? The commentary has, for practical reasons, often been referred to as a 'religious writing'; but it is problematic to call the basic intention religious, all the more since the meaning of that very term (*dharma*, religion) is one of the most important issues under negotiation in the commentary and its related texts. Baṅkim is concerned with the *Gītā*'s *dharmatattva*, its 'principles' of *dharma* (*ŚBhG*:34). The broad sense in which the pair of *dharma* and religion is again and again used, transcends any historical, empirical 'religion'; and those principles are independent even of belief in God or the immortality of the *ātman*.[9] It is devoid of metaphysical, 'supernatural' elements (cf. *ŚBhG*:22): although he states his personal beliefs in a number of instances, Baṅkim does not attempt to make them compulsory for his readers. The centre of his thought, its universal and truly normative part, is *ethical* rather than religious: it is religion reduced to ethics. This reduction, however, is in no

[5] Baṅkim himself implicitly admits this eclecticism in his *Letters on Hinduism*: 'And this [the general dissemination of progress] was the cause, why the revolt against the Vedic polytheism, instead of forming the later religion into a simple and homogeneous monotheism like Mohammedanism led to the development of an immensely complicated system, embracing within it every variety of belief, monotheism, pantheism, even atheism, and ultimately to *that highly elaborated eclectic religion which absorbed them, and which is modern Hinduism*.' (italics H.H.; *BR* III:266). Eclecticism is also seen as a characteristic of the *Bhāgavata-purāṇa* and the *Bhagavadgītā* (ibid.:268). This is quite in accordance with the very critical analysis of modern Hindu thinking by Agehananda Bharati (1971), who speaks of the 'boundless eclecticism' in the process of the modernisation of Hinduism (p. 89), into which the *Gītā* fits very well because it is likewise characterised by 'attractive eclecticism' (p. 95) — the evaluation of this eclecticism is however the opposite of Baṅkim's.

[6] Sisir Kumar Das (1984:173).

[7] Ibid.

[8] This has often been stressed with regard to *Kṛṣṇacaritra* which methodically moves along the same lines as *Śrīmadbhagabadgītā*. Cf. Ṭhākur (1978 [1894]: *Kṛṣṇacaritra*) and Buddhadeb Basu (1974:24): '[...] wherever the cunning Kṛṣṇa could in no way be caught into the ideal intended by him, he settled the problem by taking the part as interpolated — very easily, and also not always trustworthily.' Śaṅkarīprasād Basu (1990:31) once speaks of the *"prakṣipta" astra* [Beng.]' ('the weapon of interpolation'), thus suggesting that it was a device for an eclectic reading.

[9] Cf. Dvijendranāth Ṭhākur's critique of *Dharmmajijñāsā*, *Nabya hindusampradāy*: '[...] it is not the teaching of the *Bhagavadgītā* that *dharma* can be achieved also by abandoning life after death, the *ātman* and the *paramātman*.' Quoted in *BJ*:337.

way exteriorised terminologically in Baṅkim's argumentations. It is bracketed by the many-facetted term *dharma*. This term is taken from its original, central place within traditional Hindu thought and made to undergo a process of cleansing or destillation, in the course of which it acquires the meaning, at least in one of its facets, of 'essential religion/ethics', leaving behind all particular religions. It must be stressed that the definitory process leading to this meaning in *Dharmmajijñāsā* is *not* based on traditional textual material, but mainly on F. Max Müller's exposition of religion.[10] The outer appearance of the term being unaltered, Baṅkim'candra is now able to re-attribute this cleansed meaning to a few selected occurrences of *dharma* in the *Gītā*, i.e. to a traditional Hindu text. The similarities to what Bharati describes as the 'pizza effect' can hardly be overlooked.[11]

It is hard to determine, and shall not be attempted here, how and to what extent Baṅkim's personal religious belief was connected with his theoretical speculations.[12] He was, however, aware, in principle, that many Hindus would find it difficult to accept his version of Hindu *dharma*.[13] But the point is that even Baṅkim's construction of a cleansed religio-ethical system still has an aspect of instrumentality about it. His interpretations usually start from the *Gītā*'s text into ascending contexts in a step-by-step manner. The order varies, but more or less the steps are as follows: first comes his translation, then the determination of the *Gītā*'s immanent meaning (often given in the form of a paraphrase); these are followed by occasional philological examinations and determinations of the ethical purport. The hierarchically highest of these ascending levels on which meaning is assigned to the *Gītā*, i.e. the level on which he reaches his conclusions, is not this level of ethical purport. The ultimate conclusions he reaches are the recurring assertions of the superiority of the *dharma* proclaimed in the *Gītā*, i.e. in his view, of the essence of Hindu *dharma*. This superiority is what must finally be established. Accordingly the passages where Baṅkim infers this superiority have a serene tenor, a self-contained and *mantra*-like quality about them, filled as they are with statements in the superlative. Once this level is reached, his line of argumentation has come to its end.

Cultural self-assertion, then, is the most basic intention of the commentary, its fundamental impulse.[14] Superiority is shown for the past of Hindu civilisation; the

[10] Cf. Baṅkim's essay *Dharmmajijñāsā* and the discussion thereof in Chapter 2.2.2.

[11] Cf. Agehananda Bharati 1971:88ff.; 'pizza effect' roughly means a re-import of something formerly exported and refined abroad (i.e. in the case of the pizza, from Italy to North America and back). The term is handy, but based on what seems to be an imprecise view of the history of that dish.

[12] For a discussion of Baṅkim's religiosity (on the basis of the testimonies by contemporaries included in *Baṅkim prasaṅga* [1982]), cf. Śaṅkarīprasād Basu (1990:10-13 and 38-40), who traces the change in Baṅkim's attitude towards religion and concludes that he indeed was a *kṛṣṇabhakta*. Also *BJ*:329.

[13] For instance, his opposition to the hereditary nature of the *varṇāśramadharma*; in *Dharmmatattva*, the *śiṣya* reacts to it by saying: 'No Hindu will agree with this kind of Hinduism [*hinduẏāni*] of yours', and the guru answers: 'They may not, but this is the genuine inner significance of *dharma*.' *BR* II:618; also quoted in Sisir Kumar Das (1984:169) who interprets *dharma* to mean Hindu *dharma* in this instance.

[14] Hacker (1978 [1970]:607) identifies nationalism as the chief impulse of neo-Hindu thinking. I prefer to call it cultural self-assertion because the (Bengali, Hindu, Indian?) 'nation' which was to become the object of such nationalism was still not defined in clear terms by Baṅkim. He was of course a proto-nationalist, but the chief impulse had *not* yet crystallised. Bad'rul Hāsān choses the term *deśānurāg* (Beng.): 'If the whole creation of Baṅkim'candra is discussed in synthesis, then one will have to say that the

superior ethical system is visualised as inherent in Hindu tradition. All that remains to be done on the part of Baṅkim's contemporaries is to realise this and put the *Gītā* into practice. The political implications of such an implementation can easily be inferred, and are in fact alluded to in the commentary:

> If the Indians had kept in mind the harmony or unification of the doctrine of action and the doctrine of knowledge proclaimed by the Lord in the above-mentioned maxim, and had acted according to it, if both knowledge and action had equally been their goals, they would never have fallen into the present state of inferiority to more civilised nations; they would not have become subjugated, dependent on others and endangered by the education given by another nation. (*ŚBhG*:128)

His establishment of *svadeś'prīti* (the love of one's own country) in his ethical system is also a clear step towards the political dimension.[15] These instances remain, however, only faint foreshadowings of any concrete political action throughout his religious writings and also his novels.[16]

Why did Baṅkim'candra choose the *Bhagavadgītā*? As was shown in 2.2.3, he regarded *bhakti* as the most important element of any *dharma* and found it lacking in Vedic literature. The most important merit of the *Gītā*, for Baṅkim, was the harmonisation of *jñāna* (knowledge) and *karman* (action) in subordination to *bhakti* (devotion); the downright contradictions inherent in the *Gītā*[17] itself would in the further course of his commentary have been accounted for by his philological equipment. In *Dharmmatattva*, he states with reference to the first eleven *adhyāyas* of the *Gītā*:

> In these eleven *adhyāyas*, there is the praise of all three — *jñāna*, *karman* and *bhakti*. Also that is there which is nowhere else: there is the harmonisation[18] of *jñāna*, *karman* and *bhakti*. Precisely because there is

---

source of all inspiration was passion for his country [*deśānurāg*].' (1990:129) Cf. also Tapan Raychaudhuri (1988:11) who describes the 'anxious and neurotic effort at cultural self-assertion' as 'a major trait of the milieu in late nineteenth century Bengal'. The reception of Baṅkim in later years of course emphasised his political potentials, not his *dharma*, as Rām'kṛṣṇa Bhaṭṭācārya (1994:48f.) stresses ('In the field of religion [*dharma*], he [Baṅkim] is still a *śiṣya*-less guru.'); the term Bhaṭṭācārya uses to describe the claims to Hindu superiority is *atipūraṇ*, *overcompensation* (p. 50; the English equivalent is given in Bhaṭṭācārya's text). Lastly, Amiya P. Sen, in his accurate discussion of Baṅkim's attitude towards politics, explains what Baṅkim meant by 'non-political patriotism' in his *Dharmmatattva*.

[15] Cf. Chapter 24 of *Dharmmatattva*, entitled *Svadeś'prīti* (*BR* II:660-1) as well as his commentary on *Gītā* 4.19 (*ŚBhG*:152ff.).

[16] Cf. Pārthapratim Bandyopādhyāy̌ (1990) who points out that Baṅkim's novels were not political in any concrete sense, but had strong political potentialities in their treatment of Hindu-Muslim relations (p. 37f.). According to Baṅkim's own conception, ethical renewal had to precede any direct political action (Somendranāth Basu 1964:37f.); this distinguished him from reformers like Malabari or Bidyāsāgar (Vidyāsāgar) (Rākhāl Candra Nāth 1988:85). Cf. also Tapan Raychaudhuri (1988:15 and esp. 154), drawing a parallel to Dayānand Sarasvatī, Keśab'candra Sen and Bibekānanda (Vivekānanda) who all saw 'religion and its reform as the road to patriotic ends'.

[17] Cf. e.g. Arvind Sharma (1986:xii-xvi), who distinguishes between theological, soteriological, metaphysical, liturgical, canonical and ethical contradictions in the *Gītā*. Larson (1981:513) calls the *Gītā* 'a remarkable Hindu daughter, beloved and pampered by all in the family and combining in her person the best, as well as the most puzzling, qualities of her heritage'. Already Garbe (1905).

[18] [*sāmañjasya* (Beng.).]

> this harmonisation it can be called the most excellent book on *dharma* of all. But the true meaning of that harmonisation is that the final state[19] of these three is *bhakti*. Therefore, the *Gītā* is genuinely a *bhaktiśāstra*. (*BR* II:626)

If he was convinced of the *Gītā*'s outstanding position among Hindu scriptures, the *Gītā* would also not contradict other, more strategic considerations. In spite of being written from a *Vaiṣṇava* background, the *Gītā* had for centuries been considered as an authoritative text beyond sectarian confines and could thus, better than other texts, function as a symbol for Hindu tradition in general[20]. If the *Gītā* could be shown to teach a superior ethical system, then the same could be claimed for 'Hinduism' as such.[21] The *Gītā*'s wide acclaim beyond *sampradāyas* is of course based on its harmonising character; while admitting several paths to salvation, it remains sufficiently imprecise about which one is preferable and puts them together in an atomistic way. In this way space is left for the most variegated exegesis, as the history of its commentaries shows.[22] Moreover, the harmonisation in the *Gītā* is not only crucial for its acceptability among all Hindus, but also furnishes Baṅkim the foundation for an important argument: in applying it to all religions and even beyond them, Baṅkim describes it as the *general*, universal religion which resides over the other particular religions.

The most crucial point involved in this choice of the *Gītā*, however, appears to be the search for authority — quite in accordance with the basic intention which was, on a different level, identified as cultural self-assertion. *Dharmmatattva*, written before the commentary, argues for the authority of Hindu *dharma* and the *Gītā* from an independent position, and the array of arguments is very much influenced by Western catechisms on morality; in the commentary, Baṅkim merges his authority with the *Gītā*'s. He attempts to speak *through* the *Gītā*, thereby letting the new speak through the old, and constructing a continuity which allows the nineteenth century colonial subject to identify with the most universal and generous *dharma* of all times. Superior authority is there on the cultural inside, it only has to be re-appropriated. The focus of his discourse is moved to the centre. 'Funnily,' Rām'kṛṣṇa Bhaṭṭācārya (1995:86) remarks, 'it was by virtue of the *Gītā-bhāṣya* and *Kṛṣṇacaritra* that Baṅkim got the designation *Ṛṣi*.'

In the commentary, Baṅkim construes his trajectory as an untrodden middle path between two very common cognitive main roads. At the base of these main roads lies what might tentatively be called a 'geo-doctrinal equation system': *modern* equals *West*, and *traditional* equals *East*. This, according to the terminology Partha Chatterjee (1986) uses, is the *thematic* setting; the hermeneutical frame within which things were argued

[19] [*caramābasthā* (Beng.).]

[20] Cf. Huber's (1991:4ff.) survey over research concerning the historical relevance of the *Gītā*; though having been regarded as an important text for centuries by paṇḍits, and although there was an edition of it in Calcutta by Bhabānīcaraṇ Bandyopādhyāẏ in 1835, it did not apparently become popular before the second half of the nineteenth century, i.e. during Baṅkim's lifetime. This rings true for Bengal at least, but not so much for other parts of India. Mediaeval Marathi literature especially contains several commentaries on or translations of the *Gītā*, Jñān'dev's *Jñāneśvarī* and Tukārām's *Mantragītā* being the most known ones; consequently, the *Gītā* must have found popular acclaim much earlier in Mahārāṣṭra.

[21] This criterion of general acceptibility was not less important in the choice of textual groundings in other reform movements of that time, namely, Rām'mohan Rāẏ's *Vedānta* and Dayānand Sarasvatī's Veda.

[22] Cf. Minor (ed.) (1991), *Introduction*.

out. It may be questionable whether at the end of the nineteenth century, there was still any considerable number of the population in Bengal consistently paying heed to the equation system — in either possible combination of evaluations — in the organisation of their social and personal conduct. Still, it played a major role throughout the nineteenth century (and after) as a fundamental model of categories to classify and evaluate phenomena in a situation of cultural contact. Baṅkim, as we have seen, directs his polemical remarks against the followers of this model from either side, traditionalists and modernists, alike. He rejects the notion that one of these equations is to be given legitimacy and priority over the other. And what is more, he attempts to reject, from a distinctive standpoint, the classificatory model it represents as such.

Basically, the equation system has a historical dimension as well as one of identity. Baṅkim cannot deny, historically, the 'geographical' origin of enlightenment and evolutionist thought which frames his approach, and it is certainly within this concept of gradual, stage-wise development that he sets out on his re-evaluation of Indian culture. But 'the West' is no longer the monolithic block, the prototype of civilisation, which it used to represent, at a certain point, for the Derozians. The 'other West' is also perceived, e.g. in the commentary when he alludes to the Sicilian vespers,[23] or in his critique of modern European nationalism in *Dharmmatattva* (*BR* II:661). On the other hand, his interpretations are designed to bring out the 'other' Indian tradition. Yet, despite all demystifications, the geo-doctrinal equation system continues to be a platform to many of his arguments, and he sometimes also falls back upon it in his positive argumentations, e.g. when he denies the modern West, in the form of Indologists, hermeneutical access to traditional India in the form of the *Gītā*.

As a model of identity, Baṅkim rejects the system altogether. Neither of the two equations could be sufficient to form a 'modern' Indian identity. Thus new criteria, different from the geographical ones, had to be defined in order to deliminate the boundary between things to be accepted and things to be rejected. A rough outline of such a programme for his late writings is given in *Ānandamaṭh*:[24] Indian tradition is sufficient, even superior, as far as the knowledge of 'inner objects' is concerned; the knowledge of 'outer objects' (i.e. natural sciences as well as all kinds of this-worldly concerns) must however be learnt from the Europeans. In this context, Baṅkim's religious writings appear as an attempt to live up to the claim regarding traditional knowledge of inner objects; inner and outer knowledge have to be reconciled and integrated into one system. But the scheme he develops in *Ānandamaṭh* does not overcome the thematic frame, i.e. the geo-doctrinal equation system, but simply elaborates it further. The *problematic* aspect — to employ again the terminology Partha Chatterjee uses — is shifted by assigning a new value to at least one part of traditional Indian culture.

If cultural self-assertion is the main impetus of Baṅkim's religious writings, the case is different with his early novels, where it does not yet come to occupy the foreground. It comes up first in the *Confessions of a Young Bengal* in 1872, plays an important role in his satirical essays of *Lok'rahasya* and *Kamalākānta* and develops fully in *Ānandamaṭh* and the following novels and religious writings. The problem, his search for cultural identity, is formulated in its full-fledged impact already in the *Confessions*,

[23] *BhG* 3.37.

[24] Chapter 2.1.

one of the most desperate of his essays. He refers to Hinduism's 'semi-barbarous restrictions concerning food — and drink', 'expensive superstitions', 'old-fashioned ascetic purity of life', 'literature, full of false history, false geography and false physics' and 'perpetual widowhood', and states:

> The necessary minor premises being assumed, sound logic compels us to cry with one voice, Hinduism must be destroyed. Agreed. But the spiritual nature of man abhors a vacuum. Between our various *isms*, the Hindu code of personal and social ethics has been wellnigh [*sic.*] wholly repealed, and its precepts are universally seen and felt to be more honoured in the breach than in the observance. Where is our new code of morality? (*BR* III:140f.)

As early as in 1872, then, Baṅkim poses his questions, questions which would basically remain the same throughout his later writings, and which virtually bring into focus the dilemma of a colonised society. Mere acceptance and emulation of the West is not a viable path, and is most heavily attacked from *Kamalākānta*'s marginal position; the opium-eater *Kamalākānta*, in a context of power, is the most effective symbol of marginalised indigenous norms Baṅkim has created. It is in these essays, in a paradoxical way directly corresponding to the paradoxical situation of the colonised, that Baṅkim comes *into his own*; the paradoxical reversal of norms is built into the constituent narrative structure itself.

In his late writings, Baṅkim'candra goes beyond questioning contemporary values and tries to give an answer; the focus is shifted from subversion to construction, and satirical critique is changed into didactic self-assertion. In other words, the issues formerly dealt with from a marginal position are now taken into the centre. It must, however, be stressed again that Baṅkim's underlying perception of the problem he was dealing with — search for cultural identity — remained the same. It was only his mode of dealing with it that changed. Baṅkim's self-assertive mode, unlike the satirical, is apologetic; it is forced to fix a position from which to argue, to define the boundaries between a cultural inside and outside. And the cultural inside must be compatible with complex contemporary realities. In the process, the emphasis is put on indigenousness; certain earlier issues — as social equality in his *Sāmya* — lose ground: 'Bankim looks for an ethico-religious site for the Hindu people whose dominant priority is not what is socially just but what is truly indigenous — i.e., Hindu.' (Tanika Sarkar 1994:2555)

In Baṅkim's later years, it appears, self-assertion became an utter psychological necessity; the claim to superiority — decidedly a compensatory claim, as Tapan Raychaudhuri rightly (1988:136) remarks — was his way of restoring meaning to his personal life and to Hindu society as he perceived it. Despite the rationalist outlook he tried to keep up, the emotional need for self-assertion proves to be more basic to his thinking.[25] The inconsistencies in his interpretation, then, are due precisely to the overriding

[25] Cf. Āh'mad Śarīph (1990b:115): 'Although he was mainly led by reason in this work [the interpretation of *dharma* and elaboration of cultivation], he was driven by emotion too without himself being aware of it. By the force of that emotion, he unconsciously became a Hindu revivalist. Worn out by various diseases and tired of family quarrels, the son-less Baṅkim was a *bhaktivādin* driven by emotion, clad in saffron, vegetarian and desiring liberation at the end of his life — Baṅkim was then a seeker of liberation free from the obligation of reason and given to devotion. His life came to an end in the middle of these mental and behavioral inconsistencies produced by distaste. Thus the origin of both the Hindu revivalism he adopted and the *bhaktivāda* he followed was incidental, not well-planned — emotional, not reasonable.'

predominance of this basic impulse, which tended to subjugate and thus render inconsistent his other intentions. The attempt at a synthesis of *dharma* and nineteenth century Western conceptions of religion is not an objectionable enterprise. It becomes inconsistent only when this new definition of *dharma* is claimed to be intended in traditional texts. But this is the very step Baṅkim has to make in order to assert the inherent superiority of Hinduism.[26] In the discussion on reincarnation, the desire to establish, in the eyes of his readers, the value of that doctrine does not allow him to be too choosy about the means with which to operate, and makes him use authorities whose very legitimacy he denies elsewhere.[27] Further, the desire to build an objective, self-conscious readership — as a model of future Bengali society — makes him use a first person plural that does not have any real *signifié* if one is to take seriously his more empirical descriptions of his readers.[28] Formally, these inconsistencies are due to the intermeshing of two levels of argument, the empirical and the normative, or, as Asit'kumār Bhaṭṭācārya (1964) puts it, the 'ideal' and the 'real':

> In establishing the superiority of Hinduism, he compared it in many cases with Western ideals [*matādarśa* (Beng.)]. In almost all of these comparisons, a *confusion of categories* [Lat.] has occurred. Because for the Westerners he has given their real [*bāstab* (Beng.)] examples, and for the Hindus he has given examples from the ideals [*ādarśer* (Beng.)] of Hinduism, examples of the Hindu Śāstras. (p. 145)[29]

In this way, indeed, Baṅkim 'in proving the superiority of the Hindus came down, in many cases, from the form of a philosopher to that of an advocate' who knows the truth beforehand (p. 146).

Baṅkim's approach was, to put it in another way, caught up between two different procedures, an inductive and a deductive one: the results to be inferred from the text could also be deduced from various preconceptions regarding essential Hinduism; his *dharma* is an *a priori* construction.[30] Baṅkim was in the contradictory situation that while moving towards a goal or a *demonstrandum*, he had to claim that this goal had already been reached long ago, i.e. that it was already a *demonstratum*. In this regard, it may indeed be stated that his contradictoriness was shared by many of his contemporaries; given the apologetic orientation on the background of an asymmetrical cultural encounter, such inconsistencies threatened the conceptions of quite a range of

[26] Cf. Chapters 2.2.2 and 2.2.3 of the present analysis. Tapan Raychaudhuri calls this a projection: 'He projected this new ideology as essential Hinduism.' (1988:145)

[27] Cf. Chapter 2.3.3.

[28] Cf. Chapter 2.3.1.

[29] Bhaṭṭācārya focusses on *Dharmmatattva* in his critical discussion of Baṅkim's religious thought (1964:115-51) and traces exemplary cases like the following (p. 144): First Baṅkim treats the king formally as the holder of the throne obeying whom is *dharma* by definition — except in certain cases: 'as long as the king is a protector of his subjects he is a king. When he has become a torturer of his subjects, then he is not a king anymore.' Bhaṭṭācārya insists upon the 'realness' of a tyrant, thereby criticising Baṅkim's unreflected idealistic flaw. — Cf. in this connection also Agehananda Bharati's (1971:92) sharp remarks on the confusion of 'is' and 'ought' statements of 'the modern Indian' with regard to the abolition of caste; although certainly too generalised, they indicate a mechanism similar to the one at work in Baṅkim's arguments.

[30] Cf. Amales Tripathi (1967b:481).

thinkers.[31] Contradictory positions on a larger scale, e.g. his social utopia in the famous essay *Sāmya* as contrasted with the apology of a hierarchical order of society in the commentary (cf. *ŚBhG*:40ff.), can mostly be accounted for by his switch, around 1880, from subversion to construction as outlined above. His later writings were forced to stay within the parameters of a — however eclectic — Hindu tradition.

From a political and historical perspective, the most problematic aspect of Baṅkim's approach to Hindu tradition was its search for identity in exclusively Hindu terms. Islam, the religion of the greater part of Bengali population even in his times, hardly enters the picture.[32] Muslims could not possibly be expected to, and in fact did not, feel included in Baṅkim's ethical system within which their faith was ultimately seen as directed to 'that one God', i.e. Kṛṣṇa.[33] Baṅkim's choice of 'Hinduism' for cultural self-assertion was however not a free choice at all; it was arguably decisively framed by the foregoing process of intercultural perception in colonial Bengal. Ashis Nandy points out that colonialism includes certain 'codes which both the rulers and the ruled can share'[34] (i.e. Partha Chatterjee's 'thematic' frame). On an intellectual level, the admiration of the achievements of 'brahmanic speculation', to use the term Hastie employed in the controversy with Baṅkim, had been such a shared code (for parts of the century even a dominant one). From the beginning of the intellectual encounter between Europe and India, the predominant object of discussion was religion; research focused on Hindu scriptures or 'Sacred Books'; ancient India was equal to 'Hindu India',[35] the locus of the 'golden civilisation'. Thus it was ancient India which became the object of an essentialist perception. The 'Muslim' period was not of avail for similar reconstructions; rather the Muslims were conceived as the scapegoats of present Hindu India's decline and, in Baṅkim's *Ānandamaṭh*, became the victims of compensatory Hindu aggression.[36] Baṅkim's treatment of Muslims is rather complex and shall not be dealt with further here.[37] His scheme of *dharma* was however not able to surmount the basic assumptions underlying the British policy of 'Divide and Rule',[38] namely, the notion of mainly two distinct portions of population, Hindus and Muslims, and Baṅkim's cultural self-perception could not help but be considerably determined by the foregoing and contemporary Western perception of India.

[31] e.g. Brahmabāndhab Upādhyāẏ, Aurobindo, Nabīn'candra Sen, Vivekānanda, etc.

[32] In the present context, this issue cannot be dealt with at length. For a more detailed analysis, see Tanika Sarkar (1994); also Hans Harder (1996).

[33] Cf. e.g. Rezaul Karim's (1994) statement, assigning no value to Baṅkim's religious writings.

[34] Nandi (1983:2).

[35] James Mill (1817); cf. Introduction.

[36] Cf. Hans Harder (1996:esp.59-61 and 67ff.) for a discussion. Also Tapan Raychaudhuri (1988:12).

[37] It is much too simple to call him the prototypal communalist as some authors do, but it cannot be denied that he helped in constructing a Hindu-biased nationalism, if despite his underlying intentions. One would have to ask whether he did integrate Muslim society in any way; the issue is not settled by merely stating that his attacks were only meant against Muslim rulers. The latter point has often been made; cf. Amales Tripathi (1967a:17), who holds that the target was 'not the upright Moslem but the decadent tyrant'. Āh'mad Śarīph (1990b:39) writes that his insults applied to 'foreign, foreign-speaking rulers. There were no insults against Bengali-speaking Muslims.' Also Chitta Ranjan Bandyopadhyay (1994), Sāroẏār Jāhān (1984:155ff.).

[38] Cf. Gopāl Hāl'dār (1985:134,139).

Baṅkim's presentation of Hinduism has been dealt with under quite a large number of labels, such as reformed Hinduism, new Hinduism, political Hinduism, modern Hinduism, Hindu revivalism, neo-Hinduism, and even neo-Hindu revivalism.[39] The decision about which of these terms is preferable is complicated by the well-known problems connected with the term 'Hinduism' itself which have often been pointed out in contemporary Indology as well as by 'modern Hindus'.[40] Hinduism originated as a designation[41] coined by 'non-Hindus'. When about the beginning of the nineteenth century it started to be appropriated by 'Hindus', along with equivalent terms in Indian languages (such as Baṅkim's *hindudharma* in the sense of 'Hindu religion'), this appropriation was only a partial one, and usually a sign of contact with Western culture on the part of those who used it. In other words, Western-educated 'Hindus' started subsuming their traditional 'Hindu' compatriots under the term Hindu while those continued to call themselves by various names. To conceive of Hinduism as such already demanded a changed, non-traditional outlook and thus indicates a perceptive gap. If then, from a purely empirical perspective, one tended to call Baṅkim's scheme simply Hinduism (in contrast to several single, premodern religions such as *Vaiṣṇavism*, etc.), one would in that case ignore his and his contemporaries' usage of Hinduism which extended to all those religions. In view of this state of things, it is illusory to imagine that a superimposed terminology could be replaced by any unproblematic self-designation;[42] and while it is of crucial importance to be conscious of the problems involved, one will nevertheless have to stick to Hinduism as a common denominator of a variety of religions.

Baṅkim himself once uses the English term 'modern Hinduism' (*BR* III:266), although it is unclear, on the one hand, whether it means anything apart from his own interpretation, and all too clear, on the other, that it is value-loaded, in the sense of an ascending line of progress. 'Modern Hindu' (in capitals) was used similarly by the journalist Girish Chandra Ghose as early as in 1867.[43] Freed from its ideological baggage, however, 'modern Hinduism', as a technical term, stresses the encounter

[39] These terms are used differently by different authors and do not in themselves seem to indicate any regular approach. Kamal Kumar Ghatak (1991:VII) suggests that conceptional differences are implied in the choice of either neo-Hinduism or Hindu revivalism, but does not further substantiate his thesis, which appears difficult to maintain.

[40] Cf. R.E. Frykenberg's critical remarks (1989:29-49). Wezler speaks of Hinduism '— *womit bekanntlich eine Vielzahl von indischen Religionen bezeichnet wird, deren erstes und wesentlichstes, wenn nicht gar einziges, Element der Gemeinsamkeit darin zu sehen ist, daß andere, autochthone wie nicht-autochthone Religionen sich — jedenfalls ursprünglich und über längere Zeit hin — als selbst von ihnen verschieden verstanden haben*.' (1995:99). Von Stietencron aptly states that 'In popular parlance, most people in the West today speak of Hinduism as if it was *one single* religion, comparable, for instance, with Islam or Buddhism or Christianity. However, scholars who study the history of the Hindu religion more closely discover such a plurality of religious doctrine and practice within Hinduism, that the current practice of subsuming them under one religion appears inadequate.' (1995:51). Sarvepalli Radhakrishnan, himself an exponent of modern Hinduism, (1939:313) calls Hinduism 'a mosaic of almost all types and stages of religious aspiration and endeavour.' (Quoted from Nisith Ranjan Ray [1967:554]) See further the sober refusal to substitute the negative (*netibācak* [Beng.]) definition of Hinduism by a positive one in a popularly written article by Bimal kṛṣṇa Matilāl (1988:164-73).

[41] In the sense of German '*Fremdbezeichnung*'.

[42] German '*Eigenbezeichnung*'.

[43] Quoted by M.K. Halder (1977:67f.); Ghose uses it appreciatively for Rādhākānta Deb.

between religion and modernity which is an essential aspect of this phenomenon, and may thus be regarded as a valid expression.

The polemical reply to Baṅkim's 'modern Hinduism' (with reference to his *Dharmmajijñāsā*) by Dvijendranāth Ṭhākur in 1884, in turn, is entitled *Nabya hindusampradāẏ* ('The class of new / neo-Hindus' or 'The new class of Hindus'),[44] and *nabya* is definitely a negative term here. Dvijendranāth, however, apparently takes the term from Baṅkim himself who uses it much in the sense of 'modern Hindu' in his *Deb'tattva o hindudharmma* (*BR* II:791f.); Brajendranath Seal speaks of 'New-Hinduism' (probably by translating it from Bengali) as applying to the 'movement led by Babu Bankimchandra Chatterji', and his devastating critique suggests that the term itself is used derogatively. But in the following years, the term *nabya hindu* seems to have lost its evaluative tendencies in either way; and Priyaranjan Sen uses the term 'Neo-Hinduism' without any value judgement in 1932.[45] The first proper definition of neo-Hinduism is the one by Hacker; maybe because of his influence, the term is relatively firmly established in German discussion.[46] It has from then on been used frequently in anglophone publications and also evoked some amount of criticism.[47]

Compared to 'modern Hinduism' and 'neo-Hinduism', 'Hindu revivalism', along with the variant 'renascent Hinduism', has more specific implications, and in these is not less problematic than the term 'Renaissance'.[48] Further, both rest on the notion first established by the British Orientalists of a past age of flourishing civilisation succeeded by a long period of gradual decline. What was to be revived? Certainly not Hindu culture as such since it did after all exist the whole time, but the culture of that golden age which in itself was an eclectic fiction of (mainly) the nineteenth century.[49] The term was used, together with the neologism *punarutthāna*, by members of the various

[44] Both translations are possible; despite the dissociation of *nabya*, the first reading appears more likely since in such cases the attribute often refers to the first part of the compound in Bengali.

[45] In Priyaranjan Sen (1932). The term is thus older (probably considerably older) than one might be led to assume by Hacker's indication who, while stating that he does not know who invented it, takes it from an article by Robert Antoine published in 1953.

[46] Cf. e.g. a brochure, in a series of the Protestant Church, entitled 'Neo-Hinduismus' (Dockhorn 1972).

[47] Cf. Oddie (1991:141f.): '[...] it is unfortunate that the writers selected for examination are labelled "neo-Hindu". "Neo" certainly means new, but it also carries the connotation that these thinkers cannot be considered authentically Hindu. [...] how would modern Christians like to be called "neo-Christians"?' Also Bimalkrishna Matilal (1994) who reacts with irritation: 'Bankimchandra has been called a neo-Hindu by the Indologists (Paul Hacker). I believe that the term "neo-Hinduism" is a term without a content foisted upon certain cultural and religious movements in India, by the Indologists.' (p. 243) The irritation is understandable, but the belief expressed is, by all appearance, inaccurate.

[48] Cf. Hacker's remarks about the inadequacy of the terms 'renaissance' and 'reform'; 'renaissance', according to Hacker, 'indicates the atmosphere of Hindu nationalism', whereas 'reform' describes the phenomena in question 'from the angle of European culture' (Paul Hacker 1978 [1970]:580f.). Tapan Raychaudhuri (1988:8f.) dismisses the term 'revivalism' as too problematic. Rākhāl Candra Nāth (1988:xiii) prefers *nabyahindu āndolan* to *hindu punarutthān* because the 'movement', he argues, went beyond the traditional confines of religion.

[49] Cf. however, in this context, Amiya P. Sen's (1993:8-12) defence of the term: he basically points out that the term was used at the time, and that the parts of tradition that were being revived had in fact been close to dead. He further rightly stresses that many movements of that time could not be explained in terms of larger cultural continuities. Despite his considerations, the term remains problematic.

movements thus labelled.[50] The same is true, however, of the term 'modern Hinduism'. As a historiographic term, revivalism appears to be situated on a slightly different level than e.g. neo-Hinduism, which belongs, strictly speaking, to religiology and not to historiography; if conceived thus, both terms could coexist (contrary to Ghatak's [1991] and Rākhāl Candra Nāth's [1988] opinion). 'Political Hinduism' as used by Klimkeit (1976, 1981) emphasises one specific dimension of the entity to be named; but it remains uncertain in which way these more recent political elements in Hinduism should be distinguished from political elements in pre-modern Hinduism.

In these circumstances, 'modern Hinduism' and 'neo-Hinduism' appear to be the most suitable religiological terms to designate a more or less systemised set of new interpretations of ancient Hindu ideas, together with the culturally self-assertive trend which motivated them.

Baṅkim'candra was not the inventor of all of these interpretations, as the present analysis has shown; in many cases he built upon pre-existing argumentative patterns of traditional Hinduism and the Bengali nineteenth century. But he was the first to set them down systematically, and at least his modern formulation of *dharma* and *svadharma* seems to be originally his own. Baṅkim had direct influence on some later modern or neo-Hindu thinkers such as Vivekānanda,[51] Aurobindo, Bipin'candra Pāl and Nabīn'candra Sen[52] and was read by many others including M.K. Gāndhī.[53] Some of his interpretations of the *Gītā*, certainly his conceptions regarding *svadharma* and the plurality of worship, have been developed into what may be called standard positions held by modern Hinduism.

The analysis of Baṅkim'candra's commentary has, I hope, helped demonstrate once again in which way the cultural encounter with Europe and colonial power relations have combined in bringing about this new interpretation of Indian tradition labelled neo-Hinduism or modern Hinduism. It has, however, also shown that a clear-cut division between colonialist agency and colonised reaction is far too simplistic to account for the dialectic mechanisms of this encounter. Thus the criterion of authenticity must be defined differently for this process of assimilation: it is not despite, but *by virtue of* its heterogeneous character and its inconsistencies that Baṅkim's commentary can claim authenticity.

In these circumstances, I believe, it cannot be the whole point of research to historically elaborate on the 'non-Indianness' of neo-Hinduism and, on the sole ground of detected heterogeneity, disqualify large areas of subsequent Indian thought as 'derivative', 'adapted', 'imitative' or the like. This would inevitably mean pushing the Orientalists' essentialisation and reification of Oriental cultures (which after all did play its part in this process) to another level. It appears more promising to ask: At what point does 'non-Indian' become 'Indian'? Baṅkim is, I think, one of these points, a focal one. What grants him this status is not that he achieved a smooth blending of traditions thereafter undiscernibly interwoven (he did not), but the way in which he positioned his

[50] Also again and again by Baṅkim (*punarutthān* [Beng.], *punarujjīban* [Beng.], etc.).

[51] e.g. in his portrayal of Kṛṣṇa; cf. Śaṅkarīprasād Basu (1990:35f.).

[52] Cf. William Smith ([1996]) and Hans Harder (1994).

[53] Gandhi (1994:97) mentions Baṅkim'candra in his *Discourses on the 'Gita'*; he read *Kṛṣṇacaritra* during imprisonment in Yeravda, as the editorial remarks inform us.

thinking. The demarcation line between East and West, so prominent in his thought, here becomes itself a part of the Indian cultural fabric and has remained operative ever since. So there is no way of calling Baṅkim's thought, nor Baṅkim's West, 'non-Indian'. It is, I think, up to 'modern Indian tradition' and especially to 'modern Hindus' themselves to decide about the validity and authenticity of neo-Hinduism; and to Indologists not to dismiss it as non-Indian, but to remain on the scene as critical observers of still another integral, if problematic, part of modern Indian culture.

Bibliography

Adorno, Theodor W. (1990): *Der Essay als Form*; in *Noten zur Literatur* (*Schriften* Vol. 11); Frankfurt/M; 9-33.

Anderson, Benedict (1991): *Imagined Communities: Reflections on the Origin and Spread of Nationalism*; London/New York; revd edn (1st edn 1983).

Antoine, Robert (1953): *A Pioneer of Hinduism*; *Indica*, The Indian Historical Research Institute Silver Jubilee Commemoration Volume; Bombay; 5-21.

Argov, Daniel (1967): *Moderates and Extremists in the Indian Nationalist Movement 1883-1920: with special reference to Surendranath Banerjea and Lajpat Rai*; London.

Ashby, Philip H. (1974): *Modern Trends in Hinduism*; New York.

Assmann, Jan (1995): *Einführung*; in *idem* and B. Gladigow: *Text und Kommentar: Archäologie der literarischen Kommunikation IV*; München; 9-33.

Aurobindo, Sri (1940): *Bankim-Tilak-Dayananda*; Calcutta.

—— (1947): *Essais sur la Gītā: Traduction des sept premiers chapitres revue et corrigée par l'auteur*; Pondichéry.

—— (1954): *Bankim Chandra Chatterji*; Pondicherry.

—— (1986): *The Renaissance in India*; Pondicherry, 1st edn 1920; first published serially in *Arya* from Aug. to Nov. 1918.

Baird, Robert D. (ed.) (1981): *Religion in Modern India*; New Delhi.

Bandyopadhyay, Asit Kumar (1994): *Bankimchandra and Neo-Puranism*; in *BCEIP*:246-59.

Bandyopādhyāẏ, Cittarañjan (1983): *Ānandamaṭh: racanār preraṇā o pariṇām, tat saha baṅkim'candrer ānanda maṭher pratham saṃskaraṇer phaṭokapi*; Kalikātā.

Bandyopadhyay, Chitta Ranjan (1994): *Anandamath*; in *BCEIP*:220-6.

Bandyopādhyāẏ, Indranāth (1925-6): *Indranāth racanābalī*; Kalikātā, 1332 BE.

Bandyopādhyāẏ, Jaẏanta (1986): *Samālocanār rūp'rekhā: baṅkim'parba*; Kal'kātā.

—— (1990): *Upanyāse samāj'dṛṣṭi: baṅkim o rabīndranāth*; Kalikātā.

Bandyopādhyāẏ, Jaẏantānuj (1993): *Mahākābya o maulabād*; Kalikātā, 2nd edn

—— (1994): *Samāj'bijñāner dṛṣṭite bhagabadgītā*; Kal'kātā.

Bandyopādhyāẏ, Kālīprasād (ed.) (1972): *Baṅkim smārak grantha*; Kalikātā.

Bandyopadhyay, Manabendra (1985): *Novel, Bengali*; in *Comparative Indian Literature*, Vol. 1; ed. K.M. George; Trichur.

—— (1994): *My Husband, Good or bad*; in *BCEIP*:327-39.

Bandyopādhyāẏ, Pārthapratim (1990): *Upanyās rāj'naitik*; Kal'kātā.

Bandyopādhyāẏ, Sandīp (1993): *Agniyuger bāṃlāẏ biplabīmānas*; Kalikātā.

Bandyopadhyay, Saroj (1994): *The Man and the Artist*; in *BCEIP*:448-57.

Bandyopādhyāẏ, Śibājī (1991): *Aupanibeśik śikṣānīti o ādhunikatār pāṭh*; *Ākādemi Patrikā* 4, May 1991; 96-123.

—— (1993): *'Punar' biṣaẏe punarbibecanā*; *Bāromās Śāradīẏa* 1993, 26-43.

Bandyopādhyāẏ, Śrīkumār (1988): *Baṅgasāhitye itihāser dhārā*; Kalikātā, 8th edn

Bandyopadhyay, Sunil (1994): *Bankimchandra and Indological Research*; in *BCEIP*:264-70.

Bandyopādhyāẏ, Sunīl Kumār (1984): *Sāhitya śilpī baṅkim'candra*; Kalikātā.

Bandyopādhyāẏ, Yogendracandra (1974): *Yogendracandra Basu*; Sāhitya-Sādhak-Carit'-mālā 38; Kalikāṭā, 1381 BE.

Basu, Bikāś (1989): *Sāhitya niẏe*; Kal'kāṭā.

Basu, Buddhadeb (1974): *Mahābhārater kathā*; Kal'kātā.

Basu, Nimāisādhan (ed.) (1992): *Śāśvata bibekānanda*; Kal'kātā.

Basu, Rāj'nārāyaṇ (1952): *Ātmacarit*; Kalikātā, 3rd edn

Basu, Śaṅkarīprasād (1990): *Baṅkim'candra rabīndranāth o nānā prasaṅga*; Kalikātā.

Basu, Somendranāth (ed.) (1989): *Kācher mānuṣ baṅkim'candra*; Kal'kātā; 2nd edn

Basu, Svapan (1985): *Bāṃlāẏ nabacetanār itihās*; Kal'kātā, 2nd edn

Bentham, Jeremy (1970): *Collected Works of Jeremy Bentham*; ed. J.H. Burns, H.L.A. Hart; London.

Bharati, Agehananda (1971): *Hinduism and Modernization*; in *Religion and Change in Contemporary Asia*; ed. Robert F. Spencer; Bombay; 67-104.

—— (1986): *Hindu-Faschismus*; *Forum*, 30.9.1986; 29-35.

Bhaṭṭācārya, Amitrasūdan (ed.) (1975): *Baṅkim'candrakṛta sāhitya samālocanā: duṣprāpya racanā saṃgraha*; Kal'kātā, 1381 BE.

—— (1986): *Baṅkim bidyā*; Kalikātā.

—— (1991): *Baṅkim'candrajībanī* [BCJ]; Kal'kātā.

Bhaṭṭācārya, Arūp'kumār (1989): *Upanyās-śilpī Baṅkim'candra*; Kalikātā.

Bhaṭṭācārya, Asit'kumār (1964): *Bāṃlār nabayug o baṅkim'candrer cintādhārā*; Kalikātā.

Bhaṭṭācārya, Biṣṇupada (1982): *Raṅgamañce Baṅkim*; Kalikātā.

—— (1987): *Baṅkim manīṣā*; Kal'kātā, 1394 BE.

Bhaṭṭācārya, Jyoti (1992): *Jīban, dharma, rāj'nīti*; in *Yuktibādīr cokhe dharma*; ed. Prabīr Ghoṣ; Kal'kātā; 31-44.

Bhaṭṭācārya, Rām'kṛṣṇa (1994): *Baṅkim'candrer dharmacintā: asaṅgatir ut sa*; *Cāraṇ Parba*, 19th Year, 2nd No., Caitra 1401 (1994); 30-64.

—— (1995): *Baṅkim'candrer darśan'cintā: bahugrāhitār bipad*; *Paścim'baṅga Bāṃla Ākādemi Patrikā* 7, Caitra 1401 BE; 79-96.

Bhattacharjee, K.S. (1986): *The Bengal Renaissance: Social and Political Thoughts*; New Delhi.

Bhattacharji, Sukumari (1994): *Bankimchandra and Ancient Indian Literature*; in *BCEIP*: 280-91.

Bhattacharya, Amitrasudan (1994): *A Biographical Sketch*; in *BCEIP*:557-62.

Bhattacharya, Pradip (transl.) (1991): Bankimchandra Chattopadhyay: *Krishna-Charitra*; Classics of East Series; Delhi.

Bhattacharya, Ramkrishna (1997): Review of Sudipta Kaviraj (1995); *Society and Change Vol. XI*, *No.2*; July-September 1997; 77-80.

Bhattacharya, Sabyasachi (1994): *Kapalkundala's Destiny*; in *BCEIP*:300-8.

—— and Thapar, Romila (ed.) (1986): *Situating Indian History*; Delhi.

Biśī, Pramathanāth and Cakrabartī, Bīthikā (1971): *Baṅkim sāhitya bicār*; Kalikātā 1377 BE.

Biśvās, Kṛṣṇakali (1986): *Uniś śatābdīr nabajāgaraṇer āloke rebhereṇḍ kṛṣṇamohan bandyopādhyāẏ*; Kal'kātā.

Bouez, Serge (1992): *La Déesse Appaisée: Norme et Transgression dans l'Hindouisme au Bengale*; Paris.

The Brahma Sutras: with the Commentary of Sankaracharya; trans. Rev. K.M. Banerjea Calcutta, 1870.

Brookman, David M. (1990): *Sarvepalli Radhakrishnan*; Bhubaneswar.

Broomfield, J.H. (1968): *The Non-Cooperation Decision of 1920: A Crisis in Bengal Politics*; in *Soundings in Modern South Asian History*; Berkeley/Los Angeles; 225-60.

Brückner, Heidrun (1995): *Bewahren und Erneuern: Philosophische Kommentartradition im indischen Mittelalter*; in: Assmann, J. and B. Gladigow (eds.) (1995); 237-47.

Bühler, Georg (1886): *The Laws of Manu translated with Extracts from Seven Commentaries*; The Sacred Books of the East 25; Oxford.

Carpenter, William Benjamin (1869): *Principles of Human Physiology*; London, 7th edn

Caṭṭopādhyāẏ, Baṅkim'candra: *Baṅkim racanābalī*, 3 vol. (*BR*); ed. Bāgal, Yogeś'candra; Kalikātā, Sāhitya Saṃsad, Vol. I 14th edn 1401 BE (1994); Vol. II 11th edn 1397 BE (1990); Vol. III (*Bankim Rachanavali*: English Writings) 2nd edn 1990.

- *Ānandamaṭh* (*BR* I:581-644) (Engl. trans.: see Roy, Basanta Koomar 1992).
- *Anukaraṇ* (*BR* II:200-4).
- *Baṅgadarśaner patrasūcanā* (*BR* II:280-4).
- *Bāṅgālā bhāṣā* (*BR* II:368-74).
- *Bāṅgālā sāhityer ādar* (*BR* II:44-7).
- *Bijñān'rahasya* (*BR* II:129-58).
- *Debī caudhurāṇī* (*BR* I:645-717).
- *Deb'tattva o hindudharmma* (*BR* II:776-822).
- *Dharmmajijñāsā* (1884): fully reprinted from *Nabajībān* in *BCJ*:647-59.
- *Dharmmatattva* (*BR* II:584-679) (Engl. trans.: see Ghosh, Manomohan 1977).
- *Durgeś'nandinī* (*BR* I:1-72).
- *Gauṛadās bābājīr bhikṣār jhuli* (1884-5) (*BR* II: 263-70).
- *The Hastie Controversy* (*BR* III:186-224).
- *Kamalākānta* (*BR* II:49-112) (Engl. trans.: see Chatterjee, Monish Ranjan 1992).
- *Kṛṣṇacaritra* (*BR* II:407-583) (Engl. trans.: see Bhattacharya, Pradip 1991).
- *Larḍ ripaṇer ut saber jamā-kharac* (*BR* II:919-20).
- *Letters on Hinduism* (*BR* III:225-69).
- *Lok'rahasya* (*BR* II:1-48).
- *A Popular Literature for Bengal* (*BR* III:97-102).
- *Prāpta granther saṃkṣipta samālocan* (*BR* II: 873-7)
- *Rāj'siṃha* (*BR* I:489-579).
- *Sāṃkhyadarśan* (*BR* II:221-34).
- *Sāmya* (*BR* II:381-406).
- *Sītārām* (*BR* I:719-92).
- *Śrīmadbhagabadgītā* (*ŚBhG[a]* — *BR* II:680-775).
- *Sūcanā* (to *Pracār*) (*BR* II:911-3).
- *Vedic Literature* (*BR* III:149-69).

——*Śrīmadbhagabadgītā* (*ŚBhG[b]*): Baṅkim-śatabārṣik saṃskaraṇ; eds. Brajendranāth Bandyopādhyāẏ and Sajanīkānta Dās; Kalikātā, Baṅgīya Sāhitya Pariṣad, 2nd edn 1357 BE (1950) [1st edn 1347 (1941)].

Caṭṭopādhyāẏ, Bhabatoṣ (1991): *Baṅkim'candra: sṛjan o bīkṣaṇ*; Kal'kātā.

Caṭṭopādhyāẏ, Pūrṇacandra (1964): *Baṅkim'candrer bālyaśikṣā*; in Basu, Somendranāth (ed.) (1989): 88-93; 1st edn 1915.

Caṭṭopādhyāẏ, Rabirañjan (1989): *Baṅkim sāhitye kṛṣṇakathā*; in Gupta, Kṣetra (ed.)

(1989): 123-33.
Caṭṭopādhyāy, Śacīś'candra (1988): *Baṅkim-jībanī (BJ)*; Kalikātā, 1395 BE (1st edn 1318 BE [1911-2]).
Caudhurī, Nāj'mā Jes'min (1983): *Bāṃlā upanyās o rāj'nīti*; Kal'kātā (1st edn Ḍhākā, 1980).
Caudhurī, Nārāyaṇ (1987): *Baṅkim-carcā*; Ḍhākā, 1395 BE.
Chandra, Bipan (1984): *Communalism in Modern India*; New Delhi, etc.
Chatterjee, Bhabatosh (ed.) (1994): *Bankimchandra Chatterjee: Essays in Perspective*; New Delhi.
Chatterjee, Monish Ranjan (trans.) (1992): Bankim Chandra Chatterjee: *Kamalākānta: a collection of satirical essays and reflections*; Calcutta.
Chatterjee, Partha (1986): *Nationalist Thought and the Colonial World — a Derivative Discourse?*; London.
—— (1993): *A Religion of Urban Domesticity: Sri Ramakrishna and the Calcutta Middle Class*; in *Subaltern Studies*, Vol. VII; ed. *idem* and Pandey, Gyanendra; Delhi; 40-68.
—— (1995): *History and the Nationalization of Hinduism*; in Dalmia, Vasudha and von Stietencron, Heinrich (eds.) (1995): 103-28.
Chatterjee, Visvanath (1994): *Bankimchandra and Rabindranath*; in *BCEIP*:474-82.
Chattopadhyay, Dilip Kumar (1990): *Dynamics of Social Change in Bengal (1817-1851)*; Calcutta.
Chaudhuri, Nirad C. (1967): *The Intellectual in India*; Tracts for the Times I; New Delhi, 2nd edn
Clark, T.W. (1961): *The Role of Bankimchandra in the Development of Nationalism*; in: *Historians of India, Pakistan and Ceylon*; ed. Philips, C.H.; London; 429-45.
Comte, Auguste (1949): *Cours de Philosophie Positive: Discours sur l'esprit positif*, 2 vols; Paris.
Creel, Austin (1977): *Dharma in Hindu Ethics*; Calcutta.
Dae, Ar Cy [*sic.*] (1877): *The Literature of Bengal / being / An Attempt / To Trace the Progress / of the / National Mind in its various Aspects, as Reflected in the Nation's Literature / from the Earliest Times to the Present Day; / With Copious Extracts from the Best Writers*; Calcutta.
Dalmia, Vasudha and von Stietencron, Heinrich (eds.) (1995): *Representing Hinduism: The Construction of Religious Traditions and National Identity*; New Delhi.
Dās, Jñānendramohan (1994): *Bāṅgālā bhāṣār abhidhān*; Kal'kātā, 4th edn
Das, Manoj (1994): *The Rishi as Sri Aurobindo sees him*; in *BCEIP*:260-3.
Das, Sisir Kumar (1966): *Early Bengali Prose: Carey to Vidyasagar*; Calcutta / Patna / Allahabad.
—— (1971): *Western Sailors, Eastern Seas: German Response to Indian Culture*; New Delhi.
—— (1974): *The Shadow of the Cross: Christianity and Hinduism in a Colonial Situation*; New Delhi.
—— (1984): *The Artist in Chains: The Life of Bankimchandra Chatterji*; New Delhi.
Das Gupta, R.K. (1994): *A Religion of Man*; *BCEIP*:182-201 (transl. of Dāś'gupta, Rabīndrakumār (1988-9).
Dasgupta, Alokeranjan (1994): *Madhusudan und Bankimchandra: die unzufriedenen Vorreiter*; in *idem*: *Der König und der Barde: Literarische Begegnungen mit Indien*;

Kassel; 75-96.
Dāś'gupta, Alok'rañjan and Bandyopādhyāẏ, Debīprasād (1969): *Bāṃlā sāhityer rekhālekhya*; Kalikātā.
Dāś'gupta, Rabīndrakumār (1988-9): *Baṅkim'kalpita mānab'dharma*; *Deś*, Sāhitya Saṃkhyā; ed. Ghoṣ, Sāgar'maẏ; 1395 BE; 41-9.
Dāś'gupta, Śaśibhūṣaṇ (1993 [1944]): *Bāṅ'lā sāhityer ek'dik*; Kalikātā, 6th edn
Datta, Bhabatoṣ (1987-8): *Cintānāẏak baṅkim'candra*; Kal'kātā (1st edn 1961).
Datta, Bhabatosh (1994): *A Rational Quester*; in *BCEIP*:425-31.
Datta, Hīrendranāth (1940-1): *Dārśanik baṅkim'candra*; Kalikātā.
Datta, Hirendranath (*idem*) (1994): *Philosopher and Seer*; in *BCEIP*:64-70.
Datta, Michael Madhusūdan (1990 [1961]): *Nil Durpan or the Indigo Planting Mirror*; in: *Madhusūdan racanābalī*; ed. Gupta, Kṣetra; Kalikātā, 11th edn; 745-809.
Datta, Rameś'candra (1994 [1893-4]): *Hindu śāstra*; Kalikātā, 2nd edn 1401 BE. (1st edn 1300 BE).
Datta, Rameshchandra (1994): *Bankimchandra and Modern Bengal*; in *BCEIP*:73-7.
Davies, J. (1882): *Hindu Philosophy, Bhagavad Gita: the Sacred Lay*; London.
De, Amalendu (1974): *Roots of Separatism in Nineteenth Century Bengal*; Calcutta.
Derrett, J. Duncan M. (1976): *Dharmaśāstra and Juridicial Literature*; in *A History of Indian Literature*, Vol. IV; ed. Gonda, Jan; Wiesbaden.
Desai, Shantinath K. (1994): *History as Setting*; in *BCEIP*:508-11.
Devaraja, N.K. (1975): *Hinduism and the Modern Age*; New Delhi.
Dhar, Niranjan (1977): *Vedanta and the Bengal Renaissance*; Calcutta.
Dimock, Edward C. (1975): *Hinduism and Islam in Medieval Bengal*; in *Aspects of Bengali History and Society*; Asian Studies at Hawaii 12; ed. Van M. Baumer, Rachel; Hawaii.
Dockhorn, Kurt (1972): *Neo-Hinduismus: Indiens Auseinandersetzung mit dem 20. Jahrhundert*; Arbeitstexte Nr.11, Evangelische Zentralstelle für Weltanschauungsfragen; Stuttgart.
Dumont, Louis (1976 [1967]): *Gesellschaft in Indien: Die Soziologie des Kastenwesens* [*Homo hierarchicus*]; Wien (1st edn 1967).
Embree, Ainslee T. (1989): *Imagining India: Essays on Indian History*; ed. Juergensmeier, Mark; Delhi.
—— (1972): *India's Search for National Identity*; New York, 1972.
Encyclopedia of Indian Literature (1987): 5 vols.; ed. Datta, Amaresh; New Delhi, 1987.
Farquhar, J.N. (1924): *Modern Religious Movements in India*; London.
Ferguson, C.A. (1959): *Diglossia*; *Word*, Vol. 15 1959; 325-40.
Forbes, Geraldine Hancock (1975): *Positivism in Bengal: A Case Study in the Transmission and Assimilation of an Ideology*; Columbia.
Frykenberg, R.E. (1989): *Emergence of Modern 'Hinduism'*; in *Hinduism Reconsidered*; ed. Sontheimer, Günther D. and Kulke, Hermann; New Delhi; 29-49.
Gandhi, Mahatma (1994): *Discourses on the 'Gita'*; in *The Collected Works of Mahatma Gandhi*, Vol. XXXII; New Delhi, 1st edn 1969; 95-376.
Garbe, Richard (transl.) (1905): *Die Bhagavad-Gita; aus dem Sanskrit übersetzt, mit einer Einleitung über ihre ursprüngliche Gestalt, ihre Lehren und ihr Alter*; Leipzig.
Ghatak, Kamal Kumar (1991): *Hindu Revivalism in Bengal: Rammohan to Ramakrishna*; Calcutta.
Ghoṣ, Bārid'baraṇ (1986): *Prasaṅga śib'nāth śāstrī*; Kalikātā.

—— (ed.) (1989): *Baṅkim cintā: bipin candra pāl*; Kalikātā.
—— (1993): *Ākrānta baṅkim'candra*; Kal'kātā.
Ghoṣ, Jagadīś Candra (undated): *Śrīkṛṣṇa o bhāgabat dharmma*; Kalikātā, 5th edn.
Ghoṣ, Prabīr (ed.) (1992): *Yuktibādīr cokhe dharma*; Kal'kātā.
Ghoṣ, Tapobijaẏ (1989): *Mātṛbhāṣā o baṅkim'candra*; in Kṣetra Gupta (ed.) (1989); 30-52.
Ghosal, Kshitindra Chandra (1994): *Patriot and Humanist*; in *BCEIP*:227-36.
Ghose, Benoy (1978-81): *Selections from English Periodicals of 19th Century Bengal*, Vols. I-VIII; Calcutta.
Ghose, Sankar (1969): *The Renaissance to Militant Nationalism in India*; Bombay, etc.
Ghoṣ, Binaẏ (1957): *Bidyāsāgar o bāṅālī samāj*; Bombay, etc., 1364 BE.
—— (1983): *Sāmaẏik'patre bāṃlār samāj'citra*, Vol. 6; Kal'kātā.
—— (1984): *Bāṃlār nabajāgṛti*; Kalikātā, 2nd edn 1391 BE (1st edn 1965).
Ghoṣāl, Jaẏantakumār (1992): *Bāṃlā upanyāse samāj'bāstabatā (baṅkim'candra, rabīndranāth, śarat candra o tārāśaṅkar)*; Kal'kātā.
Ghosh, J.C. (1976): *Bengali Literature*; London/Totowa (1st edn 1948).
Ghosh, Manomohan (transl.) (1977): *Essentials of Dharma* [*Dharmmatattva*] by Bankimchandra Chattopadhyay; Calcutta.
Giri, Satyabatī (1988): *Bāṃlā sāhitye kṛṣṇakathār kramabikāś*; Kal'kātā.
Glasenapp, Helmuth von (1980): *Religiöse Reformbewegungen im heutigen Indien* (1928); in *Ausgewählte kleine Schriften*; eds. Bechert, Heinz and Moeller, Volker; Wiesbaden; 115-93.
Goethe, Johann Wolfgang v. (1842): *Wilhelm Meister*, 3 vols.; transl. Carlyle, [Thomas]; London.
Guha, Ranajit (1982): *On some Aspects of the Historiography of Colonial India*; in *Subaltern Studies*, Vol. 1; ed. *idem*; New Delhi; 1-8.
Gupta, Bipin'bihārī (1989): *Purātan prasaṅga*; Kal'kātā.
Gupta, Kṣetra (ed.) (1989): *Baṅkim'candra: ādhunik man*; Kal'kātā.
—— (1990): *Baṅkim'candra, bāstabikatā ebaṃ*; Kal'kātā.
—— (1991): *Baṅkim'candra caṭṭopādhyāẏ: sekāl, ekāl, anek'kāl*; in *Prasaṅga bāṃlā upanyās*; ed. Aruṇ Sānyāl; Kalikātā; 1-16.
—— (1994): *The Art-Form*; in *BCEIP*:483-9.
Gupta, Mahendranāth (Śrī'ma') (1989): *Śrīśrīrām'kṛṣṇakathāmṛta*; Kalikātā (1st edn 1882).
Haberman, David. L. (1994): *Divine Betrayal: Krishna-Gopal of Braj in the Eyes of Outsiders*; *Journal of Vaiṣṇava Studies*, Vol. 3, No.1, Winter 1994; 83-111.
Hacker, Paul (1978 [1958]): *Der Dharma-Begriff des Neuhinduismus*; in *Kleine Schriften* (KS); ed. Schmithausen, Lambert; Wiesbaden; 580-608.
—— (1978 [1961]): *Schopenhauer und die Ethik des Hinduismus*; KS: 531-64.
—— (1978 [1964]): *Zur Geschichte und Beurteilung des Hinduismus*; KS:476-83.
—— (1978 [1965]): *Dharma im Hinduismus*; in KS:496-509.
—— (1978 [1970]): *Aspects of Neo-Hinduism as Contrasted with Surviving Traditional Hinduism*; KS:510-24.
—— (1978 [1971]): *Der religiöse Nationalismus Vivekānandas*; in KS:565-79.
—— (1995): *Philology and Confrontation: Paul Hacker on Traditional and Modern Vedanta*; ed./trans. Wilhelm Halbfass; Albany.
Haithcox, John Patrick (1971): *Communism and Nationalism in India: M.N. Roy*

and Comintern Polica, 1920-39; Princeton.
Hak, Ābul Kāsem Phaj'lul (ed.) (1990): *Baṅkim'candrer sārdhaśata janmabarṣe*; Ḍhākā.
Halbfass, Wilhelm (1981): *Indien und Europa: Perspektiven ihrer geistigen Begegnung*; Basel/Stuttgart.
—— (1990): *India and Europe: An Essay in Philosophical Understanding* (Translation and revd edn of Halbfass 1981); Delhi.
—— (1991): *Tradition and Reflection: Explorations in Indian Thought*; Albany.
—— (1995): *Practical Vedānta*; in Dalmia, Vasudha and von Stietencron, Heinrich (eds.) (1995):211-23.
Hāl'dār, Gopāl (1985): *Gopāl hāl'dārer śreṣṭha prabandha*; Kal'kātā.
—— (1994): *Bankimchandra: His Continuing Relevance*; in *BCEIP*:140-9.
Halder, M.K. (1977): *Renaissance & Reaction in Nineteenth Century Bengal: Bankim Chandra Chattopadhyay; an English translation of the Bengali Essay SAMYA written by Bankim Chandra Chattopadhyay, the father of Indian Nationalism*; Calcutta.
Harder, Hans (1994): *Traditionalistische und neohinduistische Gedanken in dem bengalischen Roman* Bhānumatī *(1900) von Nabīn'candra Sen*; *ZDMG* 144,1, 1994; 92-113.
—— (1995): Review of Bhabatosh Chatterjee (ed.): *BCEIP*; in *BSOAS* 1995,3:174-6.
—— (1996a): *Bankimchandra Chatterjee: Unfreiwilliger Begründer kommunalistischer Ideologien?*; in *Religion — Macht — Gewalt: Religiöser 'Fundamentalismus' und Hindu-Moslem-Konflikte in Südasien*; eds. Weiß, Christian et al.; Frankfurt/M; 57-70.
—— (1996b): *Brahmabāndhab Upādhyāẏ (1861-1907) und die Befreiung von den* Feringhees *durch den* varṇāśramadharma*: Gedanken eines frühen Svadeśī-'Revolutionärs'*; *ZDMG* 146,2, 1996; 492-506.
Hāsān, Bad'rul (1990): *Uniś śatak: nabajāgaraṇ o bāṃlā upanyās*; Kal'kātā.
Haug, Martin (1863): *The Origin of Brahmanism*; Poona.
Heimsath, Charles (1964): *Indian Nationalism and Hindu Social Reform*; Princeton.
Hoffmann, Karl (1967): *Der Injunktiv im Veda: Eine synchronische Funktionsuntersuchung*; Heidelberg.
Horsch, Paul (1967): *Vom Schöpfungsmythos zum Weltgesetz*; in *Asiatische Studien*, XXI (1967), 31-61.
Horstmann, Monika (1995): *Towards a Universal Dharma:* Kalyāṇ *and the tracts of the Gītā Press*; in Dalmia, Vasudha and von Stietencron, Heinrich (eds.) (1995): 294-305.
Huber, Friedrich (1991): *Die Bhagavadgita in der neueren indischen Auslegung und in der Begegnung mit dem christlichen Glauben*; Erlanger Monographien aus Mission und Ökumene, Band 12; Erlangen.
Jāhān, Sāroẏār (1984): *Baṅkim upanyāse mus'lim prasaṅga o caritra*; Ḍhākā.
—— (1985): *Baṅkim'candrer upanyās: mūlyāẏaṇer pālābadal, 1865-1900*; Ḍhākā.
—— (1991): *Bāṃlā upanyās: sekāl-ekāl*; Ḍhākā.
Joarder, Safiuddin (1977): *The Bengal Renaissance and the Bengali Muslims*; in *Reflections on the Bengal Renaissance*; eds. *idem* and David Kopf; Rajshahi.
Johnson, Samuel (1885): *Oriental Religions and their relation to Universal Religion*; London.
Jones, Kenneth W. (1976): *Ārya Dharma — Hindu Consciousness in 19. Century Punjab*;

New Delhi.
Julien, Stanislas (ed./trans.) (1853): *Histoire de la vie de Hiouen-Thsang et de ses voyages dans l'Inde* by Hui-Li; Paris.
Kane, P.V. (1930-62): *History of Dharmaśāstra*, 5 vols.; Poona.
Kant, Immanuel (1836): *Metaphysics of Ethics*; transl. Semple[, ?]; Hamilton.
—— (1977): *Die Metaphysik der Sitten*; Werkausgabe, Bd.VIII; ed. Weischedel, Wilhelm; Frankfurt/M.
Kar, Śiśir (1988): *Britiś śāsane bājeỳāpta bāṃlā bai*; Kal'kātā.
Karīm, Rejāul (1944): *Baṅkim'candra o musal'mān samāj*; Kalikātā.
Karim, Rezaul (1994): *In the Eyes of a Non-Hindu*; in *BCEIP*:177-81.
Karunakaran, K.P. (1965): *Religion and Political Awakening in India*; Meerut / Delhi / Calcutta.
Kāỳ'sār, Śāntanu (1990 [1982]): *Baṅkim'candra*; Ḍhāka, 2nd edn (1st edn 1982).
Kaviraj, Sudipta (1993): *The Imaginary Institution of India*; in *Subaltern Studies*, Vol. VII; eds. Chatterjee, Partha and Pandey, Gyanendra; Delhi; 1-39.
—— (1995): *The Unhappy Consciousness: Bankimchandra Chattopadhyay and the Formation of Nationalist Discourse in India*; Delhi.
Kaṭha-Upaniṣad; ed. Swāmī Śarvānanda; Madras, 8th edn 1956.
King, Ursula (1977): *'True and Perfect Religion': Bankim Chandra Chatterjee's Reinterpretation of Hinduism*; *Religion* 7, 1977; 127-48.
Klimkeit, Joachim (1976): *Der politische Hinduismus der Neuzeit*; in *Der Religionswandel unserer Zeit im Spiegel der Religionswissenschaft*; Darmstadt; 94-108.
—— (1981): *Der politische Hinduismus*; Wiesbaden.
Klostermaier, Klaus K. (1992): *Vaiṣṇavism and Politics: The New Dharma of Braj?*; *Journal of Vaiṣṇava Studies* Vol. 1, No.1, Fall 1992; 166-82.
Kofman, Sarah (1978): *Aberrations: Le Devenir-Femme d'Auguste Comte*; Paris.
Kohn, Hans (1928): *Geschichte der nationalen Bewegung im Orient*; Berlin.
Kopf, David (1969): *British Orientalism and the Bengal Renaissance: The Dynamics of Indian Modernization 1773-1835*; Berkeley/Los Angeles.
Larson, Gerald James (1981): *The Song Celestial: Two Centuries of the* Bhagavadgītā *in English*; *Philosophy East and West*, XXXI, No.4, Oct. 1981; 513-41.
Lassen, Christian (1846): *Bhagavad-Gita, id est Thespesion melos, sive Krischnae et Arjunae colloquium de rebus divinis*; Bonn (1st edn 1823).
Lingat, Robert (1973): *The Classical Law of India*; Berkeley, etc.
Lucretius (1965): *De Rerum natura*; eds. Leonard, William Ellerly and Smith, Stanley Barney; Madison.
Madan, T.N. (ed.) (1991): *Religion in India*; Delhi.
Mahābhārata; critically edited by Vishnu S. Sukthankar (from 1943/Vol. 4 ed. by S.K. Belvalkar); Poona, Bhandarkar Oriental Research Institute; 1927-59. [Vol. 3: Āraṇyakaparvan 1942, Vol. 6: Bhīṣmaparvan 1947].
Mahaffey, Patrick J. (1994): *Interpreting Religious Plurality: Patterns of Argument in Hindu Thought*; in *Aspects of Religion: Essays in Honour of Ninian Smart*; Toronto Studies in Religion 18; eds. Masefield, Peter and Wiebe, Donald; New York, etc.; 291-311.
Majum'dār, Karuṇāmaỳ (1984): *Candranāth basu: jīban o sāhitya*; Kal'kātā.
Majum'dār, Mohit'lāl (1949-50): *Baṅkim-baraṇ*; Kul'gāchiỳā (Hāoṛā), 1356 BE.
—— (1963-4): *Ādhunik bāṃlā sāhitya*; Kalikātā, 1370 BE.

—— (1994): *Prabandha saṃgraha*; Kalikātā.
Majumdar, Mohitlal [*idem*] (1994): *A View of the Highlands*; in *BCEIP*:111-20.
Majumdar, R.C. (1963): *History of the Freedom Movement in India*, Vol. 1; Calcutta.
Majumdar, Śrīś'candra (1964): *Baṅkim'bābur prasaṅga*; in Basu, Somendranāth (ed.) (1964); 1-28.
Matilāl, Bimal'kṛṣṇa (1988): *Nītī yukti o dharma — kāhinī sāhitye rām o kṛṣṇa*; Kal'kātā, 1395 BE.
Matilal, Bimalkrishna (*idem*, 1994): *Images of India*; in *BCEIP*:242-5.
Māẏ'hār, Āh'mad (1991): *Bāṅālī manīṣīder kathā*; Ḍhākā.
Mill, John Stuart (1969 [1861]): *Utilitarianism* (1861); in *Collected Works*, Vol. X; ed. F.E.L. Priestley; Toronto, 1969; 203-59.
—— (1969): *Auguste Comte and Positivism*; ibid.:261-368.
—— (1969): *Three Essays on Religion*; *ibid*:369-489.
Minor, Robert (1991): *Sri Aurobindo as a* Gita-*Yogin*; in: *idem* (ed.): *Modern Interpretations of the Bhagavadgītā*; Delhi.
Mitra, Pyārīcād (n.d. [1855-7]): *Ālāler gharer dulāl*; in *Satsāhitya-granthābalī* Vol. 1, Kalikātā.
Moore, Peter (1994): *Religions as Systems*; in *Aspects of Religion: Essays in Honour of Ninian Smart*; ed. Peter Masefield and Donald Wiebe; Toronto Studies in Religion 18; New York, etc.; 39-57.
Muir, John (ed.) (1858-63): *Original Sanskrit Texts on the Origin and Progress of the Religion and Institutions of India*, 4 vols. and Index; London, 1858 (Vol. 1), 1860 (Vol. 2 [2nd edn 1868]), 1861 (Index to Vol. 1 and 2, Vol. 3), 1863 (Vol. 4); London.
Mukherjee, Sukhamoy (1994): *Vande Mataram: The Texture of a Song*; in *BCEIP*:237-41.
Mukhopādhyāẏ, Belā (1981): *Baṅkim'sāhitya o lok saṃskṛti*; Durgāpur.
Mukhopādhyāẏ, Bhāskar (1988): *Sañjīb'candra: jīban o sāhitya*; Kalikātā; 1395 BE.
Mukhopādhyāẏ, Biśvanāth (1993): *Biruddha samālocanāẏ baṅkim-sāhitya*; Kalikātā.
Mukhopādhyāẏ, Jīban (1983): *Ānandamaṭh o bhāratīya jātīyatābād*; Hāoṛā, 1389 BE.
Mukhopādhyāẏ, Śyāmāprasād (ed.) (1938): *Baṅkim-paricay*; Kalikātā.
Müller, F. Max (1878): *Lectures on the Origin and Growth of Religion as Illustrated by the Religions of India* (*Hibbert-Lectures*); London.
—— (1890): *Natürliche Religion: Gifford-Vorlesungen*; transl. by Engelbert Schneider; Leipzig.
Nandakumar, Prema (1994): *Bankimchandra and Subramania Bharati*; in *BCEIP*:400-11.
Nandi, Ashis (1983): *The Intimate Enemy: Loss and Recovery of Self Under Colonialism*; Delhi.
—— (1987): *Traditions, Tyranny and Utopia: Essays in the Politics of Awareness*; Delhi.
Naravane, Vishwanath S. (1978): *Modern Indian Thought*; New Delhi.
Nāth, Rākhāl'candra (1988): *Uniś śatak: bhāb saṃghāt o samanbaẏ*; Dillī/Kal'kātā.
Neevel, Walter G. Jr. (1976): *The Transformation of Śrī Rāmakrishna*; in *Hinduism — New Essays in the History of Religions*; ed. Smith, Bardwell L.; Leiden; 53-97.
Nicholson, R.A. (1930): *A Literary History of the Arabs*; Cambridge.
Nyāẏ'ratna, Rām'gati (1991 [1872]): *Bāṅgālā bhāṣā o bāṅgālā sāhityabiṣaẏak prastāb*; ed. Bandyopādhyāẏ, Asit'kumār; Kalikātā.
Oberhammer, Gerhard (ed.) (1983): *Inklusivismus: eine indische Denkform*; Wien.
Oddie, G.A. (1991): Review of Sharma, Arvind (ed.) (1988); *South Asia. Journal of*

South Asian Studies; New Series, Vol. XIV, No.2, December 1991; 141-2.
Odud, Kājī Āb'dul (1936): *Hindu-musal'māner birodh*; Visva-Bharati Studies No.6; Kalikātā; 1342 BE.
O'Flaherty, Wendy Doniger and Derrett, J. Duncan M. (ed.): *The Concept of Duty in South Asia*; New Delhi.
Pal, Bipin Chandra (1932): *Memories of my Life and Times*; Calcutta.
—— (1994): *The Literary Works of Bankim*; in *BCEIP*:78-84.
Pāl, Sabitā (1994): *Bāṃlā samālocanā sāhityer itihās 1850-1885 (ādi parba)*; Kal'kātā, KLM.
Pātañjala yogadarśana (Patañjali 1987); with a commentary in Sanskrit and Hindi by Āraṇya, Hariharānand; Dillī (1st edn Lakh'naū, 1953).
Patrī, Pūrṇendu (1996): *Baṅkim'yug: pratham khaṇḍa: 1838-1858*; Kal'kātā.
Pattrea, Purnendu (1994): *A chronicle of Fifty-Six Years*; in *BCEIP*:563-78.
Poddar, Arabinda (1970): *Renaissance in Bengal: Quests and Confrontations, 1800-1860*; Simla.
—— (1988): *Renaissance in Bengal: Its Character*; in *Culture of Bengal through the Ages: Some Aspects*; Burdwan.
—— (1994 [1951]): *Baṅkim-mānas*; Kal'kātā, 7th edn (1st edn 1951).
—— (1994): *A Rationalist's Predicament*; in *BCEIP*:432-8.
Prabhakar, Vishnu (1994): *The Great Predecessor*; in *BCEIP*: 166-71.
Radhakrishnan, Sarvepalli (1939): *Eastern Religions and Western Thought*; Oxford.
Rām'kṛṣṇa Param'haṃsa: *Śrīśrīrām'kṛṣṇakathāmṛta* — see Mahendranāth Datta (1989).
Ray, Ajit (1986): *Bankim Chandra Chatterji's New Hinduism and the* Bhagavadgita; in *Modern Indian Interpreters of the* Bhagavadgita; ed. Minor, Robert N.; Albany; 34-43.
Rāẏ, Āśālatā (1984): *Cintānāẏak bhūdeb mukhopādhyāẏ*; Kal'kātā.
Rāẏ, Gopāl'candra (1979): *Anya ek baṅkim'candra*; Kalikātā.
—— (1981): *Baṅkim'candra*; Kalikātā.
Rāẏ, Jībendu (1984): *Baṅkim'candrer bhārat cintā: sūtra o prakṛti*; Kalikātā, 1391 BE.
Ray, Nisith Ranjan (1967): *Religion: i. Hinduism*; in: *The History of Bengal (1757-1905)*; ed. Sinha, Narendra Krishna; Calcutta; 554-561.
Ray, Rajat Kanta (1984): *Social Conflict and Political Unrest in Bengal, 1875-1927*; Delhi.
Rāẏ, Rām'mohan: see Roy, Rammohun
Ray, Sibnarayan (1994): *Ambivalent Genius*; in *BCEIP*:211-19.
Rāẏ, Śyāmal (1990-1): *Bāṃlā upanyāse svadeś'cintā, 1882-1926*; Kalikātā, 1397 BE.
Rāẏ'caudhurī, Gopikānāth (1991): *Bāṃlā kathāsāhitya: prakaraṇ o prabaṇatā*; Kal'kātā.
Rāẏ'caudhurī, Sunītirañjan (1981): *Uniśer śatake nabya-hindu āndolaner kaẏek'jan nāẏak*; Kalikātā, 1388 BE.
Raychaudhuri, Tapan (1988): *Europe Reconsidered: Perceptions of the West in Nineteenth Century Bengal*; Delhi.
Reiche, Kurt (1927): *Auguste Comtes Geschichtsphilosophie*; Tübingen.
Renan, Ernst [*sic.*] (1864): *Das Leben Jesu*; trans. Eichler, Ludwig; Berlin, 6th edn
Rhys Davids, T.W. (1877): *Buddhism: the Life & Teaching of Gautama*; London.
Rocher, Ludo (1993): *Law Books in an Oral Culture: The Indian* Dharmaśāstras; *Proceedings of the American Philosophical Society*, Vol. 137, No.2, 1993; 254-267.
Rothermund, Dietmar (1965): *Die politische Willensbildung in Indien 1900-1960*; Schriftenreihe des Südasien-Instituts der Universität Heidelberg, Bd.1; Wiesbaden.

—— (1970a): *The Phases of Indian Nationalism and other Essays*; Bombay.

—— (1970b): *Traditionalism and Socialism in Vivekananda's Thought*; *Quest* No. 67, 1970.

Roy, Basanta Koomar (trans.) (1992): Bankim Chandra Chatterji: *Anandamath*; London; 2nd edn (1st edn Delhi 1941).

Roy, Gopal Chandra (1994): *The Prime Place of Pilgrimage*; in *BCEIP*:588-90.

Roy, Rammohun (1901): *The English Works of Raja Rammohun Roy*, 3 vols.; ed. Ghose, Jogendra Chunder; Calcutta.

The Sāṃkhya Sūtra Vṛtti or Aniruddha's Commentary and the Original Parts of Vedāntin Mahādeva's Commentary to the Sāṃkhya Sūtras (*SSV*); ed. Garbe, Richard; Calcutta, Baptist Mission Press, 1888.

Śaṅkara (1983): *Srīmad Bhagavad Gītā Bhāṣya of Sri Saṃkarācārya: with Text in Devanagari & English Rendering, and Index of First Lines of Verses* (*ŚaBhG*); trans. Warrier, A.G. Krishna; Madras.

Sānyāl, Hīreṇ (1994): *Bhārat sandhāne baṅga*; Kal'kātā.

Samāj'pati, Sureścandra (ed.) (1982): *Baṅkim-prasaṅga*; Kalikātā, 2nd edn (1st edn 1922).

Śarīph, Āh'mad (1990a): *Ālocanā*; in *Baṅkim'candra sārdhaśata janmabarṣe*; ed. Hak, Ābul Kāsem Phaj'lul; Ḍhākā; 37-51.

Śarīph, Āh'mad (1990b): *Bāṃlādeśer sāmpratik cāl'citra*; Ḍhākā.

Sarkar, Benoy Kumar (1937): *The Positive Background of Hindu Sociology*; *Book 1: Introduction to Hindu Positivism*; Allahabad.

Sar'kār, Bīrendra Candra (1983): *Baṅkim'candrer kṛṣṇacaritra: tāttbik o tathyabhittik paryālocanā*; Kalikātā.

Sar'kār, Sudhīr'candra (ed.) (1981-2): *Paurāṇik abhidhān*; Kalikātā, 4th revd edn 1388 BE.

Sarkar, Sumit (1977): *The Swadeshi Movement in Bengal 1903-1908*; New Delhi, 2nd edn (1st edn 1973).

—— (1990-1): *Ramakrishna and the Calcutta of His Time*; in *The Calcutta Psyche*; ed. Geeti Sen; Calcutta; 99-121.

Sarkar, Susobhan (1979): *On the Bengal Renaissance*; Calcutta.

Sarkar, Tanika (1994): *Imagining a Hindu Nation: Hindu and Muslim in Bankimchandra's Later Writings*; *EPW*, Sept.24, 1994; 2553-61.

Śāstri, Haraprasād (1981): *Haraprasād śāstrī racanā-saṃgraha*; Vol. 2; Calcutta.

Śāstrī, Śib'nāth (1967 [1903]): *Rām'tanu lāhiṛī o tat kālīn baṅgasamāj*; Kalikātā, 2nd edn (1st edn 1903).

Schlegel, August Wilhelm von (1846): *The Philosophy of History*; transl. Robertson[, ?]; London.

Schwab, Raymond (1950): *La Renaissance Orientale, avec un préface de Louis Renou*; Paris.

Seal, Anil (1968): *The Emergence of Indian Nationalism: Competition and Collaboration in the Later Nineteenth Century*; Cambridge.

Seal, Brajendranath (1994): *Neo-Hinduism*; in *BCEIP*:85-8.

Seeley, John Robert (1869): *Ecce Homo: A Survey of the Life and Work of Jesus Christ*; London, 10th edn

—— (1895): *Natural Religion*; London/New York, 4th edn (1st edn 1882).

Seely, Clinton B. (1997): Review of Kaviraj, Sudipta (1995); *South Asia Research 17,1*, Spring 1997 (Special Issue: Bengali Studies); 93-102.

Sen, Amiya P. (1993): *Hindu Revivalism in Bengal 1872-1905: Some Essays in Interpretation*; Delhi.
Sen, Dinesh Chandra (1911): *History of Bengali Language and Literature*; Calcutta.
Sen, Priyaranjan (1932): *Western Influence in Bengali Literature*; Calcutta.
Sen, Sukumār (1987): *Bāṃlār sāhitya-itihās*; Natun Dillī, 3rd edn (1st edn 1965).
—— (1994): *Bankimchandra*; in *BCEIP*:127-30.
Sen Bhaṭṭācārya, Supriẏā (1996): *Ūnabiṃśa śatābdīr svadeś'cintā o baṅkim'candra*; Kalikātā.
Sengupta, S.C. (1958): *Bankimchandra Chatterji (1838-1894)*; in *Studies in the Bengal Renaissance*; ed. Gupta, Atulchandra; Jadavpur; 67-78.
—— (1987): *Baṅkim'candra*; Kal'kātā; 2nd edn (1st edn 1976).
Sen Gupta, S.C. [*idem*] (1994): *Bankimchandra and the Bengal Renaissance*; in *BCEIP*: 133-9.
Sen'gupta, Gaurāṅgagopāl (1994): *Svadeśīya bhārat-bidyā sādhak*; Kal'kātā.
Sen'gupta, Pradyot (ed.) (1982): *Nakśā: sekāl-ekāl*; Kalikātā.
Sen'gupta, Subodh'candra (1989): *Baṅkim'candra*; Kalikātā/Niu Dillī.
Sengupta, Subodh Chandra (1977): *Bankimchandra Chatterjee*; Makers of Indian Literature; New Delhi.
Sharma, Arvind (1986): *The Hindu Gītā: Ancient and Classical Interpretations of the Bhagavadgītā*; London.
—— (ed.) (1988): *Neo-Hindu Views of Christianity*; Leiden.
Shastri, Haraprasad (1994): *The Precious One*; in *BCEIP*:21-6.
Siṃha, Kālīprasanna (1882-3): *Maharṣi kṛṣṇadvaipāẏaṇ bed'byās praṇīta mahābhārat: svargīya mahātmā kālīprasanna siṃha mahodaẏ karttṛk mūl saṃskṛta haïte bāṅgālā bhāṣāẏ anubādita*, 3 vols.; ed. Basu, Candranāth; Śyām'pukur; 3rd edn
Sinha, N.K. (1994): *In the Little World of a Civil Servant*; in *BCEIP*:579-87.
Smith, Bardwell L. (1976): *Hinduism: New Essays in the History of Religions*; Leiden.
Smith, William ([1996]): *Great India: Nabinchandra Sen and the Mahābhārata of the Nineteenth Century*; paper read at the 14th European Conference on Modern South Asian Studies, Copenhagen 21-24 August, 1996; unpublished.
Sontheimer, Günther D. (1980): *Die Ethik im Hinduismus*; in *Ethik der Religionen: Ein Handbuch*; ed. Ratschow, Carl-Heinz; Stuttgart, etc.; 349-436.
Spencer, Robert F. (1971): *Religion and Change in Contemporary Asia*; Bombay.
Śrīdhara Śvāmin (1972): *Srimad Bhagavad-Gita: Text, Translation of the Text and of the Gloss of Sridhara Swami* (*ŚrBhG*); ed./transl. Swami Vireswarananda; Madras.
Stevenson, Robert W. (1991): *Tilak and the* Bhagavadgita's *Doctrine of Karmayoga*; in *Modern Interpretations of the Bhagavadgītā*; ed. Minor, Robert; Delhi.
Stietencron, Heinrich von (1995): *Religious Configurations in Pre-Muslim India and the Modern Concept of Hinduism*; in Dalmia, Vasudha and *idem* (eds.) (1995): 51-81.
Stokes, Eric (1963): *The English Utilitarians in India*; Oxford; 2nd edn (1st edn 1959).
Tagore, Debendranath (1909): *The Autobiography of Maharshi Devendranath Tagore*; ed./transl. Tagore, Satyendranath and Devi, Indira; Calcutta.
Tagore, Rabindranath (1953): *The Religion of Man*; Hibbert Lectures for 1930; London, 4th edn.
—— (1961): *Reminiscences*; London, etc. (1st edn 1917).
—— (1994): *Bankimchandra*; in *BCEIP*:7-15.
Tapādār, Satyabrata (1985): *Se yuger rāj'karmacārī baṅkim'candra*; Kalikātā.

Teoẏārī, Rām'bahāl (1993): *Baṅkim bīkṣā*; Kal'kātā.

Ṭhākur, Rabīndranāth (1978 [1894]): *Ādhunik sāhitya* (comprising the essays *Baṅkim'-candra* [1894] and *Kṛṣṇacaritra* [1894]); in *Rabīndra racanābalī*, Vol. 9; Kalikātā, enlarged edn 1978; 397-526.

—— (1978 [1902]): *Nababarṣa* (1902); in *Rabīndra racanābalī*, Vol. 4; Kalikātā, enlarged edn 1978; 367-77.

Telang, Kashinath Trimbak (1990 [1882]): *The Bhagavadgītā with the Sanatsujātīya and the Anugītā*; Sacred Books of the East, Vol. 8; Delhi (1st edn 1882).

Thapar, Romila (1977): *Communalism and the Writing of Ancient Indian History*; in *Communalism and the Writing of Indian History*; ed. *idem*; New Delhi, 2nd edn; 1-23.

Thomson, J. Cockburn (trans.) (1855): *The Bhagavad-Gita: or a discourse between Krishna and Arjuna on divine matters; A sanskrit philosophical poem*; Hertford.

Tilak, Bal Gangadhar (1935): *Śrīmad Bhagavadgītā Rahasya or Kara-Yoga-Śāstra*; transl. from Marāṭhī by Sukthankar, Bhalchandra Sitaram; Poona.

Tripathi, Amales (1967a): *The Extremist Challenge: India between 1890 and 1910*; Bombay, etc. (Bengali version: *Bhārater mukti saṃgrāme caram'panthī parba*; trans. Datta, Nirmal; Kal'kātā, 2nd edn 1991.)

—— (1967b): *Bengali Literature in the 19th Century*; in *The History of Bengal (1757-1905)*; ed. Sinha, Narendra Krishna; Calcutta; 472-513.

—— (1991): *Svādhīnatā saṃgrāme bhārater jātīya kaṃgres (1885-1947)*; Kal'kātā, 2nd edn 1398 BE (1991).

—— (1994): *Itālīr ryaneśāṃs bāṅālīr saṃskṛti*; Kal'kātā.

Trivedi, Ramendrasundar (1994): *The Holy Seat*; in *BCEIP*:53-63.

Tylor, Edward B. (1913 [1871]): *Primitive Culture: Researches into the Development of Mythology, Philosophy, Religion, Language, Art, and Custom*, 2 vols.; London, 5th edn (1st edn 1871).

Umar, Bad'ruddīn (1990): *Īśvar'candra bidyāsāgar o uniś śataker bāṅālī samāj*; Ḍhākā.

Vācaspatyam (*Śrīvācaspatyam: bṛhat saṃskṛtābhidhānam*); compiled by Tārānātha Tarkavacaspati; Varanasi (1st edn 1873-84).

Van M. Baumer, Rachel (1969): *Bankimchandra's View of the Role of Bengal in Indian Civilisation*; in *Bengal Regional Identity*; ed. Kopf, David; East Lansing, Michigan; 61-72.

—— (1975): *The Reinterpretation of Dharma in Nineteenth-Century Bengal: Righteous Conduct for Man in the Modern World*; in *Aspects of Bengali History and Society*; ed. *idem*; Asian Studies at Hawaii 12; Honolulu; 82-98.

—— (1994): *India and the Modern Age*; in *BCEIP*:538-46.

Vedāntasāra of Sadānanda; ed. Jacob, G.A.; Bombay, 1894.

Viṣṇumahāpurāṇam; ed. Śarman, Rājendranātha; Delhi, Nag Publishers, 1985.

Vṛddhagautamasaṃhitā; in *Dharmaśāstrasaṃgraha*, Vol. 2; ed. Vidyasagar, Pandit Jivananda; Calcutta, 1876; Vol. 2, 497ff.

Wackernagel, Jakob (1954): *Altindische Grammatik*; Göttingen.

Waligora, Melitta: *Bengalische Renaissance: Eine begriffliche und methodische Annäherung an das Thema*; unpublished.

Weightman, Simon and S.M. Pandey (1978): *The Semantic Fields of Dharm and Kartavy in Modern Hindi*; in *The Concept of Duty in South Asia*; eds. O'Flaherty, Wendy Doniger and Derret, J. Duncan M.; New Delhi; 217-28.

Wezler, Albrecht (1995): *Der Tod als Mittel der Entsühnung*; in: *Im Tod gewinnt der Mensch sein Selbst: Das Phänomen des Todes in asiatischer und abendländischer Religionstradition*; ed. Oberhammer, Gerhard; Wien; 97-140.

Wilson, H.H. (1861): *Essays and Lectures on the Religion of the Hindus*; 2 vols. (Vol. 1: *Sketch of the Religious Sects of the Hindus*; Vol. 2: Miscellaneous Essays and Lectures); ed. Rost, Reinholt; London.

—— (tr./annot.) (1864-77): *The Vishṅu Purāṅa: A System of Hindu Mythology and Tradition*, 5 vols. and Index (Vol. 1 1864, Vol. 2 1865, Vol. 3 1866, Vol. 4 1868, Vol. 5 1870, Index 1877); London.

Winternitz, Maurice (1967): *History of Indian Literature*, 3 vols.; amended by Jha, Subhadra; Delhi.

Young, Richard Fox (1981): *Resistant Hinduism: Sanskrit Sources on Anti-Christian Apologetics in Early Nineṭeenth-Century India*; Publications of the De Nobili Research Library, VIII; Vienna.

Zbavitel, Dušan (1976): *A History of Bengali Literature*; in Gonda, Jan (ed.): *A History of Indian Literature*; Vol. IX, Fasc. 3; Wiesbaden.

Index